Autobiography of
HERBERT W. ARMSTRONG

D1224821

Volume 1

HERBERT W. ARMSTRONG
1892–1986

Table of Contents

Introduction

FROM BEGINNINGS humble and small without parallel, to the magnitude of today's enterprises and worldwide impact is the story of GROWTH unbelievable! It is the incredible story of something never done before—never done *this way*—a seemingly impossible achievement utterly unique in the world!

By all the criteria of organizational and institutional experience, it simply could never have happened.

Every phase of this globe-girdling Work has been something altogether UNIQUE—a *first*—the blazing of a new trail.

• Ambassador College is astonishingly UNIQUE among institutions of higher learning.

• The *Plain Truth* magazine is utterly UNIQUE in the publishing field.

• The *World Tomorrow* program, viewed and heard by millions worldwide on both television and radio, is

1

entirely UNIQUE in broadcasting.

• And the Worldwide Church of God, behind these global enterprises, is altogether UNIQUE on the earth—practicing, as it does, the revealed *ways* of the living Creator God, and for the first time in 18½ centuries, thundering His all-important Message of the way to World Peace over all continents of the earth.

This entire Work has belied all traditional experience. It has *reversed* accepted procedures. Yet, I hasten to add, these have *not* been ways of *my* devising!

But *how* did it all start?

And since this is the life story of a man, what led a man who had been unusually successful in the world of mammon, with his energy and drive solely directed toward self-gain and status in the business world, to come to reverse his entire life goal and become dedicated to the things of God? Why would a man turn his back on material rewards, and devote his life to GIVING instead of getting?

How I came to receive the eye-opening shock of my life, and in due time to be literally *thrust* into the very *last* calling and profession I would ever have chosen, was an experience as UNIQUE as everything done since.

Coming to the present, *why* do heads-of-state— kings, presidents, prime ministers of many governments around the world invite personal meetings with a private citizen of my status? Why do governments officially confer highest honors on such a private alien?

I repeat, this reversing of trends, ways and procedures has not been that of *my* devising. As I look back over the years, I can only shake my head in wonderment. I have not done these things—no man could. I cannot take credit. Yet, paradoxically, I have

2

been privileged to have the leading part in these activities.

This, truly, is one of the most incredible success stories of our time. There is a very significant reason! For it is the story of what the living God can do—and has done through a very average human instrument, called and chosen by Him—one whose eyes He opened to astonishing truth about the real *cause* of the troubles and evils heads of governments face, and the *way* to World Peace—one He reduced to humble obedience, yielded in faith and dedicated to *God's way!* God promises to prosper His own Work. And *HOW GREATLY* He *has* blessed and prospered it! Like the grain of mustard seed, it GREW!—*and GREW!*

Ask yourself: What company, business, enterprise or institution in *this* world's ways, ever experienced a steady GROWTH averaging nearly 30% every year for decades?

This activity did!

Most commercial businesses and enterprises do well to hold about even over the years. But a growth averaging 30% every year, regularly and steadily, for decades? It must be a record unmatched. It meant doubling in size and scope and power every 2⅔ years. It meant *multiplying* itself in size eight times in every eight years, 64 times every 16 years, 4,096 times in 32 years!

Most, if not all major corporate institutions began with sizeable capital. But this worldwide Work started *giving*—(reversing objectives and procedures) with absolutely no financial capital!

These globe-girding enterprises included the founding and operation of a co-ed college in the field of the liberal arts and humanities. I'm sure anyone experienced in the administration of a private-owned college would say: "No one could start to build such a college without money, endowment, government aid, or grant from any foundation, making no appeal to the public for financial support, and build such a college, of outstanding quality and beauty with the most modern facilities, and in so doing gain an enviable financial status recognized by major banks in New York, Philadelphia, Los Angeles, London and Geneva. IMPOSSIBLE!"

But much more! In every way, Ambassador College is unique. In magnificence of its campus—in the tone and character of its buildings and grounds—the physical setting in which it has produced tone and character in young men and women—Ambassador College is certainly unique in a world where education has drifted into materialism. Ambassador has dared to recapture the TRUE VALUES; to restore the most necessary MISSING DIMENSION in knowledge; to become a cultural *character-building* institution, concerned with moral, spiritual and ethical values as well as with the intellect. It started without money—with four students and eight members of faculty and administration. There have been no protest marches, no friction between students and faculty and administration, no hippie-type students. Ambassador is indeed UNIQUE!

These enterprises include the *World Tomorrow* television and radio broadcast, aired weekly in nearly every market throughout the English-speaking world and in numerous other areas worldwide. There is no solicitation for financial support. The programs are UNIQUE in the broadcasting field, with worldwide impact on MILLIONS!

There is *The Plain Truth*—a finest quality mass-circulation magazine in full color in seven languages, with about eight million copies monthly. This, alone, would rate as "BIG BUSINESS" if it were a commercial profit-making operation. But this enterprise was built, starting without capital, without advertising revenue and without subscription price income. It is indeed UNIQUE in the publishing field.

Also there are other publications, including *The Bible Correspondence Course* issued monthly, with scores of thousands of students enrolled; the *Good News* magazine and a *Youth* magazine. There are scientific expeditions, in association with the Leopold III Foundation for the Exploration and Conservation of Nature. This Work, further, has been engaged in large-scale archaeological projects in joint-participation with Hebrew University of Jerusalem and with the Japanese government; with other institutions in Syria, as well as cultural and humanitarian projects in Southeast Asia, the Kingdom of Jordan and in Africa.

Yes, truly, this has been "Mission Impossible"— ACCOMPLISHED! And still being accomplished in ever-increasing magnitude! It has been and is, as stated above, an example of what the living God can do, has done, and is doing through human instrumentalities yielded to Him and obedient to HIS WAYS!

I had been, over wide areas, conducting surveys on conditions and trends. I was greatly concerned over learning that most people are not happy—the world is full of evils. But WHY? My surveys revealed the worsening *conditions,* but not the *cause.* Nor could it be found in science, nor in education, nor in government, nor in religion.

In the autumn of 1926, my wife said she had discovered, in the Bible, a God-ordained WAY OF LIFE—a way contrary to accepted Christianity. It became controversial. I was challenged into the most intensive study of my life.

I had been born and reared of upstanding and

stable parents of a traditional orthodox Christian denomination. I had never had any particular religious interest, and by age 18 I dropped out of Sunday school and church attendance. I assumed, as probably do most, that the denominations of traditional Christianity had received their beliefs and doctrines from the Bible. I had always said, "I simply can't understand the Bible." But now I set out to prove, *by the Bible,* that "all these churches can't be wrong!"

Soon I encountered the most astonishing shock of my life! I was shocked to discover not only that traditional Christianity taught *contrary* to the Bible— that the Christian religion, with more adherents than any religion, did *not,* as I had supposed, get its teachings from the Bible, *BUT* that the Bible contained teachings and revelations of *facts* not known or taught by *any* religion.

It was amazing! I began to see plainly, in the Bible, that what I had been taught from childhood was primarily the *very opposite* of what the Bible teaches in plain language! At first I was confused. My head was swimming! My foundations seemed to be crumbling beneath me.

Simultaneously I was making a renewed in-depth study of the theory of Evolution. I was researching it and at the same time the Biblical claims of special Creation.

Was there a God, after all? What *could* a man believe? It was, for a while, a frustrating dilemma.

Gradually, as these months of 12- to 16-hour days of study progressed, the real truth began to emerge. It didn't come easily or quickly. It required effort, zeal, determination, patience. And above all, a willingness to confess error when proved, and to confess truth even against my own will.

6

I *did* find absolute PROOF that the Creator, God Almighty, exists and RULES the universe. I found many proofs of the inspiration and authenticity of the Bible. And I found the *CAUSE* of all this world's ills, as well as *the solution that will be made*—if even against the resistance and opposition of humanity! I found the MISSING DIMENSION in KNOWLEDGE—*what* man is, *why* man was put on earth—the PURPOSE for which we were made alive. I found THE WAY that was set in living motion to CAUSE and produce PEACE, HAPPINESS, ABUNDANCE! I found what neither science, religion, nor education has revealed—what had been overlooked, though available.

And IT ALL MADE SENSE!

I found THE REVEALED ANSWERS—rational, obvious answers—to humanity's problems, troubles and evils. Answers not found in science, education, government nor religion! And I found that the very GOSPEL—which means *good NEWS*—brought to the world by Christ had for 18½ centuries been rejected or ignored by that world!

How all this came about is the story of an experience as unique as it was heartrending and difficult to go through—for it became a battle against my own self and my human—my *very* human nature. In the end, I lost that battle in an unconditional surrender. And the incredible accomplishments in which I have been privileged to have the leading part, have been the result.

Sometime ago, a leading American news magazine, reviewing the frightening state of today's world, commented to the effect that it would seem the only hope for human survival now lies in the intervention of an unseen "Strong Hand from Someplace." What has been developed in such astonishing manner in this Work is directly creditable to the direction, inspiration, and empowerment of that "Strong Hand."

It is a historic fact that many times the unseen One has prepared in advance those to be used as His instruments for getting His purpose accomplished. In my personal case, looking back in retrospect, I have felt that the advance preparation, even from childhood, was a thrilling succession of unusual and intriguing experiences.

Thousands have requested that I write the details of those experiences.

Too often, it seems to me, leaders in science, in government, or other fields of activity hastily ask only, "How soon can we?" instead of *"Should we?"* I did ask myself, *should* the story of my life be written and published? For some time, I felt it should not. I felt it was my responsibility to get on with *getting the job done,* not to talk or write about myself.

But when listeners, viewers and readers ask to know what's back of this Work—how it started, what led to it, *how* it has been done—I came to realize they have a right to know.

As a young man I read Benjamin Franklin's *Autobiography* three times—over a period of a few years. It had a considerable impact and influence on my life. I owe much to having read it. The reading of life experiences of many other men, whether biography or autobiography, have been of great value and inspiration.

There was the autobiography of Bernard Baruch, biographies of George Washington, Abraham Lincoln, Theodore Roosevelt and many others.

Then there was the Apostle Paul, a man of God, who told his life experiences, recorded in the Bible. The first four books of the New Testament consist, primarily, of those portions of the life-story of Jesus

8

helpful to the reader. The Old Testament is replete with biographical sketches of the life experiences of many men—Noah, Abraham, Isaac, Jacob, Joseph, Joshua, Samuel, David, Elijah, many others.

I came to realize that the recording of one's life experiences can be inspiring and helpful to others— provided there has been something of real value in those experiences. The influence exerted on me by personal association with numerous leaders among men, in business, industry, education, government, and by reading of such lives, played their part in carrying me through an eventful life, filled with interesting, exciting and unusual experiences. They have helped solve problems, meet difficulties, sorrows, sufferings. They have contributed also to successes, and the joy of participating in great accomplishments.

And now, looking back on a long life well filled with action, effort, travel, important personal meetings with the so-called great and the near-great, many world leaders, kings, presidents, prime ministers, educators, industrialists, heads of great banks, scientists—a life replete with exciting events and unusual experiences, I feel that the recording of all this might impart some measure of inspiration and help to the reader.

For one thing, I had felt, years ago, that the story of these experiences might be helpful and of value to my two sons. Benjamin Franklin addressed his *Autobiography* to his son. But there never seemed to be time to write it, just for them.

But after so many radio listeners and *Plain Truth* subscribers requested the background facts, it seemed that I owed it to them, and I decided to write it in serial form, an installment each month, in *The Plain Truth*.

Consequently, the Autobiography began appearing with the September, 1957, issue.

AUTOBIOGRAPHY

It is my sincere hope and desire that the reader will be helped to a richer, fuller, more abundant life by this *Autobiography*.

10

1

Boyhood

EVEN FROM EARLIEST memory, life always has seemed unusual, eventful, exciting.

I was born July 31, 1892, of respected and upright parents who were of solid Quaker stock. My ancestors had emigrated from England to Pennsylvania with William Penn, a hundred years before the United States became a nation. My ancestry, through a paternal great-grandmother, traces back to Edward I, King of England.

I first saw the light of day in a red brick two-apartment flat on the northwest corner of East 14th and Grand Avenue, in Des Moines, Iowa. Of course I remember absolutely nothing of the day of my birth—even as you remember nothing of the day you were born. But my mother always remembered it, especially since I was her firstborn, as my father was a firstborn son before me.

A friend in Des Moines, some years ago, jestingly remarked that I "became famous too late"—the flat in which I was born long since had been replaced by a business property.

The earliest events that linger in memory occurred when I was three years of age. Our family then was living on West Harrison Street in Des Moines, near 14th. We lived in a modest cottage, and my father's parents lived in a two-story house next door. I remember scampering through the rear side door of their house to sample the delicious apple pies my grandmother made.

Also there is still memory of my maternal great-grandfather Elon Hole, then between 92 and 94, often taking me up in his arms—and the tragedy that occurred when he fell down the stairs, and died from the fall. Then there was an uncle, Jesse Hole, in my memory—also in his nineties.

I started kindergarten at age 5. I can still hear in my mind the mournful clang of the school bell, one block south.

Swearing Off Chewing

It was at this advanced age of 5 that I swore off chewing tobacco. A ditch was being dug in front of our house. Of course ditches were still being dug with shovels, by hand in 1897. This was quite exciting for a five-year-old. I spent most of my time out in the front yard watching. Ditch diggers in those days universally chewed tobacco. At least these particular diggers did.

"What's that there?" I asked, as one of them whipped a plug of tobacco out of his hip pocket, and bit off a corner.

"This is something good," he answered. "Here, sonny, bite off a chaw."

I accepted his generosity. I can remember distinctly

struggling to bite off "a chaw." That plug was really tough. But finally I got it bitten off. It didn't taste good, and seemed to have a rather sharp bite. But I chewed it, as I saw him chew his, and when I felt I had it well chewed, I swallowed it.

And very soon thereafter—a minute or less—I swore off chewing tobacco for LIFE!!! I say to you truthfully, I have never chewed since!

This was very shortly after the days of the old horse-drawn street cars. The new electric trolley cars had just come in—the little dinkys. I remember them well. The conductor on our line was Charley, and the motorman was old Bill. The most fascinating thing in the world was to park myself up at the front of the long side seat, on my knees, so I could look through the glass and watch old Bill run that car. I decided then what I was going to be when I grew up. I was going to be a street car motorman. But something in later years seems to have sidetracked that youthful ambition.

I do remember, though, that my father had a different idea of what I would be when I grew up. I was constantly pestering him with questions. I always seemed to want to know "WHY?" or "HOW?" I wanted to UNDERSTAND. At age 5 I can remember my father saying: "That youngin is always asking so many questions he's sure to be a Philadelphia lawyer, when he grows up."

That obsession for understanding was to have great influence on founding *The Plain Truth* magazine and Ambassador College in later years.

Those Important First Years

When I was 6 the family moved to Marshalltown, Iowa, where my father entered the flour milling business.

I remember the events of those days at age 6 much better than I do those of age 56. The mind is much more receptive, and the memory far more retentive, in the earlier years.

Believe it or not, every baby learns and retains more the very first year of life than any year thereafter. Each year we learn and retain a little less than the year before. Few, however, realize this fact. For each succeeding year, the total fund of knowledge increases. Knowledge accumulation is *additive,* that of each year is added to the fund of previous years. Writing up these early experiences brings this forcibly to mind. Occurrences are coming back to me in my mind now, as I write, that I have not thought of consciously for years.

Old Century Out — New Century In

After a year or so the family moved back to Des Moines. It was while we lived there that my brother Russell was born, Jan. 26, 1900, when I was 7½.

Another milestone event that lingers vividly in memory was the turn of the century. (Actually, the true turn of the century was Jan. 1, 1901.) *That* particular New Year's Eve was a once-in-a-lifetime event. Then and there I formed an aversion to church "Watch-nights" on New Year's Eve.

I couldn't see any fun, at 7½ years, in having to sit quietly in church from about 8 o'clock until midnight, unable to get up and play or run around, just quietly "watching" the old century out and the new century in. We were only watching the passing of a humanly calculated point of time, anyway. I only knew that it was a droll and dismal evening for me. I went to sleep once or twice, only to be awakened.

This new-century watch-night event occurred 26 days before my brother Russell was born. When my little baby brother was a few months old we moved to

14

Union, Iowa, probably spring of 1900, where my father went into partnership in a hardware store.

The "Pigeon Milk" Hunt

One day I wandered into the town job-printing shop. I must have been on one of my usual information-seeking forays, asking so many questions that ways and means had to be thought up for ridding the printers of the nuisance.

"Say, sonny, I wonder if you'd run an errand for us," asked the printer. "Run over to the grocery and ask them for a half pint of pigeon milk."

"What's it for?" I asked. "Why do you want it?" I always had to understand "WHY?" and "HOW?"

"To grease the presses with," explained the printer.

"How'll I pay for it?"

"Tell 'em to charge it," was the answer.

At the grocery store the grocer explained:

"Sorry, bub, we're just out of pigeon milk. They carry that now at the jewelry store."

From the jewelry store I was sent to the furniture store, then to the drug store, and after almost every store in town I went to my father's hardware store. Dad explained that I had been chasing all over town on a fool's errand. Anyway, I added to my store of knowledge the fact that pigeon milk is not to be found in stores. And I didn't think it was a more foolish errand than the one a rookie sailor was sent on when his ship was anchored at Pearl Harbor. Older sailors sent him to a dour Commandant on shore to get the key to the flag pole—and he got thrown in the brig.

While at Union I sold the *Saturday Evening Post* every week. I remember the special canvas bag with the magazine name on the side very well.

Our barn in Union was badly infested with rats. I determined to do something about it. I obtained a large cage rat trap at the hardware store, and almost every morning I had a number of rats in the trap.

I remember a birthday party my mother had for me on my 9th birthday, July 31, 1901, probably because a picture taken at the party has remained in the family box of old pictures.

Back to Des Moines we moved again in 1901, in early fall, after a year and a half in Union, this time near East 13th and Walker. I was now in the 4th grade. We lived a short distance from a Seventh-Day Adventist Sanitarium, with a bakery shop near the front entrance. I remember being sent often to this bakery for special "health" bread—probably whole wheat. The thing that most impressed me, however, was the impression on my boyish mind that these Adventists must be some kind of odd religious people, because they "kept Saturday for their Sunday." Even at that age, anything different from common custom and general social acceptance automatically seemed strange—and if strange, then of course it seemed WRONG. Why do people assume that the rank-and-file of PEOPLE can't be wrong?

It seems most of us, unless we do stop to think a bit, are like Mrs. O'Rafferty, watching her son march with the soldiers down Broadway, just returned to New York after World War I.

"I was that proud of Dinny," she said, "for, d'ye know, they were *all* out-of-step but him."

Well, perhaps it *was* Dinny who was properly *in* step—who knows? The point is, we blindly assume that the majority of PEOPLE can't be wrong. But I was to learn, in later years, that people as a whole can be wrong—so terribly wrong that PEOPLE are now bringing the END of their wrongly built civilization crashing down on their own heads.

Only, most people are still unaware of it!

When I was eleven, 1903, the automobile was in its earliest infancy—mostly built like the horse-drawn carriages, hard solid rubber tires, steered by a stick or handle rather than a wheel. We often called them horseless carriages. My father was always jolly, and he loved a joke. It was while we were living in this house that he called out to us:

"Hurry! Come quick! Here goes a horseless carriage!"

Seeing one of these early automobiles was a rare sight. We came running to the front window. A carriage was going by. It was a *horseless* carriage all right. It was drawn, not by horses, but a pair of mules. My father's strong bass voice boomed forth in hearty laughter.

Wrestling became a favorite sport in those days. These were the days of Frank Gotch, Farmer Burns, Zbysco, and others, when wrestling was a real sport and not a fakery show. "Clayt" Schoonover's older brothers had set up a real wrestling mat, and they taught us all the main holds.

I think I loved ice skating perhaps more than any other sport, however. I had learned to take wide, sweeping strokes in a style so that my body would sway way over, from one side to the other, using the force of gravity to help propel forward. There was a rhythm and sort of sensation to it that was thrilling.

At that time, 1902-3, many of the streets in the city were as yet unpaved. The sidewalks were wood slats nailed down on two-by-four runners, with narrow cracks between slats. I remember this, because of an incident. One day someone dropped a dime—a ten-cent piece—and it fell onto the sidewalk and disappeared through one of the narrow cracks. Neighbors must have spent two or three man-hour days tearing up the sidewalks hunting that lost dime. I learned then that people will expend far greater effort to prevent *losing* something than they will to gain something. Later I used this bit of psychology with good effect in advertising copy.

When a Boy Is Eleven

I have often said that the HAPPIEST year in any human life is that of a BOY at age eleven. At that age a boy experiences something, I believe, which a girl never knows. He has no sense of responsibility to weight him down. He has no burdens but to HAVE FUN. Of course boys that age will do foolish things, sometimes dangerous things. How any boy lives to adulthood I will never know—unless there is a guardian angel watching over and protecting each boy.

Another condition of the time illustrates how recently this world has become really modernized. The street lights in our neighborhood were gas lights. Electricity had not yet reached that stage of modernization in 1902-3. A man came by on horseback every evening about dusk, with a lighted wick on the end of a stick, with which he reached up and lit each light. Then, about sun-up next morning he had to ride by again turning the lights off.

During these days I did a great deal of bicycle riding, developing big calf muscles on both legs. By this time my father had invented the air-circulating jacket idea around a furnace, and had gone into the furnace manufacturing business, with a small factory on East 1st or 2nd Street. I worked summer vacations in the factory.

Our transportation, 1903-4, was horse and buggy—

and my bicycle. Going to the factory in the morning, we had to use the whip on the horse occasionally to keep him trotting. But returning home in the evening, it was necessary to hold tight rein on him. He needed no urging to trot. He seemed to know his oats were waiting for him in our barn.

Early Religious Training

I think it is time, now, to explain what boyhood religious training was mine.

Both my father and mother were of solid Quaker stock.

From earliest memory I was kept regularly in the Sunday school and church services of the First Friends Church in Des Moines.

From earliest boyhood I was in a boys' class in Sunday school, and we all sort of grew up together. I can't remember when I first knew those boys. I guess we were all taken there as babies together.

Anyway it was interesting, some twenty-five years ago, to learn what had become of most of them—for I had drifted away from church about age 18, and had gotten completely out of touch. One of them had become Dean of Student Personnel at San Francisco State College, with a Ph.D. from Yale. I contacted him, and he gave me considerable and valuable assistance and counsel in founding Ambassador College in 1947.

Another, who had been perhaps my principal boyhood chum through those early years, was a retired retail furniture merchant, who had enlarged and successfully maintained the retail establishment founded by his father. Another was a successful dentist. The son of the Pastor of my boyhood days had died apparently early in life. Another had become director of a large relief agency in the Middle East. On the whole, the boys of that class had grown to become successful men.

The Awakening —
Spark of Ambition Ignited

During the years between 12 and 16, besides school, I had many Saturday and vacation jobs. I carried a paper route, was errand boy for a grocery store, special delivery boy for a dry goods store, spent one summer vacation as draftsman for a furnace company, and there were other odd jobs.

But at age 16, during summer vacation, I obtained my first job away from home. The job was waiting on tables in the dining room of a semi-resort hotel in Altoona, the next town east of Des Moines. There was an electric line—an interurban street car—that ran out through Altoona and on east to the little town of Colfax. This Altoona hotel served food of a standard that attracted many guests from Des Moines.

The owner was a single man of perhaps 45. He complimented my work highly. Soon he began to tell me that he could see qualities in me that were destined to carry me to large success in life. He constantly expressed great confidence in me, and what I would be able to accomplish, if I were willing to put forth the effort.

The effect it had on me reminds me of an experience my wife has related which happened when she was a little girl. She was in her father's general store. A man came in, placed his hand on her head, and said:

"You're a *pretty* little girl, aren't you?"

"I'll thank you," spoke up her mother indignantly, "not to tell my daughters they are pretty! That's not good for them."

Promptly little Loma ran to a mirror and looked

into it. She made a discovery. She said to herself approvingly: "Well I *am* pretty amn't I?"

I had never realized before that I possessed any abilities. Actually I had never been a leader among boys. Most of the time I had played with boys older than I who automatically took the lead. But now, for the first time, I began to believe in myself. This hotel owner aroused ambition—created within me the DESIRE to climb the ladder of success—to become an important SOMEBODY. This, of course, was vanity. But it also was ambition for *accomplishment*—for self-improvement. And he also stimulated the WILL to put forth whatever effort it would require to achieve this success. He made me realize I would have to study, acquire knowledge and know-how, be industrious and exercise self-denial. Actually this flowered into grossly overrated SELF-confidence and conceit. But it impelled me to *driving* effort.

Life's Turning Point

It is impossible to estimate the importance of this sudden arousal of ambition—this injection of an intense desire for success—this igniting of the spark of determined energy to achieve worthy accomplishment.

This was the turning point of my life.

Suddenly life became a whole new "ball-game." There had awakened within a totally new outlook on the future.

This, I believe, is the vital ingredient that has been missing in most human lives. Most continue through life as I was prior to this arousal of ambition. As I have stated, up to this point I played with boys older than I. It seemed natural for them to assume leadership. I simply "went along." The idea of looking forward to achieving success, or an accomplishment of any note never intruded itself into my mind. Nor does it, probably, in the average mind. And it was like an intrusion, for my mind was uninterruptedly occupied only with the interests, pleasures and enjoyments of the moment.

Suddenly all this was *changed!* Drastically changed! What a tragedy the vast majority of human minds cannot be given this HOPE—this DESIRE—this ambitious expectation—this CONFIDENCE—in their future! The general attitude of hopelessness for the future has spawned the modern mod rebellions—the hippie movement—the campus protests, riots and violence.

Of course, as yet, at age 16, there had formulated no definite GOAL to work toward, further than the general ambition to SUCCEED. Of what that success was to consist had to crystalize later.

Also, so far, it was pure VANITY. But it was a positive vanity, and that might be vastly preferable to a negative, purposeless humility. It was the first *start* toward later accomplishment.

Some few years later, I was considerably inspired by one of Orison Swett Marden's "inspirations" books, titled, "He CAN Who Thinks He Can." What a pity that there seems to be a famine of such books today.

Returning to Des Moines I continued as a student at North High School. I began to spend extra hours outside of high school at the city library, mostly in the Philosophy, Biography, and Business Administration sections. I began to study Plato, Socrates, Aristotle and Epictetus. It was at this time that I first read Benjamin Franklin's Autobiography.

My first date with a girl took place at about this time—a date to escort a next-door neighbor girl in my class in high school to some school function. At that stage I was pretty much in awe of girls, and felt awkward

22

in their presence. It has always been a puzzle to me that so many boys around that age are afraid of girls, ill at ease before them, and yet girls seem not to be shy or bashful in any way in the company of boys. For the next 8 years I continued to date this girl on and off, (not what today is termed "going steady," however), but never did I put my arm around her, kiss her, or as they would say today, "neck with her." (It was called "loving up" in those days.)

North High had a total enrollment of only 400 then. In high school I went out for football, and for track, and played a small amount of basketball in the gym. In football I played end or halfback. I weighed only 135 in those days, and was too light to make the team, but I suited up with the team in all of its home games, usually played in the Drake University Stadium. In track I went out for the mile run in my Sophomore year only, but never was entered in the state meet. The best time I ever made was 5 minutes flat, on the Drake track, where the annual Drake Relays, nationally famous, are still run. Today the world's best milers run the mile under 4 minutes!

I was an average student in school. But in final exams I always got grades of 95% to 98%.

But as yet there had been set no definite GOAL in life. At the tender age of 16 the idea of fixing a definite objective—of finding the true PURPOSE of life—occurs to few teenagers. Ambition had been aroused. I was *burning* with DESIRE to go somewhere in life—to become a success. But exactly *where*, or precisely *what* constituted the "SUCCESS," had not as yet crystalized.

2

Learning Important Lessons

AT AGE 18 I found a book in the public library, titled, "Choosing a Vocation." It took the reader through a searching self-analysis, and a survey of vocations, occupations and professions, to place the candidate where he best fit.

A thorough study of this self-analysis and survey indicated that I would probably be most successful in the profession of journalism and advertising. And this, to me, was one of the truly exciting, thrilling professions.

It so happened that my uncle in Des Moines, Frank Armstrong, my father's younger brother, was the most prominent advertising man in the state. He had led the movement of establishing Ad-Clubs in other cities over the state, and he was the first president of the state association.

I went to my uncle for counsel and advice. From

that time, since I had chosen his field, he practically steered my life for the next eleven years, and I owe much to him. To me he seemed like a sort of second Benjamin Franklin, and on the whole I felt he had unusual insight, understanding, and sound judgment.

The place to begin in the advertising profession, he advised, was the want-ad department of a daily newspaper. This was the freshman class of the advertising school of hard knocks.

It was late December, 1910. Now the big question came: should I stay in school, and take courses in advertising and journalism in college or university?

"Well, Herbert," he counselled, "that depends on you and how much ambition and drive you have. It happens that no college or university in the country has yet offered a course in this profession that is worth a plug nickel.

"Now I know," he continued, "that nearly everybody has the delusion that an education is something you get at school—and higher education at the university. It's like going to a hardware store or department store to purchase a lawn mower. People seem to have the idea that an education is something they have all wrapped up at the university, ready to hand it over to you when you buy it by paying the tuition. But it has always seemed to me that traipsing across the door-sill of a college classroom, or sitting in an arm-chair, is not putting an education into your mind. Education comes from study—from books—from lectures—from contacts—from travel—from thinking about what you see and hear and read—and from experience.

"The reason we have to maintain schools and universities is simply that most people are too lazy—most lack the ambition and persistence, the drive—to procure an education outside of schools and colleges. Most people must have someone do their thinking and planning for them, assign lessons and homework, and force students to study and learn by a system of rewards and punishments in the form of grades, and finally, a sheepskin with a degree.

"Now if you have the initiative, and the will to drive yourself to study, without these prods of rewards and penalties, you can acquire just as complete an education outside the classrooms as in. You can gain a much more thorough and practical knowledge of the profession you have chosen outside than in. And so far as general education is concerned, you can acquire that, if you have the gumption and the will. I can help you choose the proper textbooks to study in general educational areas, as well as in advertising and journalism, and psychology—which, by the way, you'll have to understand and use. Actually, Herbert," he continued, "a majority of corporate heads, presidents and board chairmen of New York and Chicago Banks are primarily self-educated beyond high school education. The doctors, dentists, scientists and technologists, of course, went on through university."

At that time a small percent of high school graduates went on to matriculate in college or university. Today that condition has reversed, and as high as 90% of high school graduates enter the mad scramble to gain entrance into the institutions of higher learning. Also, in 1910, a much smaller percent went on to graduate even from high school.

I went home and thought it over thoroughly. Ambition is not only the DESIRE, but the determination and the *will* to *achieve* the desired goal. For two years ambition had burned fiercely within me. I wanted both success and to become a well-educated person. I knew I wanted these goals intensively enough to *drive* myself to any needed extent to succeed.

I told my uncle my decision. He assigned me to one year's experience in want ads, and advised that I get a job in the want-ad department of the Des Moines *Daily Capital,* then published by Lafe Young, senior United States Senator from Iowa.

Applying Laws of Success

I didn't know, as yet, what later I came to learn were the seven laws—or seven steps toward SUCCESS—but I was starting out with the first four of them.

Well, ALMOST! The first law is to choose the right goal. I had chosen my life's goal. I thought then I had chosen carefully, intelligently, wisely, and the RIGHT goal. I had put myself through a thorough self- analysis, and survey of professions and occupations. I had not unthinkingly stumbled onto whatever job, field, or occupation that was nearest me.

Most people, I have observed, are victims of circumstance. They have given no intelligent thought to choosing where they live, what they do, or planning for the future. They have no specific aim or goal in life. They are headed toward no definite PURPOSE. They are where they are by circumstance.

I was to learn later that the RIGHT goal was one I knew nothing, as yet, about. But I *had* chosen the field that was to provide the precise needed TRAINING for the RIGHT goal, when my eyes became opened to it. I was getting the precise needed training, education and experience.

The second law of success is EDUCATION—the specific specialized education and training needed for success in the chosen goal, *in addition* to the general

27

balanced education one needs to develop the whole person.

With the determination and drive to study, and by applying myself to the task, the course of study and training had been laid.

And next comes good HEALTH, to which I gave much thought and diligence. And fourth was the DRIVE to push oneself into getting these things done. My ambition was so strong—the desire to succeed so intense—that I was imbued with almost excessive drive. And on this first assignment I became a hustler.

The fifth requisite is resourcefulness—the ability to think a problem or obstacle through—to find a BETTER WAY—to find the SOLUTION to problems—to THINK about what one is doing WHILE he is doing it.

And my very first experience on the new job was to demonstrate that.

I did not ask *The Capital* if they needed any help. That was too negative—might have resulted in being turned down. I went straight to the manager of the want-ad department, told him I was entering the advertising profession, and had decided to join his staff because it offered the best opportunity to LEARN, and to advance. I got the job. The starting salary was $6 per week.

I had no conception, then, that the advertising profession was not, after all, to be my final life profession—or that *this* experience was merely the preliminary training needed for the ultimate bigger job later in life.

In those days I had developed a very excessive case of self-confidence. I was snappy, confident, self-assured—yet *sincere,* and in the intent of heart, honest.

On this want-ad job I soon became known as a "hustler." On the street I hurried—walked rapidly. I was a dynamo of energy. Off nights I studied. Books were procured on advertising, on psychology, merchandising, business management, and English. All the leading trade journals were subscribed to and diligently read—primarily *"Printers Ink,"* and *"Advertising & Selling,"* the two leading trade journals of the profession.

My uncle directed the training in learning an effective *style* in writing. Constantly I studied the writing style of Claude Hopkins, president and chief copywriter for the Lord & Thomas Advertising agency. This man reputedly drew a salary of $50,000 a year (big money in those days) writing the advertising copy for Quaker Oats, Pepsodent, Palmolive, Goodyear tires, Blue Jay Corn Plasters, Ovaltine, and others. His rapid style, unique, yet plain, simple and easy-to-read, *built* multimillion dollar businesses for those firms.

Also my uncle started me reading Elbert Hubbard, with his two magazines, *The Philistine* and *The Fra*—primarily for ideas, writing style, vocabulary. Later I was to become personally acquainted with Elbert Hubbard.

The "Goat Work"

The first day in want ads I was started out, bright and early, on a job they called "the Goat Work," tutored by a young man now ready to graduate from that job.

This job in the newspaper business might be compared to "boot camp" in the Marines. It is a most undesirable, tough, breaking-in job. I soon learned what it was.

We each armed ourselves with a copy of the previous night's paper, a want-ad blank, and a pencil. Then we started out afoot. We headed up the hill on West Fourth and Fifth—the rooming house district.

"I'll stop in at a couple of rooming houses," said my predecessor-instructor, "just to show you how to do it; then I'll go back to the office, and you're on your own."

Stepping boldly up to the first rooming house door, he rang the bell. The landlady opened the door, instantly recognizing the folded newspaper in his side pocket and the want-ad blank in his hand.

"NO!" she snapped decisively, before he could say a word, "I don't want to run any want ads."

"But *lady,*" my instructor put a foot in the door being slammed in his face, "you know Mrs. Jones down in the next block, don't you?"

"Never heard of her!" Of course not. Neither had the boy with me.

"Well, Mrs. Jones put her ad in the *Capital,* and at least a dozen men came trying to rent the room. The reason you didn't get results is that you put your ad in the wrong paper."

But by this time the madam had managed to dislodge his foot and slam the door.

This same procedure was repeated at the next house.

"Well—" said my want-ad buddy, happily, "that shows you how to do it. Hope you sell a lot of ads. So long—see you at the office."

Finding a More Effective Way

But it didn't seem that he had demonstrated how to do it—but rather, how NOT to do it.

I waited until he was out of sight. I hid both the newspaper and the want-ad blank in my inner pocket, covered with my overcoat. Then I walked briskly up to the next rooming-house door.

"I hope you haven't rented your room yet," I smiled

as the landlady opened the door. "May I see it?"

"Why, certainly," she smiled back, opening wide the door.

I trailed her to the second-floor room. No doors were going to be slammed in my face.

"Why," I smiled, "this is a delightful room, isn't it?" The landlady beamed expectantly. I whipped out the want-ad blank and began rapidly writing.

"Here!" she exclaimed suspiciously, "what are you doing with that want-ad blank?"

But she could not slam the front door in my face now—nor did she appear big enough to attempt throwing me out bodily.

"Now look," I said calmly. "This is a lovely room. Do you know why your want ads have not rented it for you? The want-ad solicitors have told you it was because you put it in the wrong paper. You know that's bosh as well as I. The reason you didn't rent your room is that *you are not a professional advertising writer!*"

By this time I had the want ad written—at least two or three times longer (and costlier) than the average.

"Listen," I continued, "imagine *you* are a young man reading all the room-for-rent ads, looking for a room that is going to be your *home*. Now think how all those other ads are written—then listen to this, and think!—which room would YOU go to see, and rent?"

I read the ad, which certainly made the room sound very desirable. In fact, its glowing terms probably flattered her. She just *couldn't* resist seeing that flowery description of her room in print in the paper.

"Why, I'd certainly want to rent *that* room, instead of those ordinarily described in the want ads," she replied. "That *does* make it sound good." She bought the ad—as large as three ordinary ads.

And the ad did rent her room!

31

That was the first advertisement I ever wrote that was printed. But I had already been diligently studying textbooks on advertising writing.

Since 1958 we have been large purchasers of double-page and full-page advertising space in several of the world's leading mass-circulation magazines, including, in the United States, *Life, Look, TV Guide,* and around the world, double pages in many editions of *Reader's Digest,* half pages in London Sunday *Times,* full pages, full color, Sunday *Times* magazine; *Hörzu* in Germany, other leading magazines in Australia, South Africa, The Philippines, and others.

The twenty years experience in the advertising and journalism profession, starting with this first want ad, was the preparation that supplied the know-how for effective use of this type media, reaching a readership in excess of 150 million worldwide. Results were more than gratifying. Two such double pages in English in *Reader's Digest* brought 20,000 new subscribers in India for *The Plain Truth.*

After an energetic morning I was back at the want-ad office about 1 p.m., the deadline for getting ads to the composing room. I had a handful of want ads.

"Much-a-Welcome"

Soon I thought of a faster, more pleasant way to sell *more* room-for-rent ads, in less time.

The rival papers were *The Register & Leader,* and *The Daily News.* The *News* didn't count as a want-ad medium, but the "R&L" as we then called it was the city's big want-ad medium. Today *The Des Moines Register* is recognized by many as one of the nation's ten great newspapers. In 1924 I was offered the job of

32

advertising manager of *The Register,* and refused it—but that's getting ahead of the story.

The "R & L" printed perhaps three or four times more room-for-rent ads than *The Capital.* Rooming-house landladies had become smart. In order to prevent newspaper solicitors annoying them on the telephone, or prospective roomers turning them down on the phone before actually seeing the rooms, they usually gave the street address *only,* in their ads.

I knew that the "information" office of the telephone company indexed according to street addresses, as well as by name, but the information operators were not supposed to give out names or numbers for a given street address.

So I called the information office, and first engaged the operator in a jocular conversation. After a while I persuaded her, this once, to give me the name of the rooming-house landlady at a certain street address.

"Well MUCH-A-WELCOME" I said jokingly.

"Oh, you're entirely welcome," she said.

"No!" I came back, *"I'm* not welcome—I said *you're* much-a-welcome."

She was a little confused at this 18-year-old kidding.

"Well, what am *I* supposed to say, then?"

"Why, *you're* supposed to answer, 'you're entirely OBLIGED!' "

She had a good laugh. That joke sounds about as "corny" as Iowa's tall corn, now—but it certainly got me results with that information operator.

Next morning I called "information," and said, "This is Much-a-welcome again!" It brought a friendly laugh. I was, in my self-confident assurance, a reasonably glib talker. Somehow I managed to talk this information operator into giving me the names and telephone numbers of every room-for-rent want ad in the morning paper that we had not carried the evening before.

Always I ended by saying "Much-a-welcome," and she would laughingly reply, "Oh, you're entirely obliged." Silly, perhaps—but it got me the names and telephone numbers I wanted. Quite a telephonic friendship was struck up with this information operator. Often I wondered how old she was—what she looked like. I never knew. It did not seem appropriate to suggest a face-to-face meeting. But this daily morning procedure continued as long as I was on Rooming House ads.

Getting Ads by Phone

Once I had the names and telephone numbers, they were called by phone.

"Good morning. Is this Mrs. Smith?" I would start off, cheerily.

While I was only a boy of 18, I had inherited a strong bass-baritone voice from my father, even lower-pitched then than now, and sounded quite mature on the telephone. I discovered, even then, that I was possibly more effective audibly than visually. Indeed, this was the first prelude training for radio broadcasting that was to follow, beginning 24 years later.

"I wonder," I would continue the telephone conversation, "if you would describe your room to me." While getting the description, prompted by repeated questions from me, I was rapidly writing a very descriptive want ad. Then I explained that she had not described it well enough in the morning-paper ad to cause anyone to really want to walk out to see it, and told her that I was an expert ad-writer, and quickly read the ad that would tell enough about the room to cause

34

prospective roomers to want to see it. I explained that the reason she had not been getting results was the fact her ad was written so inexpertly.

A large majority of these hastily written telephone ads were sold. The rooms were usually rented—unless they failed to live up to the description after prospective roomers called to see them.

Soon we were carrying more room-for-rent ads than the "R&L." Whenever one of our rooming-house customers had a vacant room, they automatically called for me on the telephone, and soon rented the room again.

One of the seven laws of success, I repeat, is resourcefulness. Also an important point I have always stressed to students in Ambassador College is to THINK—and *constantly* to THINK about what you are doing *while you are doing it!* This experience in thinking of a more effective way of selling room-for-rent want ads might offer a helpful example to some of my readers.

My First Display Ads

It was not long until I was promoted out of the room-for-rent columns and into the Real Estate section.

But first came a challenging test—the toughest of all. The want-ad manager, a young man (older than I) named Charles Tobin, had an ambition. He hoped to increase his salary to a point that would enable him to wear a fresh-laundered shirt every day. Immediately, that became one of my ambitions, too. The assignment he gave me was to sell a special section on the want-ad page, of single-column *display* ads to the second-hand furniture dealers.

These stores were all owned by a type of men who

35

did not believe in advertising, and valued every penny as if it were a million dollars. To me, this was an unpleasant task, because so many of these stores were dirty and dusty and musty, cluttered and ill-arranged—an unpleasant atmosphere to enter.

Here, again, however, ads were sold by *writing the ads,* and making attractive-appearing layouts. These were the very first display ads I ever had printed. I remember staying up until midnight studying a book on advertising and selling psychology. It took the combination of all the selling psychology, attractive advertising layouts and copy, and persuasive personality I could muster to accomplish that assignment. But it was accomplished—a total of about a third of a page or more, as nearly as I can now remember.

During this "special number" crusade, I encountered a somewhat handicapped Jewish boy of about my age, the son of one of these "used furniture" merchants. The store owner was delighted to learn that I had some influence over his backward boy. It seemed like a responsibility that had come to me, to encourage him to go back to school, to study hard, and to begin to believe that he could be a success some day, and to start working, and *fighting,* even against sluggish impulses of self, to make something of himself. For some months I continued occasionally to drop in at this store to give this lad another "pep talk." It seemed to be doing good. I hope the progress continued, but after about a year we lost contact.

The $2 per Week Lesson

But after "putting over" this special number, I was given a Real Estate beat, and the salary raised to $8 per week.

I was put on a regular "beat," calling daily on a

certain number of Real Estate brokers to pick up their ads. Here again, I started writing ads for them. Results were increased. More and more the dealers on my route began using large ads in the *Capital,* using less space in the "R & L."

It was on this job that I became known as a "hustler." I walked at a pace that was almost a run. It was drive, *drive,* DRIVE!! all morning long—until the 1 p.m. deadline. Then the afternoons were spent in the office preparing form solicitations, to which were attached clipped want ads from the other local papers, or even those of other cities, which were mailed out. Thus I learned to sell want ads by mail. This knowledge landed an important job, later.

It was not long until Ivan Coolidge, then want-ad manager over at the "R & L," asked me to drop over and see him. He offered me $10 a week if I'd leave *The Capital* and join the *Register* staff. Later on, Ivan established an advertising agency of his own in Des Moines, which, I believe, gained some prominence—but he was unfortunately cut off somewhere in mid-life by premature death.

I told Ivan I wanted to consult my uncle before giving him my decision.

"So," chuckled my Uncle Frank, with the wisdom of a Ben Franklin, "the opposition is beginning to *feel* the pressure, eh? Want to hire you away from the *Capital*—willing to pay $10 a week to stop the competition, are they? Well, now listen, Herbert, a little encouragement once in a while is very helpful. It shows you are making good. You can get some inspiration out of it to provide incentive to keep driving yourself on. But I've noticed that there has been a tendency in some branches of our family to keep shifting around all the time from one thing to another—never staying with one thing long enough to make a success of it. There's a good deal to the old adage, after all, that a rolling stone gathers no moss. One of the great success lessons you need to learn is persistence—to stay *with* a thing.

"Now suppose you quit the *Capital* and go over to the *Register*. You wouldn't *learn* any more about the advertising profession over there than you're learning where you are. The only advantage is the $2 per week. You'd probably blow that in, and ten years from now you wouldn't remember having had it. I think the time has come for you to pay the $2 a week to learn the important lesson of staying *with* a thing. Every week, when you draw your $8 at the *Capital,* remember you are paying the extra $2 you might be getting at the *Register* as the price of that lesson, and I think you'll remember it."

I had started out to spend *one year* in want ads at the *Capital*. The temptation had come to weaken and get off that schedule.

I took my uncle's advice and stayed on the schedule.

Learning Rules of Success

Thus, at the early age of 18, some of the seven important rules of success were being learned.

The first success rule—I emphasize by repeating it—is fixing the right GOAL. Avoid fitting the "square peg in the round hole." I was yet to learn the real PURPOSE of life, and the one true supreme GOAL. Actually I had set out on a wrong goal—that of becoming someone "important," achieving business success and status for the purpose of making money. But at least I had made the self-analysis and the survey of vocations to find where I should fit *within* the realm of business, the field of this goal.

At least, ambition had been kindled.

And, though little realized at the time, all this experience was building the necessary foundation for the worldwide activities of later life.

The second success rule is EDUCATION—fitting oneself for the *achievement* of the goal. I was getting, *not* mere impractical and theoretical classroom book education, but the *combined* education of book study at night and practical experience in the daytime. And even here, the self-education being received was precisely that required to properly prepare me for this present worldwide Work of God, without which this Work today could not have become a success.

The third rule of success is good, vigorous HEALTH. Food plays a major part in this, and I was not to learn of the importance of food and diet until I was 38 years old. But I *had* learned the importance of sufficient exercise, deep breathing, daily bathing and elimination, and sufficient sleep.

The fourth rule, *drive,* putting a constant *prod* on oneself, seems to have come naturally as a result of the ambition that had been generated at sixteen. There was always the sense that I *had to hurry!* I was learning to plunge into a task with dynamic energy.

The fifth, *resourcefulness,* or *thinking about* the problem at hand, was unconsciously being developed by experience. For example, the experience of the "goat work" job, and then in *finding a way* to get in room-for-rent ads faster by telephone, was an example of learning this rule by experience—*thinking* through and applying initiative, to a *better way* of solving a problem. Most people do such a job just as they are shown, without ever applying thought or resourcefulness to the activity.

And now, the sixth rule, *perseverance,* never

39

quitting when it appears to everyone else one has failed, was being learned at the very low price of $2 per weekly lesson. In 1947, and again in 1948, Ambassador College appeared hopelessly to have failed. It seemed everyone else *knew* we had come to the "end of our rope." It has happened many times. But that $2 per week lesson learned at 18 turned a seeming hopeless failure into a worldwide ever-expanding success.

The seventh and most important rule I was not to learn until much later.

The First Sidestep From the Goal

But now came a big mistake in judgment.

Humans do not learn well from experience, nor all at once. The lesson of the forbidden fruit has not been learned by humanity in 6000 years. My $2 a week lesson was not really *learned* until later.

As the scheduled year of training in daily newspaper want ads drew to a close, a flattering offer came. And this time I failed to seek out the advice of my Uncle Frank who had wisely steered my business career thus far.

On *The Daily Capital* staff was a book critic, Emile Stapp, who edited a Book Review department. Her desk was on the second floor adjacent to the want ad and display advertising section. She had, apparently, observed my work, noted I was energetic and produced results. She was a sister-in-law of W. O. Finkbine, one of two millionaire brothers who owned and operated the Green Bay Lumber Company, with lumberyards scattered all over Iowa; the Finkbine Lumber Company, a large lumber manufacturing company in Wiggins, Mississippi; and operating a 17,000-acre wheat ranch in Canada.

Miss Stapp lived with her sister, Mrs. W. O.

Finkbine, "out on the Avenue," as we called it— meaning the millionaire residence street of Des Moines, West Grand Avenue. I doubt very much that all the residents of that fabled street were millionaires, but at least so it seemed to those of us who were of ordinary means in Des Moines.

One day, near the end of my year at *The Capital,* Miss Stapp told me she had spoken to Mr. Finkbine, and I was being offered the job of Timekeeper and Paymaster at the big lumber mill in southern Mississippi. I was first to work a short period in the company's commissary store, managed by her brother, whose name was Hal Stapp.

The job sounded flattering. The prospect of travel to far-off southern Mississippi had alluring appeal. I succumbed to it, going off on a tangent from the planned advertising career.

The First Meeting With a Millionaire

Before leaving, I was to go to the office of Mr. W. O. Finkbine for a short talk of instruction. I shall never forget my visit to the headquarters' offices of this lumber firm. I met also Mr. E. C. Finkbine, President of the corporation. W. O. was Vice President.

It was my first experience meeting millionaires. It made an intensive impression. I was awed. There seemed to be something in the appearance and personalities of these men that simply *radiated* POWER. It was instantly apparent that they were men of higher caliber than men I had known—men of greater ability. There was an expression of *intensity* which seemed to radiate an aura of positive confident *power* about them, and affected one who came within proximity of it. I could see that they were men who had studied, used their minds continually, dynamically, and positively.

Of course I was over-impressed, due to the plastic susceptibilities and inexperience of youth. A very few years later I began meeting so many millionaires that they began appearing quite ordinary, after all—just HUMAN!

I was taken into the private office of W. O. Finkbine. He wanted to give me a little general advice before sending a young man so far away from home. I have never forgotten what he said.

"We are going to send you down with the manager of our Canadian interests," he said. This man's name I do not remember now. It was early January, and he was going down to Wiggins for a vacation, and to inspect the company's operations there, during the off-season in Canada. I had never been farther from Des Moines than Omaha and Sioux City. It was a THRILL to look forward to the trip, first to seeing Chicago, then the deep South.

"First, I want to give you some advice about travelling," said Mr. Finkbine. "Most people look upon it as an extravagance to ride in the Pullman cars on trains. They are wrong. As you're starting on your first long trip from home, I want to impress on you the importance of always travelling in a Pullman car, except when you do not *have* the money to do so.

"First of all, especially at your age, we humans are influenced by everyone we come in contact with. On the Pullmans you will come in contact with a more successful class of people. This will have more influence than you can realize, now, on your future success in life. Then, in the Pullmans it is not only cleaner, but safer.

"Now," he continued, "whenever you stop at a hotel, the same principle applies. Always stop at the *leading* hotel in any city. If you want to economize, get the minimum-priced room, but always go to the *best* hotel. You are among more successful people, which will influence your own success. The best hotels are either fireproof or more nearly so—always safer—worth the little difference, if any, in cost as insurance against accident or fire. You are a young man, just getting started in life. Try to throw yourself into the company of as many successful men as possible. Study them. Try to learn WHY they are successful. This will help you learn how to build a success for yourself."

I did not disdain his advice. There have been many times in my life when I did not have enough money to travel on Pullman cars, or stay in the best hotels. Under such circumstances, I have travelled as I could afford—and I have travelled a great deal since that eventful day in early January, 1912—in fact a goodly portion of my life has been spent in travelling, as you will see as this autobiography progresses.

Since we moved to Pasadena, I have learned that these Finkbine brothers later retired from business, and moved to Pasadena. Very often, these days, I drive past the home where W. O. Finkbine lived in retirement, and died. One lesson in life he apparently never learned. When a man decides he already has achieved success, and retires—quits—he never lives long. I expect to stay in harness as long as I live.

Introduction to the South

As I look back now, after a travel-filled life, on this first real trip away from home, it seems strange that I could have been so absolutely inexperienced in travel. But I suppose one must be initiated, and learn, and this was my introduction to a life of travel.

We boarded a Pullman car in Des Moines one night—my first experience riding in one. I think I was too excited to sleep much, wanting to see as much of the scenery as possible—especially my first glimpse of the great Mississippi River as we crossed it between Davenport and Rock Island.

There was a cold blizzard on our arrival in Chicago next morning. The ground was covered with snow. We went over to see Michigan Avenue. I was thrilled. We went through "Peacock Alley," a very long and narrow lobby, nationally famous, in the Congress Hotel, and walked through the tunnel under the street connecting it with the Auditorium Hotel. I think we visited the Stock Yards, taking the first ride in my experience on an "L" (Elevated train).

Near mid-day we boarded the famous all-Pullman "Panama Limited" on the Illinois Central Railroad at 12th Street Station. Going into the diner for lunch and again for dinner was an exciting experience—I had never seen the inside of a dining car before. It was a new experience to learn about tipping waiters, redcaps, porters, bellboys—but my companion was an experienced traveller, and this initiation into the "ropes" of travelling was under good tutelage. I learned fast. Night came all too soon, and this time I slept soundly in my berth.

The next morning the train arrived in Jackson, Mississippi, where we changed for a local train on the "G. & S. I." Line.

This was the strangest experience of my life up to this time. We had left Chicago in below zero temperature and a blizzard. I had gone to sleep that night somewhere near Cairo, Illinois. And now, this morning, after a brief sleep, here it was—SUMMER!

I had never seen southern Negroes before, and in those days, January, 1912, they were quite different from the colored people I had known up north. (Readers will understand that in those days blacks were called "Negroes" and "colored people.")

Here in Jackson, Mississippi, it seemed that there were more black people than white on the streets, and they were utterly *different* from any people I had seen in the north—and, for that matter, than southern blacks today. Today the blacks of the South are comparatively well educated, on the average, but then very few had been privileged to receive much, if any, education. I was especially attracted to the dresses of the black women—bright and loud colors—such as a bright yellow or orange, clashing with a loud purple.

Arriving in Wiggins, I found a room in town, over a mile walk from the commissary store and the lumber mill, just outside of town, and was quickly introduced to my job in the store. Saturday night was the big night at the store. The mill employees were paid Saturday evening, and thronged the store. I was broken in immediately as "soda-fountain jerker."

One of the first men I met was a Negro I shall never forget—whose name was Hub Evans. One of the men in the store brought him around to me.

"Hub," he said, "tell Mr. Armstrong how many children you have."

"Thutty-six, suh," replied old Hub, promptly and proudly—"hope t' make it foty 'fo Ah die!"

I was not merely amused—but intensely interested. "Tell me, Hub," I responded, "how many wives have you had?"

"Only three, suh!" Hub was a proud man.

The New Job

After not more than a few weeks, I was transferred over to the mill office as timekeeper and paymaster. Later I learned that only a short time before, this job had been shared by *three men,* and all of them men of ability—one of whom was now the leading real estate dealer in Wiggins, another was now the company's bookkeeper, and the third the assistant manager of the company.

The company was logging timber off a big tract east of Wiggins. It had its own railroad, by which the logs were brought into the mill. About 350 Negro men were employed, beside various department managers and top-ranking skilled employees, all white.

As mentioned above, Negroes of 62 years ago had received little or no education. There was not a man of this entire force who could write his own name. All statements were signed with an "x"—"His mark." This was a legal signature.

I learned at once that the black employees had to be paid three times a day—morning, noon, and night. They had never been trained in the handling of money. Had they been paid only once a week, they and their families would have starved before next payday, for they were nearly always "broke" before Monday morning.

But the company paid them in *cash* only on Saturday night. At all other times, they were paid in trade-checks on the commissary store—good only in trade. What a contrast from the condition of today. This was in 1912. Only some 45-48 years from slavery. The terrible years after the war had done little toward giving our black people the economic, educational and social advantages the nation owed them.

But, even though we do not yet have the Civil Rights problem fully solved, the black people certainly *have come a long way!* These problems require *time,* patience, understanding, and replacing prejudice with a love of fellowman. I am here recording only true factual history, which should help us understand today's problems.

46

A Fish Out of Water

I was to learn that I was a square peg in a round hole. I had fixed a life GOAL in the advertising profession, where self-analysis had shown I fit. The glamor of getting to travel to far-off southern Mississippi, combined with the flattery of being offered such a job as a result of my record during that year in want ads, had momentarily blinded me to my previously fixed purpose. Of course, *travel* is an important phase of education—so this six-month sidetracking was not altogether wasted time.

I have mentioned that this job combined the work previously done by three capable men, now risen to more important jobs. But it was not the kind of work into which I fit. It was, as we say, out of my line. I was a fish out of water. A square peg in a round hole.

In order to keep up with the job, due to inadaptability and resultant slowness, it became necessary to work nights. I established a system. I worked alternately one night until ten, the next until midnight, rising at 5:30 every morning. Time had to be taken out to walk the one or two miles from my room to the mill, and also to walk over to the boarding house where I took meals. I kept awake on the job nights by smoking a pipe—my first habitual smoking. In just six months this overwork and loss of sleep exacted its toll, and I was sent to the hospital with a very severe case of typhoid fever.

Escape From Death

But during this six months in Wiggins there were a few social events. One was a pre-World War I encounter with a German, in which I narrowly escaped being shot to death.

47

I took meals at a boarding house out near the mill. The daughter of the landlady was an attractive southern brunette near my age. I had a few dates with her—but, I think, quite unlike most dating today. There was no "necking" as today's youngsters call it. Indeed I had never yet kissed or had my arms around a girl. It just wasn't done, then, on the universal scale of these postwar years. Two world wars have brought greater social and moral changes than most people realize—and mostly bad.

That girl's name was Matti-Lee Hornsby. The few dates I had were on Sundays, and consisted of walking and of conversation.

That kind of date would seem pretty "dull" to most 19-year-olds today, I suppose. I wonder if it isn't because they have lost the art of interesting conversation. I have always found that a scintillating conversation can be far more interesting than a prefabricated daydream in a movie or before a TV set—far more stimulating, enjoyable, and beneficial than the lust-inciting pastime called "necking."

But more of the dating experiences later. I had not had a great many dates up to this time. One thing, however, sticks to my memory—whenever Matti-Lee became a little provoked with me, her dark eyes flashed and she snapped out the epithet: "YANKEE!" It was of course, half in fun—but I found that epithet was supposed to be insulting. I had never heard it before.

One acquaintance I made there was a young German. He must have been about 21 at the time. His father was a lumberman in Germany, and had sent the son to America to study American lumber methods. He was spending some few weeks at the Finkbine mill in Wiggins.

This German, whose name I do not remember,

48

bragged at length on the superiority of German products, methods and systems. One day, in his room at the boarding house, he was demonstrating to me the superiority of his German-made revolver over a Colt or other American make.

In play, he pointed the revolver straight at me.

"Don't point that at me!" I said, dodging.

"Oh, it isn't loaded," he laughed. "Look, if you're afraid, I'll point it away from you and show you."

He pointed the revolver a couple of feet to one side of me, and pulled the trigger.

It was a very superior weapon, all right. It drilled a hole completely through the wall of his room, and let a little round ray of sunlight shine through from outdoors!

My German friend turned white, and trembled in confusion.

"Why," he stammered in frightened embarrassment, "I was *sure* it wasn't loaded."

It is the gun "that isn't loaded" that has killed many people. And before I leave *this* little digression, may I respectfully suggest to all who read this that you teach—yes, really TEACH your children *never,* under any circumstances, to point even a *play*gun at any person. The life you save *may* be your own!

In the Hospital

My stay in southern Mississippi was brought to a sudden and rude halt. By summer, weakened by overwork and loss of sleep in the desperate struggle to make good on a job I didn't belong in, a tiny typhoid germ, according to medical theories, found fertile soil. I became delirious. The mill officials, on doctor's orders, had me taken to the Southern Mississippi Infirmary at Hattiesburg. I entered there with the most severe case in the hospital's history. I was unconscious for two or three days.

But just to be able to stay in bed, after that six months' grind with all too little sleep seemed *so good* that somehow I "snapped out of it" quicker, apparently, than any previous typhoid patient at that hospital, and recovery was rapid.

One thing I want to mention here, for the benefit of a very large portion of my readers. It isn't often considered "nice" to talk about it, but constipation is called by some medical men "the mother of all diseases." A large percentage of people are plagued with it. For some two years I had been. Cathartics give only temporary relief. There isn't a cure in a carload.

In the hospital I was forced to *fast*. Daily they gave me castor oil. UGH! I have never taken it since, but I can taste the nasty stuff yet! They fed me only lemon juice, and occasionally buttermilk.

When I left the hospital the constipation was cured. Fasting, on raw fresh fruits (no bananas), will cure it, if you will keep it up long enough. I did not undervaluate the blessing of being rid of this thing. I appreciated it *enough* to be SURE that I kept regular. I have never permitted that condition to return. *That fact alone is responsible for a large part* of whatever dynamic energy I have been able to give to our great Work—and for long life. One of the 7 basic rules of SUCCESS is GOOD HEALTH! I hope this is enough said. You can't overestimate its importance.

In the hospital I was the favorite patient of practically all the nurses. Most of them were just a few years older than I—but not so much that we did not enjoy a great deal of conversation while I was convalescing. My room became a sort of social rendezvous for the nurses. Often there would be five or six of them in there at a time. I really *enjoyed* this rest in the hospital—the release from that frightening responsibility of trying so desperately to keep up with a job in which I did not belong, getting ample rest and sleep at last.

But I have always believed in the admonition: *"Whatsoever thy hand findeth to do, do it with thy* MIGHT," even though I didn't know it was in the Bible (Eccl. 9:10) until much later. I gave that job all I had. Now, in later life, there is some satisfaction in looking back on that.

The doctors told me I would have to return back north to protect my health. Thus, by forces outside my control, I was jerked out of this misfit detour job, and I *thought* I had *learned,* now, the lesson for which I sacrificed $2 a week the year before.

Arriving back in Des Moines, Iowa, mid-summer, 1912, I went this time to seek my uncle's advice. Now began my *real* advertising career. I think the story picks up in interest at this point.

3

Learning to Write Effective Advertisements

T HIS detour was my first experience in real travel. But on this job I was a total misfit.

I had now learned my lesson—at least temporarily. Now I was going to get back on the main track—the advertising field.

Stopping off in Chicago between trains en route to Des Moines, I went up to the Mahan Advertising Agency headquarters, and succeeded in getting a job. But since it was still more than two weeks before I could become active again, I went on out to Des Moines to spend the time at home.

Hiring Myself a Job

Naturally I went almost immediately to my uncle Frank's office.

"Well, Herbert," he said approvingly, "I'm glad you've got that bookkeeping fling out of your system, and are ready to get back in the advertising field where you belong."

I told him about the job with the Mahan Agency in Chicago.

"No, Herbert," he said, seriously, "you're not ready for agency experience yet. Mahan is one of the major agencies, and it would be years before you'd even work up to being noticed by any of the top men, who are the only ones over there that could teach you anything. They wouldn't know you existed.

"Besides," he continued, "although faraway pastures may look greener, often the best opportunity is right where you are. Now it so happens that on a national magazine, right here in Des Moines, are two men that I regard as the two best advertising and merchandising men in the country. These fellows really know advertising psychology. They know *people,* and how to deal with them. They know merchandising and business *principles.* They specialize in finding which business methods, selling methods, and advertising principles are successful, and which are not.

"They are two men over at *The Merchants Trade Journal.* It's a trade journal in the retail field—read by owners and managers of retail stores—but they circulate among *every* line of merchandising, and it's the biggest trade journal in the country, with a very large national circulation.

"One of these men is R. H. Miles, who is advertising manager, and the other is Arthur I. Boreman, manager of their Service Department, which is a sort of trade-paper advertising agency."

"Why," I interrupted, "I *know* Mr. Miles. He's a neighbor of ours."

"Well," continued my uncle, "go hire yourself a job. Don't let them turn you down. Over there you'll be in daily personal contact with these two men. You'll *learn more* there than anyplace I know. Don't forget, you're still going to school—you still have a lot to learn."

I walked briskly over to *The Merchants Trade Journal* offices, gained admittance to the advertising manager's office.

"Why, hello, Herbert," greeted Mr. Miles, surprised to see me in his office.

"Mr. Miles, I have decided that I'm going to join your organization, here in your advertising department. The doctors have told me I can't start work for two more weeks. I will report for work the first Monday in next month!" This came out real snappy—very positively.

"You—you—WHAT!" It caught Mr. Miles' breath.

I repeated my affirmative statement.

"Well!!—so you've just hired yourself a job—is that it?"

"Exactly!" came the positive reply.

"Well, now—just back up a minute!" Mr. Miles began to recover. "You can't come barging in here and hire yourself a job, just because you're a neighbor of mine. *We haven't any openings!*"

"Oh, that's all right! You've got two whole weeks to *create* an opening," I came back promptly, in full self-assurance.

"Now, look!" Mr. Miles was beginning to get a little impatient at this youthful aggressiveness. "It seems you don't understand plain English. I said, WE DON'T NEED ANY HELP!"

Now it was my turn to become a little nettled.

"Mr. Miles," I came back, more positively than ever, "I'm surprised at you. Isn't this a NATIONAL magazine? Isn't this an institution of *national* importance?"

"Yes, of course," he responded.

"Well then, do you mean to tell me that an organization of national scope and influence is not interested in finding a way to create an opening for an ambitious, energetic young man like me? Do you realize that you probably don't get a chance once in several years to add to your staff a man of my caliber, my talents, and ambition and *will* to work! Why, you can't afford to pass up this opportunity. I'll *grow* with your organization. *Of course* you can create an opening! As I said, I'll report for work the first Monday in next month."

"Well, I haven't the slightest idea what we'd have you do," Mr. Miles was beginning to weaken a little.

I became more confident than ever.

"Oh, poppycock, Mr. Miles," I snapped, disgusted. "Hand me a copy of that lousy sheet of yours!" This was commonly used advertising terminology.

On the back cover I saw two or three small ads, want-ad style, advertising stores for sale.

"Do you call these want ads?" I inquired.

"Oh, we don't have a want-ad section. We only solicit display ads. Occasionally a merchant decides to quit and sell out, and sends in a small want ad to sell his business."

"Well, I happen to know that hundreds of small merchants are going broke all the time, over the whole country. Now, supposing you had a full page, or even two pages of these store-for-sale ads every month. The rate for these small ads is a lot higher than the display rate by the page. One page of want ads would bring in as much advertising revenue as three or four pages of display ads, wouldn't it?"

"Well, yes," admitted Miles, rather reluctantly, "but we have no way of selling ads of that sort."

I was real cocky and confident by now. "I can put

one or two full pages of want ads of businesses for sale in every issue of *The Journal.* One thing I've learned is how to bring in want ads by mail. So, if I have to create *my own opening,* I'll report for work the first Monday morning in next month."

"Well," came a last objection, "we can't pay you a very high salary. We couldn't pay you over $10 a week."

"Who said anything about salary?" I rejoined. "I still live at home with the folks. I'm not coming up here for the salary I make *now,* but for what I can *learn,* and the salary I *will* make, later. I'm *hired* at $10 per week," rising and extending my hand. "All I ask is that you agree to *raise* my salary as fast as I earn it. See you in two weeks."

My First Display Ad

All this was along about July or August, 1912. I do not remember now, after more than 60 years, whether I was actually put to work on building a page or two of want ads by direct mail solicitation; but it seems, in the dim distance of memory, that I did bring in a page or more of want ads the first two or three issues.

In any event, I was not long on want-ad work. I was assigned to the Service Department, directly under A. I. Boreman. For some little time I was given routine office work, with a certain amount of correspondence to answer. For this work, I was given a stenographer and a dictaphone. During this period it was my job to break in a number of different stenographers. As soon as a new girl became experienced enough to be efficient, she was taken away from me, and a new green girl fresh out of business college assigned to me.

It was not long until I was given opportunity to start writing and designing display ads. As mentioned

56

above, this Service Department was a sort of trade-journal advertising agency. We handled the trade-paper division of the advertising budget of manufacturers who sold through retailers. As a rule the larger advertising agencies were glad to relinquish the trade-paper portion of any client's advertising. They were primarily interested in consumer media.

I shall never forget the first ad Mr. Boreman assigned to me to write and lay out. I have mentioned before that I had been studying every book on advertising writing I could acquire. I was studying books on psychology, and on advertising psychology. I had diligently read the trade journals in the advertising field —*Printers Ink* and *Advertising & Selling.* I had studied diagrams of design and layout of ads. But as yet I had received almost no experience in actually writing the copy and designing the layout of an ad.

I do not remember at all the nature of the commodity or service or the name of the manufacturer whose ad I was to write.

But I shall *never forget* Mr. Boreman's left-handed compliment when I laid the "dummy" and typed copy before him.

"Mm-hmm—well, Herbert, that's a pretty good ad," he drawled, slowly, examining it critically.

"Now, that headline, of course, will have to be changed," he continued. "You've used too many words. There's nothing in that headline that will catch the eye. The average reader will be scanning past it to something else. You have only the fleeting fraction of a second to *stop* the eye. There's nothing in your headline to arouse instant *interest* and create immediate suspense— nothing to make the reader say, 'Well, I never thought of *that!* I want to read that!' or, to say 'Now I've always wondered about that!'—so he'll want to read on.

"The headline is not displayed correctly on your layout. Not enough white space around the headline to create contrast between a bold, black, short headline and white space around it. Never be afraid of wasting white space around your headlines. Never *waste* white space around the text matter.

"Now next," continued Mr. Boreman, "your major subhead above the text matter is all wrong. You must grab *attention*—stop the eye—in the main headline—but you must go on to arouse interest and create suspense in the subhead, if you are to win a reading for your copy. This subhead is in the wrong place in your layout, the wrong size and kind of type.

"Now, coming to the main text matter—that opening sentence won't do, Herbert. It should have been indicated on the layout to be in larger type than the balance of the text matter, and the first word should have started out with a large initial letter. Unless this opening sentence follows up the headings by cementing interest, and arousing more curiosity or suspense, no one is going to read past it. No, this first sentence will have to be rewritten, just like the headlines.

"Now, these smaller subheads through the text matter don't add anything. They must create interest, make the reader want to read what's under them. And they, too, are in the wrong kind of type. And this text matter will all have to be rewritten. It doesn't *hold* the interest, if you *had* created interest in the first place. It doesn't *arouse desire* for this thing you're selling. It doesn't make the reader—if he ever reads this ad—*want* to buy this product.

"And then, finally, there's no emotional ending to arouse the reader to *action*—IF you had first stopped his eye and gained his attention, aroused interest, created suspense, made him actually *read through* your ad, made him WANT what you advertise. The signature isn't right, either—and the border around the ad will have to be eliminated.

"But, outside of that, Herbert," he said encouragingly, *"that's a pretty good ad!"*

No, I shall never forget that experience!

That kind of encouragement was pretty hard to take—but *I learned more* about how to write an ad in that one analysis of this first ad, than many copywriters and layout men in big agencies have ever learned, or ever will learn! This one experience was well WORTH all the time I spent on the staff of the *Merchants Trade Journal*—and I was to be with them three years.

I went to work with a *will,* writing that ad all over. Practice makes perfect. It was probably two or three years later before I was able to write ads that actually STOPPED roving eyes, grabbed instantaneous *interest,* created suspense, *held* the reader's interest throughout, convinced the reader, and then moved him to action. It took time. But I was on the way.

Not long after returning from the South, and starting with *The Merchants Trade Journal,* my father went out to Idaho, where he bought a small ranch near Weiser. The household goods were packed and stored, ready to be moved after he became located.

My mother, two younger brothers and sister, went to the home of one of my mother's sisters, on a farm some 25 or 30 miles south of Des Moines, for a visit. After my father was located in Idaho, they followed and joined him there.

Learning Effective Ad-Writing

For something like a year and a half I was kept in the Service Department of *The Journal.* There I received a most intensive and *practical* basic training in the true psychological principles of writing and designing advertisements.

It has always seemed to me that the advertising profession generally has "missed the boat." It's the same in many professions.

The ad-men have progressed into a system of intricate display designs, complicated art work, and overly rhetorical text matter which, after all, doesn't really say much or *do* much to the readers—*if any.*

Take a look through the advertising pages of a magazine or newspaper today. It's a confused, jumbled hodgepodge of fancy art work, and small bits of text, artistically blocked off—usually in such a manner that no one reads it! Nothing stands out to catch, *and stop,* the fleeting eye trying to get to the next *news* or *article* headline. Nothing snatches attention away from all surrounding matter. There's nothing to arouse instantaneous *interest* at the very point where the eye is drawn for that fraction of a second glance—nothing to *hold* that interest until it creates suspense sufficient to induce a reading of the text matter.

The ads I was trained to write, during those formative years between ages 20 and 23, always *got results.* Often they were more plain and simple in appearance than the more fancy, artistic, highly illustrated ads around them. But they *stopped* roving eyes—drew attention from surrounding matter— aroused and *held* interest—*convinced* readers, and moved them to *act!* (This early training was destined to serve a great purpose!)

Today all that early training and the years of subsequent experience are being put into the production of full-page ads which are selling, *not* a commercial product or service for profit, but God's truth, without price or profit.

60

Overhauling and Simplifying a Vocabulary

For some two years, prior to joining the *Merchants Trade Journal* staff, I had been striving diligently to acquire a large vocabulary. Ever since I had read Elbert Hubbard's boast of possessing the largest vocabulary of any man since Shakespeare, it had been a challenge! I was determined to acquire a greater! To be able to pour out a torrent of big words incomprehensible to any but the highly educated had appealed to intellectual vanity.

But—at age 20—Mr. Boreman changed all that.

"When you write advertising," he explained, "the purpose is not to impress the readers with your superior vocabulary. Your purpose is to *sell goods, services, or ideas!* The purpose of words is to convey thoughts, facts, ideas—a message! When 98% of the people do not understand your words, they do not receive your message. They only become confused and turn to something *interesting.* In advertising we must reach the 98%—not the 2%.

"Use only plain, simple words. Use words that readers of no more than a third or fourth grade education can UNDERSTAND. Try to achieve good literary quality with a *large* vocabulary of common, simple words, and by the *manner* in which you weave those words into the sentence structure."

Immediately my vocabulary underwent an overhauling. Deliberately I began dropping out of my speaking and writing vocabulary all the big words not in common usage. Every person has three vocabularies: smallest of all, his speaking vocabulary, consisting of the fund of words with which he is able to speak readily; next larger, his *writing* vocabulary; and largest, his *reading* or *listening* vocabulary. Everyone can *under-*

stand many words which he may read, or hear spoken by others, which he could not readily use himself in conversation.

My effort, then, became that of developing ability to use the largest variety of words readily comprehensible by most people when heard or read.

But effective writing is far more than memorizing a store of words. It is the manner in which those words are put together in sentence structure that determines effectiveness. So I began to study a STYLE in writing. Immediately I set out to develop a distinct and effective style. It had to be fast-moving, vigorous, yet simple, *interesting,* making the message plain and UNDERSTAND-ABLE.

All this advertising instruction was the most valuable possible training for the real mission in life to which I was later to be called—our worldwide enterprises of today. It was a training such as one could never receive in any university. It was the most practical training.

Some speakers and writers seem to think they impress their audiences or readers by their ability to use big words beyond the comprehension of the audience. Others succumb to the temptation to become too "scholarly," speaking *over* the *minds* of their hearers—but never plainly *into* their minds. The same rules that attract attention, arouse interest, create suspense, win conviction and stir emotions to *action* in advertising accomplish the same results in public speaking.

Another *most* important principle—I was taught to *avoid* the academic "outline" form of presentation. This is the manner in which nearly all students are taught in colleges to organize their writing or speaking. This is the one, two, three, a), b), c) form of outline. It is orderly and precise, but dull, dry, uninteresting to the readers.

But in writing advertising, I learned always to *tell a story* —to make it *interesting*—and to tell it in *story form.* That is, first, put a question in the minds of readers they really *want* answered—or make a statement that is so unusual it either raises a question in the readers' minds, or challenges them to demand an explanation and want to read on to get it. It must arouse instant *interest.* It must create *suspense!* Like a mystery play, it must not tell the reader the answer at the beginning. It must develop, rapidly, lucidly, increasing the interest, toward the final solution or answer. It must HOLD the interest until the story is told.

The advertising headline should, when possible, make people say either: "I've always wondered about that!" or, "I never thought of that—say, *that's interesting—I want to know the answer!!*"

I learned in those early days to put a *story flow* into the text of an advertisement, holding the interest of readers to learn the answer. An ad of this nature *may contain hundreds, or even thousands of words—and people will be glued to it until they have read it all.*

I remember an incident that happened many years later.

This was in 1925, when I had established an advertising service of my own in Portland, Oregon. One of my clients was a laundry in Vancouver, Washington. I had a number of other clients in Vancouver—a retail clothing store, a jewelry store, a large drug store, and others. One of the banks had installed a new Safety Deposit Department, with new vaults and safety deposit boxes. The president of the bank called me in.

"Mr. Armstrong," he began, "we have noticed the

attractive and compelling ads you have prepared for clients here in Vancouver, and we would like to retain your services to prepare a short campaign to announce the opening of our new department.

"Now," he continued, apologetically, "we think your ads are fine—they certainly stand out—they're interesting—but we have just one criticism. We think those ads you write for the laundry are too long—too many words. People won't read so many words in an ad."

"Well now, Mr. Jones," I replied, "in the first place, your advertising requires entirely different advertising treatment, because you have a totally different advertising problem. The laundry is up against adverse public opinion, and suspicion in regard to supposed harmful laundry methods. Their problem requires what we call 'EDUCATIONAL ADVERTISING.' It must *educate* women to the true facts—it must change public opinion. This requires more words—totally different advertising treatment.

"But, as to whether people ever read so many words, I wonder if you remember an ad of a month ago, captioned, 'Is MOTHER Worth *Saving?*' "

"Why, yes!" he replied quickly. "Yes, I do remember that ad, very well. That was unusually interesting."

"How much of it did you read?"

"Oh, I read *all* of it," he responded. "It aroused my curiosity, and I couldn't stop till I found the answer."

"Well, Mr. Jones, how many *other* ads do you remember reading in that same edition of the newspaper?"

"Why—why—" he stammered, "I—I don't remember reading *any* others."

"Exactly!" I had won my point. "That ad was the

longest, wordiest ad in that newspaper—and yet it's the *only* one you remember reading, and you read it clear through! Moreover, it is the *longest ad I ever wrote!*"

"Yes," he protested, "but that ad was *interesting!*"

"That's just the point," I concluded. "If what you write is sufficiently *interesting*—if it has created suspense, and *holds* the interest or even increases it as the reader is led along through it—people will read it all the way through, no matter how long.

"It is not a matter of HOW LONG an ad is, or *how many words,* it is altogether a matter of whether you have been able to catch readers' attention, arouse their interest, and HOLD that interest. How many words are there in a complete novel? Yet the book stores sell such thick books by the millions—and people read them clear through!"

That is the principle I was taught under Mr. Boreman and Mr. Miles, between ages 20 and 23.

Applying All These Principles Now

The principles that make for effective advertising copy, which I *began* learning during those three years, apply also in broadcasting, and in magazine writing, as well as in straight advertising copy.

Let me add here that, in advertising, there are different types of merchandising problems. The ads I wrote for the laundry required educational advertising. They had to re-educate the public in regard to laundry *methods.* They had to remove prejudices, create confidence, change habits.

But perhaps most advertising is in the field called *convenience goods.* This includes such products as tooth-paste, shaving cream or soaps, cigarettes, where popularizing a brand name is the objective. This depends more on repetition than on lengthy educational copy. *Such ads have few words.*

I have been amused by the problems confronting the writers of cigarette ads. With the restrictions imposed by laws, there is not much an ad-writer can say about a cigarette, anyway. I have marvelled at the hundreds of millions of dollars spent saying NOTHING that means anything about cigarettes. The "kick the habit" commercials (1971) by the cancer society, however, seem really to have had a message.

I was to learn, later in life, that far more people will listen to a solid half-hour all-speech radio program applying these principles, than will listen to a one-minute DRY talk or commercial that arouses no interest. For many years, the *World Tomorrow* program has enjoyed *highest* ratings of listener-interest on most stations we use—and second highest on most others. That is in comparison to all programs in most markets around the world where we are heard. The various editors of the *Plain Truth* magazine and our other publications have received training in these same principles in Ambassador College. And that is one reason why *The Plain Truth* is so avidly read, and its circulation continues growing so phenomenally, while other leading mass-circulation magazines are in deep financial difficulties, and several have gone out of publication. *Plain Truth* and *Good News* articles and the *Correspondence Course* lessons are INTERESTING— they SAY SOMETHING, and say it in a manner extremely easy to read!

But, to return to the story.

Mr. Miles had, perhaps, the snappiest, fastest-moving style of copy-writing I have ever read. I thought it was *too fast*—too many short, terse sentences. Long sentences tend to *slow down* the reader. Short sentences tend to speed him up. But when writing consists of nothing but a succession of overly short, terse, staccato sentences, it becomes monotonous and unnatural. I strove for a style that gave *change of pace!* A proper balance between quick, short sentences, and occasional longer ones.

To hold a mass reading, writing should be reasonably crisp and lucid, not "dry" or slow. But a monotony of very short, terse sentences seemed to me to lack *sincerity,* and writing should, above all, be sincere!

In any event, this early training resulted in literally thousands of letters during recent years from radio listeners and readers of *The Plain Truth,* saying that the FACTS are being made more plain, more clear and understandable than they ever heard them before! Today that early training SERVES and helps millions of people all over the world!

But there is another principle in advertising even more important than any of these. That is to be *honest*—to stick to the TRUTH!

I attended many Ad-Club luncheons, and even the national Ad-Club conventions, during the many years I spent in the advertising field. From the start I was much impressed by the Associated Advertising Club's slogan: *"TRUTH in Advertising."*

But do you really know how much TRUTH there is in most commercial advertising today? If you knew *how little,* you'd be shocked.

I spent twenty years in the advertising field. I got to know advertising men. The average advertising man, preparing to write advertising copy, searches for what IDEAS or statements he might make about his product will cause the public to BUY. It never seems to occur to most advertising men to check up and see whether the statements or claims are true! If a certain claim or statement about the product will *sell* it, the ad man grabs it and makes that claim in his copy with enthusiasm.

You will see, later in this autobiography, that when I became a publishers' representative in Chicago, I built a business on HONESTY that produced CONFIDENCE. The advertising agencies, the banks, and the manufacturers with whom I did business came to know that I knew my field—I had the *facts* they needed—and that I was accurate and TRUTHFUL, and they could RELY on whatever I told them.

Another principle I was taught is this:

"A CUSTOMER is more profitable than a single sale." Win the confidence of a customer through honesty and integrity, and *many* repeat sales will come your way without selling expense.

One other ingredient is absolutely necessary, along with telling the TRUTH. And that is SINCERITY!

I Was Never Insincere

I was never insincere. True, I had swung from a sense of inferiority, to one of supreme self-confidence.

But I was entirely *sincere.* Usually a bragging, conceited young lad who is cocky, is also an insincere flippant smart aleck. I was not. It seems I was, by nature, deeply sincere and in earnest, and although excessively self-confident, even snappy and cocky in manner, there was always with it a sense of earnestness and dignity. At least I *thought* I was right, and in my heart *meant to be.* Human nature wants to *be* good—but seldom does it want to *do* good. That natural desire in one to wish to consider himself *good,* I suppose, led to an attitude of *sincerity.*

Later, God had to take the self-confidence, conceit,

68

and cockiness out of me. He replaced it with a *different* kind of confidence—an unbounded FAITH in God. I have far more ASSURANCE for the future today than I had then—many times over. But today it is based on what *God* is going to do—not what *I* am able to do.

All these are the principles I was taught under Mr. Boreman and Mr. Miles during the three years with *The Merchants Trade Journal.* I owe them much.

In the Service Department of *The Merchants Trade Journal* I was sent on occasional trips to places like Waterloo and Cedar Rapids, Iowa, Albert Lea, Minnesota, and others, selling ads I had prepared to manufacturers.

I remember vividly, at this point, a trip of this kind to Waterloo. I think it was a refrigerator account. I worked carefully on the advertising copy and layout in the hotel, then went over to see the manufacturer. This, I believe, was the first magazine display ad I ever sold.

What a *thrill* it was! As I walked from the factory back to the hotel, I was floating on air! Ah, sweet SUCCESS! It was elation! Thrills ran all through me!

Playing With a Million Dollars

The *Journal* regarded a Waterloo department store merchant as one of the best merchandisers in the nation. His name was Paul Davis. There were two department stores in Waterloo—the James Black Company, and the Paul Davis store. The Black store was the older-established and larger, but the Davis company was catching up.

Then Paul Davis had a fire. His store was totally destroyed. The next time I was in Waterloo, after his misfortune, I found the Paul Davis store in temporary quarters in a two-story building in the middle of a block. It was only a fraction the size of the department store occupying a prominent corner that had burned down. At that time, Mr. Davis said he was planning to build a new building, larger than the Black Company store.

But on my next visit, some six months later, there was no sign of any new building activity.

"What happened to that big new quarter-block multiple-story building you were going to erect?" I asked.

"Oh, that!" Mr. Davis laughed. By this time he called himself my "second Daddy." "Well, I'm not going to build it for a while yet. I'm having a lot of fun. I have one cool million dollars, CASH, in the bank. It's the insurance money. It was no time at all until every manufacturer in New York knew we had that million dollars cash. Every time a manufacturer gets overloaded with some stock, or needs to raise some quick money, he comes or sends a representative out here to Waterloo. I am able to buy chunks of merchandise in this manner, by sharp trading, at far less than any competitors. Then I put on a BIG SALE. I take a small profit, cut the price way down, and the public simply streams into our little two-floor store here. We have low overhead. We have a small inventory, compared to what we carried in the bigger store. We sell fast, turn our stock *more times a year*. And the secret of success is not the total volume of sales, but TURNOVER—the number of times you turn your stock a year—the number of times you make a profit on the same capital!

"I find that money *attracts* money! That's a principle of life. Don't ever forget it! Truly, 'to him that HATH shall be given, and to him that hath not shall be taken away even that which he hath!' I can do things with a million dollars cash I never dreamed could be done. *It's a lot of fun.* I'm enjoying it! No, I'm not going to put that million into a new store building right away.

I'm going to keep it in the bank, and *working for me* a little while longer!"

I never did forget the lessons this successful merchant, Paul Davis, taught me.

Soon after this, I became "the Idea Man" of *The Merchants Trade Journal.* I was sent on long trips, either to the Atlantic Coast or to the Gulf of Mexico and back, interviewing merchants, businessmen and Chamber of Commerce secretaries, looking for IDEAS and material for articles in the magazine.

On one of these trips, a challenge from an angry merchant resulted in what I believe was the *pioneer* experience in all these surveys and samplings of public opinion. So far as I know, I was the originator of such polls.

4

"Idea Man" for a National Magazine

MY WIFE was reflecting on what *might* have happened to us. "What if we had never met," she mused. "What if we had never been brought through the failure of our own plans? We probably never would have found the way to *abundant living*—the joys of *right living!* Think how drab and dull and empty our lives might have been! How *grateful* we ought to be!"

WHY This Is Written

Yes, our lives have been eventful, exciting, filled with action, effort, unusual experiences, travel. There have been problems, reverses, chastenings, persecutions, sufferings, but there has been success, accomplishments, happiness and JOY! We have been kept *busy*. We have *really lived!*

So, let me repeat, this autobiography is being written in the hope that these unusual life experiences may bring inspiration, encouragement, and benefit to many.

I have been greatly influenced by the tremendous impress on my life that resulted from a triple reading of Benjamin Franklin's autobiography. After reading that, I sought to learn by the experiences of other successful men.

And so it is in the hope that this story of my own life may be a means of bringing to many, in inspirational and interesting manner, the very same useable help that other biographies brought to me, that this is written.

Learning Magazine Makeup

For one six months' period, during the first two years on *The Journal*, I was given the job of "making up the magazine." That is, of taking all of the galley proofs of articles, proofs of all the ads, and pasting them in a dummy magazine the way each issue was to be designed.

During this six months I was given a desk out at the *Successful Farming* plant in their composing room.

I learned, as the publishers of *The Journal* knew, that a smaller-circulation magazine can have their publication printed each month in the plant of a larger magazine, or some large-operation printing establishment, at less cost than operating their own printing plant. The reason is obvious. The presses turn only one or two days a month on a single smaller publication. To keep all the machinery idle, besides printers, most of the month is to tie up capital that is not working. It doesn't pay.

This lesson was of very practical benefit in our present activities. For years *The Plain Truth* has been printed by large commercial printing plants in the United States and abroad.

Beginning about 1945 or 1946 we did operate our own small printing shop—first with one Davidson duplicator press, then with two, and later with three larger, but still comparatively small Miehle presses. They did our minor printing only—booklets, letterheads and such things.

All these earlier experiences were precisely what was needed to build, later, the worldwide activities of today.

Coddling a Temper

One rather dramatic incident occurred at the *Successful Farming* printing plant. It contains a lesson worth, I think, the telling.

The foreman of the printing plant at *Successful Farming* was an old experienced printer named Ed Condon. It seemed to me that printers were, in those days at least, more profane than any class of men. Perhaps it was because, in the days of hand-setting all type, a printer often would "pie" the type—that is, it would slip out of his hand and fall in a jumbled mass, whereupon every single letter of type would have to be sorted out, put back into the case and then set all over again. It was a severe test on patience. Mr. Condon not only could "cuss"—he also had a *temper!*

The only thing wrong with Mr. Condon's temper was that he made no attempt to control it. He was proud of it. He pampered it. He bragged about it.

One day he "flew off the handle" at me for some reason I no longer remember. He raved, swore, shouted, called names. I left the composing room, returned to the *Journal* offices. Mr. Boreman either went out or called him on the telephone. He received the same treatment—only more violently. He then went into the office of our publisher and editor, Mr. W. J. Pilkington.

Mr. Pilkington called Mr. Charles E. Lynde, then general manager of *Successful Farming*. He asked Mr. Pilkington if he would have Mr. Boreman and me come to his office.

When we arrived, Mr. Condon was called into Mr. Lynde's office.

"Ed," said Mr. Lynde sternly, "we cannot have our good customers insulted. You may either apologize to Mr. Boreman and Mr. Armstrong, and also give me, and them, your word of honor that this burst of temper will never be repeated, or you are fired on the spot."

Ed Condon humbly apologized.

"May I say a word to Ed?" asked Mr. Boreman.

"Ed, you're a very competent printer, and a fine and likeable fellow—except when you let loose a burst of temper. I'd like to give you a little advice as a friend—for we like you. I've noticed that you have *bragged* about that temper of yours. You've been proud of your ability to lose your head. You've nursed it along as if it were your baby you love. You've never tried to control it. Now a temper is a mighty good thing—*as long as it is under perfect control* and directed by the mind in good judgment. When you learn to *control* it, then *that's* something to be proud of! You've just been proud of it in the wrong state of action, Ed—that's all that's wrong."

Mr. Condon took the advice—*he had to*, standing in front of his top boss. He said he'd never thought of it that way, and thanked Mr. Boreman.

Perhaps some of our readers never thought of it that way. Mr. Boreman's advice was very sound! Never let tempers get out of control!

Becoming "the Idea Man"

After about one and a half to two years of training in

advertising copy writing and layout, selling advertising space, office work in dictating and letter-answering, and composing room makeup with *The Merchants Trade Journal*, I was put on a new and unique activity.

I have never heard of anything like it. I became *The Journal's "Idea Man."*

This was the most unusual training and experience of all. I was now transferred into the Editorial Department, under Ben R. Vardeman, Associate Editor. Also, on this job, I was kept partially under supervision of Mr. Boreman.

Mr. Vardeman was a tall, dignified man who was author of a book on the principles of retail salesmanship, and a Chautauqua lecturer. Also, I believe, he had written a correspondence course on retail salesmanship. He wrote most of the articles that composed the reading content of *The Journal*.

The editorial and reading columns of *The Journal* were devoted mainly to IDEAS that had been successfully used by retail merchants in increasing sales, speeding up turnover, reducing costs, principles and methods of business management, training of personnel, improving public relations. Also they put emphasis on community betterment and chamber of commerce activity.

This reading material was not written out of theoretical imagination. *The Journal* maintained an "Idea Man" who travelled all over the country, visiting stores in all lines, discussing problems and methods with merchants, checking on community and social conditions. The actual experiences of successful merchants, as sought out and reported by the "Idea Man" were written up by the editors into article form in the magazine.

I was equipped with a Hotel Credit Letter and a large postcard-size folding camera. The Credit Letter authorized me to cash checks, or write out and draw drafts on *The Merchants Trade Journal,* up to a total of $100 per week, ample in those days to cover travelling expenses. A book of instruction in photography was given me. I had to learn to take pictures of a quality worth publishing.

Expense Account Troubles

I was allowed a reasonably liberal expense account, but no extravagances or luxuries. The *Journal* expected their men to stop at leading hotels, but I always took a minimum-price single room if available. Breakfasts were nearly always taken at the lunch counter, lunches at the coffee shop or lunch counter, but the evening meal quite often in the hotel's main dining room.

I had not been out long before I put down on my expense account: "Ice Cream Soda—" and "Movie—" —or whatever the prices of those items were in those days. Mr. Vardeman was meticulously careful of details. He frowned on these expense items, and was about to disallow them, when Mr. Boreman came to my rescue. He urged Mr. Vardeman to let it go, this time, saying that he, Mr. Boreman, would write me proper instructions about these expense items.

"Next time, Herbert," Mr. Boreman's letter advised," put any little items like that down included under 'Miscellaneous.' " So after that the occasional ice cream sodas and movies were bulked together into one item, called "Miscellaneous."

This is an incident that I had forgotten. But just at this juncture (written February 1968), in order to refresh my memory on one or two other incidents as I had come to the writing of this stage of my experiences with *the Journal,* I called Mr. Boreman by long distance telephone. This expense account incident was one of two that he remembered vividly after all these years. He seemed to enjoy immensely reminding me of the incident.

This incident reminds me of an experience Benjamin Franklin related in his autobiography. During the Revolutionary War all people were required to contribute for the purchase of gunpowder. The Quakers of Pennsylvania found it contrary to their doctrine and conscience to do this. Yet they wanted to be loyal. So they solved their dilemma by contributing money for "corn, oats, and other grain." The "other grain," Franklin explained with a chuckle, was gunpowder!

The other incident which Mr. Boreman recalled to my memory was the time I "discovered" a most remarkable and practical invention being used in a grocery store. It was only a few days after I had started on my first trip. I was still pretty "green" on this job of recognizing good ideas used by merchants.

It was a vegetable rack, with water dripping down slowly over the vegetables. Now this was not only ingenious, I thought, but a most *practical* idea. It attracted attention, and kept the vegetables fresh. So I carefully took several camera shots of it, as I remembered it. But as Mr. Boreman remembered it, I hired a photographer to come and photograph it for me. Enthusiastically I sent in a glowing report of my new discovery.

There was, apparently, quite a reaction in *The Journal* office when this report, with pictures, reached them. It seems that their laughter almost shook the building down. Groceries had been using this type of vegetable rack for many years—but never having been in the grocery business, and being new and inexperienced in my "Idea" job, they somehow had escaped my attention. I thought I had made a wonderful new discovery. This demonstrated again that most of us learn, not by observation, but by cruel experience.

Ending Sluggishness

The first "Idea Man" tour took me to New York state and back. This trip started in November, 1913.

I must have visited a number of towns across Iowa and Illinois, but the first that comes back to mind, now, is traveling across southern Michigan. I remember staying overnight at the Post Tavern in Battle Creek. My mother had been an ardent Postum drinker, but I had never liked it. Here at the Post company's own hotel, however, I was induced to order their specialty, iced Postum with whipped cream. The way they prepared it, it was so delicious I have never forgotten it. It seems to me that Mr. C.W. Post was still alive, and that I saw him either in the hotel lobby or in the dining room.

I remember stopping off at Ann Arbor, home of the University of Michigan. Probably I went south from there, making stops at Toledo, Fostoria, Upper Sandusky, Bucyrus, Mansfield, Wooster, Massillon, Canton, Alliance, and Youngstown in Ohio.

Next, I entered Pennsylvania, with Franklin as the first stop. By this time I was feeling so sluggish, I hunted up an osteopath in Franklin. I had occasionally taken osteopath treatments, not as a medicine for any sickness, but more to take the place of an athletic "workout" at times when I was not getting sufficient exercise. At this time I thought a treatment might make me more alert and help the sluggish feeling I was having to fight.

"Well now," said the osteopath, "I'll be glad to give you a treatment and take your money for it if you insist, but I can tell you something without any charge that will do you a lot more good. *Quit eating so many eggs!"*

"Why," I exclaimed in surprise, "how did *you* know I've been eating a lot of eggs?"

"By your color, and condition of your liver," he said.

He explained that I had a somewhat torpid liver that would not readily assimilate an excess of eggs, corn, or peanuts. Some people seem to be able to eat eggs every morning for breakfast without harm. I found, from this osteopath's advice and subsequent experience, that my liver is apparently different. I can eat eggs occasionally without harm—but I must avoid eating them regularly. I have found that lemon juice seems to be the antidote. Accordingly, ever since that experience in Franklin, Pennsylvania, I have eaten sparingly of eggs, and taken generously of lemon juice. If I may seem to have some fair degree of energy, vitality, and physical stamina, it is largely due to being careful about diet, among other things.

I mention this because some of our readers may be suffering from the same inert sluggishness, feeling dopey, and drowsy a good deal of the time, caused by the same kind of liver. If so, try eliminating the eggs, corn and peanuts for a while, and start drinking lemon juice every morning before breakfast (without sugar).

The Niagara River Lesson

Next I went north, stopping at Oil City and Titusville in Pennsylvania, and on to Buffalo. I spent December 25th, 1913, at Niagara Falls. I shall never forget that first visit to Niagara Falls. There had been a silver thaw, then a refreeze. All the trees glistened in the bright sun like millions of brilliantly sparkling diamonds, especially over on Goat Island.

This visit to Niagara Falls allowed me to leave the United States for the first time in my life—walking across International Bridge into Niagara Falls, Canada.

There was an experience on Goat Island I shall never forget. I had walked up the island, away from the falls, some little distance. The Niagara River is very swift at that point. Out in the river I noticed one huge rock. It seemed like a great, insurmountable barrier standing in the way of the swift on-rushing waters from above-stream. To me it was like the insurmountable barriers that frequently confront us—that threaten to *stop* us in our progress. So many people get discouraged and quit.

But not those waters!

The waters of that river swirled *around* the great rock, struck it head-on and splashed *over* it. One way or another the waters got past it, and hurried on to their destination—the falls, and then down the swift rapids of the river on into Lake Ontario. The waters didn't lie down. They didn't become discouraged. They didn't quit. They found a way *around* the impassable barrier, and on to their destination.

I decided that if inanimate, mindless elements could surmount and find a way past obstacles, so could I. This experience has often come back to mind when the going has gotten tough, or when I was tempted to become discouraged and quit.

While at Niagara Falls I went through the Shredded Wheat plant. They had many visitors, who were taken through the plant on guided tours. At the end of the tour the guests are served shredded wheat the way the factory serves it. Always before it had tasted like straw, or a miniature bale of hay to me, but the way they served it—with sliced bananas and rich cream, and with a wonderful cup of coffee—it was simply delicious.

Visiting Elbert Hubbard

Having a Sunday layover in Buffalo I was able to indulge a personal adventure and pleasure. On two or three occasions I had met Elbert Hubbard, world-famous writer, author, publisher, and lecturer. Hubbard edited and published two national magazines with a literary flair—*The Philistine*, and *The FRA*. He himself managed to write most of the contents.

Elbert Hubbard was no shrinking violet. He readily admitted to possessing the largest vocabulary of any man since Shakespeare. In his own ranking of American authors from the days of Washington, Franklin and Jefferson, he "modestly" rated himself number one. When the dictionary contained no word to fit his need, he coined a word that did. He wore semi-long hair, a great broad-brimmed hat, and an artist's bow tie. He hobnobbed with the great and the near-great, wrote them up in flattering rhetoric—for a price befitting his superlatives.

He wrote *A Message to Garcia*, which, next to the Bible, sold more copies than anything ever written in that day.

For a few years now, I had been reading Elbert Hubbard regularly. I read his "stuff," on my Uncle Frank Armstrong's advice, for style, for flair, for vocabulary, and for ideas in philosophy—though my uncle had cautioned me against absorbing without question his philosophies and ideas of religion. Hubbard was an agnostic. He seemed to possess a deal of wisdom about men and methods and things—but he was utterly devoid of spiritual knowledge.

And now my opportunity came to visit this noted sage at his famous Roycroft Inn and Shops, in East Aurora, New York, a short distance south of Buffalo.

The morning was spent at the Inn, browsing around among books and booklets and copies of *The FRA* and *The Philistine*. After lunch at the Inn, Elbert Hubbard came in. He remembered me, from former meetings in Chicago and Des Moines on his lecture tours.

He led the way out on the wide veranda, and started throwing the medicine ball around. As I remember, there were four of us—Hubbard, his daughter Miriam, not far from my age, and another guest. Once I caught Hubbard napping, and socked him on the side of the head with the big medicine ball—and daughter Miriam soon returned the compliment, jolting me with a lalapalooza. It was fun.

Next, Fra Elbertus, as he liked to style himself, piloted me and the other guest on a tour of the Roycroft shops, where artistic and quality printing was done. Along the way, he picked up a deluxe leather-bound copy of *A Message to Garcia*, inscribed my name in it with his autograph, and presented it to me; and a little later, inscribed in the same manner, he gave me a copy of his *American Bible*.

When my mother heard that Elbert Hubbard had published a new Bible of his own, she was gravely shocked—until I explained. Hubbard's own explanation was that the word "bible" simply means "book." It comes from the Greek *biblia*, and by itself has no sacred meaning, merely designating any book. Of course Hubbard's *American Bible* was intended as an agnostic's answer to *The Holy Bible*, which he regarded merely as the literary and religious writings of the Hebrews.

Since the Bible is composed of a collection of various Books written by various men, combined into one large Book, Hubbard had assembled together a selection of writings of outstanding Americans, including Washington, Jefferson, Franklin, Emerson and Lincoln—and, of course—HUBBARD! A faint insight into Hubbard's rating of the value and importance of the writings of these Americans may be gleaned from the fact that slightly more than half of the whole book was filled with the writings of all other American writers *combined*, while the writings of Hubbard *alone* filled almost half of the entire book!

Somewhere, through the years since 1933, these two books personally autographed and presented by Elbert Hubbard have become lost.

Happiness Out of WORK?

Returning to the Inn, Hubbard called out: "Everybody down the basement!"

Here I was put to work, beside Mr. Hubbard, wrapping large scrubbed Idaho potatoes in tissue paper, for packing in "Goodie Boxes." The Roycrofters at that time were advertising in their publications as deluxe gifts these "Goodie Boxes" which were attractive wooden boxes filled with choice vegetables, fruits, nuts, and other "goodies."

As Mr. Hubbard and I chatted away, he began suddenly to chuckle.

"What's so funny?" I queried.

"I was just wondering what you really think of me," he mused. "You visit me as my guest. I charge you full price for your lunch. I try to induce you to stay overnight as a paying guest in my hotel. And at the same time I put you to work without wages."

"Well, who," I asked, "was that self-admitted great philosopher who said: 'Get your happiness out of your work!'?"

That pleased him. It was his own quotation, oft repeated in his magazines.

84

I continued, "I was trying to decide what I really think of you once, and I asked a Unitarian minister who reads your stuff whether he knew what your religion is. He said he wasn't sure whether you have any, but if you do, he was quite sure it originated in your pocket book."

"Ho! Ho!" roared the Fra gleefully, and then he quickly replied, "Well, anyway, I get away with it, don't I?"

After perhaps an hour of this "getting happiness out of our work" we adjourned to the music salon of the Inn on the ground floor. Sunday evening concerts were frequently held in this room, which contained three Steinway grand pianos. By this time, mid-afternoon or later, several other guests had arrived. Hubbard ascertained that three of us played the piano. We compared notes and found only one tune all three could play from memory, the waltz "The Pink Lady."

So, with Elbert Hubbard leading like a maestro with great gusto and sweeping arm motions, the three pianos rang out while those assembled sang or waltzed.

As we broke up, Hubbard again urged me to stay overnight, but I had to be on the job early Monday morning, so caught the late afternoon train back to Buffalo.

Sent to Interview Henry Ford

From Buffalo I continued on east to Rochester, Syracuse, Rome, Utica. I may have stopped off at a number of towns and small cities through Ohio, Indiana and Illinois on the return trip. I do not now remember whether I did this, or returned on a through train to Chicago, and then directly to Des Moines.

I had been scheduled to continue on to Troy and

Albany, New York state, but on January 5, 1914 a sensational news story broke in Detroit. The Ford Motor Company raised basic wage rates from $2.40 per 9-hour day to $5 per 8-hour day. It was banner-headline front-page news nationwide.

On that day I reached Utica, New York, and the Journal editors telegraphed me to go immediately to Detroit and interview Henry Ford. They wanted a story on this labor bombshell based on personal interview by a Journal representative.

The $5-a-Day Plan

Arriving in Detroit, I registered at the Hotel Statler—no, on second thought I believe this was before the Statler was built and I stopped at the Hotel Tuller—and took a cab out to the Ford Motor plant, located at that time in Highland Park. There was a many-storied office building in the front—I believe fronting on Woodward Avenue, with the large factory buildings to the rear.

Stepping up to the receptionist desk, I stated my mission and asked for an interview with Henry Ford.

"Mr. Ford," replied the receptionist, "is not a difficult man to see, and if you wish I can arrange an interview for you, but if it is information about the new wage plan you want, I can tell you that Mr. Ford himself really is not as familiar with all the details of it as Mr. John R. Lee, head of the Sociological Department. You see, this whole new plan was originated by Mr. Lee, through his department. He presented the plan to Mr. Ford and the Board. They looked into it and approved it, but that's all. They simply turned it over to Mr. Lee to administer through his department. He's the man who has all the facts about it."

I was there to get the facts, not to glorify my vanity

by being able to say I had gained a personal interview with a man as famous as Henry Ford. I said that I would prefer to talk to Mr. Lee.

I remember well my opening statement and his reply.

"Mr. Lee," I began, "you are now paying the highest wages in the automobile industry—or perhaps in *any* industry. I'd like to get all the facts about it."

"No, Mr. Armstrong," he replied, "we do *not* pay the highest wages, but on the contrary we pay the *lowest* wages in the industry!"

"But," I stammered, "don't you now pay a standard minimum scale of $5 per day, and don't the other factories pay only about $3.50 per day?"

"Quite true," smiled Mr. Lee, "but still, we are paying the *lowest* wages in the automobile industry. You see, we don't measure the *actual* wage by dollars paid, but by the amount of production we receive per dollar paid. Our sales volume is by far the largest in the industry. This has made it possible for us to install an assembly-line system of production. The Ford cars start at one end of this production-line. As they proceed along this line, each worker adds his own part. At the end of the line each car is a finished product. In this manner we are able to set the pace of production. As each car unit goes past each man, he is required to complete his part in the assembly of the car within the time-limit before it has moved past him. You see, we actually set the pace at which each man must work. There can be no stalling, no loafing on the job, no slowing down. We gear the production speed of each man to a high level of work per hour.

"We pay some 43% more dollars per workman per day, but we get 100% more production out of each

87

man—and pay only 43% more money to get it. So you see, we actually pay the *lowest* wages in our industry for what we GET from the labor of our men."

"Well if this plan pays the Ford company so well, why don't the other motor companies adopt the plan?" I asked.

"They can't," said Mr. Lee, "on their present volume of production. But of course if and when they get their sales volume up to a level that will make possible the assembly-line system, they will naturally come to it."

"How about labor unions?" I asked.

"Oh, we have nothing to do with them. Our men are free to join the union if they wish, but there's no point in their paying out labor union dues when they already receive 43% above union scale. We don't recognize the unions in any way, nor will we negotiate with them. As long as we pay so high above union scale, we are simply not concerned with them."

I learned that Mr. Lee's department actually checked into the very homes of employees, and regulated their living standards, thus keeping their men at peak efficiency for turning out extra-volume production.

"But," I pursued, "don't your employees object to this interference and regulation of even their private home life—and also to being forced to keep up such a stiff pace of work?"

"The whole answer to that is economic. Of course they have to work harder, and submit to certain of our regulations even in their private family lives—but enough men are *willing* to submit to these conditions in return for receiving almost half-again more pay than they could obtain elsewhere."

There, as I remember it after 60 years, is the story

of the $5-a-day wage plan that was such a sensation in its day.

But its day came, and has gone. Other automobile factories *did* expand into the assembly-line production system, and then the Ford company found itself on a level with other companies so far as the labor situation was concerned. Ford fought off union recognition and negotiation for many years, but finally was forced to bow to it.

Mr. Lee insisted on driving me, himself personally, back downtown to my hotel. The cars of the company officials were parked in a wide breeze-way between the office building and factory. He took me into the factory for a glimpse of it. As we returned back to the breeze-way, we saw Henry Ford himself about to step into a car some twenty feet away. Mr. Lee asked me to excuse him for a moment, saying he had something he wanted to speak to Mr. Ford about. So I did see Henry Ford but did not meet him or speak to him.

How Christ Is Creator

Much later, after my mind became opened to Biblical understanding, this experience came back to mind forcibly as an illustration of how the Bible represents that God Almighty is the One Supreme Creator, and yet everything that exists was created by Jesus Christ (John 1:3; Col. 1:16).

In Ephesians 3:9 it is stated that GOD created all things *by* Jesus Christ. Henry Ford was, while he lived, the *manufacturer* or *maker* of the Ford cars. But when I visited the Ford factory, I saw Mr. Ford standing there in a well-pressed business suit. It was *his employees* who were doing the actual *work* of making the automobiles. They did it *for* him—at his command. And they did it with tools, machines, and electric *power!*

89

In like manner, God is Supreme Creator. But He delegated the actual *work* of the creating to the One who became Jesus Christ—to the "Logos," or the One who was the WORD—the SPOKESMAN. But He, Christ, utilized the POWER of the Holy Spirit. In Genesis 1:2, we read that the SPIRIT of God moved or was brooding upon the face of the waters. He, Christ—the WORD—*spake,* and it was done! (Ps. 33:9.)

Write Your Autobiography as You Go!

At this point I am constrained to offer the reader some advice on how to write an autobiography. Don't wait until you are 65 to write it. Start writing it at age 3 or 5, and turn it out on the installment plan—as you go. Write it while the events are fresh on your mind. Of course you'll find this method has its drawbacks, too. You won't know at the time which events will stand out in later life as important or interesting, and probably you'll write down about fifty times as much as you'll finally use.

But I find that trying to write the whole thing in retrospect later in life is rather frustrating, too. A lot of things begin to seem all jumbled up. I was sure, when I started writing about these "Idea Man" trips, that the very first one took me west as far as Grand Island, Nebraska, south through Kansas, Oklahoma, and Texas, east through Louisiana and Mississippi, then north through Alabama, Tennessee and Kentucky. I started to write it that way, but found it wouldn't work out. Then it came back to mind from somewhere in those mysterious recesses of memory how the first trip was the one into New York State and back. So that portion had to be rewritten.

Even now, it seems I must have started on this "Idea Man" work earlier than I had remembered, and that the period spent on the magazine "makeup" at the *Successful Farming* composing room was spent somewhere in between these editorial trips. In any event every effort is being made toward accuracy, and this account, as you are reading it, is approximately accurate.

One reason why I am mentioning the names of most of the towns and cities visited on these trips is that *The Plain Truth* has readers in all these places, and I have felt it might add a certain interest to those particular readers to know I had visited their towns. I think that in most of them I could still name the hotels where I stayed.

Becoming an "Early Bird"

The second Idea Tour began a few days after returning to Des Moines, early January, 1914. It took me to Atlanta, Georgia, up the Atlantic Coast to Virginia, and back across from there. I do remember some events from this tour, and a few may be worth recording.

On this trip I travelled some days down the Mississippi River on a large river steamer.

I went first to Davenport, Iowa, making stops in search of ideas at Iowa City and other towns along the way, and travelling by riverboat to Muscatine, Ft. Madison, and Keokuk, Iowa, where the boat was lowered through the locks of the big dam; then terminating the riverboat mode of transportation at Quincy, Illinois. This riverboat travel was quite intriguing at the time.

The itinerary next took me across Illinois to Springfield, Decatur, and Mattoon, and to Terre Haute, Indiana; then south to Vincennes, and Evansville, then Henderson and Hopkinsville, Kentucky. At Hopkinsville, I remember, I was assigned to the "Bridal Suite" of the hotel, of which the hotel employees seemed effusively proud. It was a large room, rather old-fashioned, but dolled up in a manner the staff thought quite distinguished. There were stops at Clarksville and Nashville, Tennessee, and then a night I well remember at the Patton Hotel in Chattanooga.

At this time I was sleeping so well nights that I was having a fight with willpower to awaken and get up mornings. Everything I had read about the lives of great and successful men on the subject indicated that all such men are early risers.

There's the old saying: "The early bird gets the worm." Not that I desired worms, but I did want to be a success. A successful man must discipline himself. I had determined to establish the habit of being an early riser. I could not always depend on hotel clerks getting me up by a call in the mornings, especially in smaller town hotels, so I had purchased a Baby Ben alarm clock which I carried with me.

But I found myself drowsily turning off the alarm, turning over, and going back to sleep. I was becoming determined. At the Hotel Patton, before retiring for the night, I called for a bellboy.

"You going to be on duty at 6 in the morning?" I asked.

"Yassuh, Ah'll be heah," he assured me.

"Well then, do you see this half-dollar on the dresser?"

His eyes glistened. The usual tip in those days was a dime. A half-dollar was a very extra special big tip.

"You pound on my door at 6 a.m. until I get up and let you in. Then you stay here until you see I am dressed, and that half-dollar is yours."

You may be sure I didn't roll over and go back to sleep at 6 a.m. next morning. This system worked so well

92

I kept it up until the "early-bird" habit was established. This was one more example of having to put a *prod* on myself, to *drive* the self to do what *ought* to be done, instead of giving in to inclination or impulse.

Silk Gloves

This trip was started in early January, immediately after the New York State trip. In Iowa we had worn gloves in the winter, kid gloves for dress. In Atlanta it was too warm for kid gloves. I'm not at all sure, now, that any gloves were needed. We never think of wearing gloves in Southern California, and it is not noticeably colder in Atlanta. Probably the main incentive was to "look sharp," rather than cold hands, but I bought taupe-colored silk gloves with three stripes of black braid trim on the back. If vanity is the main ingredient of human nature, I had my share of human nature. I suppose a peacock feels about like I did.

In Atlanta I stopped at the narrow but very tall Wynecoff Hotel—the hotel made nationally famous by a terrible fire several years ago. I remember I went there because it was "fireproof."

Starting back north, stops were made in search of merchandising ideas at Gainesville, Ga., and then Greenville, South Carolina. Near Greenville was a famous rustic-fenced ranch. A Sunday was spent there, and with other travelling men the day was spent going out to this unusual ranch. I still have a picture or two taken at the place.

Then on to Spartanburg, Charlotte, and Greensboro, North Carolina, and Lynchburg, Virginia, from which point I turned back west, stopping at Roanoke, then Bluefield, West Virginia, and on to Ironton and Portsmouth, Ohio. Next stops were made at Chillicothe, Columbus, Springfield, Piqua, Dayton, in Ohio.

You Can't TASTE Smoke

Next, another Sunday layover was spent in Richmond, Indiana. On the mezzanine floor of the hotel a Sunday afternoon argument ensued between five or six travelling men.

One of the men made the ridiculous and outlandish statement that no one can *taste* smoke. The other fellows laughed at him.

"You're crazy," exclaimed one. "Why, all the cigar and cigarette manufacturers advertise that *their* brand TASTES better!"

"Sure," answered the "crazy" fellow, "But it isn't true. You only *smell* the smoke of tobacco—you can't taste it!"

He offered to prove it. We went to the cigar counter and bought about three sets of cigars, two of each exactly alike, then returned to the mezzanine. The first doubter was asked to put the two identical cigars in his mouth, one at a time, lighting only one of them. Then he was blindfolded, and one of the other fellows held his nose so he could not smell. The lighted cigar was then put in his mouth.

"Now tell us which cigar I put in your mouth—the lighted one or the one not lighted. Go ahead, puff on it. Tell us which cigar you are puffing on." This was the challenge of the "crazy loon."

The guinea pig gave two or three big puffs.

"Aw," he exclaimed, "this is silly. Why should I puff on *this* cigar? It isn't lit. There's no smoke coming out of this."

The blindfold was jerked off his eyes, and he was amazed to find himself puffing out smoke like a smoke stack!

The experiment was tried on two or three others,

with cigarettes as well as cigars. All of us were convinced that you CAN'T TASTE SMOKE—but then, *you* probably will say we were *all* crazy! Nevertheless, from that time it has been difficult for me to believe any manufacturer's brand of cigarettes "taste better," for the simple reason I became convinced they don't TASTE at all—they *SMELL!* I mean that, literally!!

After visiting Muncie, Anderson, Indianapolis, and Lafayette in Indiana, I went on to Chicago and back to Des Moines.

5

Pioneering in Public Opinion Polls

A PPARENTLY the "Idea Man" trip from Des Moines to Atlanta and return ended along in April, 1914. It was then that the assignment as makeup man for *The Merchants Trade Journal* came, related in the beginning of the preceding chapter. This assignment, with a desk in the composing room of the *Successful Farming* plant, interspersed with writing advertising copy for clients of *The Journal's* Service Department, lasted six or seven months.

Becoming a Typist in Two Weeks

It was about the beginning of November, 1914, that I was assigned to the next, and last, "Idea Man" trip. This time I was to proceed west as far as Grand Island, Nebraska, then zig-zag south to Houston, Texas, then east to Birmingham, Alabama, then north to Detroit, and back to Des Moines.

Earlier that year the first portable typewriter had been put on the market. It was only some six months after the first little folding Corona had come out that Mr. Boreman presented me with one.

"Herbert," he said, "here is one of the new portable typewriters. We want all the idea material sent in typed hereafter."

"But," I protested, "I've never learned how to use a typewriter. It would take me a week to peck out one single day's reports on that thing."

"Well that's *your* problem," grinned Mr. Boreman. "The way to get things accomplished is to put a *prod* on yourself. Most of us never get around to doing a thing until necessity drives us. So I guess necessity forces you to learn how to type—and *quick!* For we are requiring that all your notes, data, and reports be typed on that baby Corona, and we require that all reports arrive here *on time!*"

What an assignment!

But the *prod* was on! Hurriedly I procured an instruction book on typing. But I saw at once that I did not have sufficient time to learn to type with all eight fingers and two thumbs as instructed in the book. I threw the book away, and began to teach myself my own way, using the first two fingers of each hand, and occasionally a thumb on the space bar.

I proceeded west through Atlantic and Council Bluffs, Iowa; through Omaha, Fremont, Columbus and Grand Island, Nebraska.

At Columbus, in the Evans Hotel, I ran across a man who bore a startling resemblance to Elbert Hubbard. He even wore his hair semi-long, with an artist's bow tie and wide-brimmed hat. He seemed very pleased when I told him he was Hubbard's double, and that I knew the famed "Sage of East Aurora," and had visited at Roycroft Inn. I forget his name, but it seems he was a state senator.

The quest for interesting and practical ideas used successfully by merchants was unusually productive, on this tour. The material for live and useful articles in *The Journal* was accumulating much faster than I could get them typed by the "hunt and peck" system. I worked late nights hunting for letters on the keyboard and pecking at them. I put the typewriter on my lap in train seats and pecked away furiously while traveling to the next town. But my notes were piling up on me.

From Grand Island, I cut south and east through Hastings, St. Joseph, and arrived in Kansas City Saturday night. By now my plight was desperate. I knew my week's reports had to be in the *Journal* office by Monday. I went to the old Baltimore Hotel, then Kansas City's leading hotel, but long since torn down, and hunted keys and pecked away on that little Corona all night long, going out two or three times through the night to an all-night restaurant for coffee—and kept up the ordeal until Sunday afternoon, getting my week's reports finally into the post office.

Starting out early Monday morning the tour continued through Lawrence, Topeka, Hutchinson, Wichita, and Arkansas City in Kansas; then through Oklahoma, stopping at Blackwell and then Enid. An uncle, my mother's elder brother, was ticket agent out at Goltry, Oklahoma some twenty miles west of Enid, and I was able to take an evening train to Goltry and catch an early morning train back, so it was possible to spend the night visiting relatives I had not seen in years.

Indians!

Next was El Reno. And there, for the first time in my life, I saw real Indians. In the dime stores and the

98

department stores, stout Indian squaws, when tired, would just squat down on the floor in the center of an aisle and remain there until rested. Other shoppers were obliged to squeeze by, if possible, or go around another aisle. Out on the main street, I saw a flash of bright red streak by, leaving a cloud of dust.

"What in the world was that?" I asked in astonishment.

"Oh," replied a local man, "that's a young Indian just returned from Carlisle University. He recently inherited a sum of money from the government, and spent it all for the most expensive bright red racing automobile he could find. Since returning from college, he has reverted back to a semi-savage state, and drives his car recklessly wide open down the main street."

Again on a Saturday night I arrived, this time, in Oklahoma City, with a notebook full of ideas piled up on me. Once again there was the all-night ordeal at the folding portable typewriter. But by this time my four fingers seemed to begin finding the right keys almost automatically, and from that time on I was able to keep up with the typed reports. Before this three months' tour was ended, I was pecking away on the typewriter at a speed more rapid than most stenographers.

And, come to think of it, I am this very minute, still rapping out these lines with these same four fingers. Only today, I am privileged to click the words off on a large electric typewriter.

However, the present worldwide enterprise, in its present phase, was actually begun, back in 1927, by clicking off articles on one of those early model folding Coronas. It could not have had a more humble beginning. But we shall come to that phase of the story in due time.

Leaving Oklahoma City early Monday, Chickasha

came next—another Indian reservation town—then Ardmore. Next were Gainesville, Ft. Worth and Dallas, Texas. Thanksgiving Day was spent at the Adolphus Hotel in Dallas.

The Adolphus in Dallas in those days carried the architectural appearance of being a slightly smaller sister of Chicago's Blackstone—though additions have made it several times larger today. In those days the most exclusive hotel in America, with the possible exception of the Waldorf-Astoria in New York, was the Hotel Blackstone in Chicago. It was commonly reported that guests were not admitted into the main dining room of the Blackstone in the evening, unless they were in full evening dress; and that the noted diva Mary Garden, coming in after an evening performance at the Blackstone theatre, was refused admittance because she was not in formal attire.

Also, in those days, The Adolphus maintained, as nearly as possible in a city not much over 100,000 population, as Dallas then was, the atmosphere of The Blackstone.

The main dining room was plush and ornate, serviced with a *maître d'hôtel* and two or three head waiters, besides waiters and bus boys. Most everybody was home for Thanksgiving dinner, and the hotel dining room was almost empty. The *maître d'hôtel* ushered me to a table and spent the entire time of the meal chatting with me.

"I'm a long way from home on Thanksgiving," I said, "and on a reasonably generous expense account. I wish you would order my dinner for me. This is once I'm not going to keep down the cost. Go ahead. Shoot the works. Order the finest dinner you can serve."

He did, and I have never forgotten that Thanksgiving dinner a thousand miles away from home. In these

100

days of jet aircraft, that would not seem far, but it did
then.

A Strange New "Coke"

Sunday was spent at Waxahachie. Directly across from
the hotel was the largest drugstore in any town of 5,000
in America. (Waxahachie is listed at more than 12,000
population in the 1965 Atlas. But it was around 5,000 in
1914.) Waxahachie also had the largest cotton ginning
center in America, as I recall. But this drugstore
interested me.

Sunday afternoon I walked over to the drug store
soda fountain, and ordered a "coke." After the
attendant squirted into the glass the coca cola syrup,
and then the soda water, he took the mixing spoon and
dipped the edge of it into a saucer containing a few
drops of some liquid which looked like milk, shook it off
the spoon, then stirred the spoon into the coca cola.

"What kind of strange new 'coke' do you call that?"
I asked. "What was that you dipped the spoon into and
then shook off?"

"Milk," answered the attendant.

"Why," I inquired, "what's the idea? You shook the
milk all off the spoon. You didn't mix enough into the
'coke' to even notice it. What's that supposed to do?"

I was really puzzled.

"Well," grinned the soda fountain attendant,
"that's the only way I can serve it to you, according to
law."

I was more puzzled now than ever.

"You see," he explained, "it's against the law to
serve coca cola on Sundays—but it's perfectly legal for
us to serve *food*. Milk is food. That tiny portion of a drop
of milk I stirred into it made it *food*."

I had heard of a lot of ridiculous Sunday "blue

101

laws," but that one really took the prize. However, Texas or the municipality of Waxahachie must have gotten "fed up" with it and abolished that law long since.

I Saw General Funston

I continued in the search of interesting and usable ideas in retail stores and checking community and general social conditions in Waco, Temple, Austin, Houston, and Galveston, Texas. It was quite an event to catch my first glimpse of an ocean at Galveston, on the Gulf of Mexico. I went in swimming on the beach, so I could say I had been in the ocean.

Also I was quite impressed with the Hotel Galvez. General Funston, at that time General Pershing's boss, was there, and I rode up the hotel elevator with him. He was short, not tall, but wore a short goatee beard, and carried himself with very dignified military bearing. However, the dignified military bearing was a little lacking that night, as he was being helped from the bar up the elevator to his suite.

From Galveston I proceeded on through Beaumont, and Lake Charles, Louisiana.

The Crucial Letter

At Lake Charles, I received a letter from Mr. Boreman. It was very critical. By this time he had taken over a large part, or all, of the editorial duties from Mr. Vardemann. Mr. Boreman's letter threw me into consternation.

He was not pleased with my work. I was going to have to step on it—get on my toes—produce more and better material.

I was really frightened. I saw visions of being fired. That was a disgrace I felt I could never take. But Mr.

Boreman had not directed me to take the next train home. Apparently I was to be allowed to wind up this trip, at least.

Nevertheless, from that time on, I brooded over the thought of "having a can tied to me" upon return to Des Moines. The vision built up in my mind. I did really "step on it," from that moment. I hustled harder than ever before. I feared being suddenly called in and fired.

Actually, I learned afterward—too late—that Mr. Boreman had not the slightest intention of discharging me. I had apparently gotten into a temporary slump, and he wrote me a rather sharp letter in an effort to help me snap out of it. But all through the remainder of this trip the fear of being fired built up in my mind.

Nevertheless I kept on working with increased zeal.

From Lake Charles I continued on through Lafayette and Baton Rouge to New Orleans, Louisiana. I remember picking up quite a story of how an aggressive dry goods merchant in Baton Rouge beat the big city competition of New Orleans and held his trade at home. This was my second visit to New Orleans.

Too Conceited? Yes!—But

Perhaps I was entirely too proud in those days. Actually there is no "perhaps" about it. I was! Later I was forced to suffer for years to have this vanity and conceit crushed out, before I could ever have been fully prepared for the responsibilities of today.

But I was young then. And I have often wondered if it is not really *better* for a young upstart to *be* conceited, self-confident, cocky—and with it, ambitious, energetic in trying to accomplish something, than to be an ambitionless, spineless, lazy, shiftless fellow utterly

lacking in spark, drive, and the zeal to try to accomplish
something worthwhile.

Such ambitious fellows, of course, may not have
right goals—they may not know the real PURPOSE of life,
or the true *way* of life, and they may be energetically
pressing on only toward more vanity, and "a striving
after wind," as Solomon puts it. But at least they are
mentally ALIVE, and not dead! And once circumstances
do shake them and bring them to themselves, and
humble them and open their minds to the true values,
they are already in the *habit* of exerting enough energy
so that, turned at last in the right direction, something is
REALLY accomplished.

At least one reader of this autobiography—and so
far as I know, only one—has written very disapprovingly
of it, condemning me for having been vain and conceited
in those early formative years. I have stated all the facts
about that over-abundance of self-assurance. Indeed I
have put emphasis on it.

This, then, is one of the things I had to be changed
from! This is a candid and true life story, and the bad is
being told along with what good there may have been.
But, if there was ego and cocky conceit, there also was
ambition, determination, fire, drive, and honest and
sincere *effort* toward what then seemed to be a right
goal.

When the Unseen Hand mentioned in the
introductory chapter took a hand, shook me up,
knocked me down, took away what financial success I
appeared headed toward, beat out the proud conceit
and punctured the inflated ego, my eyes were opened
to what they had not seen before. The goal was
changed. The self-confidence was replaced with faith.
But the fired-up desire now flamed forth in the new
direction. The sincere *drive,* and energy now was

104

applied with increased zeal to the new and far better goal.

And if FAITH, and CONFIDENCE, and positive ASSURANCE in what GOD has set out to do through a poor human instrument has been by some critics misapplied as vain conceit, then I offer no apology—but the dynamic and ever-expanding work of the living God cannot stop, just to please the whim of critics who stand on the sidelines, themselves *doing nothing* except to carp and complain and criticize. My zeal and dynamic drive toward a wrong goal did not exceed that of Saul of Tarsus. But when his eyes were opened, look what a power *he* was!

Jesus was *perfect* in every respect, yet He had His critics who always thought He was doing everything the wrong way. Yet, like the critics of His work today, they did not do better—they simply didn't *do,* period! They sat on the sidelines and watched the procession empowered by the Spirit of God speed by, on to the true goal of accomplishing God's PURPOSE here below!

So I have deemed it proper that the full truth about that self-conceit of those formative years be brought out. But let me emphasize, it was not DECEIT. It was honest and sincere.

Challenged into a Survey

The "Idea Man" tour continued on through Hattiesburg and Meridian, Mississippi, then Selma, Montgomery, and Birmingham, Alabama. What route was taken from Birmingham north I do not now remember. It seems that the next stop was Decatur, Alabama. I think I must have made stops at Columbus and Nashville, Tennessee, and Bowling Green, Louisville, and Lexington, Kentucky.

In any event, the next distinct recollection is in

105

Richmond, Kentucky. Apparently I backtracked some distance south to arrive there. I had heard from travelling men along the way that Richmond was the "deadest" town in all America, and I thought there might be a worthwhile story in finding the reasons for this.

I do distinctly remember getting into a discussion with a furniture merchant in Richmond. I might better have said a heated argument. For I had instantly formed the impression that Richmond was then the most backward, lifeless town of around 5,000 population I had ever visited.

I hope that the bombshell I exploded before the merchants of that town had something to do with waking it up—for apparently the town did come to life, since I noticed in the latest census it is now over 12,000 population.

In any event, I was so utterly disgusted with the lack of civic pride and development, and the lackadaisical inertia of the merchants after interviewing several of them, that I must have expressed my disappointment to this furniture merchant. He argued heatedly that Richmond was a very live town.

"Is that so!" I came back. "Do you realize that probably more than *half* of the trade of the consumers in your town and immediate trade territory is going to the mail order houses, and to the stores in Cincinnati and Lexington?"

"Why, we don't lose *any* trade to outside competition," he yelled.

I shot back. "That shows how sound asleep you are! Why, you don't know what's going on right under your nose here in your own town. I'll tell you what I'm going to do! I'm going to show you that an outsider can come into your town and learn more of the REAL FACTS of merchandising conditions here in three days than you've learned in a lifetime!"

I was good and mad! I was determined to show this sleepy storekeeper, whom I felt unworthy to be dignified with the name "merchant," just how ignorant he was of conditions, of just how dead the businessmen of this town were.

The prod was on! I was only supposed to spend one day in Richmond. I knew I had to work fast. I had to account for my time at the office. This was not routine "Idea Man" work. I was doing this on my own. So I had to hurry. I was fired up! I was determined to *get the facts!*

I had no pattern to go by. To my knowledge no survey—no sampling of public opinion—or investigation from a representative portion of the people, according to the law of averages, had ever been made. I had to think my own way through. But I was so angered that I did a lot of fast thinking—and planning.

The Pioneer Survey

Early each of the three mornings I went to the freight house and the express office. I knew well the big Chicago mail order house methods of shipment. The tags did not contain the mail order house names. Only the street addresses. But I knew well the Homan Avenue address of Sears Roebuck and the street address of Montgomery Ward. Also the smaller mail order houses. Rapidly I jotted down notes of the names and addresses of all local citizens receiving merchandise from Chicago mail order houses, listing the description of the merchandise.

As soon as the banks were opened on that first morning, I went to the bankers, told them of the survey I was making, and asked their cooperation in checking through their stubs and giving me the amount of bank drafts that had been purchased for mail order houses during the past 30 days. Also to go through the cancelled vouchers of customers, and add up the total, over a given period, of checks that had been sent by local depositors to either mail order houses or stores in Lexington and Cincinnati. All agreed to cooperate fully.

Next I went to the postmaster. I asked if he would cooperate to let the merchants know conditions by checking back thirty days through the stubs of money orders purchased for mail order houses or big city stores. There was a postal regulation allowing the postmaster to use his own judgment about giving out such information, and this postmaster was willing to cooperate.

Then, while they were tabulating this information, I devoted the three days to house-to-house and farm-to-farm interviews. For this latter purpose I hired a "rig," for there were very few automobiles in service as yet in 1915, especially in towns of this size. So I drove with horse and buggy ten miles out in two or three directions from town.

I learned that the farmers west of town were so indignant at Richmond merchants that they were actually organizing to boycott these stores altogether. Housewives in town were eager to talk to an investigator. They vehemently poured forth their scathing denunciations of their local merchants.

The women universally said they were *forced* to go either to Cincinnati or Lexington to buy clothes. The stores there sent their expert buyers to New York seasonally to select the latest styles. But the styles at local Richmond stores were completely out of date, and of poor design, quality and workmanship.

The main street, downtown, was not paved, and

108

often shoppers were forced to walk through mud ankle-deep in crossing the main intersection.

The merchants and their clerks were sleepy, unaccommodating, uncheerful, and seemed to feel they were imposed upon to wait on a customer. If merchandise was unsatisfactory and returned, the customer was always *wrong,* and the merchant always wroth.

I went to the ticket agent at the depot.

"These so-called merchants of ours," he said, "have no idea at all of what goes on. In order to go to Lexington—or to Cincinnati—the women shoppers have to take an early morning train leaving at 5 a.m. Lexington shoppers have to change trains at Winchester. Whether they go to Lexington or to Cincinnati, they have a whole day for shopping, and the return train doesn't arrive until long after stores close in the evening. So local merchants are never up early enough to see them go, or late enough to see them return. But we have a train load every shopping day."

My First Public Speech

After working furiously daytimes on this quick survey, I typed rapidly of evenings, writing up reports of every interview. On the third day I collected all the data from the banks, post office, and express office. Then I carefully tabulated all the information, reduced the equations, by the law of averages, to indicate the whole picture of the conditions of the town—and the results were truly ASTOUNDING!

Among all these drowsy storekeepers, I had found one live and alert merchant—the local Rexall druggist. Consequently I had kept him informed as to what I was uncovering in Richmond. He was intensely concerned, and urged me to stay over in Richmond one more day, so he could have opportunity to arrange a dinner for the following evening and get all the merchants to attend, and hear my report.

I felt I could not remain another day in Richmond. I was already three days behind schedule. I did not, at that time, realize that this survey would be of any use or value as editorial material in the magazine. The fear that I was slated to be fired on return to Des Moines had been haunting me. Actually I wrote up this complete report of the survey for the express purpose of explaining this three-day loss of time—and I actually felt I would be reproved for it, and now, more surely than ever, fired.

But this druggist was very persistent.

"Mr. Armstrong," he argued, "you simply do not have any *right* to come into our town, unearth all these sensational facts, and then slip on out and refuse to share this information with our local merchants. Why, *this* is what we've all been needing for years. It will wake this town up."

When he put it as a moral DUTY, and an obligation, I could not refuse. I think I must have had some kind of illusions about sacrificing my job, however, to fulfill this obligation. However, it gave me this fourth day to complete the typing of my report on the survey, together with all tabulations, and final recommendations.

So on this fourth evening here was a dinner arranged by this Rexall druggist. How he ever managed to induce all those merchants to attend I did not know, but apparently all were present.

This was probably the first public speech I ever made in my life. But I was so *filled* with sensational facts that I forgot to be self-conscious or embarrassed.

I remember making the recommendation that, since no local ready-to-wear department was large enough to hire an expert woman buyer and send her to New York on buying trips, they all go together and cooperate, employing one buyer for all of them; and that on her return from New York at each buying season, they have her give public lectures in their various stores, giving the women advance information on what would be the styles for the coming season.

Possibly some of these suggestions of mine, based on the survey, had something to do with the fact that Richmond today is a growing town more than twice as large as it was then.

My First Magazine Article

It was some weeks later that I received the shock of my life. I received a copy of the latest issue of *The Journal* in the mail. I had heard nothing from Mr. Boreman or anyone at the office in regard to the long report I had sent in about the survey. At least, no news had been good news. They had not fired me for it—yet!

But now, some weeks later, I opened the latest copy of *The Journal,* and there, in big headlines as the leading article, I was told of the most sensational article *The Journal* had ever published.

They played it up BIG!

And, for the first time—*under my own by-line!*

The accompanying editor's note explained that they were publishing this astonishing report verbatim, just as their "Idea Man" had written it.

Also, it seems now that in this same issue was another smaller article under my by-line. For the past several weeks, I had begun to write up my material in article form. Always before, however, the editors at *The Journal* office had done a complete rewrite job on my material. But now, my own articles began to appear.

6

Discovering Rules of Success

Following the original survey of business conditions in Richmond, Kentucky, instructions came from the home office of *The Merchants Trade Journal* to do another investigation. They wanted this one from a larger town. Lansing, Michigan, was suggested.

So, leaving Richmond, Kentucky, I proceeded north through Cincinnati and other towns and cities in Ohio.

I am reminded at this point of a visit to the National Cash Register Company plant in Dayton. Again, I am not sure whether it was on this particular tour. But I learned there of an incident which *has* always been remembered.

A Sales Lesson

At that time NCR, as this company was familiarly called, had something of a reputation of being the most

112

aggressive sales organization in American business. And its president, John R. Patterson, was more or less generally reputed to be the country's most successful sales genius.

This is what I learned: Mr. Patterson's mind had caught a sudden sales inspiration. Immediately he did a sensational and unprecedented thing. He sent telegrams to every NCR salesman in the United States, ordering them to come to the factory in Dayton immediately—at company expense. I was shown, while touring the plant, a large auditorium in the company's office building. Here, I was told, the hundreds of salesmen assembled, filled with curiosity. Mr. Patterson addressed them.

"Men," he began, "you are wondering why I called all of you here. Now I will tell you. Every one of you loses sales because your prospects put up objections you are unable to overcome. An idea flashed into my mind the other day that will enable you to turn *every* objection into your strongest selling point. It's so simple you'll all wonder why you never thought of it. *Whatever* the objection, you are to answer immediately, with a smile of complete assurance: 'Why, *certainly*—and *that's* the *very reason* you need this National cash register!' "

Then Mr. Patterson asked a few salesmen to come to the platform and pretend they were prospective customers, putting up to him the objections that each salesman had failed to overcome.

One said, "I simply can't *afford* to buy a cash register."

"Exactly!" responded Mr. Patterson, "and *that's* the very *reason* you *need* this National Cash Register. When you have all the records this register will give you—when it protects you from losses—pays for itself and *saves* you money, then you *can* afford things!"

One by one John R. Patterson answered every sales

objection which his salesmen had been unable successfully to answer.

I have found this principle of salesmanship effective, perhaps hundreds of times.

A Disappearing American Institution

At this point I must indulge another digression. I had written this chapter of the Autobiography in our bedroom of a Pullman car on a train. Mrs. Armstrong and I were en route to Texas, on the Dallas car of the streamlined "Sunset Limited." At El Paso our car was switched onto a "T & P" train for Dallas.

We had just returned from the dining car. Between our streamliner car and the diner we passed through one of the oldtime Pullman cars. I had not seen one in some time. The modern Pullmans are all-room cars. But these older models contained mostly open Pullman seats that make up into berths in sections at night. This is the kind of sleeping cars I rode constantly on these "Idea Man" trips.

The newer streamliner cars provide private toilets in every room, but these old-timers provided one large men's washroom at one end and a ladies' rest room at the other end. These men's washrooms contained a long leather lounging seat at one end, and a chair or shorter seat on the side. They were also the men's smoking rooms. With the disappearance of men's washrooms on Pullman cars has departed a real American institution! I suppose few women know anything about it.

In these washrooms, especially on long trips, men would sit or stand and talk by the hour. In these washrooms no introduction was needed. Conversations were opened as a matter of course. Men conversed familiarly, as if they had been acquainted for years, rarely introducing themselves by name. And what would

114

you women suppose they talked about? Their wives? Laughing at dirty stories? NOT AT ALL! I don't believe I ever heard one off-color story being told in a Pullman washroom. Men always had something more important to discuss than idle gossip about their wives. The discussions were always impersonal.

It was here, in this great but vanishing American institution that the political, economic and social problems of the nation and the entire world were "solved!" Questions of religion were usually avoided. Heated arguments or angry controversy were rarely, if ever, indulged.

If only the heads of state of the world's great nations could have had the Pullman washrooms wired, and the conversations tape-recorded, they could have had the solutions to all their knotty and perplexing problems! TOO BAD! Tape recording came in after this honored American institution went out!

I spent many an hour in thought-provoking conversation in this "institution" of a bygone day, from the days of these "Idea Man" tours, until the modern streamliners relegated this meeting place of business men to a vintage of the past.

But in all seriousness, this digression about washroom conversations truly *belongs* in this story of formative life experiences. For I verily believe that these hours of contacts over the years with many important, thoughtful and successful men contributed their share in the preparation for the responsibilities of today, and for the years still ahead of us. We are influenced by every person with whom we come in contact. The most successful men—the LEADERS—the men of accomplishment—rode the Pullman cars. These washrooms afforded a meeting place where I was privileged to enter invigorating, stimulating, and often enlightening conversation with men I could never have contacted otherwise. Here was a place where men were free and relaxed, always willing to converse with other men on a social parity, regardless of social distinctions outside the Pullman washrooms. Contacts and conversations with scores and scores of prominent and important men—many of them in Pullman washrooms, are among my most treasured experiences.

WHY Men Fail

On all these "Idea Man" trips, one assignment had been to observe, and to question businessmen, in all parts of the country, to try to learn why one man succeeds and another fails. An alarmingly large percentage of retail merchants over the nation were operating "in the red"—on their way to failure and bankruptcy. WHY?

Two men might start out in business under almost identical conditions. One would succeed in building a thriving and profitable business, while the other would "go to the wall." *The Merchants Trade Journal* wanted to know WHY!

I had questioned literally hundreds of businessmen, as to their ideas or opinions on this question. The majority gave the same answer—lack of ability.

While in Detroit on this trip I had a nice interview with the manager of Detroit's large department store, the J. L. Hudson Company. He, with a minority of other businessmen I interviewed, insisted that the main reason for failure in business was lack of sufficient capital.

Of course both of these were factors. But, based on observation, getting at the FACTS that led either to success or failure in hundreds of businesses, I found a third important cause of failures was the fitting of the proverbial square peg in the round hole—in other

116

words, so many men are misplaced—in the wrong line of business, for *them;* this, coupled with the fact that the seven laws of success are not known or followed by most people.

One Sad Experience

I remember a perplexed and frustrated merchant in southern Indiana. He was coming out on the short end, without any profit, and he couldn't figure why.

"I have figured to the very penny every item of cost in doing business," he explained. "It costs me exactly 20% to do business—including every expense—salaries, rent, utilities, advertising, even cost for wrapping paper and string—and it runs exactly 20 cents on each dollar of sales. Now I have figured that a 5% profit is fair. So I add the 5% profit to my 20% cost of doing business, and I mark up all my goods 25% above wholesale price. But at the end of the year my 5% profit just simply isn't there—it has vanished, clean as a whistle! I can't figure where it went!"

"I think I can," I replied. "Suppose you buy a certain item at a cost of $12 per dozen. What are you going to retail that item for?"

"Why, $1.25, of course. $12 per dozen is $1 each. I add an overall of 25%—to cover 20% cost of doing business and 5% profit, and mark the selling price at $1.25."

"I thought so!" I exclaimed. "That's where you've made your mistake. Now look! You say your expenses run 20% of your sales—right?"

"Sure!" he said.

"All right. Now I want you to figure 20% of that $1.25 selling price, and subtract it from the $1.25."

He did, and couldn't believe his eyes!

"Let's see—20% of $1.25 is 25 cents. WHY, when I

117

subtract my expenses from the selling price, I am right back to my cost price! *Where did my 5% profit go?"*

I felt like laughing, but it was no joke—it was too tragic!

"You see," I explained, "you figure your cost of doing business as a percentage of your SALES—not of your buying price. But when you figured your markup, you figured it on the BUYING price, instead of the selling price. Actually, you should have marked your price up 33 1/3% above the BUYING price, in order to sell the item at a price to allow you 20% on the SELLING price for expenses, and 5% for profit."

I left this merchant in a rather dazed condition. WHY was he failing? Lack of capital? Lack of ability? Square peg in a round hole? Or, perhaps, lack of proper EDUCATION, the second law of success!

I found many retail merchants in small towns who were former farmers. It seemed that many farmers in those days had a habit of grumbling and complaining. They knew they worked hard. It seemed to them that the merchant in town had it mighty easy, compared to their lot. The mail order houses kept telling them how the retail merchants gouged them and took big profits. It looked like running a store was a luxurious EASY LIFE, with big profits.

So, many farmers sold their farms and bought retail stores. Then they began to learn that a merchant had *worries* a farmer never thought of. They were untrained and unskilled in merchandising, advertising, selling, cost accounting, shrewd buying. Salesmen from manufacturers and wholesalers overloaded them with the wrong goods. They didn't know how to figure markups. They didn't know how to meet the public, or sell goods. They didn't know how to manage clerks, if they hired any. They were MISFITS—square pegs in round holes!

Then, there are those seven LAWS of success!

Most people—men and women alike—probably do not think of, or apply a single one of these seven laws. These are of such importance that we have issued an attractive free booklet on the subject which the reader may receive upon request.

The Lansing Survey

I continued on to Lansing, state capital of Michigan, to put on the second survey of retail business conditions.

Here conditions were found to be very much like those in the smaller town of Richmond, Kentucky. Although Lansing was much larger than Richmond, and had better and larger stores, yet I found, on actual investigation by house-to-house and farm-to-farm interview and reports from banks, post office, etc., that the Lansing merchants were losing untold thousands of dollars' worth of business to the mail order houses and the larger stores and exclusive shops of Detroit and Chicago.

I had one very good interview with the superintendent of the Reo automobile plant in Lansing. He explained in detail why his plant, and all others, were unable to compete with Ford's new wage plan. They were not yet on the assembly-line production basis.

Somehow, I do not remember so much about this particular survey. It was mostly a repetition of the Richmond investigation, only on a larger scale. It was the Richmond survey which shocked its way into memory, because it was a new revelation to us.

Hiring Myself Another Job

My next definite memory, after concluding the Lansing investigation, was an interview with the secretary of the Chamber of Commerce in South Bend, Indiana.

119

I have mentioned that, in addition to interviewing retail merchants, I usually interviewed also the secretaries of Chambers of Commerce, for *The Journal* was interested in general community activity and betterment, as well as successful business methods.

Of all the Chamber of Commerce secretaries I had interviewed, this man, whose name was Spaulding — I do not remember his given name or initials—impressed me by far the most. He is the only one still retained vividly in memory. He impressed me as being the most able and resourceful of any chamber secretary I had met.

After leaving South Bend, I had jogged back east as far as Ft. Wayne, Indiana. From there I was scheduled to cut southwest toward Indianapolis, and then on back to Des Moines. My biggest "Idea Man" tour was now nearing its end.

The imminence of the return to Des Moines brought back to mind the fear of being "fired." The thought of the disgrace of this now mounted to a mighty crescendo. I felt I had to "beat them to it," by resigning, avoiding the stigma of being discharged.

So on the impulse of the moment, I entered a telephone booth and got Mr. Spaulding at South Bend on long distance. Once again, I "hired myself a job."

"Hello, Mr. Spaulding!" I said. "Since I was in South Bend, I've been thinking a lot about you and your Chamber there. I've decided I want to get into Chamber of Commerce work for a while. I've decided to resign from *The Merchants Trade Journal* and come back to South Bend as Assistant Secretary of your Chamber of Commerce."

"You have!" exclaimed Mr. Spaulding incredulously. "Well, I don't know what we'd have you do, or how I could manage to pay any salary."

■ Horace Elon Armstrong and Eva Wright Armstrong in wedding dress, parents of Herbert Armstrong.

Photograph was taken in September 1887.

■ *Family of Horace Elon Armstrong—as they appeared in 1895. Pictured in this family portrait are Herbert Armstrong, who is standing between the knees of his father, and his sister Mabel, who is seated on the lap of her mother. Herbert Armstrong, approximately three years old, is dressed in a Scottish kilt, then the style for little boys. Left, Eva Wright Armstrong.*

■ *Above, Herbert
Armstrong,
elaborately dressed
in the style of
the 1890s, in his
first year.*

■ *The paternal grandparents of Herbert Armstrong: Nathan and Lydia Hole Armstrong, seated; his father Horace Elon Armstrong (standing, left), his uncle Frank (center), the youngest of the three brothers, and his uncle Walter (standing, right).*

■ *Above, Herbert Armstrong at the age of one year with his great grandfather Hole —then age 92!*

■ *The cottage on West Harrison Street, above, where Herbert Armstrong lived. In photo his grandparents Nathan and Lydia Armstrong stand in front of their home. Left, Thomas and Sarah Armstrong, great-uncle and great-aunt of Herbert Armstrong.*

■ *Herbert W. Armstrong—about three and a half years old—standing with sister Mabel. This was the dress style for boys and girls in the 1890s.*

■ *Family of Horace Elon Armstrong—as they appeared in 1897. Horace Armstrong, sporting mustache typical of the period; his children Mabel and Herbert, who is about five years old; and Eva Wright Armstrong.*

■ *Herbert Armstrong is shown at age nine with sister Mabel—then seven—and younger brother Russell, age one year. Photo was taken in 1901.*

■ *Two memorable turn-of-the-century school photographs. Above, Herbert Armstrong, seated center on the ground, in his early school days. In the photo above left, he is standing to the right of center, behind the lad kneeling in the foreground. Left, Mary Ann Maxwell, who married John Wright and was the mother of Eva Wright Armstrong.*

■ *Mr. Armstrong at the age of 19, seated in front of the depot at Wiggins, Mississippi, with the town's real estate agent and child. Bottom photo shows him in front of Mr. Stapp's residence in Wiggins, January, 1912.*

■ *Top left, Mr. Armstrong on a formal date in suburban Chicago. Right, above, Herbert W. Armstrong, in his early twenties, was on another date when a girl friend snapped this picture. Many years later Mr. Armstrong would write about the principles of dating that would change the lives of thousands of young people. Left, Frank Armstrong, the uncle of Herbert W. Armstrong, as a young man.*

■ *Top, Herbert Armstrong, age 21, on Sunday afternoon visit to farm near Greenwood, South Carolina. Beneath artistic arbor at the farm. Below, at falls that furnished power for large cotton mill at Greenville.*

■ An article published in the Merchants Trade Journal as a result of Mr. Armstrong's fact-finding "Idea-Man" trips. Also illustrated is a bound survey. Mr. Armstrong pioneered the field of opinion polls.

■ *Dixie Highway boosters, Logansport, Indiana. On this old photo Mr. Armstrong appears with his hands on his hips in the front center of the crowd. Mr. Armstrong on one of his surveys in the Deep South.*

"Oh, that's all right," I responded with the usual cocky confidence. "I'll have to go on out to Des Moines, and check out finally with *The Journal,* and you'll have a couple weeks or so to figure it out before I return."

This self-assurance and positive approach must have been difficult to resist, for Mr. Spaulding said he'd try to think of *something.*

Thereupon I sent in to Mr. Boreman a letter of resignation, saying I would finish this trip and then would leave immediately to return to South Bend.

My First Big-League Game

It was about this time, or on one of my "Idea Man" trips through Chicago, that I saw my first major-league baseball game. Ralph Johnson, manager of *The Journal's* Chicago office, and I went together.

The Detroit Tigers were playing the Chicago White Sox in an American League game at Comiskey Park. I had seen a number of minor league games. I had played a great deal of baseball as a boy, between ages eleven and eighteen. But it seemed to me that this major-league brand of baseball was the most monotonous and least exciting of all.

Then I began to understand the reason. They were better players. There was no wasted motion. When a shortstop picked up a hot grounder, he didn't get all excited, and wildly wind up before throwing to first. He scooped up the ball as his throwing arm was smoothly moving into throwing position, and effortlessly it was thrown with speed straight to the first baseman. The players were not making as many motions, but actually the ball was traveling faster.

It's the same in all branches of athletics. The novice makes work of it—goes to unnecessary effort. The champion does it smoothly, with precision.

The same is true with workmen. A greenhorn beginner as a carpenter wastes a lot of motions with his hammer, plane or saw, and quite frequently his hammer misses the nail altogether. The experienced carpenter does it smoothly, effortlessly to all appearances, but he is getting the job done faster.

This particular baseball game really was a monotonous, dull, unexciting game. Even the experienced regular customers were talking about it. We endured the game down to the last half of the ninth inning. The White Sox led, 3 to 1. Detroit was at bat. There were two outs, none on, and one strike on the batter, who happened to be the famous Ty Cobb. We arose trying to get out of the stands before the rush.

A regular "dyed-in-the-wool" fan, sitting in front of us, turned around and said earnestly, "Please take my advice and don't go yet. No baseball game is over until the last out. Ty Cobb hasn't failed to get a hit in any game this year. Don't worry—he'll get a hit."

Why Ty Cobb was Famous

We sat down again, a little dubiously. "Ball one!" droned the umpire.

"Ball TUH!"

"FOUL ball! Strike TUH!" the umpire's drone continued.

"Ball THREE!"

"This is *it!*" exclaimed the fan in front of us, excitedly. *"Now* watch what happens! Old Ty Cobb won't miss getting that hit!"

He didn't! The next pitched ball cracked squarely off Cobb's bat, driven like a bullet straight between left field and center. It was a two-bagger at least—maybe a triple, if Cobb rounded the bases fast enough!

But Cobb didn't! To our utter amazement, he jogged leisurely to first, sat down on the bag, stretched, and yawned drowsily!

But as soon as the ball was thrown back to the pitcher, he was up and alert, dancing friskily at a dangerous distance off first, beginning a taunting, razzing line of chatter at the pitcher.

"Hey YOU PITCHER! *Thanks* for that two-bagger you handed me! *Yea!* Thanks for NUTHIN! I didn't want it as a *gift!* I'd rather STEAL it from ya! Come on, now! I'm goin' a STEAL second. Try and catch me! Ya can't throw straight enough to catch me!"

The pitcher whirled and whipped the ball to first. But Ty slid back under the ball safely. Now he razzed the pitcher more than ever, taunting him, telling him he was no good—he was going to pieces—daring him to catch Cobb off base.

The pitcher threw a ball and a couple of strikes at the batter, meanwhile whipping the ball a couple more times to first trying vainly to catch Cobb off base.

Then Cobb dashed off and stole second.

The batter finally connected. This, too, might have been good for two bases. But the batter was forced to stop on first. Ty Cobb lay down on second, feigning sleep, snoring loudly. But as soon as the ball was again in the pitcher's mitt, he was up and dancing wildly far off second, his torrent of contempt for the pitcher pouring violently from his mouth.

Two or three times the pitcher made a vain attempt to snap the ball to second in time to nail Cobb off base and end the game with the third out. But each time only brought a fresh outburst of contemptuous discouragement from Cobb. This strategy was beginning to have its effect on the pitcher. Before the next batter could get a hit, strike out, or a base on balls, Ty had stolen third.

There, again, he sat down and continued taunting the pitcher.

WHY didn't Cobb race, on his own hit, for second, third, or even to stretch his hit into a home run? WHY, when he was on second, and the next batter cracked out a line drive, didn't he race on to round third and score a run? Usually a single drives in a run if a man is on second.

The answer is that the score was 3 to 1 against Detroit. One run was not enough. Had Cobb scored a run on either his own hit, or that of the batter following him, the White Sox probably would have put out the next man, and the game would have ended 3 to 2 for Chicago. Cobb's strategy was to exasperate the pitcher psychologically until he "went to pieces" so that following batters might succeed in driving in a total of THREE runs needed for a Detroit win. As long as Cobb remained on base, he was allowed to taunt and razz the pitcher.

So he remained on third, shouting ridicule at the pitcher, who now walked a batter, filling the bases. The pitcher now was thoroughly rattled, nervous, his confidence gone.

The next batter drove out a double, scoring all three men on bases. Thus the game ended. Score, Tigers 4, White Sox 3!

This game turned out to be one of those rare, once-in-a-lifetime thrills most people never see, though they may attend ball games regularly. It was the topic of conversation of all Chicago next day.

On arriving in Des Moines I learned, to my dismay, that Mr. Boreman had had no thought of "firing" me, but merely wrote the letter I had received at Lake Charles, Louisiana, in an effort to snap me out of a slump and prod me on to better effort. I gathered the impression that he was genuinely sorry to see me leave *The Journal.*

Actually, now, having been myself an employer for several years, I think I can better understand. The almost three years I had spent with *The Journal* had been largely preparatory years, and Mr. Boremen probably figured they had invested quite a little time, instruction, supervision and money toward developing a man who had some slight promise of becoming a really valuable man in the organization some day. And to see me quit and drop out, just as I was beginning to be worth something—beginning to be able to write articles and advertising copy professionally—meant the investment was now wasted and a total loss, except for whatever value I had been while there.

While with *The Journal* my salary had been raised a number of times. The raises had never been large, but they were fairly constant, as frequently as I deserved, and I probably was in line for another raise about the time I resigned. I was then getting $20 a week, which was not a high salary, but with the expense account, travelling most of the time, the salary was mostly clear. There was no room or board to pay out of it.

I must have had another conference with my Uncle Frank Armstrong while in Des Moines this trip, but do not remember his reaction to my latest detour from the main track. But even though it was another sidetrack, nevertheless it was to provide valuable *experience* and training for the later BIG JOB.

Building a Highway

Leaving Des Moines this time was destined to be leaving it as "home" forever. I had been born and reared there. But now I was almost twenty-three. Perhaps it was time to fly the home nest.

125

I arrived, I believe, one evening in South Bend and obtained a room at the YMCA which was to be my home for some three or four months. Next morning I reported to Mr. Spaulding at the Chamber of Commerce.

Actually there had been no need of an Assistant Secretary, so there was no salaried job awaiting me. But, as I had detected on my one interview with him, Mr. Spaulding was a resourceful man, and he did come up with something for me.

The automobile was just beginning to come into its own in America in 1915. Of course most families did not, as yet, own automobiles, but the number was increasing annually. And the cross-country highway idea was just beginning to make its first bit of headway. Of course all roads outside of towns and cities were unpaved. But a great deal of work had been done on the Coast-to-Coast "Lincoln Highway" (now U.S. 30), and this already had been built—in the manner they were then built—routed through South Bend.

This manner of building consisted of doing considerable additional grading, and surfacing of already existing roads. Few if any of the old "horse and buggy" square corners were straightened out. Surfacing consisted, at best, of a certain amount of graveling—but few even dreamed, as yet, of paving or hard-surfacing highways between cities.

At this particular time the highway activity centered on getting through the new "Dixie Highway," from Canada to the Gulf. As planned by its promoters, this north-south highway was to pass through South Bend. But the right-of-way, and cost of road improvements had to be approved by, and paid by, each township and county. The Federal Government had not, apparently, gotten into the highway business as yet. Nor were there any State highways.

126

Mr. Spaulding explained to me that they were running into a snag. Although there was a Dixie Highway Association, more or less privately promoted but endorsed, as nearly as I remember the set-up, by civic groups such as Chambers of Commerce, the right-of-way over existing roads or for any new roads, if necessary, had to be voted and approved by a majority of property owners of each township and county along its route. The big obstacle was the northern township of Marshall County, which was next south of St. Joseph County, of which South Bend was County Seat.

In order to hurdle this barrier, and to promote the construction of the new highway generally, Mr. Spaulding had conceived the idea of forming a local Motor Club. It was in no sense like the AAA, or associated automobile clubs of today. Its primary aim and purpose was good roads, and the promotion of this Dixie Highway.

One idea we had was to name or number every country road in St. Joseph County. I am not sure now whether this was Mr. Spaulding's idea or mine. It was very difficult for a farmer to direct anyone unfamiliar with the neighborhood to his farm. He would have to direct one to go about a mile and a quarter in a certain direction to a certain windmill; then turn left to a road where he would see a red barn; then right until he came to a certain cow in a pasture, then to the fourth house on the left—or some such crazy and incomprehensible direction. Our idea was to name and number country roads like city streets, with road signs plainly designating the name or number of each road.

Mr. Spaulding's idea was for the Chamber of Commerce to sponsor the Motor Club, which I believe we named the St. Joseph County Motor Club, and memberships were to be sold to automobile owners for

$2 each, with the more prominent citizens expected to purchase the multiple block of memberships.

How to Swing a Group

When I arrived, Mr. Spaulding had the germ of the idea, but it remained for me to "put it over." First, we had to propose the idea to the Chamber's Board of Directors, and win their approval.

One of the first lessons learned in this new school of Chamber of Commerce activity was how to swing a group of hard-headed businessmen to vote the way you want them to. Mr. Spaulding had the know-how. It was an interesting experience.

First, he selected three of the more prominent and influential Board members whom he felt sure of winning to the idea. He and I went to these men, and "sold" them on the Motor Club idea privately. He arranged for one of them to spring to his feet in the Board meeting as soon as Mr. Spaulding had presented the general idea, and enthusiastically endorse it, saying he was most definitely in favor of this idea. The other two men were to follow suit, rising promptly before any other Board members could rise to object, and heartily endorse the idea.

Then, at the Board meeting, after Mr. Spaulding had outlined his proposal for the Motor Club and these three members in rapid-fire succession had generated enthusiasm by their vigorous endorsements, Mr. Spaulding exclaimed that it seemed useless to ask for more discussion — and brought it to an immediate vote before any member could object.

In this meeting were several multimillionaires. South Bend was home of a number of very prominent industries, including the Studebaker automobile factory, Oliver Chilled Plow Works, L. P. Hardy sales book

128

manufacturers, and many others. It was a new experience to me to see the psychological effect of this strategy on these supposedly hardheaded businessmen. Like all humans, they had the "sheep" instinct. The impression had been created in the mind of every Board member that every *other* member, except possibly himself, was enthusiastically in favor of this proposition, and not wishing to be on the losing side, or a lone dissenter, each one voted YES—it was unanimous!

So the Motor Club became a reality. My commission was to be 25%. I learned later—too late—that the proper rate of commission on a thing of that kind should have been 50%. But the whole idea was a new one to all of us. Actually, my work was very successful, but I was only half paid, and was unable to "hold body and soul together" as they say, on what I was making—so after a few months I was forced, of necessity, to move on.

But there were some exciting experiences in putting through this Dixie Highway during those few months.

7

How to Put Resourcefulness into Practice

As I mentioned, there were no national or state highways in those days, late spring of 1915. These pioneer cross-country highways were privately promoted with the cooperation of civic bodies. They were merely graded and gravelled. A paved highway between cities was as yet unheard of. I do not remember how the funds were provided, but probably by popular subscription from property owners along the right of way. I do remember we had to get all the farmers along the way signed up for it.

The South Bend Chamber of Commerce had endorsed this Dixie Highway project. But the promoters had run into a provoking snag. The farmers of the northern township of Marshall County, next south of St. Joseph County of which South Bend is County Seat, were refusing to sign up. They were stubborn. One little township might block the entire project from the Gulf of

Mexico to Canada. A chain is no stronger than its weakest link.

It was my job, among other things, to sign up these adamant farmers.

For some little time, however, probably the first three or four months at South Bend, my activities were bent on selling memberships in the new St. Joseph County Motor Club. This brought me into close personal contact with some of South Bend's prominent millionaires. I worked fairly closely with Mr. E. Louis Kuhns, a millionaire capitalist. I believe he was Vice President of the Chamber of Commerce.

Several times I went out to the Studebaker works to chat with the sole remaining member of the famous Studebaker Brothers. Mr. J. M. Studebaker was then 84 years of age, hale and hearty, still somewhat active, and arrived at his office precisely at eight every morning. He arrived always with a rose or a carnation in his lapel. Two or three times, on my visits to his office, he removed his carnation from his lapel and stuck it in mine. I remember Mr. Studebaker as a very kindly man, and I always counted it a rare privilege to have been able to spend a while in conversation with him. He and his brothers originally founded the Studebaker Brothers Wagon Works, long before the days of the automobile. But by 1915 they were one of the leading automobile makers.

Also I knew Mr. A. R. Erskine, at that time president of the Studebaker works. I believe Mr. Studebaker was Chairman of the Board.

Mr. L. P. Hardy, head of the L. P. Hardy Company, which I believe was the country's largest sales-book manufacturer, also was very active in Chamber work and I knew him well. The last time I passed through South Bend, driving a new car home from the factory, I looked in the telephone directory and failed to find the L. P. Hardy Company listed. They must have moved elsewhere or gone out of business.

Most of these prominent and wealthy men bought multiple blocks of Motor Club memberships, which sold for $2 each.

Frugality of the Wealthy

The one man reputed to be the wealthiest of all South Bend's multimillionaires at that time was Mr. J. D. Oliver, head of the Oliver Chilled Plow Works. He was reputed to be worth one hundred and ten million dollars.

Here, I thought, was a man who could easily afford to purchase even a few *thousand* memberships. I began to count my commission in advance. As explained previously, Mr. Spaulding had not been able to create a salary job for me, and I was promoting this Motor Club on a commission basis of 25%.

In order to psychologically build up to my one BIGGEST order of multiple memberships, I had planned first to contact all the other prominent men. I felt it would have a good effect on J. D. Oliver to be able to tell him how many memberships the others had taken. He, I figured, would want to outdo them.

I had a nice talk with Mr. Oliver. He listened to my entire explanation of the purposes of the Motor Club—the need of better roads—the benefit that would accrue to the community and every business in South Bend. He listened to the explanation of how generously the other prominent businessmen of South Bend had purchased multiple memberships. He seemed quite interested. My hopes for a BIG commission rose.

"Mr. Armstrong, I think this Motor Club is a

splendid activity. It will be a fine thing for the community. Yes, you may surely count me in. I want to join!"

MAN! Now my hopes *soared!*

"That's certainly splendid, Mr. Oliver. How many memberships shall I put you down for?"

"Just one single membership. Two dollars!" came the businesslike reply.

Did you ever have a bucket of ice water thrown in your face at the moment of greatest anticipation?

It was incredible! A man who had $110,000,000—and he took one little, tiny, measly membership—just $2—just the poor widow's two mites! But that's what he said.

"Maybe," I thought, as I left the Oliver Chilled Plow plant, "that's why Mr. Oliver *has* a hundred and ten million dollars. He holds on to what he gets." I was a disappointed young man. But I still had a job to do.

Learning to Drive

After selling Motor Club memberships to most of the important businessmen, I went after those running smaller businesses, and even citizens who were employed. I needed to get out into the country and neighboring suburbs.

I suppose the dealers who handled some of the leading automobile makes might have loaned me a car for this civic-betterment work, but they didn't. It remained for the dealer of the smallest, lowest priced of all to offer me the free use of a car.

No—it wasn't a Model-T Ford. It was a smaller and lower-priced car—a little baby Saxon. Not many of my readers today will remember the Saxon, and my memory of it is pretty dim, but I believe it was smaller than today's German Volkswagen. I had never before driven a car. This is where I first learned—with a baby Saxon in South Bend, at age 23.

While I was there Ralph DePalma, then the world's most famous automobile racing driver, came to South Bend with his famous racing car. I don't remember much of the occasion, but I do remember DePalma—he made quite an impression on me.

Also while I was in South Bend two then famous movie stars came through. They had soared to the top in a serial thriller, "The Million Dollar Mystery." It created about the same national sensation in that day that the TV show "The $64,000 Question" did in 1955. These two actors told me that they had personally made very little money out of it. No one knew how it was going to catch fire with the public before it started, and they were employed on straight salary by contract. It made a big fortune for its owners, not its actors. Then, in an effort to cash in on their popularity, these two actors put all the money they had into promoting the sequel, titled "The HUNDRED Million Dollar Mystery."

But, as they should have known, had they been better psychologists, the sequel was a total dud. They lost all they had. A million dollars seemed like an unheard-of amount of money, and those words in the title coupled with the magic word "MYSTERY" captured the fascination and interest of the American public back in the early "silent" days. But it was like a child with a new toy. Once the glamor and excitement of the toy wears off, it becomes "old stuff." Give the child another toy just like it, only bigger, and he won't be interested.

The star of these serials was James Cruze. The other actor was Sid Bracey.

Cracking the Adamant

It must have been about mid-summer or a little later

that the time came when the Dixie Highway project could not be delayed any longer.

The farmers to the south of us, in the north township of Marshall County, were adamant. The road was approved through Marshall County up to this township line, and again as soon as it entered St. Joseph County. This little three- or four-mile strip of road was the only link incomplete along the entire length of the highway from Mobile to Canada.

It was now my job to crack through that human stone wall.

I had been quite intrigued in watching the strategy Mr. Spaulding had employed in "selling" the Motor Club idea, and a job for me, to the Board of Directors of the Chamber.

One morning we received a telegram at the Chamber of Commerce from the Director of the Dixie Highway project in Atlanta, Georgia. It stated tersely that he would be in South Bend in a few days, and unless we had the highway completed through this county south of us, the entire highway would be re-routed by way of Chicago, and South Bend would lose out altogether.

This was the ammunition I needed.

This was the signal to spring to action, *in high gear!*

I decided our only chance was to utilize the same principle of psychology Mr. Spaulding had used in putting the Motor Club through with the Chamber directors. But this was tougher. I decided it needed a big show—a real "whoop and hurrah!" The only way to break through the obduracy of those farmers was through their emotions. I had learned, as an advertising principle, that you can move people to action easier and quicker through their emotions than through their reason.

135

I decided we had to appeal to both—with terrific impact!

Hurriedly I called Mr. Hardy and Mr. Kuhns. I told them I planned to stage a big rally that night at the little town of Lapaz, in the very center of this reluctant township. I asked them if they would come down and make an impassioned speech to the farmers in favor of the Dixie Highway. When they had agreed to this, I asked them if they would approve the expense, to be paid by the Chamber of Commerce, of a big brass band to help get out the crowd at Lapaz. Having agreed to speak, they couldn't well refuse to approve the expense of the band. Mr. Spaulding agreed to call other Board members and get the band approved.

Then I arranged for a big platform to be built during the afternoon at Lapaz. These arrangements made, I borrowed my little Saxon car and drove to Plymouth, county seat of Marshall County. There I arranged with the telephone company to put through a "general ring" on every rural party line in that township, and notify all the people that there was to be a BIG RALLY that night at Lapaz—with a big brass band and noted speakers from South Bend.

Excitement of this kind was a very rare thing in such rural areas in those days. I knew this would get all the people out. In Plymouth I went first to the hotel, and wrote out the message I wanted the telephone operators to announce over all their telephone lines in that northern township. You may be sure I put all the advertising punch I knew in that message.

This accomplished, I went to the office of the county attorney. I explained my mission, and what the South Bend Chamber was trying to do, and its value to Plymouth and Marshall County. Then I asked him to draw up for me a legal petition for the completion of the road improvements through this northern township, with several sheets attached for signatures. He dictated the legal document and his secretary typed it while I waited.

Armed with this, I drove back to the vicinity of Lapaz. I had previously obtained the names of four leading farmers in this township, thought to be less hostile than most to the new highway.

Now my REAL task began. I had to "sell" these four men on the project in person, and I didn't dare fail on a one. I was armed also with the telegram from Atlanta received that morning. I had facts and figures on how the new highway would increase the value of their farms, bring more trade to the towns of the community, and in every way benefit the farmers.

The Big Show

With necessity as a prod, I succeeded. One by one these four key farmers were won over. I explained that they would have to appear ENTHUSIASTIC. All four finally agreed to act according to my plan.

Now the stage was all set—and not a bit too soon—it was by that time sundown.

The crowd began to arrive. The platform had been erected. The delegation from South Bend arrived, and took its place on the platform. I simply do not remember, now, whether I myself acted as Master of Ceremonies or who, but it seems that this was done by a leading businessman from South Bend.

The band struck up lively tunes, designed to whip up emotional fervor. We got the crowd to singing, laughing, dancing, shouting. It was a real show. Then the men selected as the best public speakers in the South Bend Chamber of Commerce, Mr. Hardy and Mr. Kuhns, gave their stirring impassioned speeches, reading the telegram, telling the farmers it was their last chance—tonight or *never!*—and the advantages to them, their community, and probable increased value of their land that the new highway would bring.

"Now, gentlemen, step right on up here and SIGN this petition right now! Who'll be the first?" shouted all six feet four of E. Louis Kuhns.

This was the signal. I shoved my number one farmer forward.

"I want to sign that petition right now!" shouted my first farmer.

"I'm *for* it! *I* want to sign it!" shouted out my number two farmer, crowding forward to the platform.

"Me, too!" barked my third man. "This is just what this community has been needing!"

"Hey! Let me through!" roared my number four farmer. "We ALL want in on this! Come on, men—let's ALL sign it!"

And they all did. They all crowded forward and signed to put the highway through! Every farmer who had been bitterly opposed was carried away with the emotion of things, and was convinced that everybody else was *for* it, so he might as well go along, too!

I had negotiated one more experience in learning to apply the fifth law of success—RESOURCEFULNESS—in meeting problems and handling obstacles.

The adamant wall was cracked!

The Dixie Highway was built—today known as U.S. 31, now a major paved highway from Canada to the Gulf. And, to my readers who live along U.S. Highway 31, this is the story of how the last link of your highway was put through, and how it finally came into being!

Arriving in Danville "Broke"

The two to four months spent in Chamber of Commerce

138

work in South Bend had been valuable experience as part of the groundwork for later accomplishments—but far from profitable as immediate financial return.

It seemed that I was doing as well as could be expected. Many multiple memberships had been sold. But I was running behind financially. I was living in a small room with an alcove bed in the YMCA. I ate mostly either at the "Y" cafeteria or the coffee shop in the Oliver Hotel, inexpensively. Yet I was running into debt. And the "cream"—the multiple memberships sold to leading businessmen and Chamber members—had all been skimmed off, and it had become a matter of soliciting single memberships at $2 per person. My commission of 25% was not sufficient to keep me going.

Finally the decision had to be made to leave. I should have taken this problem up with Mr. Spaulding, or Mr. Kuhns, but I was too embarrassed to go to them about a personal financial problem. Actually I took the more embarrassing course, as I was to learn later. It is always best to face a problem and solve it. Running away from it is never the solution. I left debts behind in South Bend. Later, when they became very pressing and I was still unable to pay them, I wrote to Mr. Kuhns.

I had by then learned that the standard rate of commission on activities similar to mine in South Bend was 50%. Actually I had been only half paid. I wrote to Mr. Kuhns about this, to see whether the Chamber of Commerce could rectify the mistake and pay me the additional 25% which I actually had earned. He replied that, on investigation, he had confirmed my contention that the commission should have been 50%. But he maintained it was then too late. Had I come to him about it before leaving South Bend, he said, something might have been done to adjust the commission

139

properly. Of course he was a millionaire, and without missing the change he *could* have paid these small debts and cleared the good name of a barely 23-year-old chap, who had, in this instance, been the victim of an unintentional injustice. But that did not seem to be the way millionaires get to *be* millionaires!

A year or more before I had come to South Bend, the Chamber had employed an assistant secretary, whose name, I believe, was Vaughn. He had visited South Bend while I was there, was about my age, and I had become acquainted with him. He was now secretary of the Chamber at Danville, Illinois.

Why I took the train from South Bend directly to Danville I do not remember. Apparently I had thought, or Mr. Spaulding had thought, that Vaughn might be able to turn up something for me to do in Danville. And I *had* to get something else to do immediately! I had barely enough money to get me to Danville.

Arriving in Danville one morning, stone-"broke," not even a dime, I went first to call on Vaughn, but he had absolutely nothing for me—not even any ideas.

I walked back down on the street. I had no money for lunch. I had no money for a place to sleep that night. I was too proud to beg. Actually, that thought didn't even occur to me—I'm merely stating it now. My experience indicates that no honest man *ever* begs. I have given to many beggars on the street, and have put many of them to many different tests to see if I could find an honest one. Some had a "line" that sounded real sincere. But not one ever proved honest. I think the police will tell you there is no such thing as an honest beggar.

Perhaps some are like one I knew of in Vancouver, Washington—though most are not as successful. This fellow could throw his body into a pitiful-appearing

140

contortion, put a pleading, pity-arousing expression on his face, hold up his hat with some cheap pencils in it from his squatting position on a busy corner, and wring the hearts of passers-by. Then every evening he would get up, limp a few blocks to his Cadillac parked on a back side street, unkink his legs and spine, and gingerly hop into his car and drive home to his wife who wore an expensive mink coat!

King David knew human nature. He said, "I have been young, and now am old; yet have I not seen the righteous forsaken, nor his seed begging bread" (Ps. 37:25). No, *honest* people just never do beg!

Enforced Resourcefulness

Perhaps I should never have come to realize that RESOURCEFULNESS is one of the seven laws of success, or to have acquired any of that ingredient, had circumstances not *forced* it upon me!

If so, I'm grateful for the dilemma!

Here I was, almost 2,000 miles away from my parents, with no place I could call home, just arrived in a strange city, "BROKE!"

I had to think!—and think FAST!!

One thing came to my mind in this emergency. The surveys of retail business conditions I had made in Richmond, Kentucky, and in Lansing, Michigan, had been sensational in what they had uncovered. They had been of very great value to the merchants of those cities. While I had been in Des Moines, after resigning from the *Merchants Trade Journal,* Mr. Boreman and I had talked about the idea that there ought to be some way of *selling* these surveys to merchants so that such investigations might be made everywhere.

But no way to sell the idea had occurred to us. Unfortunately men will not pay money to hire an investigator to find out what's *wrong* about them—to discover and show them their faults and mistakes, and to criticize them.

The thought came that Danville was an ideal size city for such a survey. But *how* could I induce anyone to pay me a fee to unearth the mistakes the local retailers were making?

"I've got it!" The idea flashed to mind. "I'll sell the idea to the local NEWSPAPER. Why, this kind of information I dig up in a survey is just the ammunition the advertising department of the newspaper needs to sell bigger advertising space to the merchants! It's just the information they need to show the merchants how to write their copy—what individual merchants need to do inside their stores to make their advertising bring in better results! WHY didn't I ever think of this before?"

With brisk and confident steps, I walked into the office of the business manager of Danville's daily newspaper. Enthusiastically I told him of the surveys I had made—the national sensation they had created in *The Journal*—the value to the merchants—and how this information could be used to perhaps *double* the advertising revenue of his paper.

"I'll buy it!" exclaimed the business manager without a moment's hesitation. "How much is it going to cost?"

Caught Flat-footed

He snapped out his decision as if he was afraid I might change my mind about being willing to do the investigation if he delayed.

His answer came so suddenly it caught me flat-footed!

The FEE? I hadn't thought of that! I was so bent on solving my dilemma and getting some money into my

142

pocket before lunch time that I had not thought the idea quite that far through. I had no time to think.

"Why," I blurted out, "Fifty dollars, I guess."

Again I had far underestimated the value of my services. As I found out later, I should have said $500, and he would have paid it just as readily! Actually I did later put on a number of surveys for $500 fees. These experiences will be covered in due time.

I had outlined to this newspaperman that I proposed to get at least 100 interviews with consumers, so selected as to be representative of the whole population, even out into the country and neighboring suburban towns; I was to obtain as much information as possible from local banks, the express company, post office, freight houses, etc., as to mail-order business and trading in Chicago stores. All my information was to be typewritten in detail, accurately tabulated and summarized, with separate PRIVATE reports and recommendations for each major local store. The newspaper was to arrange a dinner at which all local retailers were to be invited, and I was to give a talk, revealing what I had found.

So, on blurting out the $50 fee, I added:

"I'd like a $10 advance right now, the privilege of drawing another $10 during the survey, and the balance when I turn over to you the complete typed report and summary on the night of the dinner." This was to be either the third, or the fourth night.

Actually I had cheated myself out of $450! nevertheless, the predicament was solved. I walked out of his office with ten dollars in my pocket! I ate lunch! And I slept that night at the "Y"!

It certainly *could* have been worse! What I *really* did was to pay $450 to learn another lesson. Experience is a DEAR teacher! But, truly, "the laborer is worthy of his hire!" This experience helped me to learn that it is not wrong to charge a fair and just price for services or commodities, and that an employer should not underpay employees.

The business manager of that newspaper must have realized, at least after receiving my 40- or 50-page typed report and analysis, that the professional effort and "know-how" that went into that investigation was worth several times the little fee I had spontaneously blurted out. But, in the business world, *"business is business!"* He paid what he agreed. No more!

This world's way is based on selfishness, greed, competition—GETTING all you can, *giving* as little as possible—the *profit* principle. Our world-girding enterprises of today have been based on the *giving, serving* principle—and *this* way of doing things has built a major-sized organization that has been eminently successful—serving and benefitting millions worldwide.

A New Job

The merchandising survey was completed, typed, summarized, data tabulated and analyzed in some three or four high-pressure days.

The dinner given by the newspaper for the merchants of Danville was well attended. My report of the investigation, as had been the case at Richmond and Lansing, was something of a bombshell. It really shook up the merchants to learn existing facts about their own businesses and their own town of which they had been totally unaware.

Nevertheless, a young man barely twenty-three is still just a "young man" to others of senior maturity. I didn't realize it then, but even the brilliancy of this report did not conceal the obvious fact that I was a youngster, and probably in need of a job. I do think, however, that this investigation and the revelations it disclosed gave these businessmen the impression that I was a fairly "live" young man who would be a valuable employee, because four or five of them tried to employ me. And I was in no position to turn down a job.

I took the job that appeared, at the time, to be most promising. It was with the Benjamin Piano Company, selling pianos. I devoted a month or two in determined effort, and never sold a single piano!

This perfect goose-egg record reminds me of the "punch line" of old "Lightnin' Bill Jones" in a play that broke all records on Broadway some 38 or 40 years ago. Old "Lightnin' Bill" was a likable good-for-nothing old codger who *knew* all, and had *done* all.

"Yep," he exclaimed at the climax of the show, "I was in the bee business once. Drove a swarm of bees clear across the desert, and never lost a bee!"

I managed to get pianos in many houses, on trial, and never sold a piano!

I learned something about the piano business. It was not conducted like other businesses. The method was to work through piano teachers. The piano teachers always had prospective customers—homes where a child was at the age for learning to play the piano. The company had a number of piano teachers working for it in Danville, and over its entire trade territory. The teachers supplied us with the names of prospects they had already approached with the idea of lessons for their children. Then I would call and try to talk the parents into giving the child lessons—which necessitated the purchase of a piano. I would induce them to let me put a new piano in the home on trial—without any obligation to buy. Then I would notify the teacher, and she would "accidentally" happen to be passing by, and drop in for a friendly call—discover the piano, play it, tell the people it had a wonderful tone, and a perfect action, and highly recommend that they buy it.

Unfair Competition

This seemed like a "sure fire" method of selling pianos.

There was just one thing wrong with this setup.

Competition!

I soon found that our competitors *also* had piano teachers working for *them!* I knew, of course, that our store paid a commission to their piano teachers if the sale was made. What I didn't know was that our competitors paid a commission to their teachers if they could knock the sale of a Benjamin piano, once it had been moved into a home on trial.

When I called back at a home a few days after placing a trial piano in it, I usually found the woman angry.

"Why did you talk me into letting you bring that old tin pan into my home?" she would demand. "I want you to send your truck and get this out of here at once! Miss Anderson is a music teacher, and she happened to call on us, and she tried out this piano and told us it was *no good!*"

I had been successful selling advertising space, but as a piano salesman I was a total flop. That kind of competition seemed to me so absolutely rotten, foul, and unfair I simply refused flatly to try to combat it. Getting a local music teacher to recommend a good piano, which I knew was worth recommending, and paying her a commission, seemed legitimate. But employing a teacher to go into homes and lie about competitors' pianos was a dishonest method I refused to engage in. Instead I permitted disgust and resentment to discourage me on the entire dirty business. Also I found there was no honesty in pricing pianos. They were usually far overpriced at the start, and the salesman was expected to keep cutting the price until he sold the instrument. This is not necessarily true of the best quality pianos. And I am talking about 1915 practices.

I never believed in price-cutting. A product or a service ought to be fairly and honestly priced in the first place, and then the price maintained.

I have learned that men fall into two classifications, so far as salesmanship is concerned. Some men are born to be salesmen —others are not. Even the man with the hereditary aptitude for it must *learn.* But salesmen are of two kinds. One can sell a commodity, the other can sell an *idea.* I was of this latter type. As a piano salesman I was a square peg in a round hole.

Back Into Advertising

Of course I had been keeping in touch with my uncle, Frank Armstrong, by occasional letter. He realized I had become sidetracked again, and came to my rescue.

About the time it became evident to me, and also to Mr. Benjamin, that I was not headed for an overwhelming success as a piano salesman, I received a letter from Uncle Frank saying he had lined up a temporary job for me, putting on a special "Bank Building" number for *The Northwestern Banker.* This publication was a leading sectional bank journal, read by bankers in Iowa, Minnesota, North and South Dakota and Nebraska.

Without delay I landed back in Des Moines. At that time a large number of banks, especially small country banks, had been erecting new bank buildings—some were small bank buildings occupied solely by the

147

bank—some were multiple-story office buildings, with the bank occupying the ground floor.

The magazine had conceived the idea of a special number devoted to the subject of new buildings. I was to sell ads to as many as possible of those banks who had constructed new buildings, showing a picture of the new buildings in the ads.

Newspapers are always working up special issues, with the purpose of selling special one-time advertising space. I did not believe in these special issues—and I detested them, after this experience, to the point that thereafter I always refused to take part in them.

Actually there was no benefit to be gained by the bank in buying a page or a half-page in this special bank building number, except to enjoy the vanity of seeing a picture of their new building in this trade journal, with the knowledge that most of the other bankers in these five states would see it also. But, that's the way business is done. One of the strongest advertising appeals is *vanity.* You'll see it constantly on TV commercials, and especially in all the women's magazines and the newspapers, utilized by cosmetics manufacturers, automobile and cigarette companies, and many other industries. Advertising men appeal to human weaknesses a great deal in order to sell goods.

I started with a trip through the southern half of Iowa. I was making very disappointing headway. The truth is, my heart wasn't really in it, for I realized I was selling nothing more valuable than flattery.

Selling a Sales Manager

One incident occurred on this trip which might contain some interest. At Red Oak, in Southwestern Iowa, was a nationally prominent calendar factory. What idea I had in mind as to how they could profitably use advertising space in a sectional bank journal I do not remember. But I do remember that I called to see the sales manager. He refused to see me.

This only made me determined. Of all people, I felt a *sales manager* had no right to refuse to see a salesman.

I went to my hotel room, and wrote him a brief and very pointed letter. I reminded him that he sent salesmen all over the United States to call on customers and sell his company's product. Also I reminded him that if his salesmen met with the kind of treatment he accorded me, his factory would soon be covered over with rustimania instead of the beautiful green ivy vines that covered it then. I didn't mind being turned down if what I had to sell did not fit in with his program or prove profitable to use. But I did demand at least a hearing!

I rushed with the letter to the post office, registered it, and mailed it special delivery, to be delivered to and signed by addressee only. I knew the special delivery mail carrier would get in to him.

This strategy got me the interview. As I remember it, I did not sell him any advertising space. But I did have the satisfaction of gaining the interview. That cockiness and conceit that pervaded my personality in those days was full of persistent determination, and a difficult thing for another to turn down.

I guess the lesson that came to mind on Goat Island at Niagara Falls on December 25, 1913, had its effect. Obstacles were things to *find a way* around, or over, or through, or under. *Resourcefulness,* coupled with determined *drive,* remember, are two of the seven laws of success. "Where there's a *will* there's a WAY!" I hope some of this will rub off on my readers. Not the egotistic

149

conceit—but the determination, resourcefulness, and right principles of a true success.

Success Out of Failure

This swing through Southern Iowa was anything but a success.

Clifford DePuy (pronounced DePew), publisher of *The Northwestern Banker,* was discouraged. I think he was willing to call it "quits" and write off the expenses and advanced drawing account of my efforts so far as a loss. But again Uncle Frank came to the rescue.

"I've always noticed," he said, "that salesmen who fail in Southern Iowa usually succeed in the northern part of the state. I don't think you'd better give up yet. My advice, Cliff, is to send Herbert up into Northern and Northwestern Iowa, and see if the results are not different." Mr. DePuy agreed to one more trial.

In the northern half of the state I began to sell ads, and it soon became apparent that we would publish the special bank building number, after all.

Several of the new bank buildings I visited had been constructed by The Lytle Company, of Sioux City. I was especially impressed by the fact that officers of these Lytle-built banks were far more than ordinarily enthusiastic about this company and its methods. They worked on the cost-plus basis. Most bankers told me they considered this the most economical way to build, provided one is certain he is dealing with a fully competent and thoroughly honest contractor. This construction company was headed by Mr. J. A. Raven, and all bankers who had dealt with the company spoke highly of him. I jotted down their comments.

An idea was beginning to perk in my mind.

Arriving in Sioux City, I waited outside the Lytle Company office building at noontime until I saw Mr.

Raven go out to lunch. I was not ready to see him—yet! Then I walked in, and from his secretary obtained all his catalogs, circulars, printed matter, and especially photographs or cuts of several of these bank buildings I had visited.

Next I proceeded to a stationery store and procured a large sheet of good quality drawing paper, somewhere near 14 x 26 inches in size. The next three days were spent in my hotel room.

Down in Des Moines, Cliff DePuy was getting grey-haired wondering what had happened to his new salesman. I had nothing to report, until I had completed my idea. I did put on the pressure, but it had to be just "right," and it took time.

At the end of three days, I had produced a very forceful complete FOUR-PAGE advertisement, with attractive layout sketched and carefully designed on this large sheet of drawing paper, replete with cuts of several bank buildings. It contained statements from these bankers, which I had jotted down while in their banks, expressing their full satisfaction with Mr. Raven's system of building construction. It even contained the endorsement of *The Northwestern Banker,* which I felt safe in offering, based on such unanimous approval from so many banks. The ad, of course, invited banks and bankers to write for catalog and a consultation with Mr. Raven with a view to constructing a new bank home for them.

Selling a BIG Ad

At last I was ready to see Mr. Raven. When I walked in and showed him this big layout of a four-page insert, he almost fainted. It happened he was a regular advertiser in *The Northwestern Banker*—he ran a tiny sixteenth-of-a-page card every month!

151

The audacity of trying to jump him from a sixteenth of a page to four full pages seemed incredibly preposterous! Of course, I knew it would. I was prepared for that.

Mr. Raven was a calm, steady, conservative type of man.

"Why!" he exclaimed, " we couldn't afford to run an ad anywhere near that big!"

"On the contrary, Mr. Raven," I rejoined, "you can't afford *not* to run it. Now let me *read* this ad to you. I want you to HEAR it, before you decide. Here! You hold this layout, and see with your eyes where each bit of text matter will be printed, among these big headlines and pictures of banks you've built."

Of course, he wanted to *hear* it. But he was convinced he didn't want to *buy* it.

One thing I had learned at the *Merchants Trade Journal* was the effective method of selling advertising copy. There must be a well-designed and very attractive dummy, or layout, with the headlines sketched in, the pictures or illustrations showing, and boxes or horizontal lines showing where the smaller text matter will be printed. The idea was to let the prospective advertiser hold and look at this attractive dummy, while I held and read the typed text matter, putting into it all the emphasis where it belonged, and the proper tone of enthusiasm and drive.

This layout *was* very attractive—Mr. Raven had to admit that! The ad certainly sounded convincing! He admitted that! Running in this special number, devoted to new bank buildings, it ought to have a terrific impact. He couldn't get around *that!*

"Yes," he said, "that's all true enough. But—FOUR PAGES! Why, that's *unheard* of! We can't afford anything like that!"

152

"Yes," I agreed, remembering John R. Patterson's sales strategy, "it is certainly UNHEARD OF! The bankers of these five states have never seen anything as audacious, as important looking, as a FOUR PAGE AD! And *that's* the very reason you *can* afford it, Mr. Raven! Now look! This entire four-page ad is going to cost only $160. The very *smallest* country bank jobs you get run around $8,000, and your bigger jobs into the hundreds of thousands. You construct on a 10% fee basis for yourself. Your profit on just one tiny little $8,000 country bank building is $800. If this big ad results in bringing you only one little $8,000 job, it will have paid you, won't it?"

"Well, yes, I suppose it *would,*" he replied thoughtfully. "I never thought of advertising in that way, I guess."

"And, be honest, now," I pursued. "How many new construction jobs do you think you really ought to get as a result of a dominating ad like that?"

"Why, I should think it ought to bring us *several* new jobs," he admitted. "Mr. Armstrong, I guess you've shown me a new and more effective way to advertise. But I, myself could never have designed and written an ad like that. Yes, I think that ad will really *pay!* All right, we'll run it, and see what happens!"

Paying for Vanity

Leaving the Lytle Company office, I literally *ran* back to the Hotel Martin, and from my room called Cliff DePuy in Des Moines.

"Where have you *been?* What in the world's *happened* to you?" he demanded on hearing my voice. "Have you sold any space yet?"

"Have I!" I exclaimed. "I've spent the past three days writing up an entire FOUR PAGE insert for this

153

special number, and I sold it to Mr. Raven of the Lytle Company!"

"WHAT!" he gasped, unbelievingly. "Say that again!"

I learned later that Cliff forgot momentarily that he was a grown man, all 6 feet 3 of him, and all 28 or 30 years of him, as his age was at that time, and that he jumped up and down for glee like a little boy, and then took off a half holiday and ran out to tell every banker in the city that we were running a whole FOUR PAGE ad in the next issue! *Never* had anything that big been heard of!

Before describing the result of that ad, I must recount, here, an incident that occurred at this same time while I was in Sioux City.

Mr. Raven told me he knew where I could sell a full page to a bank. He grinned as he explained. Up in Royal, Iowa, a little town of perhaps less than 500 population about 80 miles northeast of Sioux City, he had built two small bank buildings. On completion of the first one, the bank across the street called him in. The president said he had watched the Lytle Company's work, had checked up on them and was convinced of their reliability and honesty, and had decided to employ them to build a new building for his bank.

"Now, can you tell me how much that little new building across the street cost?" he asked.

Mr. Raven said it had cost $8,000. (Remember, this was 1915. The same building would cost immensely more today.)

"Well, Mr. Raven, we want you to draw up plans right away to build a $16,000 bank for us."

It was going to take an entire day to go to Royal and back, on the slow branch line railroads in that country. But I decided a sure-fire page ad was worth it.

154

I arrived in Royal and went immediately to this larger bank. I had a full page ad designed, with a picture of the building, which I had obtained from Mr. Raven. Also I had a layout of another full page with a picture of the smaller bank across the street, which I managed carelessly to permit this banker to see.

"Well, that ad looks nice," commented this bank president, "but Mr. Armstrong there's no reason for us to advertise in the *Northwestern Banker.* We have nothing to sell to other banks."

This was only too true. Today my conscience would not let me sell such an ad. There was only one reason for him to buy it—VANITY. And, perhaps, spite, or competitive spirit to prevent his competitor across the street from getting it. But I was prepared with the answer.

"Well," I said, "in that case, I suppose I'll have to see the bank across the street. You see, this is an EXCLUSIVE proposition. Just one ad is sold in each town. If you take it, the other bank can't run their ad. If they do, then you can't. And it really *is* too bad—for now I suppose all your fellow bankers you know and meet at the group meetings and state conventions will see the picture of that little bank across the street, and they won't even *know* that you have a building twice as big and fine."

I emphasize, I would refuse to use such a sales appeal to vanity and jealousy today. It was almost pitiful, when he asked, like a whipped dog, "How much did you say this page is going to cost?" as he reached for a pen and signed the one time space contract without another word.

Yes, I learned that there is jealousy and a spirit of competition among dignified and conservative bankers, just as there is between other humans.

155

Result-Getting Ads

After this Sioux City episode, I worked my way, selling a few page and half-page ads to banks which had constructed new buildings along the way, on over to Charles City, Iowa. In Charles City was another company which ran regular but small ads in the *Northwestern Banker,* The Fisher Company, manufacturers of bank fixtures and interiors.

They worked to some extent with the Lytle Company, since they installed most of the interior of a bank, including the cages and counters.

Here, again, I took a couple days or so, first getting their catalog, with illustrations of many of their interiors of banks, and designed and wrote a double-page spread for them. By the same method used with Mr. Raven, this double spread was sold to Mr. Fisher.

Both this two-page ad, and the Lytle Company four-page ad produced unexpected results, and each sold a number of new jobs.

Before the next issue of the trade paper went to press, I called again at both Sioux City and Charles City, and each company signed up on a yearly basis, the Lytle Company for a full page or more each issue, and the Fisher Company for a half page or more each issue.

Actually, through the following seven years each company never used less than this minimum space, but many, many times the Lytle Company used double pages, and the Fisher Company full pages, and, I believe, a few more double page ads. These ads, which I continued to write for them over a span of the next seven years, proved very profitable to them, and expanded their businesses.

For a few months I continued to work around in Iowa, using the procedure of selling advertising space for

156

ads I had already written before calling on prospective advertisers.

Developing a Business

By this process a temporary one-month special-issue job was converted into not only a steady job, but a developing and growing business of my own.

I had taken this special issue job on a commission basis, with a drawing account of, I believe, $40 per week, as an advance from the publication to cover expenses. This drawing account was deducted from commissions earned. The commission basis, common for all publications of this class, was 40%.

In other words, publishers of bank journals and similar publications had found that it actually *cost* them 40% of the sell space, regardless of the method used in paying—whether salary and expense, commission, or what.

Clifford DePuy had, at that time, been the publisher of the *Northwestern Banker* only a comparatively short time—possibly two or three years. His father had been editor and publisher before him. But when the elder DePuy had died suddenly, the entire responsibility came crushing down on Cliff's shoulders. His father had been most highly respected by the bankers of the Central Northwest, and very popular personally.

Clifford DePuy had been attending an art school or something of the kind. He had not established any great reputation as a success. But now he held a serious and a frank conference at the bank which held the publication's account.

Actually he and the elder DePuy's family were shocked to learn the magazine had been left heavily in debt. But on condition Cliff would make a real fight to

157

save the publication, the bank offered to back him as long as his efforts remained promising for the future. He agreed to roll up both sleeves, plunge into the business, do everything in his power to preserve the publication. The bankers of the Northwest had a real love for this journal. They didn't want to see it suspend publication. Although Cliff was inexperienced in this field, they agreed to back him.

I recount this experience here because it is one that frequently occurs and it illustrates a principle. The sudden plunging of heavy responsibility on one often brings him to an awakening, provides heretofore lacking incentive, arouses dormant abilities. This new responsibility suddenly descending on Clifford DePuy stirred him to intensive and dynamic action, and brought out dormant qualities and abilities. In a few short years he had developed the publication into a very profitable enterprise with adequate reserves. Later he expanded, purchasing other publications. He became a successful publisher.

Cliff and I had a business relationship together for the next seven years. He was tall, about six feet three as I remember, aggressive—a human dynamo. I respected his abilities, and I'm sure he respected mine. Later, in Chicago, he periodically came in, once or twice a year, and we would spend a couple or three days calling on prospective advertisers together. We flattered ourselves in those days that we were an unbeatable team. We both worked at a terrific pace, and we fancied prospective advertisers found us almost impossible to turn down. I think we did pack quite a persuasive wallop at that!

After a month or two of soliciting advertising accounts for the *Northwestern Banker* over the state of Iowa, it seemed advisable for me to go in to Chicago.

8

Becoming a Publishers' Representative

I T WAS now the fall of 1915. By this time I had a considerable amount of valuable experience behind me.

I had reached the age when most students had graduated from college—twenty-three. All this time I had continued my studies, delving into many subjects, including philosophy and psychology, but my "major," of course, had been journalism, advertising, selling, and merchandising, along with business management. This study had been combined with intensive "field experience" in contacts and dealings with businessmen over most of the United States, discussing business methods and problems with them.

Practical vs. Theoretical Education

This education was far more *practical* than theoretical classroom instruction out of textbooks usually written by professors utterly lacking in practical experience.

Nevertheless, I frequently wondered, in those days, how my education would stack up with that of most college graduates. Later I was to find out.

You will remember, as recounted in the earlier part of this autobiography, that at age eighteen I had faced, and answered, the question of going to college. I had chosen the advertising profession. There were no worthwhile courses available in advertising in the colleges and universities at that time.

On the advice of my uncle, Frank Armstrong, leading advertising man in Iowa, I had decided on a course of self-study combined with active experience. I had, except for deviations from my goal, chosen the jobs that would provide the training I needed for the future, rather than the jobs which paid the most.

Then I purchased books, and borrowed books from public libraries, beside subscribing to the trade journals in the advertising field, *Printers Ink,* and *Advertising & Selling.* I read a great deal of Elbert Hubbard's writings, and continually studied and analyzed the best advertisements in newspapers and leading magazines. Also, I read a great deal in certain general magazines, such as the *Quality Group* of those days, especially *World's Work.* I confined my reading in magazines to informative and thought-provoking articles, resisting fiction almost altogether. Fiction is the lazy man's reading. Like the movies, and today's TV programs, it is merely a ready-made daydream, inducing habits of mind-drifting.

These years of self-assigned study enforced mental activity, contacts with successful men in many varied fields, coupled with the practical experience that had been mine, had produced an education and training superior to the average college education.

As president of a liberal arts college with three

160

campuses on two continents today, I can say that this intensive education from the university of hard knocks and practical experience in application has made possible a college offering *today's* students a sound and practical education acquiring the *true* values! And supplying the "MISSING DIMENSION" in education.

Moving to Chicago

My work on the one issue special bank building number of the *Northwestern Banker* had been converted into a regular job as advertising solicitor, on a 40% commission basis, with a drawing account.

Right here I hope I may interject a success principle of which the vast majority seem totally unaware. Here was a temporary job, doing a special one month edition of a small class journal. But it offered larger opportunities. Those greater possibilities were *visualized,* and *acted upon!* The temporary job was turned into a steady job as advertising solicitor for one sectional bank journal. And it led from these to establishing a successful business as Publishers' Representative in Chicago.

This is the quality, rare among people (but *why should it be?*), called VISION. This job on one sectional journal later was developed into a business as publishers' representative for nine bank magazines. Most men are never able to see any possibilities of expanding their present jobs. They do merely what they are told—what someone higher up thought out and laid before them. Or they use deceit to jerk the rug out from under the man above them.

The Bible says that if we do only what we are commanded—what is expected of us—we are *"unprofitable servants"* to be cast out "into outer darkness."

Most people go to one extreme or the other. While

161

the big majority never think beyond their present jobs—never *think* out ways to do the job *better,* or to develop or expand their *own* job into something bigger, or to be preparing themselves for the better jobs ahead and promotions to them, a minority go to the opposite extreme. They are always trying to do the job ahead—or the boss's job—without adequate ability, preparation or experience, and only throw monkey wrenches into the gears, causing damage, lacking wisdom and judgment.

Most men never seem to realize how the application of some of these principles makes all the difference between employee and employer; between mediocrity or failure and success.

Back to the story. I had now developed the opportunity into a job. But the field in Iowa was too limited. The nation's advertising headquarters centered in two cities—New York and Chicago. After a month or two of developing a few accounts in Iowa, chief of which had been the Lytle Company and the Fisher Company, I moved into Chicago.

I made my home at the old Hotel Del Prado, a southside residential hotel on the Midway, adjacent to the University of Chicago. The one personal friend I had in Chicago at the time was Ralph G. Johnson, manager of the *Merchant's Trade Journal's* Chicago office, and I moved into the Del Prado because he lived there.

The old Del Prado has long since been torn down, and a new skyscraper Del Prado erected over on the lake shore. The old one was a sprawling three or four-story frame building, well maintained as a first class residential hotel. Most cities have residential hotels, and I learned that they are a most satisfactory type of residence for single people, whether young or old.

Very soon I came to know most of the residents of the Del Prado. The hotel provided a weekly Wednesday night dance for all guests. The dining room was cleared to provide the dance floor. There were spacious lobbies and lounge rooms. There was a sort of unwritten law among guests which dictated that if one desired social contact, he would find almost any of the other guests receptive and friendly; or, if he preferred privacy, or to sit alone in the lobby, no one would intrude.

I lived at the Del Prado almost two years—until a certain Iowa girl came to Chicago to become my wife. This privilege of living in a large metropolitan residential hotel was one of the cultural and valued experiences of all those formative years. It supplied one of those social-cultural influences which many college students receive by residence in a fraternity house—but without some of the evils of frat life.

I soon observed that the most popular girl at the Wednesday night dances—or chatting in the lobbies at any other time—was Miss Lucy Cunningham. Miss Lucy, as everybody called her, was a white-haired maiden lady in her seventies. She was especially popular with all the single young men. A few University of Chicago co-eds lived at the Del Prado with their mothers. But often these attractive and intelligent young co-eds were forced to play the role of wallflowers during a dance, while Miss Lucy was *always* in demand!

She was a charming conversationalist, witty, intelligent, well educated. We fellows spent many an exhilarating evening hour chatting with her in one of the lobby rooms—usually three or four young men around Miss Lucy. That was long before cigarette smoking became habitual with the female sex. In those days it was not generally accepted as being "nice" for a lady to smoke. Prostitutes smoked, but not "nice" women. Miss Lucy, however, was a "nice" woman who was a little

163

ahead of her time. She was "nice" all right, but she dared to do what she wanted. Miss Lucy smoked cigarettes! Whenever another guest walked past the grouping of sofas and lounge chairs where we were sitting with her, she would casually hand her cigarette over to one of the fellows, who would hold it until the way was clear again. Probably not many, except a number of the young men residents, ever knew her addiction to smoking.

I didn't like to see her smoke. It has always seemed disgusting to me to see any woman smoke. But, remember, I was young then, and fancied I was quite "broad-minded" about such things. I was not naive. No one is wholly good or bad, and I liked Miss Lucy for the things that were good about her.

Besides, I myself smoked in those days. You'll remember how I "swore off chewing" tobacco at age 5. But I had taken up pipe smoking during those long and frantic night hours at Wiggins, Mississippi, as an aid to staying awake while I worked over the books. I had smoked, moderately, ever since. However, I will say that I was never a heavy smoker. Never more than one cigar a day, or three or four cigarettes in a day. That's the reason I did not have the battle many men have had in breaking the habit, when I saw that it had to be broken. My battles with myself were in other directions.

An Office of My Own

The first time in my life I had an office of my own was in Chicago. On arriving there from Iowa, now representing the *Northwestern Banker,* I opened an office in the Advertising Building, at 123 West Madison Street, in the heart of Chicago's Loop. This location was only a half block off South LaSalle Street, which is the "Wall Street" of Chicago. Most of the great banks and investment houses (of Chicago) are located on this street.

The Advertising Building was occupied solely by advertising agencies, publishing firms, publishers' representatives, or those of allied lines in the advertising field. The Ad Club, a division of the Chicago Association of Commerce, had its club rooms there.

The name of this tall but slender skyscraper has been changed at least twice since then. Not many would remember it as the Advertising Building today.

Actually, I did not quite open an *office,* as yet. The fourth floor of this building consisted of one large general room, with a tier of private offices forming an "L" around the far side and the rear of the floor. This large general room was filled with a number of desks. At first, I rented merely desk space in this open room. It was about two years before my business expanded to the point where I required, and was able to afford, a private office; and then I rented one on that same floor. Altogether I maintained office facilities on that same floor for seven years.

At the entrance of this desk-space room was a telephone switchboard and a receptionist. She served all tenants on that floor, taking telephone messages when tenants were out. Through this entire seven years of my tenancy there, the same alert, quick-thinking receptionist remained at that switchboard. Her name was Olive Graham. She had an astonishingly remarkable faculty. She could remember every telephone number that had been given to her for days, and precisely *when* the call had come in.

On one occasion, a man attempted to alibi his failure to call me by claiming that he had called, and left his telephone number for me to call. I took his telephone and called our switchboard—Randolph 2-100.

"Olive," I said, "Mr. Blank says he called me three days ago, when I was out, and left his number, Blank 8-693, for me to call."

"No, Mr. Armstrong," replied Olive promptly. "No Mr. Blank called three days ago, and no one left the number Blank 8-693."

That was positive proof. Olive was never mistaken. Mr. Blank was forced to admit he had not made the call. How that girl could carry hundreds of telephone numbers in her mind I could never understand. I never knew her to miss.

Advertising Tractors to Bankers

Some little time after setting up my own headquarters in Chicago, I had what might appear to be a most absurd "brainstorm." Those on our present staff and our architects well know that these "brainstorms" have a way of continuing, even today.

They may seem ridiculous or absurd at first thought. But more often than not they have proven to be very practical and worthwhile ideas. You see, while I was touring the country as the "Idea Man" for the *Merchants Trade Journal,* my job was to look for IDEAS—practical ideas—ideas that had been put to work, and had proven successful. That experience taught me the value of IDEAS.

In the aptitude tests given prospective employees by one large corporation, one of the questions was: "Do you ever daydream?" 99 out of 100 applicants, *if* they were putting down the answers they supposed the company *wanted,* rather than the actual truth, would most surely have answered "NO!" Actually, the company was looking for men who *do* daydream in a certain manner. Not the kind of daydreaming that lets the mind stagnate and drift without thinking—but the kind of

166

thinking daydreaming that utilizes imagination—that thinks up IDEAS, and then mentally puts them to every test to see whether they will *work!*

To climb the ladder of ultimate success in accomplishment, one must exercise VISION, and, supplementary to it, IMAGINATION—the kind of active, practical THINKING that produces sound and workable IDEAS! The college in which I was trained taught me these things. The *average* college education, however, fails to inculcate anything of this nature.

This "brainstorm"—or IDEA—was the selling of large advertising space in the BANK journals to farm tractor manufacturers. Certainly no one had ever heard of such an apparently preposterous idea before. But it worked, and it paid the farm tractor industry in a big way—and, incidentally, it put me above the $50,000-a-year income class (in terms of *today's* dollar) while still a youth in my twenties.

However, that idea required time to develop.

At first, my work in Chicago confined me primarily to the solicitation of advertising from banks and investment houses which had not previously used space in the *Northwestern Banker.* Although I was required to call on, and render any desired service to the financial institutions which were already advertising in the *Northwestern Banker,* I received no commission from any of this, but only on such new accounts as I developed myself.

This journal was already carrying the advertising of many of Chicago's large banks and bond houses. But there were still others.

What a "Correspondent" Bank Is

One might wonder why the larger Chicago banks should carry advertising in journals read only by other bankers.

The answer is that these larger banks in Chicago and New York *do* have something to sell to other banks.

They are, in a sense, *bankers'* banks. Virtually every bank in Iowa, Minnesota, North and South Dakota, and Nebraska kept a goodly sum of money on deposit in at least one Chicago bank. This was a system used by banks to facilitate the clearing of checks.

Have you ever wondered how checks you send to people in other states are cleared?

Suppose, for example, you live in Ft. Dodge, Iowa. You owe a bill to a concern in Muncie, Indiana. You mail the Muncie firm a check on your local Ft. Dodge bank. The Muncie firm deposits the check in its local bank in Muncie. The Muncie bank either pays the Muncie firm the amount, thus cashing your check, or it credits the amount to the firm's account in the bank.

But, now, how is that bank in Muncie, Indiana, going to get the amount of the check from YOU? When you wrote out your check, drawn on your Ft. Dodge bank, you represented that YOU had that amount of money on deposit in the bank in Ft. Dodge. The check is merely an order for your bank in Ft. Dodge to pay to the firm in Muncie, Indiana, the amount of *your* money written on the check. Now when a bank over in Muncie, Indiana, PAYS this amount of money to this Muncie firm, the Muncie bank must have a way to collect YOUR money from your bank in Ft. Dodge. How?

Banking procedures have undergone some change, and today the Federal Reserve system is used by member banks to a great extent in the clearing of checks, and the correspondent system to a lesser degree.

But in those days it was done primarily through this correspondent system. Most banks scattered over such states as Indiana, Illinois, Iowa, Wisconsin have a

168

Chicago Correspondent. That is, they keep a sum of money on deposit in a Chicago bank, for the very purpose of clearing checks. So the Muncie bank has a Chicago Correspondent. Also the Ft. Dodge bank has a Chicago Correspondent, although it may be a *different* Chicago bank.

Here is how the system works. The Muncie bank sends your check to its Chicago Correspondent bank. On receipt of your check, this Chicago bank credits the amount of your check to the account of the Muncie bank. Now the Muncie bank has been reimbursed for cashing your check. If your check was for the amount of $100, it has $100 added to the amount it has on deposit in the Chicago bank. Now this Chicago bank must be reimbursed. Through the Chicago Clearing House system, it sends your check to the Chicago bank which is the correspondent of your Ft. Dodge bank, which has an adequate amount of money on deposit with its Chicago Correspondent bank. This bank in Chicago thereupon debits the account of your Ft. Dodge bank $100. In plainer words, it takes the $100 out of the money on deposit by your Ft. Dodge bank, which is paid through the Chicago Clearing House system to the other Chicago bank which is the Correspondent of the Muncie bank. And finally, the Chicago Correspondent of the Ft. Dodge bank sends your check back to your bank in Ft. Dodge, notifying your bank that it has taken this $100 out of the money they had on deposit. Your bank stamps your check paid, taking *your* $100 which it had on deposit, thus reimbursing itself for the $100 which its Chicago Correspondent took out of its money on deposit there. And at the end of the month you receive a statement from your bank showing they have deducted this $100 from your balance on deposit, and enclosing the canceled check.

This is all not so complicated as it probably sounds. I have taken space to explain it so simply that a little child can understand it. But I thought it might be interesting to my readers, most of whom probably never had any understanding of how checks are cleared from one part of the country to another.

Attending Bankers' Conventions

My work now brought me into contact with many of the nation's leading bankers. Solicitation among Chicago's larger banks and security firms made it necessary to cultivate personal acquaintance with those officers directly connected with the correspondent accounts. This often included one of the vice presidents, and in some instances the presidents.

Certain phases of the banking business are not generally known by the public. One of these is the personal acquaintances and contacts maintained among men of the banking fraternity.

Each state has its state Bankers' Association, with its annual Bankers' Convention. These state conventions are well attended by presidents, vice presidents, cashiers, and even some assistant cashiers, especially those whose jobs are connected with the correspondent business. Each state is divided into groups, and each group holds its annual group meeting.

Then on the national level, there is the national A.B.A. (American Bankers' Association) convention each year, well attended by presidents and top-ranking vice presidents of the nation's largest banks.

At these annual conclaves, bankers, so dignified and formal at home and before customers in their own banks, really "let down their hair," as the saying goes. They familiarly call each other by their first names.

To a large extent, this correspondent business

between banks is conducted on a personal acquaintance basis. Although there were two outstanding national magazines in the banking field, these localized sectional bank journals maintained a personal contact and hold on their banker subscribers that was not possible for a national magazine.

There were seven principal sectional or regional journals, all published by men of outstanding personality. These publishers attended most of the group meetings, and all of the state and national conventions. They mixed personally with the bankers of their districts—who were the readers of their publications. The most eagerly read pages of these monthly journals were the personal gossip pages. All these sectional journals published a great deal of personal news about individual bankers in their districts. The bankers of each section, who knew most of the other bankers personally, were naturally eager to read any personal news items about bankers they knew—and about *themselves!*

Since I was now the advertising representative of perhaps the leading one of these sectional bank journals, I began to attend several of the state bankers' conventions, and most of the A.B.A. (American Bankers' Association) conventions.

In this manner I began to form personal acquaintance with hundreds of prominent bankers—another important factor in my education which had some influence in preparing me for the real job ahead.

In Chicago were many manufacturers of products sold to banks. Of course I solicited advertising from these.

The Tractor Brainstorm

I do not remember just how this IDEA came to mind

171

about selling large-space advertising to the manufacturers of farm tractors. But in some manner, through personal contacts with scores of small-city and country bankers, I had come to realize that tractors, in those days, were sold for *cash*—there were no easy-payment plans, or financing terms offered. The farmers were forced to borrow the money from their bankers in order to purchase tractors. My conversations with bankers had indicated that bankers were not, as yet, "sold" on the idea of the farm tractor.

So, in order to get all the FACTS, I made an extensive survey. That experience in conducting the surveys at Richmond, Kentucky, and Lansing, Michigan, had shown the value of fact-finding by survey, obtaining information from a representative portion, based on the law of average.

This farm tractor survey was made primarily by mail through questionnaires. These questionnaires were sent to a thousand or more bankers, and a representative number of farmers, and a third questionnaire to scattered local dealers who sold tractors. Simultaneously, I went out on a personal tour of several states, personally interviewing bankers, tractor dealers, and farmers.

This survey unearthed some startling facts, which tractor manufacturers had never realized about their business.

The officers of the average bank in the *Northwestern Banker* territory owned eight farms. Many had come into this farm ownership through foreclosure of mortgages. Of course they did not farm, themselves. These bankers either employed managers to operate them, or rented them out. Multiplying our circulation by eight, I learned that I had a farm-owner circulation to sell at a lower cost per page per thousand circulation than the farm papers.

But the principal reason farm tractor manufacturers needed to buy advertising space in a banking journal was to win the favor of bankers so that they would readily loan money to their farmer customers for the purchase of tractors. The bankers were proving a very serious sales-resistance factor.

Whenever a farmer would come into a bank to borrow money for the purchase of a tractor, the banker, calling him by his first name, would ask:

"What do you want the money for, John?"

And when he learned John was about to buy a tractor, he discouraged John. At first, when I presented these facts to tractor manufacturers, they scoffed.

"Why, Mr. Armstrong," they would object, "if the bank they do business with refuses the loan, the farmers simply go across the street to another bank and borrow it there."

"Apparently," I replied, "you do not realize the personal relationship between country bankers and their farmer customers. The country banker is a sort of 'father confessor' to his farmer customers. They come to him with their problems—ask his advice. Do you suppose these bankers are so stupid that they would turn down a loan in such a manner that their farmer customer would be offended, and go to a competitive bank? I have interviewed scores of bankers on this point. The banker who feels his farmer customer ought not to spend the money for a tractor doesn't *refuse* the loan—he merely talks the farmer out of wanting it. He will talk to farmer John something like this:

" 'Well, John, my advice would be to go a little slow before you go into debt to buy that tractor. As you know, John, I own eight farms myself. And I'm not at all sold on the practicality of tractor farming. In my opinion, the tractor hasn't arrived yet. It's still in the experimental stage. Now I know, John, that tractor salesman has probably put up a pretty slick argument. Of course he's interested in getting a big fat commission for himself. But *I'm* interested in *your* welfare, John. Now, of course, if you decide to let that salesman talk you into it, we'll loan you the money, but my advice is, don't do it! You raise your own feed for your horses. But you'll have to BUY gasoline to feed the tractor. I don't think it would pay.' "

In soliciting the advertising of tractor manufacturers, I soon found that their advertising managers could not buy it, because they were given a definite appropriation for definite fields—the farm journals, and the farm dealer trade papers. They had no appropriation for bank magazines, and they lacked authority to change company policies.

It became necessary for me to go direct to the presidents of factories in the tractor industry.

This, again, was an experience that afforded personal contacts with several multimillionaires. Among them was the president of J. I. Case, Mr. Wallis; Mr. Brantingham of the Emerson-Brantingham Company; George N. Peak, president of Moline Plow Works, who later became prominent in President Franklin D. Roosevelt's N.R.A.; Gen. Johnson, vice president of John Deere & Company, also later head of one of President Roosevelt's N.R.A. activities.

Representing Nine Magazines

My one biggest obstacle in this farm tractor field—and also in soliciting manufacturers of items sold to banks—was the limitation of our circulation to one five-state region. These big advertisers in the Chicago district advertised on a *national* basis.

Also, because of this, I encountered stiff opposition

174

from the advertising agencies. Advertising agencies *serve* the advertiser, who is their client, but they are not paid by their clients. They are *paid* by the publishers, on the basis of a 15% agency commission on all billings.

The Agency position was this: It took just as much time, and effort, for them to prepare a page ad for our little sectional bank journal with some 2,000 circulation and an advertising rate of $40 per page, as for a page ad in the *Saturday Evening Post* with a page rate, in those days, of $5,000 (much higher, in later years!). The Agency would make only $6 for its work on a page for us, compared to $750 for the same amount of effort for a page in the *Post*.

I began to realize that I could sell big-space advertising much easier for a large *national* circulation than for one small sectional journal.

This brought about another "brainstorm." Although there were two leading national magazines in the banking field, they did not provide a sufficiently complete national coverage. The seven leading sectional journals completely dominated their respective fields. The only possible *complete* national circulation in the banking field could come only by using these nine—the seven leading sectional journals, and the two national magazines.

But there was still a major difficulty. These various bank magazines had various page sizes. Agencies usually send ads out in plate form—already set to type. The necessity of making plates of so many sizes would discourage agencies.

So, about a year or a year and a half after moving to Chicago, I had worked out a proposition to set myself up as an independent publishers' representative in the bank field.

These publications, by whatever methods, had found it cost them 40% to get business. I proposed to represent all nine magazines, and myself to finance all solicitation, and send them advertising at a reduction to them of 25% in cost of obtaining business. In other words, I was to have exclusive representation, on a 30% commission basis, but the magazines were to pay me the entire year's commission in advance on all 12-time yearly contracts, upon receipt of signed contract from the advertiser. They were all to adopt a standard magazine page size.

But there arose one overpowering obstacle in my path.

Clifford DePuy, about this time, had acquired a second of these seven leading sectional bank journals—the old *St. Louis Banker,* the name of which he changed to the *Midcontinent Banker.* He objected in loudest tones to my representation of any other publications. I had been his exclusive Chicago representative, and he was determined to keep it that way.

I, on the other hand, had become determined to expand my field. I maintained that I could send Cliff a great deal more business as the representative of a complete *national* circulation. He didn't think so. We *really* clashed on this issue.

But, before this issue was finally settled, I had met a certain *very* attractive young lady out in Iowa.

I think the time has come to relate a different phase of these life experiences—my dating girls, and the romantic side of life from the beginning up to the time of marriage.

9

How I Met My Wife

IN the chronicle of experiences that
provided the training for the activities
of later years, none exceeded in import
the dating experiences that culminated in marriage—at
least none exceeded the marriage experience.

If it be true, as it definitely appears now in
retrospect, that the Eternal God knew He would call me
to the important activity now in progress with progressively increasing power of impact, and that this
early training of formative years had some measure of
unseen and unrealized divine guidance, then it is true,
also, that the selection of my wife and life partner was
providential.

It was through her, years later, that circumstances
impelled my conversion and induction into the Great
Commission. This commission, from its beginning had
been a *team* activity commission in which Mrs.
Armstrong shared equally—even though it may not

have been evident to many.

No phase of any man's life is more important, or has greater bearing on his future success or failure, than the romantic experiences and their culmination in marriage. The same is true, conversely, in the lives of girls who have reached the dating age.

Few young people, today, realize the seriousness of this phase of life. Proper dating has become virtually a lost art in America. Young people today, it seems, do not know how to date. Most have little or no conception of the nature of true love, or the meaning and responsibility of marriage. They are men and women physically, but they are still children emotionally.

Let me repeat, here, that I was born of solid old Quaker stock. I was brought up from childhood to believe that marriage was for LIFE, and divorce was a thing unheard of in our family. Marriage was regarded seriously, and as something not to be considered by a young man until he had acquired his education and preparatory experience, and was established financially and in position to support a wife and family.

Consequently, in my dating of girls prior to age 24, there was no thought of marriage, except indirectly.

My Dating "System"

And, by "indirectly," I mean this: I had a "system." I was conceited enough to think it a pretty good system. I was aware that I did not really know what love is. But I had the conception that it was a mysterious thing that might hit a young man when he wasn't looking. He might suddenly "fall" for a girl. Once this happened, so I surmised, the poor victim lost his mental equilibrium. He was "hooked" and unable to help himself, or if the girl be the wrong one, to recognize that fact.

I was, in other words, afraid I might be caught off

178

guard and helplessly plunged into a binding lifelong marriage with the wrong girl. I had heard that love was blind. If I should fall in love with the wrong girl, I would probably be totally blinded to the fact she was the wrong one. My life would be ruined! That is, so I then supposed.

My "system" was born out of fear of this possibility. I didn't want to get serious, or think of marriage, before I was advanced enough to support a family. But, if this "love bug" *should* stab a hypo love potion into me prematurely, I wanted to have insurance against being bound to the wrong one.

Therefore my "system" was this: I would generally avoid even dating a girl unless she appeared, so far as I could then see, to be at least eligible *if* I lost my head and "fell" for her. Next, on my first date, one thing was always uppermost in my mind—to coldly *analyze* that girl from the point of view of what kind of a wife and mother she would make, *if* I lost my head over her. If she definitely didn't measure up, I firmly avoided any second date with her. If I were not quite sure one way or the other, I would allow myself a second date—if she appeared sufficiently interesting. If a girl passed my analytical test, then immediately I put all thought of marriage out of mind, but she remained on the list of girls who were eligible for dates—IF I desired them.

As a result of this "system" I *did* date girls I felt were well above the average. I enjoyed a scintillating conversation. If a girl was unable to carry on her part of such an "intellectual" conversation, or was lacking in any mental depth and brilliancy, she didn't interest me enough for another date.

My First Date

I suppose most little boys, around age 4 or 5, pick out

some girl they call their "girl friend." This is, of course, quite cute and amusing to parents and other adults. I mentioned, earlier, a little girl who took part in some church play with me, at age 5.

Then, around nine or ten years of age, a Sunday school chum and I picked out a girl whom we mutually called "our girl"—only she never knew it. We were too young and too shy to tell her.

I kissed a girl for the first time when I was twelve. Some of us kids in the neighborhood were playing "post office." I think I secretly considered that girl to be my "girl friend," though I'm sure she didn't know it. I do remember her name.

I also remember the name of this Sunday school girl I secretly shared with the other boy. But I will refrain from mentioning it, for the other boy finally did start "going with" her when he became old enough, and wound up marrying her—and I have heard that she moved to Pasadena.

But my first real date came when I was a freshman in high school. It was with a neighbor girl who also was a freshman at North High, in Des Moines. The occasion was some high school event that took place in the evening. I remember I was very self-conscious being on a street car alone with a girl.

WHY is it that so many teen-age boys are bashful in the presence of girls their age, while girls seem never to be the least bit embarrassed?

I did continue to "go with" this girl, off and on, for some seven or eight years, but never was it "going steady" as so many young people do today, and it was never serious. Never once did I kiss her.

Once, when I was probably twenty-two or twenty-three, on a date with her in Des Moines, I did start to slip an arm around her. Promptly she took my arm and placed it back where it belonged. But not because she was a "prude."

"I wish you wouldn't, Herbert," she said simply. "At least unless you are serious. You're the only fellow I've ever gone with that hasn't necked with me. I'd like to keep this one slate clean. It has really meant something to me."

I wasn't serious, so my arm stayed home the rest of the evening.

"Necking" Experiences

When I first dated this girl, at about age fifteen, and for some years after that, I never "necked" with any girl. Only we didn't call it "necking" then—it was "loving up," and back in my mother's day it was "spooning." I don't know what they called it in Abraham Lincoln's day, or back in the days of Adam and Eve. But it's been going on all these millenniums and centuries, no matter what any passing generation may call it. It speaks its own universal language. But, in this autobiography, I shall use the terminology of the present day, for reasons of clarity.

So far as I know, during the earlier years of my "dating" experience this thing of "necking" was not practiced in the promiscuous way it is today.

I dated a number of girls I regarded as unusual, and considerably above the average. One was the daughter of the president of an insurance company. She was my mother's original preference, and I think that at the time Mother would have been pleased had I married her. But neither of us held the slightest romantic interest for the other. She was an artist and sculptress. I admired and respected her, however, and, enjoyed an occasional date with her. Then there was another girl, a neighbor in Des Moines, who excelled as an artist. In fact, this girl excelled in just about everything she did. I dated her frequently in Chicago, as I passed through on those "Idea Man" trips, while she was a student at the Chicago Art Institute. Actually, both of these girls were studying at the Art Institute. There was another girl in Rock Island, Illinois, with whom I became acquainted through the above-mentioned two girls, a member of one of the oldest and most prominent Rock Island families.

But, along about age 21, it seemed that the "necking" pattern was being ushered in. In those years I wanted to be "modern" and to keep up with the times. I began to think that perhaps I was being considered a little behind the times, and decided that perhaps I ought to start "necking" a little—at least after a second or third date. I don't think many indulged in it on the first date, in those days.

At that time I was dating a girl in Des Moines who was a special "buddy" of a girl who was going "steady" with a chum of mine. The four of us double-dated frequently. So I began the popular pastime of "necking." Only it was then called "loving-up." The girl didn't object. Her father was dead. Her stepfather was an automobile dealer, and frequently, on our dates, we were taken riding in their car with her stepfather and her mother. We "necked" openly in the back seat. Her parents seemed to think nothing of it.

Then one night on their semisecluded front porch, she became especially serious. She began to tell me how much money her father had left her, and she felt we ought to begin to plan what to do with it.

This came like an electric shock. I realized she was seriously taking marriage for granted. Such a thought had never entered my mind. I told her so. This stabbed her right in her heart.

182

"But if you're not serious, and thinking of marriage, what on earth have you been 'loving-up' with me for?" she asked.

I explained that she was the first girl I had ever "necked" with—that I had come to believe I was being considered old-fashioned by the girls—that it had seemed to me that it was being done generally, and that girls expected it. I did it because I supposed it was the thing I was supposed to do.

At this she burst into tears and ran into the house. This sudden turn of affairs shocked and hurt me deeply. I knew I had hurt her, and that made me feel like a cad. Next day I called on the telephone to apologize. Her mother answered.

"My daughter has told me all about it," accused the mother with icy scorn. "She never wants to see you again!" She hung up the receiver.

So my first experience in "necking" came to an unhappy and semitragic end. I hope this girl later became *really* in love with the right man for her, and found a happy marriage. She was a fine girl and deserved it. But I have never heard from or about her since.

Truth About Necking

I have wished very much that I could have known, in those days, what I am able today to teach the class in "Principles of Living" at Ambassador College. For had I realized the TRUTH about this practice called "necking," that very fine girl would have been spared the humiliation of confessing love for one who was not in love with her.

But I didn't know such truths in those days. My standards were those of the other young people my age in the world—that is, the standards of those young people who had *ideals* and good intentions—but based on the way that seemed right to us humans.

It was totally against my code of morals to "insult" a girl—which, according to those human standards meant carrying "necking" beyond the point of "decency." That I never did in my life. I felt I knew where to "draw the line." And I *was* always careful to observe that human-reasoned line.

But all young people are not that careful. What I did not then know is that even any "necking" at all — harmless as it is supposed to be—is the very first phase of the four phases of sexual intercourse! In very plain and frank language, "necking" belongs IN MARRIAGE as a definite PART of the marriage relationship. Humans usually reverse what is right. They indulge in this preliminary act of sexual arousal *prior* to marriage as a part of dating—and then dispense with it after marriage, thus often ruining and breaking up marriages!

I didn't realize, then, how many countless acts of fornication, and premarital pregnancies, are caused by this supposed harmless and popular custom of "necking." The "new morality" has replaced the strong convictions some of us had about where to "draw the line."

I Meet Two Pretty Girls

Up until 1917 I had never thought really seriously of any girl. I liked the company of girls. In my vanity I fancied that I had been dating the real "cream-of-the-crop"—girls considerably superior to the average. But during these years I was still "going to school"—in the way I had decided was best for me—acquiring knowledge of my chosen field, gaining experience, preparing myself to make BIG MONEY later.

In my foolish conceit of those days, I was cocksure that I was headed for outstanding success. But I had certain ideals and convictions, and one of them was that a young man ought not to think of marriage *until he was prepared to assume the responsibilities of marriage*— especially that of *supporting* a wife! The idea of *my* wife having to get a job to help earn the living would have crushed my spirit—would have been the supreme disgrace!

In January, 1917, I was in Des Moines on one of my regular trips to Iowa, renewing contracts and soliciting new ones. My mother had written that her twin sister, my Aunt Emma Morrow, was stricken with pneumonia, and asked me to visit her on this trip. So I took the short side-trip to the Morrow farm, 30 miles southeast of Des Moines, and a short mile north of the crossroads town called Motor, which consisted only of a store, schoolhouse, church, and two or three houses.

I found my aunt considerably improved, and convalescing. During the afternoon a girl from Motor, two years younger than I, came to see my aunt. She was introduced to me as a cousin—but only a third cousin. Immediately I was impressed. She was pretty, and seemed to be an unusually nice girl. Her name was Bertha Dillon, and her father owned the store at Motor. He was my mother's first cousin.

I was enjoying a conversation with her, when, about 4:30 in the afternoon, her older sister, Loma—just my age—came bounding in. That's not an exaggeration. I hadn't seen such fresh, joyous, "zip and *go*" in a long time. She literally exuded energy, sparkle, good cheer, the friendly warmth of a sincere, outgoing personality.

Now I was much *more* impressed! She was even prettier than her sister. There was something *different*

185

about her—something wholesome that I liked. She was the school teacher at Motor.

"Where," I asked myself inwardly, "could I have been all my life, never to have run across *these* two cousins before?" At that time, although these girls were rather *distant* cousins, I thought of them only as "cousins."

This was about the middle of the week. My cousin, Bert Morrow (he was a *first* cousin), just one year my junior lacking a day, drove me over to the little town of Beech to take the evening train to Des Moines. My aunt's nurse was returning to Des Moines on the same train. Loma rode along with us in the "Model T" to Beech. I learned that she was planning to go to Des Moines Saturday morning to do some shopping.

"Why," I asked, "don't you bring Bertha with you, and meet me at noon for lunch, and we'll take in a movie in the afternoon?"

It was a date.

Only, when I met her Saturday noon, she had not brought her sister. I had preferred to meet Loma alone, but I had felt that propriety demanded that I ask both girls.

I took her to luncheon at Des Moines' nicest place at that time—the Harris-Emery department store Tea Room. It was one of the finest department store tea rooms in the nation.

I was really enjoying this date. She didn't know it then, but Loma was being intensively analyzed. No thought of marriage, you understand—just routine, as I always did on a first date. She seemed to be a girl of sound-minded good sense and high ideals. She had superior intelligence. There was a mental *depth* most girls lacked. I was well aware that she was utterly lacking in sophistication. She was not, in fact,

186

completely "city broke." There was none of the haughty social veneer—none of the acquired artificial mannerisms of the eastern "finishing school" products or the social debutante. Indeed, I perceived she was a bit naive. She was completely sincere in trusting and *believing in* people. She had not seen or learned much of the rottenness and evils of this world. She had that innocent, completely unspoiled freshness of a breath of spring.

Also, from the instant when she first came *bounding* in at my aunt's farm, I had noticed she was almost something of a tom-boy—active, very alert. Whatever she did, she did quickly. I learned later that her brothers dubbed her with two nicknames— "She-*bang*" and "Cyclone!" She was full of fun, yet serious—with the unspoiled wholesomeness of an Iowa country girl. And, most important of all, strength of character!

I observed quickly that although she was alert and active-minded, hers was not one of those flighty surface minds, active but shallow. She was able to discuss serious and deep things intelligently. She was very much an extrovert, but not a shallow, gossipy chatterbox.

Although I noticed, and became immediately well aware of these qualities, no thought of falling in love, or of marriage, entered my mind. I thought of her only as a cousin. Perhaps I had so disciplined my mind in regard to marriage that it automatically avoided such thoughts. But I *did* want to see more of her—*definitely!*

She Rated a Second Date!

After the luncheon conversation, which must have lasted more than an hour and a half, we went to a movie. I remember nothing whatever about the movie—I do remember holding a soft, warm hand.

187

I always stayed at the Brown Hotel in those days—a residential hotel on the edge of the business district. After the movie, we walked over to the hotel lobby. I ran up to my room, picked up a package of family pictures I happened to have in my suitcase, returned to the lobby and showed the pictures to her.

I remember that among them was a "Cousins' Letter" I had initiated. Ever since I could remember from earliest childhood, my father's generation had kept a family letter circulating. It made the rounds, perhaps once in nine months or a year, from coast to coast. Some of the Armstrong family were in New Jersey and Atlantic coast locations. Some were in Ohio and Indiana, some in Iowa, Colorado, and some in California. Each time it came around, my father removed his letter which now had gone the rounds, wrote and inserted a new one. I had organized a "Cousins' Letter" of our younger generation. It made about two rounds, and apparently died a natural death. But this big packet of letters had just finished its first round, and I remember showing it to my new-found cousin. She however, was a third cousin on my mother's side of the family. This circular family letter only included the "Armstrong" cousins.

Then I took her to her evening train to return home.

I have mentioned my "system" of analyzing girls on the first date. Loma had been duly analyzed. She passed the test with a perfect grade. She rated a *second* date!

In fact, the more I thought about it, she rated it without delay! I lived in Chicago. If I were to have another date with this very attractive young lady any time soon, I decided it had to be next day!

Accordingly I hopped the morning train, called my cousin Bert Morrow to drive over to Beech after me, and, to everybody's surprise, here I was to "see my aunt" again! I don't remember, now, how I maneuvered to get Loma up to my aunt's, but I do remember spending considerable time with her there. And *she* remembers a walk out on the country road in the deep snow.

I also remember holding her hand again—much to the dislike of my uncle and aunt. After I left, they began to warn her against me.

"Now Loma," they admonished, "you'd better let Herbert alone. He reads those magazines written by that awful Elbert Hubbard, and he's probably an atheist. He probably doesn't ever go to church anymore!"

But I had asked Loma to write, and she said she would.

So now the "dating" was continued by mail. I must have had her a great deal on my mind, for I wrote to her almost every day, and received several letters a week in return.

A year and a half before, I had felt that the Iowa territory was rather "dead" for new business for the *Northwestern Banker*. There was more business to be had in Chicago. But now, of a sudden, Iowa seemed to become very desirable territory again, requiring more frequent visits from me.

The next Iowa trip seems to have been some time in February. On a later Iowa trip in May or June, we had a double date in Des Moines with Loma's number one girl chum and her fiancé. At an amusement park, we took a roller coaster ride—Loma's first in her life—and also her *last!* She was so frightened that she unconsciously had a firm, almost death-like iron grip on my trousers just above the knee as we came to a stop—much to her embarrassment and the glee of her chum and fiancé! She was such a modest person that this was terribly mortifying!

189

But I am getting ahead of the story.

As we continued the acquaintance by correspondence, we exchanged ideas on many subjects. I wanted to know what she was interested in—what she believed—what her ideas were. She seemed to have high ideals, and I discovered that she was seriously concerned about religious truth—more so than I. I had virtually no interest in religion.

Business seemed to require my presence in Iowa again in early April, and then the first week in May.

I "Fell"

In our correspondence, we had exchanged ideas and ideals on such subjects as "necking." Of course I had never, as yet, made any advances toward her in this direction—except for holding her hand a few times. Her letters said she didn't believe in "necking." I would not have been a normal young man if I had not determined to put her to the test on that.

It was about the 7th or 8th of May that she met me again in Des Moines. During the afternoon, we went out to one of the spacious parks where wild flowers could be picked.

As we were sitting, or leaning on our elbows on the ground, opportunity came for me to slip an arm around her shoulders, and, leaning over her, plant a healthy kiss on her lips. She didn't resist.

Sitting back up, I grinned and asked, *"Now* are you angry with me?" "Uh-huh," she smiled.

I wasn't quite sure *what* to think, now, after she had expressed such disapproval of anything of this sort in her letters. But it was *not* just a frivolous kiss to her, as I was soon to learn.

We returned to the apartment of my uncle Frank Armstrong and his family. I was taking a midnight

190

sleeper for Sioux City, and she was to remain at my uncle's for the night.

When it came time for me to leave for my train, Loma came out into the corridor of the apartment building to say good-night. Suddenly, impulsively, she reached her arms around my neck and planted a good earnest kiss on my lips!

This, I suddenly realized, was *serious*.

In a daze, I left. I couldn't sleep that night for hours. Nothing had ever hit me like this before. That had not been any ordinary "necking" kiss! I knew that was, as they say today, FOR *REAL!* It came on impulse straight from the heart. She had kissed me because she really *meant* it! It produced an emotional upheaval inside me—a totally new experience. Through the mental daze I began to realize this was LOVE.

I hasten to add, however, that this emotional thrill I experienced was produced because of the *circumstances* leading to it. No one should suppose that being really in love must hit one with the kind of emotional wallop I experienced.

In Sioux City next morning, the first thing I did was to call on a doctor whom I knew. I asked him if there was any reason why third cousins ought not marry.

He only laughed. "None whatsoever," he said. "Third cousins are no cousins at all, so far as marriage is concerned."

Returning to Des Moines a few days later, I went back down to Motor. It was the night of May 13th. We walked down the roadside, past the old Quaker Church building and graveyard. I told Loma that I knew, now, that I was in love with her.

Tragedy Threatens!

This seemed to come like a shock to her. Apparently she

191

had not thought of it in just this way before, but now, suddenly, it dawned on her that if we were married it meant living in Chicago, in more cultural and, as she supposed, sophisticated surroundings than she had known. This sudden realization frightened her.

She stammered that she was not sure.

That statement fell on me like a ton of bricks! I had never doubted, in my confident conceit, that if and when I ever did fall in love it would be mutual. Now, suddenly, came the realization that *I* might be faced with tragedy! But I knew the right answer. I wish *more* young people, "falling" for one who is *not* in love with *them,* could know this right answer. Most young fellows, it seems, would start pleading with the girl to marry them, anyway. That is definitely *not* the right answer.

"In that case, Loma," I said regretfully, soberly, but firmly, "I don't want to ever see you again—that is, not unless, or until you find that you, too, are in love. I certainly wouldn't ask you to marry me if you don't love me. It would only wreck *both* our lives—and I love you too much to ruin your life."

We were walking back to her home, which was on the second floor over the store. We sat down for a while on the steps of the store.

It was momentarily difficult to understand, now, why she had kissed me as she did that night outside the door of my uncle's apartment. Was I merely receiving just retribution for causing the first girl I had ever "necked" to fall in love, when I didn't love her?

I asked Loma for an explanation.

She explained, then, how the sudden thought of marriage had frightened her. She and I had lived in two different worlds. I had been city born and city reared. I had travelled a great deal. I was worldly wise. I knew the world and was a part of it. I lived in one of the world's largest and most metropolitan cities. She was a country girl. How would she be able to act and live in the sophistication of a city like Chicago?

"Loma," I said seriously, "you're a real diamond. Maybe you haven't had the exterior polish of an eastern finishing school applied. Most of those girls have outer polish, but no qualities underneath. It's mostly a lot of put-on and make-believe. It isn't *real*. But you are REAL, Loma, and you have the QUALITY of good character all the way through. I can see to putting on what polish you'll need. I don't want, and never could love, a lot of pretense and empty-headed sophistication! YOU have the *real* qualities for a good wife and the mother of my children. It's YOU I love, and I know now I can never love anyone else. Don't worry about the lack of social training and sophistication. That stuff can be bought a dime a dozen! It's trash! I don't want it! All I want YOU to decide is whether you're in love with me, as I am with you."

Then, rising, I said finally, "Just one thing I want you to promise me. As soon as you're SURE, in your own mind, whether you're *in love*—either way—I want you to telegraph me just one word—'YES' or 'NO'—and I'll understand."

She promised. I walked away toward my aunt's house, a mile down the road. There was no good-night kiss.

10

Marriage Plans Complicated by War

I HAD no intention of returning to the store at the crossroads "town" called Motor. But next morning my Aunt Emma Morrow found it necessary to do some shopping, and asked me if I would drive her in their Model T Ford.

How my aunt maneuvered me into the upstairs rooms I do not remember. But I distinctly remember sitting on the bed in a bedroom, my aunt in front of me on a chair, and Loma Dillon sitting beside me, with the box of old family pictures on her lap.

The Unspoken Answer

As we were looking over the family pictures, my Aunt Emma told us that my Uncle George had courted her and that they became engaged to be married in those same upstairs rooms, over the store. Then suddenly, when my aunt and Bertha had their eyes on a picture,

Loma leaned over and whispered in my ear that she had something to tell me, a big secret. I "got the message" and squeezed her hand, but neither of us gave the others any idea of what had happened under their very eyes.

Not a word was spoken at the moment. But of course Loma and I knew I had received the unspoken answer. She was now sure. And the following morning, waiting at the depot for the train to take me to Des Moines, we agreed we were engaged to be married.

Actually, I had never proposed—that is, in so many words. We simply KNEW—and verbally agreed that we were engaged.

The Cloud of War

But even the happiness of knowing we were in love and engaged to be married was clouded by the war. The United States had been drawn into World War I, declaring war on Germany April 6, just five weeks and four days before we were engaged. It had left my future gravely in doubt.

Immediately after the declaration of war, or as soon as the call went out for voluntary enlistments for the Officers' Training Camp at Ft. Sheridan, Illinois, I had applied for entrance.

The Army did not have a fraction of the needed number of commissioned officers. It was impossible for West Point to graduate the required number quickly. To meet the emergency, Officers' Training Camps were set up immediately at various locations. Intensive rush training had to be given to qualified applicants in time to provide officers to train draftees and volunteer soldiers in the large cantonments all over the country as soon as they could be built.

To qualify for admission to an Officers' Training Camp, a candidate was required to be a college graduate

195

or its equivalent. Lacking a degree, the equivalent had to be testified to by three men of known prominence. I was very glad to be able to obtain a letter from Arthur Reynolds, President of Chicago's largest bank, the Continental & Commercial National (now the Continental-Illinois National), saying he had been personally acquainted with me for several years (I knew him when he was President of the Des Moines National before he went to Chicago) and considered that I had acquired considerably more than the equivalent of a college education. I obtained similar letters from an official of Halsey-Stuart Company, prominent investment bankers, and from my friend Ralph G. Johnson, manager of the Chicago office of *The Merchants Trade Journal.*

Immediately I purchased an army officers' military manual and began to study. Also I enrolled in a drill class organized for preliminary training of officer candidates at one of the armories. But as an army officer I was certainly a "greenhorn" as evidenced by a snapshot I had of Ralph Johnson and me patriotically trying to salute in front of the Hotel Del Prado, where we both lived. I had not yet learned that a soldier must keep his heels together.

Attempting to Be an Army Officer

I successfully passed the physical examination, and received notice that I had been accepted for admission, with orders to report at Ft. Sheridan on a definite date, which I do not now remember.

Then a few days before I was to enter camp, a second notice came. It advised me that in the last minute rush the Army had received six times as many applications as it could accept, and consequently first choice had been given to those with previous military experience, and secondly, to the taller men. I was only

196

average height for those days. The notice expressed great appreciation by the government for my patriotism, but regretfully notified me that I could not now be accepted. However, I was advised that I might apply for enlistment in the second session after graduation of the first, some three months later.

Immediately I applied for entrance into the second Officers' Training Camp. Again I was accepted, and notified to report on a definite date. But again, at the last minute, an overflow of applications by men of previous military experience or taller men crowded me out.

I applied for admission in the Quartermasters' Corps, feeling that if I could not enter the army as an officer, I could serve better in its business department than as a private. But here again the rush of men enlisting was too great, and this department was already filled to capacity.

"Well," I said in some disappointment, "I've tried. Now I'm going to let them throw a rope around my neck in the draft and come and get me."

Meanwhile, as related above, Loma and I became engaged on May 15th.

The Marriage Problem of Every War

And immediately we faced the age-old problem that always has confronted engaged couples in time of war. Many of my readers also faced this same problem, either in World War I, World War II, the Korean war or the war in Vietnam. Those of you who have will understand.

I felt that our marriage should be postponed until after the war, as most men feel at such times. Loma wanted to be married before I donned a uniform—as girls in love usually do.

197

Our arguments will bring back memories to those of you who also found yourselves in love in time of war.

"Suppose," I argued—as perhaps millions of men have argued—"I should be seriously wounded, and come home crippled for life. I wouldn't want you to be tied for life to a disabled man. And then you'd never be free to marry another."

"I would never *want* to marry anyone else," she countered. "And if you should come home crippled or disabled, then more than ever I would want to be your wife to help you. But if we were not already married, you'd be too proud to marry me then—you'd think I was marrying you out of pity, and you'd refuse. So I want to be your wife *before* you go into the army."

"Yes, but I might even be killed in action, and then you'd be a widow. I would rather leave you still single and free to marry someone else."

"If you should be killed," came her immediate answer, "then I would *want* to be your widow. And as for falling in love with anyone else, you look here, Herbert Armstrong! Do you think *you* could fall in love with some other girl?"

"No of course not!" I replied.

Around and around we went. As fast as I could think of another reason for waiting until after the war, she countered with a ready answer. We simply could not agree.

Finally, "Tell you what I'll do," I concluded. "I will take our problem to the chairman of my draft board. He is a college professor, Prof. J. Paul Goode of the University of Chicago."

Finally she agreed to this.

One of my strongest arguments against pre-war marriage had been the fact that thousands were getting married to escape the draft. At the outset of World War

198

I, married men were not being drafted. Those who married to escape the draft became contemptuously referred to as "slackers." I did not want to be called a "slacker." I was sure that Dr. Goode would advise me *not* to marry prior to war service.

Accordingly, as soon as I returned to Chicago, I sought and obtained an interview with Dr. Goode. He listened attentively, asked questions, got all the facts. Then he surprised me by advising me to marry Miss Dillon at once.

It is, of course, difficult to remember many details and dates of such events after forty-one years. But a letter to my mother (then in Weiser, Idaho, partially reproduced in this volume), brings much vividly to memory.

This letter was written Friday night, July 20th. The first drawings of draft numbers, to determine by lot which men would be called to camp first, had taken place in Washington, D. C. that morning. My registration number was 1858. It was one of the earliest numbers drawn. I wrote that I figured I would be among the first 80,000 men drafted in the entire country. And since an army of some four million was actually put into service, it was apparent that I would be called to training camp on the very first group.

It appeared, however, that due to delays in building and equipping the training camps the first contingent would not be sent to camp before October 1st.

I had been out to Motor, Iowa, visiting Loma on this trip and now was on my way back to Chicago. However, on getting this news of my early draft, I stated in this letter: "This is Friday night, so I am going back to Motor early in the morning, to spend Saturday and Sunday with Loma. It's getting harder to remain away from her, someway, and I can't return to Chicago now without another visit. Loma still wants to be married before I go (into service). I have put up every possible objection to it I could think of, and they are numerous, but she brushes them all aside, says she has considered them all and still wants to (be married first)."

We Set the Date

Next morning Loma and her father met me at the depot with their Ford car. I had given her, by long distance telephone, the news of the draft. For the first time she was not beautiful. She was sobbing. Leaning her head on my shoulder, her tears dripping down my chest, she sobbed that she wanted to be married before I went to camp.

What man is strong enough to resist a woman's tears?

My Aunt Emma had been on her side. Professor Goode had been on her side. And *her tears were on her side*. I was unanimously outvoted—for this swung even me over on her side—and I acquiesced, as I suppose men have done in such circumstances ever since Adam and Eve.

We decided to be married as soon as possible. She needed a week to make all preparations to come to Chicago. I needed a week to locate a place for us to live. It was now July 21st. My twenty-fifth birthday was the 31st. We decided she was to be the finest birthday present of my life.

Sunday night I caught the sleeper in Des Moines for Chicago. Loma spent a busy week sewing and preparing. The minister's wife gave a shower for her, attended by nearly everyone in the neighborhood. Mrs. Gertie Shoemaker, mother of one of her first grade little girls, Irene, worked steadily with Loma, sewing, all that week. She is still one of Mrs. Armstrong's best

200

friends, whom she visits whenever she is in Iowa—and that little first-grade daughter of Mrs. Shoemaker is today herself the mother of a fifteen-year-old daughter, Mary Kay.

Meanwhile, in Chicago, I had succeeded in renting a nicely furnished apartment for six weeks from a family going away on vacation. It was located on the North side on Wilson Avenue, between the Evanston "L" line and the lake.

The Wedding Day

On Monday, July 30th, Loma, accompanied by her father and stepmother (her own mother had died when she was twelve), did her final shopping in Des Moines, and boarded the night sleeper for Chicago. We had arranged for her to leave the train at suburban Englewood station, and I was to meet her there.

She would never let me forget that I was ten or fifteen minutes late in arriving. Never having been in so large a city before, she was frightened. She telephoned my office, but I was on an "L" train en route to meet her.

I was imbued with the advertising man's flare for first impressions. In those days I felt very proud of Chicago. I always enjoyed showing visitors the BIGGEST or the LARGEST of everything—the largest stockyards in the world, the largest store, the largest theatre (until New York built bigger). I wanted my bride's first glimpse of Chicago's "Loop" to be the impressive Grant Park view, overlooking Michigan Boulevard. So I took her on an "L" train over to the Illinois Central commuter train in Jackson Park, thence to the "I. C." commuter station in downtown Grant Park.

We walked through Chicago's "Loop," up to my office, where by this time I was sharing a private office

201

with another tenant; then a block north on Clark Street to the County Building and the Marriage License Bureau, where we obtained our marriage license.

We had lunch at the then most famous Chinese restaurant in Chicago, King Joy Lo's. We went back out to Jackson Park on the South Side, took some camera pictures, then to the Hotel Del Prado where I had lived for nearly two years. I asked Miss Lucy Cunningham, the 70-year-old most popular "girl" in residence at the Del Prado, to accompany us as a witness to the marriage ceremony. She took Loma to her room for a little relaxing rest and freshening up. Then we three walked a short distance to the residence of Dr. Gilkey, pastor of the Hyde Park Baptist Church. I much admired his preaching.

I had made arrangements beforehand for the wedding at the home of Dr. Gilkey. He had been unexpectedly called out of the city. But his father-in-law, a Dr. Brown, pastor of the Oak Park Baptist Church, was on hand to perform the ceremony. Dr. Brown was a very handsome and distinguished appearing elderly man. Mrs. Gilkey was the second witness.

And so, in what I have always felt was the nicest simple little wedding ceremony I have ever seen, with only five people present, we were married for the remainder of our natural lives, and I placed the wedding ring on her finger and kissed my own darling wife.

I myself have since officiated at so many weddings I have long since lost count of the number—some of them somewhat more elaborate, with many guests—some as plain and simple as our own. But somehow I have always felt there is no nicer wedding than a plain, simple ceremony without ostentation of formal dress, with only the minister and two witnesses present.

I think it is usually the brides' mothers who engineer the lavish weddings.

In any event, we were married, not as so many deluded people are today, "till *divorce* do us part," but "till DEATH do us part."

The Unrecognized Call

Our first home together seemed to us to be a very lovely apartment. Of course we were to have it only six weeks, but it was nice while it lasted. It had to substitute for a honeymoon. The beach was only about two blocks down Wilson Avenue. We spent many hours there.

One night my wife had a dream so vivid and impressive it overwhelmed and shook her tremendously. It was so realistic it seemed more like a vision. For two or three days afterward everything else seemed unreal—as if in a daze—and only this extraordinary dream seemed real.

In her dream she and I were crossing the wide intersection, only a block or two from our apartment, where Broadway diagonally crosses Sheridan Road. Suddenly there appeared an awesome sight in the sky above. It was a dazzling spectacle—the sky filled with a gigantic solid mass of brilliant stars, shaped like a huge banner. The stars began to quiver and separate, finally vanishing. She called my attention to the vanishing stars, when another huge grouping of flashing stars appeared, then quivering, separating, and vanishing like the first.

As she and I, in her dream, looked upward at the vanishing stars, three large white birds suddenly appeared in the sky between us and the vanishing stars. These great white birds flew directly toward us. As they descended nearer, she perceived that they were angels.

"Then," my wife wrote a day or two after the

dream, in a letter to my mother which I have just run across among old family pictures, "it dawned on me that Christ was coming, and I was so happy I was just crying for joy. Then suddenly I thought of Herbert and was rather worried."

She knew I had evidenced very little religious interest, although we had attended a corner church two or three times.

Then it seemed that, from among these angels in her dream, that, "Christ descended from among them and stood directly in front of us. At first I was a little doubtful and afraid of how He would receive us, because I remembered we had neglected our Bible study and had our minds too much on things apart from His interests. But as we went up to Him, He put His arms around both of us, and we were so happy! I thought people all over the world had seen Him come. As far as we could see, people were just swarming into the streets at this broad intersection. Some were glad and some were afraid.

"Then it seemed He had changed into an angel. I was terribly disappointed at first, until he told me Christ was really coming in a very short time."

At that time, we had been going quite regularly to motion-picture theatres. She asked the angel if this were wrong. He replied Christ had important work for us to do, preparing for His coming—there would be no time for "movies." (Those were the days of the "silent" pictures.) Then the angel and the whole spectacle seemed to vanish, and she awakened, shaken and wondering!

In the morning, she told me of her dream. I was embarrassed. I didn't want to think about it, yet I was afraid to totally dismiss it. I thought of a logical way to evade it myself, and still solve it.

"Why don't you tell it to the minister of the church

up on the corner," I casually suggested, "and ask *him* whether it means anything."

With that, I managed to put it out of my mind.

Let me say here that in about 99,999 times out of 100,000, when people think GOD is speaking to them in a dream or vision in this day and age, it is pure imagination, or some form of self-hypnotism or self-deception. I have only come to believe that this dream was a bonafide call from God in the light of subsequent events.

Do not hastily ascribe a dream to God. True, the Bible shows that God *has* spoken to His own chosen servants by this means of communication—primarily in the Old Testament, and before the writing of the Bible was completed. But most dreams mean nothing. And false prophets have misled people by telling false dreams, representing their dreams to be the Word of God (Jeremiah 23, where God says, "I am against prophets who recount lying dreams, leading my people astray with their lies and their empty pretensions, though I never sent them, never commissioned them" —verse 32, *Moffatt* translation).

Certainly I did not ascribe this dream to God. It made me feel a little uncomfortable at the time, and I was anxious to forget it—which I did for some years. I was twenty-five at the time. God left me to my own ways for five more years. But when I was age thirty, He began to deal with me in no uncertain terms, and from that time every business or money-making venture I attempted was turned into utter defeat.

The Draft Classification

Upon return of the people from whom we rented the apartment, we stayed on in the bedroom we had occupied a few days. A friend of theirs, a desk clerk at

Hotel Sherman, was looking for temporary tenants on a similar basis. His wife and children were to be gone a month. He kept one room for himself, and rented the rest of the apartment to us for the month. Then we moved to a single bedroom of an apartment occupied by a Mrs. Brookhart in the same general North Side neighborhood, where we had dining room and kitchen privileges at times when Mrs. Brookhart was not using them. By this time we knew that we were to become parents.

It was about this time, probably late September, that the draft boards had their questionnaires ready for filling out. The questionnaire included a question as to marriage status, whether there were children or a pregnancy; and also a question regarding religious affiliation. I wrote down "Quaker," but realizing the Quakers were being granted exemption as conscientious objectors, I wrote in the words: "I do not ask for exemption because of Church affiliation."

I was still expecting to go to army camp as soon as the camps were ready. But no call came, and a few weeks later I received my draft classification card. Dr. Goode had personally marked it "Class IV, Noncombatant," probably because he remembered I had married on his personal advice, with no intention of evading the draft.

I have mentioned that I sold advertising space by first writing the copy and selling that. Always these ads were carefully gone over with my wife before submitting them to prospective advertisers. The surveys made were discussed and planned with her active participation. From the time of marriage, we have always been partners in whatever was my work.

I remember her saying, not many days after we were married: "They say a wife either makes or breaks her husband. Well, you just watch me *make mine!"* But do not receive the impression that she "wore the trousers" in our family. She was a woman of purpose, of ideas, vision, depth of mind, resourcefulness and great initiative. But the responsibility of being head of the family was mine, and I have assumed it.

An Emergency Call

About one o'clock one afternoon a telephone call came from my wife. It was a desperate emergency call. She was sobbing so that she could hardly talk. "Something terrible has happened," she said between sobs. "Hurry! Come home quickly!"

"What's happened?" I asked. She couldn't tell me, over the telephone. "Just hurry home—*quick!* Oh, *it's terrible!* HURRY!"

I ran full speed to the elevator, and out to the street below, where I hailed a cab. No time to take the "L" train. I asked the cab driver to rush full speed to our address.

Dashing up the stairs two steps at a time, I ran into our apartment and took my sobbing wife in my arms.

"What on earth *is* it?" I demanded.

Then she told me, still sobbing. She had lost faith in two women!

"Those women told dirty stories!"

She had been introduced to an elderly woman by the people of the second apartment we had occupied after marriage. She had seemed such a kindly, nice old lady. My wife had gone to visit with her several times.

On this particular day, this lady was entertaining my wife and one other woman at luncheon. These two women began to tell dirty stories and laugh at them. Mrs. Armstrong was shocked. She had never heard that kind of language come from the mouth of a woman before. She was horrified! Manners or no manners, she suddenly excused herself, and ran from the woman's apartment. She continued running all the way to our apartment and immediately called me.

I looked at my innocent, naive, trusting little wife incredulously!

"Is that all!" I exploded, almost speechless. "Look here, Loma! Do you mean to tell me you called me away from an important business conference, and caused me to waste cab fare all the way out here, for nothing more serious than *that?*"

My sweet, trusting little wife was so broken up at having to lose faith in people that I found it necessary to remain with her the rest of the day. We took a long walk out Sheridan Road, and probably then went to a movie to get her mind off of it.

The disillusionment she experienced in Chicago caused her a great deal of suffering. She learned that many if not most people in a great metropolitan city become *hard, suspicious, selfish,* more mechanical than human.

11

Our First Child

FOR SOME four months after our wedding day we lived on the North Side of Chicago, near the lake. During that brief period we had occupied two furnished apartments and one furnished room.

About Thanksgiving time, 1917, we moved into a single room on the South Side. We sub-rented this room from Charley and Viva Hyle in their apartment some short distance south of 63rd Street.

Charley Hyle worked on the night shift at an automobile assembly plant. My wife and Viva became good friends. Actually, although we rented only the one bedroom with kitchen and dining room privilege, we shared the entire apartment with them—living room, as well as dining room and kitchen.

By this time we knew we were going to become parents. Our first baby was due the latter part of May.

Our First Child Born

It probably was the affirmative checkmark on the pregnancy question on my draft-board questionnaire which caused the Board chairman, Professor J. Paul Goode, to give me a Class 4, noncombatant, draft classification.

We lived with the Hyles until very shortly before the time for our baby to be born.

In January, 1918, my wife accompanied me on a business trip to Des Moines. We both wanted our baby to be born in Des Moines. Mrs. Armstrong had formed an intense aversion to the artificial and mechanical city of Chicago.

Arriving in Des Moines, my wife found that her girl chum's mother was in the hospital, having just given birth to her tenth child. The modern method of hospital delivery with anesthesia was just then becoming the vogue. This particular mother recommended it to my wife, and also her doctor, a woman obstetrical physician, Dr. Georgia Stuart.

Mrs. Armstrong preferred a woman doctor, and I did not oppose. Consequently, a visit was made to Dr. Stuart's office for a check-up and instruction, and she was retained.

Our baby was due to be born about May 25th. We made our next trip to Des Moines well ahead of time—so we supposed—arriving on Sunday, May 5. On Monday we went to the doctor's office for a check-up. I needed to take a week's business trip to Sioux City and other points.

"You are in splendid condition," Dr. Stuart assured my wife. "There is every reason to expect the baby to go the full time, and I believe it is perfectly safe for Mr. Armstrong to be away for the remainder of this week.

My wife's sister, Bertha Dillon, came to stay with her in our apartment in The Brown, a residential hotel where we always stayed when in Des Moines. I left that day for Sioux City.

About two o'clock Thursday morning Mrs. Armstrong knew the baby was about to be born. Two weeks prematurely, she called Dr. Stuart on the telephone, and the doctor told her to get dressed and she would drive past the hotel and take her to the hospital at once.

In those days women wore high-top laced shoes, and in the excitement of the emergency, much frightened due to the fact I was away and this was her first childbirth experience, Mrs. Armstrong was too nervous to lace up her shoes, and her sister had a frightful time trying to get those high-tops laced up!

Finally they made it and were ready to leave. Bertha sent a telegram to me telling me to race to Des Moines on the first train.

This trip I was staying at the West Hotel in Sioux City. For some reason I slept a little late that Thursday morning. Coming down for breakfast around eight, I looked in my box at the desk, and the clerk handed me the telegram, which had arrived there at 3:30 a.m.

"Quick!" I exclaimed, "when does the next train leave for Des Moines?"

"The only train all day to Des Moines left about 15 minutes ago," was the terrifying answer.

I was outraged!

"Look at this telegram!" I thundered at the hotel clerk. "It arrived here at 3:30 a.m., in plenty of time for me to have caught that train. WHY DIDN'T YOU CALL ME OR SEND IT TO MY ROOM?"

"Well, I suppose the night clerk didn't want to

disturb you," was the nonconcerned and exasperating answer.

I could not have been more angry!

"Now LOOK!" I said sharply, "There's *got* to be some way to get to Des Moines before that train tomorrow morning!"

"Well," said the hotel clerk, "there is a train leaving for Council Bluffs and Omaha in about thirty minutes, but I don't know whether you could make any connection from there to Des Moines."

In that thirty minutes my bags were packed, and I had boarded that Council Bluffs train. At the depot I learned that if we were on time at Council Bluffs, there was a chance to race across town in a taxi and catch a train on the Rock Island line due in Des Moines about six o'clock that very evening.

Quickly I scribbled off a telegram to my sister-in-law giving the train number, and requesting her to wire me on the train, at some town along the way, the news of my wife's condition.

A Father Suffers Birth Pangs

Nervously I kept inquiring at every train-stop for a telegram. There was no telegram. The suspense was building up. It was becoming almost unendurable.

We did arrive at Council Bluffs on time. The taxi made the mad dash across town. The taxi driver thought I might take three minutes to try to get a long-distance telephone call through. There had not been time to try to get Bertha by telephone at Sioux City—I just barely caught that train. The cab driver stopped in front of the telephone office. I raced in and tried to make the connection with Des Moines. The three minutes ran out on me before they got the call through.

212

I just caught the Rock Island train for Des Moines on the run.

But the train didn't seem to run—it seemed to slow down to a slow walk.

WHY didn't that train go a little faster? It didn't seem in any hurry. It made all the stops.

Time dragged. My nerves raced. The suspense built up.

I don't think we arrived in Des Moines at six that same night. I think it was at six several nights later. At least so it seemed to me.

After an eternity of anxious suspense, before the train came to a full stop, I was the first passenger off at Des Moines. I ran full speed to a telephone at the newsstand in the depot.

A nurse at the Methodist Hospital said sweetly, "You have a fine new seven-pound-nine-ounce daughter."

I didn't even hear *that*.

"I don't care a hang about that," I snapped back, *"HOW'S MY WIFE?"* All day long I had lived through the agonizing hours not knowing whether my wife had lived through it.

You see, this was my first experience at becoming a father. I didn't know yet, then, that the doctors will tell you they've never lost a father yet.

"Oh," said the sweet little nurse's provokingly slow voice, "she's just FINE!" At last I could relax a little, as I raced to a cab and asked him to drive full speed to the hospital.

Babies Don't Stop Breathing

Stepping briskly into my wife's private hospital room, I was greatly relieved to see her smiling happily, reaching her arms toward me. I kissed her, and almost

213

immediately a nurse brought in our little daughter, Beverly Lucile. She was the most *beautiful* baby I had ever seen! I was a very proud father.

Mrs. Armstrong has always had a penchant for naming babies. She has named dozens—perhaps scores of them—wherever and whenever other mothers would allow her to name their babies. Of course she had Beverly named long before she was born. Had she been a boy, my wife had decided to name him Herbert Junior. But by the time our first son was born, more than ten years later, we had both changed our minds about the name "Junior."

Just as the baby was born, my wife, only partially under the ether, asked:

"What is it, girl or boy?"

"It's a girl," answered Dr. Stuart.

"Girl! Beverly!" said Mrs. Armstrong with emphasis in her semi-anesthetized stupor.

After ten days the doctor released her from the hospital, and our little family of three and Bertha resumed life at The Brown. There was a small balcony off our apartment. The baby was laid on the bed, and we sat down out on the balcony.

We heard a slight sound from the baby.

"Quick!" exclaimed my young wife in nervous anxiety, "see if the baby's still breathing!"

I had to rush inside to reassure her that babies just don't stop breathing for no reason at all.

Whenever the baby made a sound, Mrs. Armstrong was sure she was choking to death. When she did not make a sound, my wife was sure she had smothered to death.

In our apartment was a small kitchenette. The baby's first bath away from the hospital was quite an experience. Mrs. Armstrong's *first* experience! She was

214

so afraid the baby would take cold, she turned on the stove until the kitchenette room was so hot the baby screamed. The young mother didn't know why the baby screamed—became frightened, supposing something terrible was wrong with the baby. Both sweat and tears rolled down my wife's face. She was afraid for any air to touch the baby, so she hurried frantically with the bath! When the baby cried and even screamed because of the excess heat and lack of oxygen, her young mother, not knowing what caused the baby's discomfort, burst out crying, too—but with determination she finished the bath! Many young mothers have many things to learn, the same as young fathers!

The Flu Epidemic

It was now after the 20th of May, 1918. The flu epidemic had struck the United States, during the very crisis of the war. People were dying all over the nation, and especially in the larger cities.

We decided against taking our baby back into the congestion of Chicago. Instead we rented a house in Indianola, Iowa, 18 miles south of Des Moines, where there were fewer people to come in contact with and less danger of being exposed to the new influenza disease. The house we rented was close to the Simpson College campus.

Leaving my wife and baby with her sister Bertha, I returned alone to Chicago to look after my business. At the railroad depots boxed caskets were being loaded on the baggage cars of most trains—bodies of influenza victims. We had not wanted to risk exposing our new baby by a train ride to Chicago. In Chicago I saw people in the congested "Loop" traffic wearing cloth masks over their mouths and noses to prevent breathing a flu germ.

After some three months we decided the family could not remain apart any longer—nor could I afford the frequent trips to Iowa to be part time with my family, so I brought my wife and baby daughter back to Chicago. This time we rented a room with a family named Bland, who had an apartment on the South Side, south of 63rd Street, not far from the Hyles, who had moved away by this time.

I began to concentrate more and more on developing the farm tractor business for *The Northwestern Banker*. As mentioned in a previous chapter, Clifford DePuy, publisher of *The Northwestern Banker,* had purchased the old *St. Louis Banker* at St. Louis, and changed its name to the *Mid-Continent Banker.*

He appointed a former acquaintance of mine, R. Fullerton Place, as Editor and manager of the *Mid-Continent Banker.* Some years before, when I was 18 years of age and a solicitor in the want-ad department of the Des Moines *Daily Capital,* Mr. Place had been Sports Editor of the *Capital.* We always called him by his youthful nickname, "Rube" Place.

Also I mentioned, in an earlier chapter, that after this "farm tractor brainstorm" hit me, I had made extensive surveys to gather facts and information not possessed by tractor manufacturers about their distribution problems.

With this information accurately tabulated and analyzed, I was able to approach the manufacturers in the tractor industry with facts they themselves did not know about their own selling and distribution problems.

I found that bankers invariably discouraged their farmer customers from buying tractors. The readers of my magazines—the country bankers—were talking thousands of farmers out of buying tractors after local dealers had talked them into it. Our readers provided a major sales resistance.

It was, therefore, important to the tractor industry to "sell" the bankers on modern mechanized farm methods.

Doing Business With Millionaires

It became necessary to do business direct with the presidents of these great corporations. Thus, once again, I was thrown into business contact with important millionaire executives. These contacts were important in the early training for the job I was destined to be called to later.

I soon learned, however, that it was difficult to induce the head of a great corporation with national distribution to advertise in one small bank journal covering only five states—or, after the purchase of the *Mid-Continent Banker,* even the two small localized sectional journals. They were accustomed to doing business in a big way—of *national* scope.

I think I must have caught some of their vision. Later, when the media of radio and the printing press were opened to me in the big Commission, it seemed natural that my thinking was constantly along lines of expansion—first from Lane County, Oregon, to the Portland area; then the entire Pacific Northwest; then California and the entire coast; then national; then, finally as of today, WORLDWIDE! I think my readers will be quick to grasp how these years of business training provided the necessary foundation for the great Work of today.

Of course all these farm tractor manufacturers placed all their advertising through advertising agencies. In the agencies, even more than in the offices of tractor corporation presidents, I was tremendously handicapped by representing only a small sectional circulation. They, by contrast, bought space on a *national* basis.

The New Brainstorm

This situation inspired the new brainstorm, also previously mentioned in this autobiography. There were seven leading sectional bank journals, and two national magazines with more scattered banker circulations. It required all nine of them to cover the entire nation with an intensive national circulation.

I compared my situation to that of actors in show business. An actor in a theatre on Broadway gets paid for one performance each night, but to play before many thousands of people he must act the part all over again night after night. But a movie actor in Hollywood, I reasoned, acted the part just once, and it was seen in hundreds and hundreds of theatres. The Hollywood stars were paid in hundreds of thousands or millions of dollars, while the Broadway actors were paid in hundreds of dollars. The movie star received *multiple* compensation for the *one* effort.

I saw that it would be far easier for me to sell a *national* circulation for a string of nine magazines on the one effort. In other words, it would be easier to make *nine* commissions on the one solicitation, than one commission.

Immediately this idea met emphatic and determined resistance from Clifford DePuy. I was his Chicago representative, and he was not going to share my services with anyone else!

I told Cliff I was absolutely certain I could send him more business under the new setup, at only 30% commission, than I could as his exclusive representative at 40%. He believed that I could not get as much business for his magazines sharing my time with seven others as I could devoting all my time to his magazines alone. It was like the irresistible force meeting the immovable object.

We were both strong willed.

It came to a climax one night in the offices of the *Mid-Continent Banker* in St. Louis. I had been in St. Louis soliciting business. Mr. DePuy was there. I needed to draw an expense check as advance commission in order to have train fare to return home in Chicago.

"O.K.," said Cliff, "agree to give up this fantastic idea of representing seven other journals, and remain exclusively my representative, and I'll give you the check."

He "had me over a barrel"—so he thought!

Actually, his ultimatum was entirely fair and reasonable, from his point of view. But I couldn't see it that way. To me it meant more business than ever for him, and at 25% reduction in cost of getting it. I felt he ought to help get me established in it.

Round and round we went. Neither would give in.

Mr. Place tried to cause me to give in. He quoted Scripture. "The Bible says, 'To him that hath shall be given; and to him that hath not shall be taken away, even what he hath.' In this case Cliff *hath,* and you *hath not!* You'll simply *have* to give in, Herbert, or you have no way to get back to Chicago."

"I'll *never* give in!" I retorted with increased determination and set jaw. "I'll start to WALK back to Chicago before I'll give up this new plan. If you won't advance me expense money, I might as well leave the office and start walking. *I'll find a way* to get home and develop this string of bank journals!"

When Cliff saw how determined I was, on the

showdown, he was not willing to let me start walking all the way to Chicago. He gave me the needed expense money.

I will say, however, that I did my best to make it a good investment, and succeeded. I *did* send him a great deal more advertising under the nine-magazine, national-circulation setup than I could have done otherwise—and at lower commission.

In those days I worked sporadically in streaks.

I seemed to have my "off" days and my "on" days. When I was "on," I was "red hot," and, as I fancied, at least, very brilliant. But on the "off" days it seemed I couldn't sell anything. I became very uncomfortably aware of this great fault, and I tried to fight it, but it took me years to overcome it. But I did overcome it eventually.

Actually, during these next few years, I did not work more than four or five days a month. But, with the nine magazines and a national circulation, the commission on a half-page, or a full-page contract for one year was rather large. I did not need to have too many of the brilliant days to make a good year's income.

From memory, my income for that year 1918 was approximately $7,300; for 1919 approximately $8,700; and for 1920 over $11,000. When you consider what a dollar in those days was worth, those were very good incomes by today's standards.

The Curtis Opportunity

Not very many knew of that fault of working in spurts on my "on" days. The business contacts didn't, because I only called on them on the "good" days. On those days I was supremely self-confident, and consequently effective.

220

Soon I knew and was known by almost every advertising agency in Chicago. Representing the nine leading bank journals—having virtually a monopoly representation in the banking field—now with an intensified national circulation to offer, enhanced my prestige greatly with the agencies. They came to know me as a publishers' representative who "knew his stuff." Also, they had learned, by the latter part of 1918, that I was absolutely honest in statements about bank journals—whether those I represented, or competitive journals.

Since bank journal circulations were very small, even though extremely high in class, the page rates were comparatively low. Agencies made very small commissions from business placed in bank journals. Having confidence in my knowledge and honesty, most Chicago agencies came to rely almost altogether on my advice relative to any space used in the banking journals.

At that time the biggest organization in the publishing field was the Curtis Publishing Company of Philadelphia, publishers of *The Saturday Evening Post, The Ladies' Home Journal,* and *The Country Gentleman.* They were regarded as the most aggressive people in the publishing business. It was a matter of great prestige to be on their staff.

Along about this time the Curtis organization was looking for a brilliant and promising young cub solicitor who showed promise of developing into a high executive position. They inquired of space-buyers and contact men in most of the leading advertising agencies for recommendations of the most promising man in the field soliciting the agencies. I was one of the top two recommended by the Chicago agencies, and was called to the Curtis Chicago office, where their western manager offered me the opportunity to join the Curtis staff.

It was a very flattering opportunity. However, I wanted to be SURE, before making a change. By this time I had finally learned the lesson of sticking with a thing, and not shifting around. I went to Arthur Reynolds, President of the Continental & Commercial National Bank—Chicago's largest bank, and second largest national bank in America—for advice.

He pushed a button on his desk. Immediately a secretary appeared.

"Bring me our file on the Curtis Publishing Company of Philadelphia," he said. The file was quickly produced. He scanned over it quickly. I noticed that the material in it was red-pencil marked, so as to call to his attention quickly the most vital information.

"I'm going to advise you to remain where you are," he concluded within a few moments. "The Curtis people are a big prestige organization. But you'd be just a cub with them, starting near the bottom. It would be years before you'd be noticed by any of the men at the top. Some of these big companies take good care of their men, others pay small salaries. The Curtis people do not have to pay big salaries for the job or office held. With them you'd be a little frog in a big puddle. Where you are, you are a big frog in a little puddle. You have your own business. You have developed it so as to bring yourself into constant contact with big and important men. In my judgment this is better training for your future success than anything you would get with the Curtis organization. It is flattering, of course, that the advertising agencies have rated you one of the two most promising and effective young advertising solicitors in Chicago. Take this as encouragement to drive yourself on to greater accomplishment. But I think you are doing well right where you are."

I took his advice. The Curtis offer was turned down.

An Irate Competitor

An incident occurred about this time which illustrates the confidence that had been built up in the advertising agencies of Chicago.

One day the space buyer of the Critchfield agency called me on the telephone.

"There's a Mr. Chazen here," he said (the name has been changed for obvious reasons). "He says he is publisher of three bankers' magazines, one circulating in Illinois, Indiana and Wisconsin; one in Nebraska, and one in Kansas and Oklahoma. Is it any good?"

It was not. It was a fake. I told him the truth.

"No, it's a plain fake. He really has a good circulation in Nebraska, but that is all. He puts a different cover with a different name on a very few copies and calls it by the name of his supposed Illinois, Indiana and Wisconsin paper; then he puts still a different cover with another name on a few copies, supposed to be a magazine circulating in Kansas and Oklahoma. I have survey reports from every bank in Illinois and Wisconsin. His supposed magazine for these states has exactly four subscribers in Wisconsin, and 17 in Illinois. That's all."

"Thanks, Armstrong," said the Critchfield space buyer.

It took this irate publisher about 12 minutes to hotfoot it across the Loop to my office.

"Armstrong," he shouted as he burst in the door, "what kind of a game are you playing, anyway? It seems you've got all the agencies in Chicago hypnotized so that no one else can get any business here without your approval. All right! I'll pay! *What's your price?* What have I got to pay you to lay off, and recommend my three magazines?"

"Sit down, and cool off, Mr. Chazen," I said. "Sure I've got a price. The price is simply whatever it is going to cost you to build an honest circulation for those two fake papers of yours, and join the Audit Bureau of Circulations, and prove your circulation by an ABC audit. Then I'll recommend your magazines for nothing."

"Why, Why!" he puffed and stammered, "that's *outrageous!* That's IMPOSSIBLE! Do you know what that would cost me?"

"Sure I know. But it's the price of being HONEST!"

"It's an OUTRAGE!" he kept shouting, as he stomped out of my office.

There was another occasion when an agency had a client who needed all the banker circulation he could get in Minnesota. In addition to the *Northwestern Banker,* I recommended a Minneapolis bank journal that had a good strong circulation in Minnesota. Its publisher came to see me and thank me. He had a good honest circulation in Minnesota, and where it fit a marketing problem I was glad to recommend it.

Our New Apartment

We were still living in our little three-room apartment at Blands when the World War I ended, November 11, 1918.

We shall never forget that day. We had Beverly with us at my office. Chicago's Loop went crazy—berserk! We joined in tearing thick telephone directories into thin strips and throwing them out our fourth story window. Everyone was doing it. It was like snow falling all over the Loop. I got out in the throng for a while—managed to elbow my way for some two blocks—then fought my way through the jam back to the office. Every whistle and siren was going—every car honking full blast!

About that time I learned of a new apartment building being built out in Maywood, third suburban town west of Chicago. I was beginning to get some of the tractor advertising for my nine magazines, and we felt that at last we could lease a full apartment. I leased this one, on the third floor, from the architect's blueprints, about the time the foundation was being laid. The apartment was on Fifth Street, a block or two north of the Northwestern railroad tracks.

It was going to be several months before the apartment building would be ready for occupancy. Nevertheless, in January we rented an old house on Second Street in Maywood, a few blocks from the new apartment building. My wife's father had decided to come to Chicago, and he bought furniture for the house. Her younger brother, Walter, had been released from the Navy and he and Bertha also lived with us in this place.

We lived there some six months. Beverly learned to walk there. The elder of my wife's younger brothers, Gilbert, returned from the trenches in France, discharged from the Army; and so, with his two sons back from the war, my wife's father shipped his furniture and moved back to Iowa.

We then moved for a few weeks into the hotel in Maywood. Maywood was a totally different type suburb in those days than it is today. It has grown immensely and has become a big factory town.

The frame hotel caught on fire while we stayed there, an incident of great excitement. In one room a couple of excited guests threw the mirror of the dresser out the window, breaking it into many fragments and

225

then they carefully carried down the stairs the dresser itself.

We soon found a furnished house on Fourth Street we could rent until our apartment was finished. While living in this house, shortly prior to occupying the new apartment, my mother came to visit us, and remained until we had moved into our apartment.

All the while business was improving. We felt able to furnish our new apartment, and engaged one of Marshall Field's decorators to work with us in the furnishings for the apartment. What we selected was of the very best. Our own apartment—the first that was our very own since marriage—seemed a joy indeed.

We had moved into the furnished house in early December, 1919, and into our apartment in April, 1920.

By this time we were expecting our second child. My wife was having difficulties. Within a week or two after moving into our new apartment, and only a few days after my mother had returned to Salem, Oregon, Mrs. Armstrong was stricken with toxemia eclampsia, with urinalysis showing 40% albumin, and rushed to a hospital. We were told that there was only one doctor in the world who could save her in her serious condition—and this specialist was called in. She survived, and our second daughter, Dorothy Jane, was born in a Des Moines hospital on July 7, 1920.

There was one lasting ill-effect from this critical illness—the treatment that was administered ruined my wife's beautiful golden hair—the most beautiful I had ever seen—and in a comparatively short time she was white-haired.

The world-famous obstetrical specialist brought in on my wife's case in Chicago, her Des Moines doctor, and my wife's uncle who was a captain in the Medical

Corps in the Army, all told us that another pregnancy would mean the certain death of my wife *and* of the baby. Although we did not know why at the time, we learned much later we were of the opposite Rh blood factor.

12

Depression Strikes!

S HORTLY after our second daughter, Dorothy, was born, I persuaded my younger brother, Russell, then twenty, to come back to Chicago and join me in the advertising business. He had been employed in an office job with the Portland Gas & Coke Company in Portland, Oregon.

My Brother's Experience

I gave him what instruction and coaching I could, and sent him out calling on prospects to sell advertising space for our magazines. But after several days—or perhaps two or three weeks—he didn't seem to be doing so well. I knew he had not had any of this kind of experience. So I decided to take him on a call with me, to observe the manner in which I talked with prospective advertisers. I decided that we should call together on someone I had never met before.

The J. I. Case tractor account had just switched to a

new agency I had never contacted. I decided to make the call on the space buyer of this agency. It was one of my "on" days, and about 10:30 in the morning.

I wanted to set a good example for Russell, to show him how it was done. We went together to the agency office. Briskly, and with dignity I stepped up to the receptionist.

"Tell Mr. Blank that Mr. Armstrong is here to see him," I said in a positive tone. I had found that this approach usually got me right in on my man.

The space buyer came out to the reception office, holding my card which I had sent in by the receptionist.

"What bank journals do you represent?" he asked.

"The nine largest—*all* of them that are worth using," I replied snappily and positively, and in a tone of authority.

"Well!" he exclaimed, "come in!"

In his office I immediately launched into the situation my surveys had disclosed, slapping down on his desk a pile of hundreds of questionnaires from bankers and tractor dealers, and taking out of my briefcase the typed tabulations and summaries of the surveys.

He was tremendously impressed.

"Mr. Armstrong," he said after we had covered the material in the surveys, "I wonder if you could prepare for me a statement of the combined circulations, page sizes, rates, et cetera, of your publications."

"I have it right here—already prepared for you," I said, handing the statement to him.

He asked me to prepare for him some other statement. I reached into the briefcase and handed it to him. He asked if I would send over to him sample copies of each of my magazines. I reached in the briefcase, and handed them to him.

"Well," he said finally, "that just about covers everything. Now tell me, Mr. Armstrong—I see you know this problem thoroughly, and you know your own publications. Just what do you advise for this J. I. Case account—which magazines, and how much space ought they to use to accomplish their objective with the bankers?"

"They should use nothing but full pages," I said, speaking authoritatively, "and they should use all nine publications for a concentrated national circulation, because the J. I. Case distribution is national; and they should use it every issue on a year-around basis because they have an educational problem which is going to require constant educational-type copy over an extended period of time. You've got to change the attitude of bankers in regard to mechanized power farming. That's a big order. It can only be done with big space, and it's going to take time. And here I have for you the data and arguments you should incorporate into the advertising copy to convince the bankers. These are the facts that will convince them if you present them in important-size space and keep it up month after month."

I handed him the typed statement of facts, data and arguments which my surveys and personal interviews with bankers had indicated would be most effective in changing banker attitudes toward tractors.

He thanked me, and Russell and I left.

Record-Breaking Contract

Out in the hall, on the way to the elevator, I asked Russell: "Do you think we will remain on the J. I. Case list, for renewal contracts for another year?"

"Boy!" exclaimed Russell, *"will we!* Why, I think he will do just what you recommended. Why, you had him literally eating right out of your hand."

"Well, did that experience help you, Russ?"

I was completely surprised at his answer.

"No! It certainly didn't! Instead, it showed me why I haven't been landing any contracts. Look, Herb! I'm only twenty years old. They think of me as just a kid. You are twenty-eight. You've been in this for years, and you've had experience I haven't had. You have all the facts right on your tongue tip. You speak with assurance and authority. You know your stuff, and men you talk to *know* that you know your stuff. They have confidence in you immediately. But I don't have all this knowledge yet, and I don't appear as mature, and I can't talk as confidently."

I was disappointed. To try to help my brother, I had really keyed myself up to "put on a good show" for him on this call. It boomeranged. It reacted in reverse. It discouraged him. And I didn't know what to do about it. What he had said was true. It would take him years to gain maturity of appearance, and the knowledge of all these merchandising and distribution problems, just as it had taken me years to acquire this knowledge and maturity.

That same afternoon the space buyer in the agency we had called on that morning called me on the telephone.

"Hello, Mr. Armstrong. I have some good news for you. I didn't tell you this morning, but while you were here, the president and advertising manager of the J. I. Case Company were here in the office of our president, making up the lists for the next year. I took all your data list."

"Splendid!" I replied, "but how much space?" I was

231

already carrying the J. I. Case account, with half-page space in only three magazines.

"Full page," he replied.

"Splendid! But how many magazines?"

"Oh," as if he had not thought to tell me, "all nine of them."

"Splendid! But how many months?" I was having to drag it out of him.

"Fifteen months," he replied. "We will start with the October numbers, using October, November and December of this year, and then the entire calendar year next year, making a total of 15 pages in each magazine."

"Wow!" It was the biggest advertising contract ever sold for bank journals, so far as I knew. And so far as I know, it probably is still the record today. By this time advertising rates on all my magazines had gone up considerably. My commission on this order was probably around $3,500—a good fee for about one hour's consultation that morning!

For some little time longer I tried to keep Russell on the job, not soliciting tractor accounts, but smaller-space advertising. But he was just too young. He procured a job with one of my clients, a burglar alarm manufacturer, selling their burglar alarm system to banks. He traveled for some months in northern Illinois and in Wisconsin, gaining some valuable experience, getting together Board meetings in banks to present his product to them. But, although he did better on this, his youth proved too great a handicap, and finally he returned to Portland, Oregon, and to his job with the Gas company.

Depression Strikes

In January, 1920, the well-known statistician Roger

Babson was the speaker at one of our Association of Commerce luncheons then being held each Wednesday in the Cameo Room of the Morrison Hotel. Through the Advertising Club, a division of Chicago Association of Commerce, I had been a member of the Association for some years.

We were then at the very height of a wave of postwar prosperity.

"Gentlemen," said Mr. Babson, "we are about to enter the worst business depression that our generation has ever experienced. I advise you all to set your houses in order. I advise against any further plans of expansion until this depression has passed over."

Seated at tables in that large room were leading bankers and business executives of Chicago. I glanced around. I saw amused smirks animate the faces of many prominent men.

Through the next few months of 1920 business activity continued its boom upswing.

In the summer of that year I attended the American bankers Association national convention in Washington, D. C. While passing the White House one day, I was stopped at the driveway for a large limousine emerging from the White House to pass. In the rear seat was President Woodrow Wilson. He smiled and waved his hand to the two or three of us who happened to be passing at the moment.

Mr. Wilson was the fourth President I had seen in person. At age five or six, when we lived in Marshalltown, Iowa, held in my father's arms, I saw President William McKinley. He was making a rear platform address from his private train. The event was so vividly stamped in my memory that I remember it distinctly, even though I was scarcely out of babyhood at the time.

I saw and heard President Theodore Roosevelt several times, both during his administration and afterward. I sat within about fifteen feet of him at an Association of Commerce banquet in the ballroom of Hotel LaSalle in Chicago. I saw President Taft, when he made a speech in Des Moines, Iowa. But since seeing and waving back to President Wilson that day in 1920, I have not seen a single President in person—though of course, since television, most of us have seen every President many times; and I had seen all presidents since Wilson in newsreels.

A highlight of that 1920 convention trip to Washington, D.C. was a long conversation I had, lasting more than an hour, with John McHugh, in the lobby of the Willard Hotel. Mr. McHugh was then president of the Mechanics and Metals National Bank of New York. Later, through consolidations of this bank and others into the gigantic Chase National Bank, Mr. McHugh was elevated to a position two levels higher than the president of the largest bank on earth, with the title "Chairman of the Executive Committee."

But one might ask: *"What price Glory?"* in the business world, after all. A very few years ago I stopped in at the Wall Street offices of the Chase National Bank, and asked for information as to the latter days of John McHugh.

"Who? Never heard of him!" was the only reply I could get from those of today's staff that I questioned. Had he been a glamour-boy movie star instead of a world-famous banker, his name might have lived after him more effectively.

I was really puzzled about one thing. John McHugh was the very epitome of a quiet, cultured, dignified gentleman. He was extremely courteous, kindly, polite. Naturally he had many friends and many who *posed* as

234

friends. How could a soft-spoken and kindly *gentleman* like John McHugh turn down a conniving, scheming, professing "friend" who might come to him for a large undeserved loan?

"Didn't friends and acquaintances take advantage of such a gentle soul?" I asked one of my bank journal publishers.

He laughed. "Oh, no," he explained. "Don't worry about the wrong kind taking advantage of John McHugh's friendliness. His judgment is very keen, else he would never have risen to such high level in the banking world. Nobody puts anything over on him. He simply remains gracious and friendly, and explains that loans of this type are handled by such and such officer. He then offers to introduce the would-be borrower, expressing confidence he will be well taken care of. He always is. Such procedure is the signal to the other officer to turn the man down. The would-be borrower friend, of course, becomes angry and furious at this other officer—but not at Mr. McHugh, who still retains the friendships."

Before the end of 1920, Roger Babson's predicted depression did strike—with sudden and intense fury. By January, 1921, we had reached and passed its lowest ebb.

"Thermometers on the Wall"

At this time Roger Babson once again was the guest speaker in the Morrison Hotel Cameo Room Association of Commerce luncheon.

"Well, gentlemen," he said, "you will remember that a year ago I warned you that within one year we would be in the throes of the worst depression our generation has ever seen. I noticed many of you smiling unbelievingly then. Well, that year has rolled around,

235

and here I am again, and here is the depression with me."

Chicago business leaders were not smiling now. Mr. Babson then proceeded to explain why he knew what was coming and business executives did not.

"It is now mid-winter," he said. "If I want to know what the temperature *is, now,* in this room, I go to the wall and look at the thermometer. If I want to know what it has been, up to now, and the existing *trend* as of the moment, I look at a recording thermometer. But if I want to know what the temperature in this room is going to be, an hour from now, I go to the source which *determines* future temperatures—I go down to the boiler-room and see what is happening down there. You gentlemen looked at bank clearings, indexes of business activity, stock car loadings, stockmarket quotations— you looked at the *thermometers on the wall;* I looked at THE WAY people as a whole were dealing with one another. I looked to the SOURCE which *determines* future conditions. I have found that that *source* may be defined in terms of 'RIGHTEOUSNESS.' When 51% or more of the whole people are reasonably *'righteous'* in their dealings with one another, we are heading into increasing prosperity. When 51% of the people become *'unrighteous'* in their business dealings with their fellows, then we are headed for BAD TIMES ECONOMICALLY!"

I have never forgotten Mr. Babson's explanation. I hope my readers today may remember and profit by it, too.

I paid with the loss of my business to learn the lesson!

Every one of my big-space advertisers in the tractor and similar industries went into economic failure in that flash depression of late 1920. It wiped out my business and source of income—literally!

236

I was not a quitter. I had learned, now, not to give up. But I had not learned that a *dead* horse is DEAD! For two years I stayed on in Chicago vainly attempting to revive a dead business.

13

Business Disintegrates

THE NEXT two years—from late 1920 until December, 1922—were discouraging years. A few nationally known business executives, unable to take the reverses of the depression, sank to despondency and committed suicide. One of these was the president of one of the large automobile manufacturing concerns whom I had known personally.

I had been knocked down, stunned, made groggy—but not knocked out. Desperately I clung on, hoping to climb back on top.

Conference with Millionaires

One morning—it must have been about February, 1921—a telephone call came from the secretary of the National Implement and Vehicle Association. An important meeting of the Board of Directors of the association was in progress. Mr. Wallis (I do not now

238

remember his initials), president of the J. I. Case Plow Works, my biggest client, was chairman of this board. He had asked the secretary to call me and ask if I could run over immediately to their meeting, being held across the Loop in the Union League Club.

I told him I would be right over.

I raced down to a clothes-pressing shop and shoe shining parlor, a half block down West Madison Street from my office, ducked into a dressing room and had my suit pressed and shoes shined while I waited—a rush job. Then I caught a taxi and hurried to the Union League Club.

Being ushered into the private room where the Board meeting was being held, I shook hands with Mr. Wallis, and in turn was introduced to six other millionaire presidents of large farm implement manufacturers. I remember there was Mr. Brantingham, president of Emerson-Brantingham, among the others. The magnetism of the powerful personalities of these seven big business heads surcharged the atmosphere of the room. It was the first time I had ever been in the presence of so many big men at once. I was deeply impressed. But they were not in a happy mood. They were a deeply concerned group of men. The depression was ruining their businesses. They faced ruin.

Advising Clients to Cancel

"Mr. Armstrong," said Mr. Wallis, "you know, of course, the extent to which this depression has hit the farm tractor industry. This meeting has been called in the interests of this entire industry. The industry cannot survive unless we can find some way to stimulate sales in this depression. We have to find some way to induce farmers to buy tractors—and they have quit buying them.

239

"Now what we want to ask you is this: can you—*will you* bring pressure on the editors of bank journals of this nation, whom you represent, to write strong and vigorous editorials urging bankers to advise the farmers to resume buying tractors. Can your editor show the bankers WHY they ought to bring pressure on farmers to buy tractors, and save this great industry?"

It was a crucial moment in my life. Here were seven heads of great corporations. They represented the entire great farm tractor and farm implement industry. And they were appealing to *me* to devise an idea, and take an action that would save this vast industry of American Big Business from bankruptcy!

What an appeal to my egotism! What a temptation to think of personal importance!

But I *did* know the FACTS! And when this test came, I *had* to be honest with these men. It was no time for a grandstand play for personal glory, or for pretense. I knew the FACTS—hard, cold stern FACTS—and I *had to be honest!* Even though I knew it meant cancellation of what tractor advertising had not already been cancelled.

Of course the implication was that, if I could induce our editors to undertake a campaign to pressure bankers into inducing farmers to purchase tractors in this depression, an unheard-of volume of big-space advertising would be handed me on a platter!

I was well aware of that. I was well aware that I had it in my power to ignore FACTS I had gathered, and start such a campaign in America's leading bank magazines. These men didn't know what I knew. But it would be misrepresentation—and deliberate dishonesty.

I was ambitious to make money. But not by falsification or dishonesty! I *was sincere!*

240

"No, gentlemen," I replied without hesitation. "I cannot do it! I have been constantly in touch with the bankers in regard to the farm tractor situation. Let me tell you what the country bankers *know*. They know that corn which normally has been selling for $1.12 per bushel has dropped down to 18 cents per bushel. I have one client now whose business has skyrocketed since the depression—the Gordon-Van Tyne Company of Davenport, Iowa. They make, as you know, prefabricated structures for temporary grain storage. Everywhere farmers are buying these, and storing their grain for a rise in the market—after the depression is over.

"Bankers know that one tractor replaces six horses. Tractors have to be fed gasoline, which is expensive right now. Horses are fed on 18-cent corn and oats and hay that have skidded likewise in price. Country bankers know their farmer customers would think they were fools to recommend buying tractors and feeding them on high-priced gasoline, when they have their horses being fed on grain they can't sell."

The next day I received a cancellation of my last remaining tractor account—J. I. Case. But I still had my honesty and self-respect.

A Child's Menu

In early May, 1921, it was necessary to take a business trip to Iowa. It was decided that I should take our eldest daughter Beverly, then almost three, for a visit with her "Auntie Bert" as she called her Aunt Bertha, while I transacted business in Iowa.

In a lower berth on the sleeper that night, as I was undressing her to put on her sleeping garment, Beverly stood up, and discovered she could reach up and touch the shiny top of the berth.

241

"See, Daddy," she exclaimed, "I'm a BIG girl now. I can touch the ceiling."

Next morning we were having breakfast in the dining room of the Hotel Savory. When the waitress brought me a menu, Beverly, in the highchair they had brought her, demanded a menu also. Laughingly the waitress gave her one. She looked up and down the menu with a studious expression—it might have been upside-down. And then, with great feminine dignity, in a very ladylike voice, Beverly gave the waitress her order.

"I think I will have," she said, pertly, "some ice cream, some string beans, and some candy."

Later, when her younger sister Dorothy became about the same age, she ordered a dinner.

"I want some ice cream, popcorn and some chewing gum," she ordered.

I never did quite agree with the modernistic psychologists who say we should always give children whatever they want—that they instinctively know what is best for them.

Our children and grandchildren, of course, like all others, have on occasion gotten off some "cute" sayings. One time my wife was putting on Dorothy's little Dr. Denton sleepers to put her to bed. It seems they were made of wool, and they scratched her skin.

"Mother," she said seriously, "nobody but just me and God and Jesus knows what a fix I'm in!"

Recuperating in Iowa

Things in my business went from bad to worse. It was discouraging—frustrating. I was taking the biggest beating of my life—but hung stubbornly on. Finally, about July, 1922, it became necessary to give up our apartment. My income had gone too low to support my

242

family, and at that time we decided that Mrs. Armstrong and the girls should go to her father's farm in Iowa, to lessen the expenses.

I rented a single room about a block away in Maywood, furnishing it with some of our very fine furniture, and the rest of the furniture was put in storage. We had a Knabe piano I had purchased new on contract, but it went back to the store when we could no longer keep up the payments. All the rest of the furniture had been bought for cash.

From this time I entered upon perhaps the blackest and most discouraging three months of my life. It was a mistake to try to face this uphill treadmill climb alone without my wife and family. If ever I needed my wife it was then.

I began palling around with two other young men who were advertising representatives of magazines. One of them was in process of separating from and divorcing his wife. The wife of the other was away for the summer and fall. We began to haunt nightclubs—then called cabarets. Often we would hang around these places of sorrowful, moaning, screeching, wailing music—if you could call such dirges "music"—until 1 or 2 a.m. We began to drink—not at all even a fraction of the volume of an "alcoholic"—but too much for efficiency. My mental attitude became one of frustration.

Finally, I got two or three weeks behind with the room rent on my single room, and I felt too humiliated to go back. I went to a northside second-rate hotel—then to another. Finally I could not even keep this up.

I reached the end of the rope in Chicago in October, 1922. I was lonesome for my wife and children. At last I, too, had to seek refuge on my father-in-law's farm in Iowa, where we would have no cost of living. I do not remember now, but I probably traveled this time in a day coach.

My father-in-law was finishing up corn shucking and I did the best I could to help him—but I was inexperienced, and unable to keep up with him.

Through that fall and winter, I spent most of the time in resting, and recuperating in morale from the crushing defeat of losing my business because my Big-Business clients had lost theirs. That winter, beside the warm fire of burning oak logs, I read through three or four books of fiction—about the only fiction reading of my entire life. I did what I could to help on the farm, but that wasn't much, and my wife, of course, did the cooking, and housework.

My First College Activity

At this time my wife's younger brother, Walter, was a freshman in Simpson College in Indianola. Along in November he came to me with a proposition.

"Herb," he said, "I've decided to go in for the college oratorical contest, if you'll help me."

A short time before had been the first day of basketball practice. Walter had been the star basketball player in Simpson Academy, which he had attended instead of High School. His greatest ambition had been to make the Simpson varsity basketball team, and to be chosen on the Des Moines *Register's* all-state team.

On opening day of basketball practice, he was the first one into the gym with a basketball suit. When the coach and other players came on the floor, the coach had frowned and walked over to Walter.

"Dillon," he said, "what are you doing here? We won't need you. We have all the material we need this year. Go to the showers and get into your street clothes."

244

This was open humiliation before all the candidates for the squad. Being rejected without a chance to even *try out* for the team was unfair, unjust, and discriminatory. He couldn't understand it. He was MAD! Later he found the reason. The coach's salary at that time was being paid by a certain fraternity, and only frat members were given consideration for the team.

"Now here's the way I figure," he said to me. "In oratory, *anyone* can compete. They can't throw me off because I don't belong to a frat. Now you are a professional writer. If you will help me write my oration—and it is allowable to have help—and work with me on delivery, I think I have a chance. The two best orators Simpson ever had are a Junior and a Senior—both members of that frat. If you can beat them, it will be sweet revenge. Will you help me?"

"Well, Walt," I replied, "I don't know a thing about college oratorical contests. I never saw one. I have never read the script of a college oration. I don't even know what they are like. But if you will bring me copies of a few sample orations, I'll sure help you if I can."

14

College Competition and "Oregon or Bust"

O
N expert advice, I had put myself through the college of EXPERIENCE— or, as it is sometimes called, the college of hard knocks. First was a year of want ads on a Des Moines daily newspaper. Later came three years on a national trade journal—the largest in the United States, involving a great deal of travel, and intensive instruction, training, and experience in writing advertising copy, dictating business letters, and later, writing magazine articles. After six months of Chamber of Commerce work, the seven-year career representing the leading bank journals of the nation began.

All these years I had studied diligently. My "major" in this study, of course, was advertising and merchandising. I studied what books were available. I read religiously the trade papers of the profession. I studied psychology. As a "minor" study, I delved into Plato, Epictetus, and other books on philosophy, and continually read Elbert Hubbard (whom I became personally acquainted with) for style in writing. I read human interest articles and other articles on world conditions and on the business of living, in leading magazines.

At the beginning of World War I, I had been able to obtain written recommendations for entrance into the Officers Reserve Corps from such prominent Chicago men as Arthur Reynolds, president of the largest bank in Chicago and second largest in America, testifying that I possessed more than the equivalent of a college education.

But I had not received my education in college.

The Challenge for College Competition

This request from my brother-in-law presented an intriguing challenge. I had taken a confidence-shattering beating in the failure of the Chicago business. But the vanity had not been crushed out of my nature by any means. Here was a chance to match wits with college students. Also it offered a total mental diversion from the Chicago nightmare. It was something I could "sink my teeth into," with energy and a new interest.

But I knew nothing of how college orations were written, or delivered, or judged. As I mentioned, I asked my brother-in-law if he could bring me copies of a few first-place winning orations.

He brought out to the farm a number of them from the college library, printed in pamphlet form. Immediately I noticed that they were all couched in flowery language—the amateur college-boy attempt at fancy rhetoric, employing five- to seven-syllable words which actually said practically nothing. All the orations were written on such altruistic and idealistic subjects as

247

peace, or prohibition, or love for fellowman. They displayed ignorance of the WAY to peace, or the problem of alcoholism, or of human experience in living. But they did contain beautiful, high-flown language!

This became very intriguing.

"Tell me, Walt," I asked, "what is the prevailing style of delivery? Do the oratorial contestants go at it hammer-and-tongs, Billy Sunday style tearing their hair out, throwing chairs across the platform, thundering at their audiences—or do they speak calmly and smoothly, with carefully developed graceful gestures—or how?"

"Oh, they try to speak with as much calm dignity as possible—with graceful gestures."

One Chance in TWO

"How many contestants will be in this contest?"

"There will be six, including me," Walter answered.

"All right—tell me, now—would you rather enter this contest with one chance in six of winning, or with one chance in TWO?"

He didn't quite understand.

"Why, with one out of two—but what do you mean?"

"Well, Walt," I replied, "I guess I'm not much of a conformist. I often break precedent. I figure it this way: if you write a flossy, flowery oration with big words that *say nothing,* and attempt to compete with these upperclassmen of greater experience on their own terms, you are only one of six contestants, and you probably do not even have one chance in six of winning.

"But if you pick for your subject some red-hot controversial topic—if you have the courage to actually ATTACK something, give the PLAIN TRUTH about it, open people's eyes about it, and work yourself up to white-hot

248

■ *Herbert W. Armstrong, at age 23, with spectacles. He needed glasses to compensate for one weak eye.*

MAY 1,'15 — ELBERT HUBBARD ON LUSITANIA 3463-5

■ *Period photo of Chicago, Illinois, traffic on May 17, 1920 at northside of Michigan Avenue Bridge. Left, Elbert Hubbard on board the Lusitania in 1915. Mr. Armstrong met the famed philosopher on several occasions. Right, a photo that Herbert Armstrong sent to his mother shortly before the flash depression of 1920.*

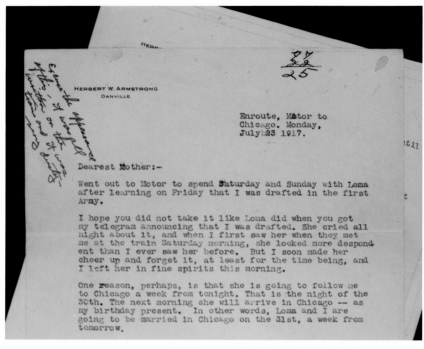

HERBERT W. ARMSTRONG
DANVILLE

Enroute, Motor to
Chicago. Monday,
July 23 1917.

Dearest Mother:-

Went out to Motor to spend Saturday and Sunday with Loma
after learning on Friday that I was drafted in the first
Army.

I hope you did not take it like Loma did when you got
my telegram announcing that I was drafted. She cried all
night about it, and when I first saw her when they met
me at the train Saturday morning, she looked more despond-
ent than I ever saw her before. But I soon made her
cheer up and forget it, at least for the time being, and
I left her in fine spirits this morning.

One reason, perhaps, is that she is going to follow me
to Chicago a week from tonight. That is the night of the
30th. The next morning she will arrive in Chicago -- as
my birthday present. In other words, Loma and I are
going to be married in Chicago on the 31st, a week from
tomorrow.

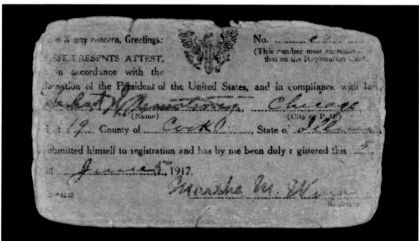

■ *Above is a reproduction of a letter from Mr. Armstrong to his mother written en route to Chicago July 23, 1917. Mr. Armstrong expected to be drafted at any moment. Front of draft card, with the signature that became known to millions.*

■ *Above, in front of Del Prado Hotel, Chicago, at age 24. Center, Mr. Armstrong and friend, Ralph Johnson, again in front of Hotel Del Prado—expecting to be drafted. Below, Herbert W. Armstrong in Motor, Iowa, his home state. Iowa, then as now, is in the heart of the corn belt and possesses the deepest and richest farm soil in the whole of the United States.*

■ *Above, Loma Isabelle Dillon (left) and her sister Edith when they were small children. Left, the family of Loma Dillon in the mid 1890s: her mother holds younger sister Edith; her father provides her back support in this photo that Mr. Armstrong came later to treasure. Right, Miss Loma Dillon sometime before Herbert W. Armstrong first met her.*

■ *Miss Loma Dillon beside pool in front of apartment building in Des Moines where she* *was overnight guest of the Frank Armstrong family. Left, Loma Dillon shortly before Herbert Armstrong* *met her. Right, Loma wearing her sister's coat which proved too large.*

■ *Herbert W.
Armstrong and
Loma Isabelle
Dillon, a vivacious
cousin, during one
of his Iowa visits in
his early to mid
twenties.*

■ *Readers will find this photo a fascinating study in the trends in swimwear. It would be better to label these garments "bathing suits" in the literal sense, as one could hardly swim effectively wearing them. On the beach of Lake Michigan, at the end of Wilson Avenue, just after honeymoon trip. In Chicago the Armstrongs lived one and a half blocks from the lake.*

■ *Top photo shows country store in Motor, Iowa. In upper right room Herbert Armstrong became engaged to Miss Dillon. Center, Loma Isabelle Dillon in Jackson Park on the morning of her marriage to Herbert W. Armstrong. Below, Loma Dillon at the time of her marriage in July 1917. She always thought of herself as a country girl.*

■ *Loma Armstrong*
with her husband at
a sporting event.
The dress is typical
of the World War I
period.

THE NORTHWESTERN BANKER
CLIFFORD DE PUY, PUBLISHER
...KER BUILDING   DES MOINES, IOWA

... who seemed to ... came from
city folks. If ... tell me I have too much
confidence in people but I used to feel they
... were deserving of confidence unless it was
be proved to me they were not, but I am find
-ing now there is a great deal of difference
between the lives of the city and the
country people and I prefer the latter—

We received a letter from John and
Hazel Wright a few days ago. John has put
in his application for the Quaker Reconstruction
work in France. I called he is going to
leave Hazel with her folks and go. If Herb
ever has to enter service that is what I
want him to do and I would like to
go too only they wont ...

I had the most wonderful dream Sat.
night. I dreamed Herbert and I were
walking down Sheridan Road and suddenly
my attention was attracted by a solid
mass of stars (it was in the evening) in
the west, shaped like a large banner
they began to quiver and separate and
at last vanished. I called Herbert's attention
to them and as they vanished another
bunch appeared and vanished in the
same way I dreamed we stopped right
out in the street and looked at them

■ *Loma's dream letter. In this letter addressed to Mr. Armstrong's mother, Loma Armstrong relates the remarkable incident of her and her husband's calling.*

■ *Top, Bertha Dillon, wife of Walter Dillon. Left, Herbert Armstrong, age 30, on the family farm. Loma Armstrong, right, and Herbert Armstrong both in their later twenties, in photo taken the Sunday before their first baby was born.*

■ *Herbert and Loma Armstrong during their early days together. Herbert Armstrong,* *though born in a small Iowa town, was by nature a child of the city and his intense artistic and* *cultural interests were reflected in his later work.*

heat of indignation and emotion, and let it fly Billy Sunday style—to start a big controversy—well, either the judges will like YOUR kind of oration, or the other kind. You have one chance in two. If they like the other kind, you lose out—you'll be voted *last place*. Then they have to choose among the other five. But if they do like your style, there is no one to choose but YOU—you'll be the only contestant with that kind of oration. So, I figure you will be either first or last. You will not be second or third."

"Say! That sounds good!" exclaimed Walter. "I don't want to be second or third. I want to WIN. If I can't win, I might just as well be last."

What to Attack?

"O.K. Now we must find something to attack and expose—something that is wrong. Something that will stir up the people. What do you hate the most?"

He didn't seem to hate anything or anybody. There was nothing I could find that he was really MAD at.

"Well," I said finally, "we'll have to find something that needs exposing—something you can really flay with forceful language. Come to think of it, right now labor leaders are resorting to some very foul practices. There have been murders, and gross injustices, both against employers and against the union members themselves. I remember when I visited Elbert Hubbard at his Roycroft Inn, at East Aurora, New York, I read a pamphlet of his that really flayed dishonest labor leaders—and he has the best, most prolific vocabulary, and the most effective rhetorical bromides of any writer I know. Suppose we attack labor racketeering."

He didn't know anything about it, but he guessed this subject would be as good as any. Immediately we wrote to Roycroft Inn for this booklet I had read. Also we wrote to Governor Allen of Kansas, who had just been on a fiery debate on labor-leader racketeering that had made national headlines.

The Herrin, Illinois massacre had occurred shortly prior to this—where many had been killed. We went all out to obtain FACTS on how labor leaders (some of them) were racketeering off of their own worker members. Walter explained to me that we were allowed to use a total of 200 words in the 2,000-word oration directly quoted from published sources. We quoted some of the most forceful phrases from Hubbard and Governor Allen.

We did not attack or oppose the PRINCIPLE of unionism. The first line of the oration stated, in the somewhat flowery language which Walter insisted on putting into it against my advice: "There was a time when the laboring man was brutalized by toil. Capital held the balance of power. Labor was cowed into meek submission."

What was opposed and exposed was the wrong economic philosophy of labor leaders who assumed that management is the enemy of labor—that the two interests run in opposite directions—that laboring men ought to use force and the strike to GET all they can, while at the same time they ought to "lay down on the job" and give in return as *little* as they could. The threat of calling a strike for blackmail purposes—asking a huge payoff from an employer to a crooked labor leader to prevent his stirring up the men for a strike—murders and violence—these things we opposed.

The First Course in Public Speaking

Now began my first real experience in public speaking. I had given talks before dinner groups of retail merchants

250

three times—at Richmond, Kentucky, at Lansing, Michigan, and Danville, Illinois, upon completion of merchandising surveys. But I had never *studied* public speaking, nor looked into any textbooks on the subject. Before this college oratory experience was over I was to become acquainted with the authors of the two textbooks on the subject used in most of the colleges and universities throughout America. As I now look back over the events of those formative years, in writing this autobiography, it becomes more and more evident that the unseen divine hand was guiding me continually into the very experience and training needed for the Great Calling.

After the oration was written, Walter memorized it. He announced that he was finally ready to begin practice on delivery. We went over to the college chapel at an hour when it was entirely unoccupied. I took a seat about two-thirds' way back. Walter went to the platform.

He started his oration. Consternation seized me. He was speaking it in his best attempt to emulate the prevailing college style—quiet, with dignity, and graceful gestures. Only, his gestures were *not* graceful. They were so obviously practiced, and not at all natural—and they were ridiculously awkward. The expression was not natural. I saw visions of "winning" last place in the contest.

This was a dilemma that had, somehow, to be solved. I saw at once that Walter did not grasp the real meaning of his shockingly powerful speech. He didn't *feel* it. This labor racketeering crisis then so prominently on front page news was something of which he seemed unaware. The oration was just so many meaningless words. Unless he could become aware of the situation, and really *feel* with white-heat indignation

251

the scathing indictment of these criminal abuses of unionism, he had no chance of winning.

What to do?

An Incident Makes It Personal

At just this time a living incident made the whole meaning of the oration *personal*. A strike was in progress at the Rock Island Railroad division point in Valley Junction—now renamed West Des Moines. The morning Des Moines *Register* reported a bombing of the locomotive roundhouse. Eleven big locomotives had been destroyed.

We went to Valley Junction, and managed to get through the lines to the office of the superintendent. The superintendent showed great interest in learning of the subject of the oration. He gave us considerable time. We went out through the roundhouse. We saw the twisted and tangled masses of steel of demolished locomotives.

We visited a home in town where the front half of the house had been blown off by a bomb. Inside the house at the time had been the wife and children of a worker who had taken up the tools the union men had laid down. For some little time the workmen who had accepted jobs after the union men had walked out had been kept behind barricaded walls day and night. Violence had become rampant. Nonunion workers had been assaulted upon leaving the yards and returning to their homes after working hours—hence they had been forced to remain behind defense barriers night and day.

Walter was now really outraged.

"When union leaders try to kill innocent wives and children just because their husbands have picked up the tools they laid down, that is just too much!" he exclaimed with heat.

252

Another nonunion home—occupied only by the innocent wife and children—had been rotten-egged.

Back in the superintendent's office he told us one of his problems with the union leaders.

"I was powerless to hire or fire a man without consent of labor leaders," he said. "In the railroad business it is just as serious a crime for an engineer to go to sleep in his cab as for a sentry to go to sleep on duty in the army in wartime. I had such a man. I tried to fire him. The labor leader refused. He said I did not have proof. I had to employ a professional photographer, and keep him here on the job constantly until this engineer went to sleep again on duty in his cab. When we presented the photographic evidence to union officials higher up, they finally consented to firing the man."

The next afternoon at the usual time we went into the college chapel for rehearsal. As Walter began speaking, the words of his oration for the first time conveyed real meaning to his mind. These words described in dynamic language exactly the way he now *felt*. I had told him to dispense with all gestures immediately after that first rehearsal. Unless gestures are *natural*, automatic and unrealized by the speaker, they are not effective anyway.

But this time Walter was gesturing. He didn't know it—*but he was gesturing!* They were not the most smooth and polished gestures of the professional speaker—but THEY WERE TERRIFICALLY CONVINCING! Today Walter was really angry! As the words poured forth, their meaning more and more expressed the very indignation he felt. The delivery was a little raw and rough—it was somewhat amateurish—but it was POWERFUL and it was CONVINCING!

"There!" I exclaimed joyfully, when he had

253

finished, "HOLD IT!" Hold it right there! Just go into the contest exactly as you went into this rehearsal! Now you have a *chance*. Of course, the judges still may not like something so radically different from the established style of college oratory. But *now* you will be either last, or first!"

Comes the Final Contest

On the night of the local college oratorical contest, Walter drew last place. He was quite discouraged. He didn't know, then, that the last speaker always has the advantage. He was terribly nervous.

The two students rated the best were, of course, very good as college speakers. Theirs were the usual suave, smooth, flowery big words, delivered calmly with smooth and much-practiced graceful gestures. They were highly applauded. *This* year the students had high hopes of winning a state championship—which Simpson had not won for eight years.

Then Walter walked out on the platform for the final oration. He started out calmly but nervously. But after some six or eight minutes the words he was speaking took him right back to Valley Junction. He *forgot* the nervousness that had seized him at the beginning. He thought only of the outrageous injustices he had SEEN with his own eyes. And for the first time he had an audience to tell it to! He began to gesture. He began to pace back and forth on the platform. He shook his fist. He was in dead *earnest!* He really MEANT what he was saying—and HE WAS *SAYING SOME-THING!*

When he had finished, he knew he had lost—but at least he had gotten a message over to that audience! He had that much satisfaction.

The judges' decision was announced. First came the

254

third-place choice. It was one of the two supposed best orators. The other was announced as second. First place—Walter Dillon!

There was little applause. The two favorites had lost out to a green, nonfrat freshman! The judges had been *moved* by his speech. They had liked it. But the student body and faculty apparently disagreed.

In the days that followed there was only one topic of conversation on the campus—the merits or demerits of labor unionism. It became a heated controversy. The professor of economics took it up in class. He disagreed with Walter Dillon's economics. He favored the union brand of economics. Apparently he had slight socialist or Communist leanings.

One senior said to me, "I hope Dillon won't disgrace us in the state contest. We might have won this year, but now, with a green freshman representing us, we haven't a chance. Boy! but wasn't Sutton's oration good?"

"Yes," I rejoined. "It was smooth and well delivered. By the way, WHAT did he talk about? I can't seem to remember."

"Why—why—" stammered the student, "I—I can't seem to remember, either. But it certainly was a great oration!"

"Well, really, *was* it—if neither you nor I can remember a thing he said? Everyone in town seems to remember what Dillon said. He really stirred up a hornet's nest! Do you really think a speech is good if it doesn't say anything?" He went away somewhat angrily.

The State Contest

A short time later came the state contest. It was held that year at Central College, Pella, Iowa. There it was the same. Walter was very nervous. I walked with him over the campus grounds while the first few contestants were speaking. Once again he was last speaker.

Once again, after a calm and somewhat nervous start—not necessarily obvious to the audience—he *relived* the scenes of violence at Valley Junction. When he came to the Herrin massacre, the bombing of the Los Angeles *Times* plant, and the other outrages of violence covered in the oration, he really *lived* it! Again he paced the floor, shook his fists, rose to a crescendo of indignant and outraged POWER at the climax, then had real pleading in his voice in his final solution of these problems.

Again third place was announced first—then second. Again we knew he was either first or last. Finally the winner—Walter E. Dillon of Simpson!

Returning to the campus we witnessed a living example of the fickleness of public opinion. After winning the home contest Walter had been in disgrace. "It was just a fluke decision," most of the students said. A freshman had spoiled their chance of winning a state contest. Walter was avoided on the streets. He was shunned.

But now, he returned the conquering hero.

Simpson had won the state championship! Walter Dillon was the hero of the campus. It was the first time any freshman had won a state contest. This was NEWS. It even made the front page of the Chicago *Tribune!* He had bids to join fraternities. The professor of economics was out of town on vacation several days—until the reverse opinion on his economics subsided. For now the student body unanimously accepted Dillon's brand of labor economics!

Well, it had been an interesting participation in college activity for me. It helped restore shattered morale. I had helped WIN something. I had begun to study public speaking. I had gained invaluable *experience* in

256

speaking, which was later to be used. My brother-in-law had been deprived without a chance of his ambition to be one of FIVE to win all-state honors in basketball. But he had won the state championship in oratory, which he didn't have to share with anybody.

Walter Dillon continued in the field of education as a life profession, and, much later, he was to become the first president of Ambassador College, and its first instructor in public speaking.

Actually, our experiences in college oratory continued on another year. I promoted a number of entertainment programs in various towns in Warren County during the following year, with Walter billed as the headliner, and charging 25 cents and 35 cents admission. We brought in some comedy and singing talent from college. A year later, by early 1924, Walter Dillon was a smooth and finished public speaker. Following the national contest of that year, its sole judge, Professor Woolbert of the University of Illinois, author of a much-used college textbook on public speaking, heard him, and told me he probably would have given Mr. Dillon the national championship, had he been entered.

Doing Surveys Again

After the rest, and oratorical contest experience of the fall and winter of 1922-23, I realized I had to find something to do.

Once before, the reader will remember, when I was stranded without a dollar in Danville, Illinois, I had brought the merchandising survey experience to the rescue by selling a survey to the local newspaper. It had been highly successful for the newspaper, resulting in a big increase in advertising volume. Newspapers derive their revenue from the advertising.

257

At Danville, I had made one colossal mistake. Caught off guard when the business manager of the paper asked what my fee would be, I had set it at $50. It should have been $500.

Now the thought of entering upon a business of conducting surveys was uppermost in mind. My brother-in-law borrowed a car, and we drove to Ames, Iowa—seat of Iowa State College. The idea of the survey was quickly accepted by a Mr. Powers, who was owner or manager (or both) of the Ames *Daily Tribune*. This time the fee was $500. The price was accepted at once.

This time I put on a more thorough survey than the previous ones. Not only housewives in the town, but students and faculty members, and heads of departments at the college were interviewed. The newspaper put at my disposal a small car. I do not remember the make, but I believe it was smaller than a Ford. This enabled me to interview farmers in all directions.

The survey uncovered some peculiar and astonishing facts. About 75% or more of the day's shopping on school days was done after 4 p.m., when rush hour began in the stores. The women of Ames seemed to prefer doing their shopping when the college girls did theirs—after class hours.

As usual, most of the trade in some lines went to Des Moines, only 30 miles south, or to the mail order houses. I found out why. Interesting facts were uncovered about certain individual stores.

Curing a Sick Store

One department store, not the largest, and one of a small chain of three or four stores, about half or two-thirds owned by the local manager, came in for the most criticism. Women were satisfied with their stocks and styles, and also with their prices. The big complaint was on the salespeople.

"Why, I've stood waiting ten or fifteen minutes to be waited on," one typical customer said, "and then the clerk said they were out of the item I wanted, when I could see it in plain sight high up on a shelf. She just didn't want to reach up that high to get it down."

Women universally reported that the clerks never smiled. I learned it would be the most popular store in town if its sales force would be transformed into smiling, helpful, enthusiastic, wide-awake people anxious to please customers.

I gave a private confidential report to each store, which the newspaper did not see, in addition to the general report and summary which was supplied the newspaper. I distinctly remember the personal report I made to this particular department-store manager. The confidential report hit him personally right between the eyes. I had discovered that he underpaid his sales force. He never smiled at them. He maintained a secret spy system, spying on clerks. He was dumbfounded to hear from me that all his clerks were well aware of this.

"The whole thing is your fault, personally," I said. "But I can show you how to correct it and double the size of your business."

"Vell," he said at last, in a Scandinavian accent, "this is the hardest ting I have ever had to take in my life—but I guess ve can take it. Vhat do you advise me to do?"

"First, raise salaries—and in a rather dramatic manner."

"Vait!" he cut in. "Look! A store can only pay a certain percent of sales in salaries. I am paying them too high a percent already!"

"Yes, sure, I know that," I responded. "But the way to get the *percent* of sales paid in salaries down is to RAISE salaries, and get your sales force on their toes—happy—smiling. Then sales will double, and the percent paid in salaries will go down."

LOWERING Salaries by Raising Them

"Tell me how ve do it," he said dubiously.

"All right, here's what I want you to do. I DON'T want you to do any additional advertising in the *Tribune* at all—until this new system has been working for at least six weeks. Big-space advertising right now would ruin your business. But, once you get this thing corrected, big-space advertising will quickly double your sales volume. First, I want you to plan a big party for the sales force. Have it on your second floor, in the women's ready-to-wear section. Try to arrange for the Home Ec. Department out at the college to prepare the biggest and finest dinner you ever saw. Hire a dance band. Don't try to beat down the cost—pay what it costs to get the BEST. Then invite all your employees. Let them know you expect them to be there. I think I can pass the word along through some of them, so they will all come. I have made friends with some of them.

"After they have had the finest dinner they ever ate, and the dance band has them feeling good—and have all these dunce caps, noisemakers, confetti to throw—everything to get them into the most gay mood—then rise and make a speech. Start out by telling them you have been making a big mistake. You have not treated them right, and they have not treated customers right—but you never realized it before, and probably they didn't either. Then tell them immediately that you are announcing a substantial raise in salaries for EVERYBODY. Tell them that from now on THEY MUST SMILE while waiting on customers. They must be *alert*. You intend to treat *them* right from now on, and they *must* treat customers right—or you'll get salespeople who will. You'll probably be paying the highest salaries in town. THEY HAVE TO SELL ENOUGH GOODS TO EARN IT—at a *lower* percent of sales than present salaries! If they don't, your high salaries will attract the best salespeople, and those who do not respond will be fired."

He said he would do it if I would come to the party, and sit by his side to bolster him up, and make a speech myself.

The party was held. It had an electric effect.

"Now," I said to the manager, "hereafter you must personally stand by the front door between 4 and 6 each afternoon, greeting customers yourself with a smile, and being sure they are promptly waited on."

Winning With a Smile

Next afternoon about 4:15 I dropped in. There he was, trying to bow and smile stiffly at incoming customers. Quickly I drew him to one side.

"No, NO!" I exclaimed. "That will never do! You are acting like you never smiled before—like your heart is not in it. LOOK at those fine people coming in here. THEY ARE CUSTOMERS! They are coming to SPEND MONEY with you. DON'T YOU LIKE THEM?"

He did, but he had never thought of them in that light before. With a little coaching, he began to realize how much he did LIKE these people. He began to smile a natural smile, like he *meant* it!

After six weeks, this store began really BIG-space advertising, with the slogans I had suggested— something like "MOST PROMPT AND INTERESTED SERVICE IN AMES." Or, "Where, you receive quick, attentive, interested SERVICE WITH A SMILE!"

I heard later from traveling salesmen who made Ames regularly that this store had more than doubled its sales volume in six months. Also an Ames shoe store, which had come in for some special criticism and correction. The newspaper DOUBLED its advertising volume.

That was my kind of salesmanship. The newspaper paid a fee of $500, and doubled the size of its business. The merchants found what was wrong with them, and doubled their business. The customers got better service, and were happy. EVERYBODY benefitted! Unless everybody *does* benefit, salesmanship is not honest! But not many salesmen know that, or the secret of intelligent and PRACTICAL salesmanship!

Important Job Offered

Next I went to Forrest Geneva, then advertising manager of both the Des Moines *Register* and the *Evening Tribune.* He had worked in want ads on the *Register* at the same time I did on the *Capital,* and we were old friends.

The Des Moines *Register* was rated (I think still is) one of the ten really great newspapers of the United States. It has a state-wide circulation, and is delivered in nearly all parts of the state early the same morning of publication.

BUT the *Register* was not getting the big department store advertising in Des Moines. This is the biggest part of the advertising revenue of any newspaper. It actually meant multiple millions of dollars to the *Register* to be able to carry the big-space store advertising.

"Forrest," I said, "the one most important thing in this world to the *Register* is to be able to crack through the barrier and carry the department store business—

262

and all the other larger stores. I CAN DO THE JOB FOR YOU.
I can crack down that stone wall and get you the
big-store business."

After I had explained in detail the method of the
surveys, and how I proposed a state-wide survey, to
show how the Des Moines stores already were drawing a
tremendous volume of trade from local stores in other
smaller towns and cities all over the state, and how a
campaign in the *Register,* with its STATE-WIDE circulation, which was tremendous, would greatly increase
their out-of-town business as well as the Des Moines
business, Mr. Geneva expressed his confidence that my
method would accomplish the result. Only one
dominant morning newspaper, as I remember, in all U.S.
major cities, was carrying the local department store
advertising. That was the Chicago *Tribune.*

"Herb," he said, "I believe you have the idea that
will do the job. Give me a few days to take this up with
the officers higher up. I'm really enthusiastic over the
idea."

A few days later I returned.

"We want you," said Mr. Geneva. "But we have run
into a certain situation. As you know, I am advertising
manager over both papers. We also have an advertising
manager for each paper, under me. Right now we have
no advertising manager for the *Register.* I cannot get the
management to approve the addition at this time of
both a new advertising manager and you as a special
expert. They want you to fill BOTH jobs."

"But Forrest," I protested, "I would be tied down
with the executive job of managing the work of your
eight advertising solicitors on the *Register,* besides all
the specialized work of the survey."

"Right," we agreed.

"But that will kill everything. I am not an

263

executive. I can't manage the work of others. I'm like a lone wolf. I have to do my own work in my own way. I often work in streaks. When I'm *'on'* I know I'm good. But on the *'off'* days I couldn't sell genuine gold bricks for a dime. I'd have daily reports to make out, and that's one thing I just never have been able to do. I'd get way behind on the reports."

"Look, Herb," he came back. "I know you *will* make good on the executive job. I won't *let* you fail. If you run into a lapse, or your reports are not in, I'll stay down myself evenings and do that part of your work for you. No one will ever know."

But I had no confidence in my ability to direct the work of eight men, and make out daily reports. So I turned down the offer to become advertising manager of a great newspaper.

I was to learn much later, beginning with 1947 when Ambassador College was founded, that I could become an executive and direct the operations and work of many hundreds of employees, besides doing about seven men's jobs myself. And long before that I learned to overcome lapses and streaks. But, had I taken that job I might be there today—an employee on a newspaper, instead of directing the most important activity on earth. We might have averted several following years of financial hardship. But I know now, in the light of events—"the FRUITS," that I was being prepared for this Work and was being brought down to the depths of defeat and frustration until I would give up the false god of seeking status out of vanity.

We Migrate to Oregon

The remainder of that summer, and through the following winter, I put on a survey for a local weekly paper in Indianola, and worked part time writing advertising for local merchants. But most of the time was devoted to working with my brother-in-law on his oratory. We wrote a new oration for the following year, which involved many experiences, although, having won, he was not eligible to enter again at Simpson College.

I was beginning to bog down in the mire. My wife was worried. We were in a rut. I didn't seem to be selling more surveys to daily newspapers. Mrs. Armstrong knew we needed some change to jolt us out of the rut. My parents were living in Salem, Oregon. A complete change of environment might get me started again.

In the late winter of 1923-24, she began to suggest the idea of a summer trip to visit my parents and family in Oregon. "But, Loma," I protested, "we can't afford a vacation trip like that."

But, she had it all planned. We would go in Walter's Model T Ford. We would take a tent and camp out nights. We would prepare our own food, avoiding restaurant costs. She would ask her sister Bertha to go along, paying her share, thus helping enough with expenses to make the trip possible. Bertha was teaching school, and had a regular income. I had earned some money and we still had a little. Along the way, I would contact newspapers and line up surveys for the future—thus getting a foundation laid for a future business.

My wife knew I liked to travel. I had been over most of the United States, but never yet as far west as the Rocky Mountains. A trip to the coast—seeing my parents and family again—was really intriguing.

Walter and Bertha were swayed by her persuasion.

In the meantime, about March 1, 1923, my father-in-law had moved from the farm he was renting from a brother-in-law, sold his stock, and bought a small-town general store at Sandyville, only a few miles distant.

I began to make preparations for our trip. On the second floor above my father-in-law's store was a sort of cabinet-making shop. I had taken manual training in high school. So I began to work out a design and to make folding wooden cots and canvas tops for our trip. Later we purchased a used tent of the type that fastened over the top of the car, so that the car formed one end of the tent. We procured a secondhand portable gasoline stove.

"D"-Day Arrives

The morning of June 16, 1924, we piled the two seats of the Model T high with bedding. We put our suitcases between the front fenders and the hood. The folded tent, boxes of food, the rest of the bedding, the folded cots, the portable stove, and all the rest of our earthly belongings were piled on a rack on the left running board high up on the side of the car. There were no trunks on the rear of Model T's.

How we piled all this stuff on that little car I can't conceive now, but we did—and an extra spare tire or two besides!

I had said to a friend of my wife, previously, "We'll be back in the fall." But when I wasn't listening, my wife told her: "That's what *he* thinks—but we are *not coming back!*"

So, "D-Day" had arrived, the morning of June 16, 1924! ("D" for Departure.) Walter cranked up the Model T, and we were off for Oregon. One thing we had on the car was air-conditioning. Except for the luggage piled high up the left side, it was *all* air—open air. The closed cars, except for very expensive limousines, had not yet come out of Detroit. But we had side curtains to button up in case of rain.

In case of RAIN, did I say?

Yes, as, unhappily, we were to experience that very night! We had reached Greenwood, Iowa, the first day out, and pitched our tent beside the car—with Mrs. Armstrong and me, our two little daughters—Beverly, age 6, and Dorothy Jane, age almost 4—Walter and Bertha Dillon—all trying to sleep on those flimsy, swaying folding cots I had made.

And then *the rains came!* We soon discovered the tent leaked! Hurriedly we arose from our rickety cots, delved into the food and utensil box, procured our one wash pan and a fry pan and a stew pan, to catch the leaking drips. There was little sleep. In Iowa, you know, there are sharp and blinding flashes of lightning, followed by deafening claps of thunder when it rains.

For three days and three nights we were marooned there. In those days there were no cross-country paved highways. We were traveling on Iowa mud roads.

Tent Cities — No Motels

Finally, we decided to make a try over the still muddy roads. A *try* is what we made. Just outside town the car skidded in the mud, and two wheels bogged down hub-deep. Walter and I started out slogging through the mud to the nearest farm house. An obliging farmer hitched up a team and pulled us out.

We managed to keep chugging along until we reached Silver City, Iowa, near Council Bluffs. Later, as we proceeded farther west, we found roads more gravel than mud. Once on dry roads we were able to amble along at a steady gait of between 18 and 20 miles per hour—when we were not stopped by some new trouble, which was much of the time.

Most days we awoke by 5 a.m., breakfasted, the women made sandwiches for noon lunch—there could be no stopping through the day—we packed everything back on the car, and climbed up on those bedding-covered seats with the car cranked up by 6 a.m.

Most days we drove until nearly dark—allowing time to get the tent pitched and staked, cots and bedding arranged, and dinner cooked before it became too dark to see. We did carry a kerosene lantern. Walter and I took turns driving. We generally managed to negotiate about 200 miles in a twelve or fourteen hour day of driving.

At night we stopped at camp grounds, provided at every town in those days. That was before the days of motels or trailer-camps. Tourists all carried their own tents and camping equipment. Every town along the way had its tent city which usually filled up by sundown. These camps provided water and sanitary facilities—of a kind. As we journeyed farther west a few cabins began to appear at some of the camp grounds. These were bare one-room, unpainted board cabins. Some had rickety old beds and metal springs—but not mattresses or bedding or linen, and little, if any furniture. There might have been an old wooden chair.

Our first stop after leaving Greenwood was Silver City, Iowa. My wife's uncle, Tom Talboy, owned a drugstore in Silver City. We drove to the store.

Visiting Relatives

"I don't know which one you are," said her Uncle Tom approaching my wife, "but I do know you're a Talboy!"

Mrs. Armstrong's mother was Isabelle Talboy before marriage. There are definite "Talboy" characteristics, and Mrs. Armstrong has them written all over her face. The Talboy family came from England. My wife's great-grandfather, Thomas Talboy, came to the United States from England somewhere near the middle of the 19th century, and started the first woolen mill in the Middle West—at least west of the Mississippi—in Palmyra, Iowa. At that time Palmyra was larger than Des Moines. There was no Des Moines—except Ft. Des Moines. The woolen mill grew and the town grew with it. But today there is no Palmyra—except a few farmhouses.

My wife's grandfather, Benjamin Talboy, was a lad of 18 when he came from England with his father, Thomas. He and his wife, Martha, whom my wife as a little girl called "little curly-haired Grandma," reared a sizeable and successful family of nine, of whom Isabelle was one of three daughters. "Uncle Tom," the druggist, as my wife called him, was named for his grandfather Thomas.

We visited the "Uncle Tom" family for a day. Grandpa Benjamin Talboy was living there, age 93. "Little curly-haired Grandma" had died at 84. She had always warned my wife against Grandpa Benjamin. He, she affirmed solemnly, was an atheist. My wife warned me against listening to him. But later we learned that he had dared to look into the Bible for himself, and, discovering these teachings diametrically contrary to the accepted popular version of "Christianity," had rejected the "Christianity." Later we learned that he was probably more of a true Christian, in *belief* if not in deeds, than his well-meaning little wife!

Our Troubles Continue!

We continued our journey westward from Silver City.

At Fremont, Nebraska, I took out time to contact the daily newspaper office. Another survey was tentatively lined up for the fall, on our return. But this newspaper call consumed a half day, and we decided not to take out any more time for newspaper calls along the way. Everybody aboard was anxious to reach Oregon.

It was at about this juncture that our tire troubles began. These tire troubles seemed to multiply, the farther we traveled. They were an excellent training in patience! We had puncture after puncture—blowout after blowout. There were eight of them within one mile on one occasion! We carried a repair kit and patched our own inner tubes. We carried along a few "boots" to plug up blowout holes in casings. Many hours were spent along the drab, dusty roadsides, one wheel jacked up, kneeling beside it, fixing tires.

We bought several used tires—we could not afford new ones—and these usually blew out about five miles out of town—just too far to go back and express our minds to the dealer who sold them!

We made an overnight stop in Central City, Nebraska, at the home of my uncle Rollin R. Wright. His son, John, was one of the two cousins (on my mother's side of the family) I had visited so often as a boy. The Wrights had then lived at Carlisle, Iowa, where my uncle Rollin was an insurance agent. He is the one who gave me and "Johnny" a good sound spanking that time when he caught us shooting off a .22 revolver. John was, within a day, one year younger than I. Now the Wrights were operating a dairy in Central City. It is always somewhat exciting to visit relatives you have not seen for several years. Next morning I went on the milk route with John. Today he is a minister in the Friends Church and has visited us a few times in Pasadena.

It seems we got as far as Grand Island, Nebraska, before our next vexation. We had made a temporary stop under shade trees because of the intense heat.

270

Little Dorothy Jane, almost four, took off one of her shoes and laid it on the right running board, from where it fell to the ground. The loss was not discovered until we had traveled too far to return to search for it. The child had to travel the remaining days of our journey with only one shoe. To buy new shoes on this trip was not within our means.

We made an overnight stop in Ogalalla, where I had intended to visit the other of these two cousins I had grown up with—Bert Morrow. He had been running some tourist cabins there, but had moved before our arrival.

It was somewhere along western Nebraska that we encountered something worse than a rainstorm. A driving sandstorm came up. The road became so clouded we could not see to drive. We had to pull over to the side of the road, button up the curtains on the Model-T, cover our heads with bedding to keep sand out of our hair, and remain marooned there until the storm subsided.

15

Launching a New Business

I SHALL never forget my first view of the Rocky Mountains from a distance. While I had traveled the Alleghenies and the Blue Mountains in the east, I had never seen any really high mountains. I had always wondered what they would look like. They seemed very lofty and awe-inspiring to me.

We drove several miles out of our way in order to dip down into the state of Colorado, before we entered Wyoming. We wanted to be able to say we had been in that state. At Cheyenne we drove up hill to the north end of town to the largest camp we had seen.

But by this time all my hand-made wooden folding cots had broken down, and the canvas tops had split down the middle. We threw them away. From Cheyenne on, we slept on the ground.

In the higher altitudes the nights became so cold we were forced to spread the bed covers on the ground

272

inside the tent, making one long bed. All six of us lined up side by side in that one bed on the ground, to keep each other warm.

At Evanston, Wyoming, the car broke down. We were detained there 1½ days while it was fixed in a garage.

During our journey across Wyoming, Dorothy's arm was bitten by a spider. It swelled up, and she was taken to a doctor. It must have been about this time that we had to telegraph my father to wire us additional funds. We had run out of food, gasoline, and money. Dorothy's arm had to be soaked in hot epsom-salts water, and held high continually. Mrs. Armstrong, Bertha, and I had to take turns, on one day's driving, holding that arm, lest it hang down.

We stopped off one full day in Salt Lake City. Walter and I played some tennis on public courts near the camping grounds—we were carrying our tennis rackets with us. We took the guided tour around the Mormon grounds and through the Tabernacle.

Premonition of Danger

At Weiser, Idaho, we visited a day and a half with the families of two of my wife's uncles, Benjamin and Walter Talboy. Walter later held a high government position in Idaho, and once ran for governor.

Leaving Weiser in the late afternoon, we were winding around the "figure eight" sharp curves of the highway following the course of the Snake River. Suddenly, my wife cried out:

"I'm *afraid* to go further! For the past hour I've been having a terrible premonition of danger! I can't explain it—but I just can't keep it to myself any longer."

"That's strange," exclaimed Walter. "I didn't want

273

to say anything—but I've been fighting off the same feeling."

That was enough for all of us. It seemed foolish, in a way. Yet we were afraid to go on. We turned back toward Weiser.

"I'm simply too nervous to drive any further," explained Walt. I took over the wheel. Just before entering Weiser, on a short down-hill slope, I made the horrifying discovery that our brakes had gone out! There were no brakes. There was no reverse! I drove the car into a garage. We were kept one more night at the Talboy relatives in Weiser. Had we not heeded those premonitions, we might have been killed crashing down steep mountain grades around sharp curves without brakes. Later we learned that at the precise hour my wife and Walter had been having their premonitions, my mother in Salem, Oregon, was also disturbed by a terrible premonition concerning our safety. It had grown so strong on her she was forced to remove her hands from the dishwater, and go to a bedroom to pray for our safety! I do not try to explain this. I am merely recording what actually happened!

At Last — We Arrive

Finally, July 3, we made our last homestretch lap from Pendleton, Oregon. That was a long day's drive in a Model T. But that night, after dark, we arrived at my father's home in Salem, Oregon, on the eve of July 4.

We had been 18 days on the way. It was fast traveling compared to the covered wagon days. Yet, today you can travel from New York to Los Angeles—coast to coast—in 4½ hours, by scheduled passenger JET plane! Allowing for the time difference, if I leave New York at 5 in the evening, after a full day of business conferences with radio stations and our

274

overseas advertising agents, I can arrive in Los Angeles about 6:30 the same evening!

Few people realize the rapid pace at which this world is traveling today—toward its own DESTRUCTION! It is time we slow down to realize HOW FAR this machine age—atomic age—space age has plummeted us in these few short years since 1924!

My Father Had Grown Up!

I had not seen my father, my youngest brother Dwight, or my sister Mary, for twelve years! Dwight and his twin sister Mary had been eight years old when they moved to the west. Now they were twenty.

But the biggest change of all was in my father. In 1912, when I was only twenty, I had felt rather sorry for my father. At that time I knew so much more than he! But I was simply amazed at how much my father had learned in those 12 years. It seems most young men know more than Dad, but they grow out of it later. I could see, now, that he knew more than I! Now I had to look up to my father with respect!

He had a nice home which he had planned and built. It was paid for. He didn't owe any man a cent. He had a comfortable salary as a heating engineer. When we found ourselves out of money on the way out—buying extra tires and such things—he had immediately wired me $200.

How many young men, getting to "know it all" from age 16 to 20, have to wait until in their middle thirties to learn how much they ought to respect their fathers! And my father was a GOOD man. He never smoked. He never drank, never used profanity. He never took advantage of another man! I honor and respect his memory. He died in April, 1933, in his 70th year.

After a few weeks' visit with my folks, we drove to

Portland to visit my wife's "Uncle Dick" Talboy, an attorney. Our elder son, Richard David, was named after him. He was an Oregon pioneer, having migrated from Iowa first in 1905. He attended Stanford University in California in 1906 and 1907. He returned to Des Moines to finish his law course at Drake University in 1907, returning to Oregon in 1913. It has been his home ever since.

The very next day Mr. Talboy had to transact some legal business at the courthouse in Vancouver, Washington—just across the interstate bridge from Portland. He invited me to go along. I had not yet been in the state of Washington, and was anxious to add one more state to my list.

Just as we emerged from the bridge, in Vancouver, I saw the plant of the local daily newspaper, *The Columbian.*

Another Survey

I asked if I might not hop out right there and contact the newspaper regarding a survey while Mr. Talboy went on to the Court House.

The owner and editor was on a vacation at Seaside, but the Business Manager, Samuel T. Hopkins—who was later to become a business partner of mine—was in. Enthusiastic over the survey idea, he felt sure Mr. Herbert Campbell, the owner, would be interested on his return. I said I would call back the following week. We were welcome to remain and visit at the home of my wife's uncle. The following week, I found Mr. Campbell as interested in the survey idea as Mr. Hopkins.

"I have only one objection," he said. "I believe it is going to take a man of your specialized merchandising and advertising experience to follow it up and make it pay. We have no such man here. Now what I want to

276

know is, can a newspaper of our size afford to employ a man of your experience and ability permanently?"

Here was a ludicrous paradox.

Here I was, down and out financially, my clothes now threadbare. And here was a newspaper publisher asking if he could afford to employ me! Yet I *had* had a training and specialized experience such as comes to few men. I had taken a severe beating by the Chicago debacle, but I still had the cocky and confident manner. I spoke with a tone of knowing what I was talking about. Evidently this impressed Mr. Campbell sufficiently that he did not notice my rather run-down appearance.

The answer came like a flash.

"No, you cannot!" I said positively.

This was a challenge. Herbert Campbell was cocky, too!

"Well, *I think we CAN!* How much is it going to cost us?"

I had to think fast. Was I going to turn down a survey, because I felt too important to take a permanent job on a small city newspaper? I made a quick compromise proposition.

"Tell you what I'll do," I shot back. "I'll put on the survey for a flat fee of $500. That will take a week or ten days. Then I will stay on your staff as a merchandising specialist for six months *only,* at a salary of $100 per week. Take it or leave it!"

"O.K. I'll take it," he snapped. I had my wife's uncle draw up a legal contract, which he signed a day or so later.

I rented a house in Vancouver, and started on the survey.

Pulling a Clothier Out of the Red

About the time we started on the survey in Vancouver,

Walter and Bertha Dillon, my wife's brother and sister started in the Model T their return trip to Iowa; Walter to enter his Junior year at Simpson College, and Bertha for another year of school teaching.

This time Mrs. Armstrong took part in the survey, and proved very adept at eliciting confidential information from housewives of their attitudes and feelings toward Vancouver stores.

The survey soon was completed, together with a complete typed summary of all data, interviews, and tabulations of statistics, as well as an analysis of conditions and recommendations.

With this data, I began counselling with merchants about individual merchandising problems.

One clothing store, for example, was running in the red. The owner asked if I could help him. I insisted on full access to his books and all information. Finally he consented.

The survey had uncovered special facts about customer attitude toward this store. One line this store carried was Hart Schaffner & Marx clothes. I knew that this firm was prepared to extend considerable dealer-help. At my request they sent a qualified representative to counsel with me and this merchant.

A new policy was inaugurated. Certain changes were made. Until now this store had not carried the more snappy styles *young* men liked. The owner, past middle age, had bought the older men's styles of his personal liking. I induced him to trust the Hart Schaffner & Marx representative fully with selections in ordering.

Also I recommended that he stock in addition snappiest young men's styles in a less expensive line.

Then we began a big-space advertising campaign in

the *Columbian.* I wrote and laid out all his ads. I induced him to spend 7% of sales in this advertising campaign.

"But," he protested, "You have shown me that Harvard Bureau of Business Research figures show that no retail clothing store ought to spend more than 4% for advertising."

"That's right," I explained, "but this big-space advertising will quickly build up your volume. The amount, in dollars, spent in advertising will remain the same. But, as sales volume increases, the advertising expenditure will become an increasingly *smaller percentage* of sales." Also I explained to him it might take six months before his total expenditures would go below his total income, and his books would get out of the red.

It took a lot of courage. But it was a matter of accept my program or go bankrupt. He finally agreed.

It did take about six months. Twice before that time he lost his nerve and wanted to quit. Twice more I talked him into staying with it. At the end of six months his business was showing a profit. The sales continued to increase. So did his merchandising turnover. And likewise his profits. Finally he was able to sell his store at a substantial profit.

Discovering a New Business Potential

Soon I became virtually advertising manager for a leading hardware store, the largest department-drug store, a furniture store, a jewelry store, a dry-goods store, and others.

But my most important client turned out to be the local laundry. The general survey had brought out some startling facts about the laundry situation. I wanted more facts. So a further separate survey was made to get the facts and more definitely learn customer-attitude toward laundries.

I found that very few housewives entrusted their family wash to the laundry. We unearthed many suspicions. Many women assured me that laundries use harsh acids and chemicals which ruin clothes. This, I soon found, was not true.

"They shrink clothes," said scores and scores of women.

"They fade colored things," women assured me.

"How do you *know?*" both Mrs. Armstrong and I began asking women we interviewed. "Has the laundry ruined *your* things—have *your* colored clothes been faded or your woolens shrunk?"

"Oh mercy, NO!" they would reply. "Why, I would never *think* of sending *my* things to the laundry."

"Then how do you *know* the laundry mistreats things in this manner?" we would ask.

"Oh, I just *know!* Why, *everybody* knows how terrible laundries are on clothes," would come the confident answer.

Scores of women said laundries would *lose* things and refuse to make good the losses. "The laundries will *never* make an adjustment or settle a claim," women assured us.

We found dozens of things wrong with the laundries—in the public mind.

Then I investigated conditions at the Vancouver Laundry, owned by a man of my name, J. J. C. Armstrong, no relation. Actually, I found that conditions were precisely the *opposite* of the general public conception.

The laundry washed clothes with a neutral chip soap—I think that particular laundry used Palmolive, a gentle facial soap. To add alkaline strength, without injury to clothes, they used an expensive soap builder—a controlled alkali, which could not harm a baby's tenderest skin, could not injure sheerest silks or finest table linens, and yet possessed the strength to get greasiest overalls spotlessly clean. This harmless but effective soap builder was not available to consumers on the retail market. It was sold only in barrel quantities direct to laundries. It was the result of then recent and specialized scientific research, manufactured by one of the largest corporations in the laundry industry, a subsidiary of the Aluminum Corporation of America (ALCOA).

Through Mr. J. J. C. Armstrong I met a laundry chemist, Robert H. Hughes, a special technical representative of this company, the Cowles Detergent Company of Cleveland, Ohio. Mr. Hughes explained to me the chemistry of laundering—why we use SOAP to wash our hands, faces, or clothes.

How Soap Cleans

It's a very fascinating story. Did you ever wonder what causes particles of dirt to cling to clothes—why clothes become soiled? Did you ever wonder how SOAP removes dirt?

I don't believe the truth will bore you. Briefly, this is the story:

Naturally, dirt would fall off clothes instead of attaching itself to cloth, were it nor for the fact that an *acid,* or oil or grease, even in slightest amount, is present. This acid holds the dirt to the cloth. Laundries *did not use acids,* as so many people seemed to believe. There is acid already present on the clothes, else they would not become soiled.

Chemically, matter is either acid, alkali or neutral. These are chemical opposites.

Soap is made from two substances—fatty acid (oil

281

or fat), and alkali. But alkali, if used alone, would injure and rot cloth. So in the soap factory the two substances, fatty acid and alkali, are mixed by a process called saponification. This converts the two into a *new substance,* which is neither acid nor alkali, but which we call SOAP.

If the soap be completely pure—a prominent soap used for faces and even babies is advertised as 99 and 44/100% pure—there is no free alkali in it. All the alkali has *combined* with the oil, tallow, or fat, and has been converted into soap. The alkaline content is now utterly harmless. Yet it has an alkaline action that will dissolve the acid that glues dirt to your skin or your clothes, so that the dirt is flushed off in the rinsing.

But a pure facial soap is not sufficiently alkaline to loosen the acid on badly soiled clothes. Therefore soap makers at the time of this story put a certain excess amount of alkali in the laundry soaps sold in stores to housewives. This excess alkali was called free alkali. It was not controlled, or neutralized, in the soap. Alkali is chemically a crystalline substance. In other words, it dilutes into and becomes part of the water. In clothes-washing, it soaks into the fiber meshes of the garment. Rinsing cannot remove it—it merely dilutes it. The *soap* and the *dirt* are flushed away in the rinsing—but the free alkali remains inside the fiber of the cloth. In the drying process it tends to eat or rot the cloth. It would even destroy shoe leather!

Now WHY does not a pure soap injure the cloth?

The answer is that, chemically, soap is a colloidal substance. In solution, or emulsion, it breaks up into thousands of tiny particles. But it does not become part of the water. Its thousands of minute particles discolor the water, float around *in* the water. In the agitation or rubbing of clothes-washing, the tiny soap particles are flushed *in between* the fiber meshes of the garment or cloth, but never soak *into* the fibers. They dissolve the acid, thus loosening the dirt. The agitation breaks up the dirt into tiny particles, loosened from the cloth. The tiny colloidal soap particles have a chemical affinity for the tiny dirt particles, which means the dirt particles *cling to* the soap particles. The rinsing flushes them away. Even if all the soap were not rinsed off, the alkali is not free but controlled by the soap, and could not eat or rot or harm the cloth.

This scientific soap builder sold by the Cowles Detergent Company contained great alkaline strength, but it was chemically in colloidal form, not crystalline, and the alkali was as completely controlled as in a 100% pure soap. Therefore it could not harm silks, woolens, or the sheerest, daintiest fabrics, although, it had the strength to wash clean the greasiest overalls. Also it restored colors, brought them out newer and sharper than before.

Since those days, however, there has been a complete revolution in the manufacture of clothes-washing detergents sold to housewives. Whether our big-space advertising of the *dangers* of the free-alkali laundry soaps to clothes then sold for home washing machines had bearing on it, I do not know.

But the chemists on the staffs of leading soap and detergent manufacturers have developed new synthetic detergents. Few housewives, if any, use soap in their home washing machines today. The first household synthetic detergent on the market was Dreft, produced by Proctor & Gamble, in 1933. Colgate came out with Vel later in the 30's. Since, there have been many developments in the field of synthetic detergents. They are not yet perfect or foolproof, but chemists have not yet exhausted the possibilities of improvement.

283

Our campaigns were in the early days of the home washing machine. These home washers were crude, compared to today's product. In our ads, and in special booklets, we "figured it out" and convinced many housewives it was less costly to send the family wash to the laundry.

A New Business Launched

I began to write big-space ads for this laundry. Armed with complete information of customer attitude and complete factual and scientific information about laundry processes, I was able to assure housewives that their sheerest, daintiest fabrics were actually SAFER at the laundry than in their own hands at home.

Soon these ads became an item of conversation among Vancouver women. It took time to dispel suspicions and build confidence. But gradually the laundry business began to increase.

Before this campaign, laundry business had consisted mainly of men's shirts, and hotel business. But now the family bundle business gradually began coming to the laundry.

I found that the laundry industry was twelfth in size among American industries—yet, in aggressive methods, and advertising and merchandising, it was the least "alive," and the most backward and undeveloped. I sensed, here, a tremendous field for a new advertising business.

I began to develop plans for a personalized, yet syndicated advertising service for leading laundries— one client in each city.

I learned that not all laundries were using as advanced methods as this Vancouver Laundry. Some laundries were still using as a soap builder plain caustic soda—free alkali. Some lacked efficiency methods of operation. Many *were* guilty of haggling with customers over claims of losses or injury, and of refusing to make losses good.

I had become closely acquainted with R. H. Hughes and his reputation among laundry owners as the leading laundry chemist and expert on production methods on the West Coast.

So, Mr. Hughes and I formed a partnership. As soon as my six months' tenure with the Vancouver *Columbian* expired, we set out to establish a new business as a merchandising and advertising service for leading laundries.

I moved my family to Portland.

I would start off every campaign with a local merchandising survey, to determine the *local* customer attitude. We would accept no client unless the laundry owner would give Mr. Hughes complete latitude and authority within his plant, to install the latest scientific methods and equipment, eliminate lost motion, and speed up efficiency.

I had to be able to make big claims in the advertising. The client had to be able to deliver what the ads promised. The client had to agree to settle every claim without a question—the customer was ALWAYS to be *right* in any complaint.

And Then . . . BANG!

The general appeal of the ads was syndicated—the same for all laundries. Yet certain factors peculiar to each local laundry were altered to comply with that particular client's conditions. We ran two large-space ads each week for each client.

The new business started with great promise. Soon we had as clients leading laundries in Eugene, Corvallis, Albany, Salem, McMinnville, Oregon City, and Portland, Oregon; and in Seattle, Spokane, Tacoma, Ellensburg, Walla Walla, Olympia, Centralia, Chehalis, and Vancouver, Washington.

In six months the business volume of some of these laundries doubled. Our advertising and merchandising service was winning big results for clients.

No matter how many clients we should acquire, I had only one general advertising IDEA to think up and write for the entire number. The new business promised to grow to be a national, universally used service.

This would mean, in another two or three years, an income larger than I had ever before contemplated. Already our fees were grossing close to $1,000 a month. They appeared to promise to rise between $50,000 and $100,000 per month within two or three more years. I began to see visions of a personal net income of $300,000 to a half million dollars a year!

And then—*the bottom fell out!*

And through no fault or cause of our making. There was one unusual condition peculiar to the laundry industry. They were highly organized in their Laundryowners National Association.

Some bright advertising man, in an advertising agency in Indianapolis, Indiana, put over on the Laundryowners National Association a $5,000,000 advertising campaign for the entire industry—the entire amount to be spent by this agency in the big-circulation national women's magazines, such as *Ladies' Home Journal, McCall's, Good Housekeeping,* etc. The campaign was to run three or more years. The Association was to pay for it by assessing each laundry-owner member within ½ of 1% of the maximum percent of sales volume a laundry could safely spend in advertising.

Every one of our customers was taxed by this

campaign up to the limit they could safely spend. They had no alternative except to cancel out all their own private local advertising. Our field was literally swept out from under our feet.

In Chicago I had built a publishers' representative business that brought me an income equivalent to well more than $50,000 a year or more before I was thirty. The flash depression of 1920 had swept away all my major clients, and with them my business.

Now, with a new business of much greater promise, all my clients were suddenly removed from possibility of access, through powers and forces entirely outside of my control.

It seemed, indeed, as if some INVISIBLE and MYSTERIOUS HAND were causing the earth to simply swallow up whatever business I started.

Reduced to Going Hungry

Soon every laundry client had been forced to drop all local advertising except one. I still had the account of one of the two largest laundries in Portland, running one ad a week in the Portland *Oregonian*. This supplied an income of $50 per month.

But $50 per month was not enough to pay house rent, and provide food and clothing for our family. We began to buy beans and such food as would provide maximum bulk and nourishment on minimum cost.

One time, a couple days before my monthly $50 check was due, we were behind in our rent, completely out of groceries except for some macaroni—we did not even have a grain of salt in the house; our gas and electricity had been shut off. We had a small heating stove in the living room, and nothing but old magazines for fuel.

My morale was fast descending to subbasement. I

was not so cocky or self-confident now. It seemed almost as if I was being "softened" for a knock-out blow of some kind.

Religious Controversy Enters

Some little time prior to this, we had been visiting my parents in Salem. My wife had become acquainted with an elderly neighbor lady, Mrs. Ora Runcorn. Mrs. Runcorn was an avid student of the Bible.

Before our marriage my wife had been quite interested in Bible study. She had been for years an active Methodist.

After marriage, although she had not lost her interest in the Christian life and the Bible, she had not had the same opportunity to express it, or participate in religious fellowship with others. While we lived in Maywood, suburb of Chicago, we had joined the River Forest Methodist Church. The fellowship there had been more social than spiritual or Biblical.

But all Mrs. Armstrong's active interest in things Biblical was reawakened when she became acquainted with Mrs. Runcorn. One day Mrs. Runcorn gave her a Bible study. She asked my wife to turn to a certain passage and read it. Then a second, then a third, and so on for about an hour. Mrs. Runcorn made no comment —gave no explanation or argument—just asked my wife to read aloud a series of Biblical passages.

"Why!" exclaimed Mrs. Armstrong in amazement, "do all these Scriptures say that I've been keeping the wrong *day* as the Sabbath all my life?"

"Well, *do they?*" asked Mrs. Runcorn. "Don't ask *me* whether you have been wrong—you shouldn't believe what any *person* tells you, but only what GOD tells you through the Bible. What does He tell you, *there?* What do you see *there* with your own eyes?"

288

"Why, it's as plain as anything could be!" exclaimed Mrs. Armstrong. "Why, this is a *wonderful* discovery. I must rush back to tell my husband the good news. I know he'll be overjoyed!"

A minute or so later, Mrs. Armstrong came running into my parents' home, with the "good news."

My jaw dropped!

This was the *worst* news I had ever heard! My wife gone into religious fanaticism!

"Have you gone CRAZY?" I asked, incredulously.

"Of course not! I was never more sure of anything in my life," responded my wife with enthusiasm.

Indeed, I wondered if she really *had* lost her mind! Deciding to "keep Saturday for Sunday!" Why, that seemed like rank FANATICISM! And my wife had always had such a sound mind! There was nothing shallow about her. She had always had a well-balanced mind, with depth.

But now, suddenly—THIS! It seemed incredible— preposterous!

"Loma," I said sternly, "this is simply too ridiculous to believe! I am certainly not going to tolerate any such religious fanaticism in our family! You'll have to give that up right here and now!"

But she wouldn't!

"Doesn't the Bible say that wives must be obedient to their husbands?" I asked.

"Yes, *in* the Lord, but not contrary to the Lord," she came back.

It was amazing how many logical arguments came to my mind. But always she had the answer.

I felt I could not tolerate such humiliation. *What would my friends say?* What would former business acquaintances think? Nothing had ever hit me where it hurt so much—right smack in the heart of all my pride and vanity and conceit! And *this* mortifying blow had to fall immediately on top of confidence-crushing financial reverses!

In desperation, I said: "Loma, you can't tell me that all these churches have been wrong all these hundreds of years! Why, aren't these all CHRIST'S churches?"

"Then," came back Mrs. Armstrong, *"why* do they all disagree on so many doctrines? Why does each one teach differently than the others?"

"But," I still contended, "Isn't the Bible the very source of the teaching of all these Christian churches? And they *do* all agree on observing Sunday! I'm sure the Bible says, 'Thou shalt keep SUNDAY!' "

"Well, does it?" smiled my wife, handing me a Bible. "Show it to me, if it does—and I'll do what it says."

"I don't know where to find it. You know I'm no Bible student, I could never understand the Bible. But I know the Bible must command the observance of Sunday, because all the churches observe Sunday, except the Seventh-Day Adventists, and they're regarded as fanatics. The Sabbath was the day for the Jews."

I even threatened divorce, if my wife refused to give up this fanaticism, though in my heart I didn't really mean it. In our family divorce was a thing unheard of—and beside, I was very much in love with my wife—though at the moment I was boiling over with anger.

"If you can prove by the Bible that Christians are commanded to observe Sunday, then of course I'll do what I see in the Bible!"

This was her challenge.

"O.K.," I answered, "I'll make you this proposition: I don't know much about the Bible—I just never could seem to understand it. But I do have an analytical mind. I've become experienced in research into business problems, getting the facts and analyzing them. Now I'll make a complete and thorough study of this question in the Bible. All these churches can't be wrong. I'll prove to you in the Bible that you are mistaken!"

This was in the autumn of 1926. My business was gone—all but the one laundry account in Portland, where we were living at the time. This one advertising account required only about 30 minutes a week of my time. I had TIME on my hands for this challenge.

And so it was that in the fall of 1926—crushed in spirit from business reverses not of my making—humiliated by what I regarded as wifely religious fanaticism, that I entered into an in-depth study of the Bible for the first time in my life.

16

Researching the Bible and Darwin

WE HAD MOVED TO the Pacific Northwest in the summer of 1924. My wife's brother, Walter Dillon, and her sister Bertha, had driven Walter's Model T Ford back to Iowa in August. Walter finished his junior year at Simpson College in Indianola, 1924-1925 school year, and Bertha continued teaching at the same school where she had taught before the Oregon trip.

During that third college year at Simpson, Walter had married a blonde girl of German background whose name was Hertha. In June, 1925, Walter and his young wife, together with Bertha and my wife's father, had returned to Oregon. With a new bride to support, it was necessary for Walter to go back to teaching school, as he had done before entering Simpson. Both he and Bertha obtained teaching jobs, and my father-in-law bought a small-town store.

During the following years, Walter attended

summer sessions at the University of Oregon, and managed also to take, part of the time, some night extension courses at the university, in Portland. Walter kept this schedule, while teaching, until he earned his B.A. at the university, and later his M.A. He soon moved up to a principalship, and finally became principal at the largest grade school in Oregon, outside of Portland.

Walter's wife had been indoctrinated with the theory of evolution in college. One day she and I became engaged in a discussion. The evolutionary doctrine came into the conversation. I mentioned that I was not convinced of its validity.

Accused of Being Ignorant

"Herbert Armstrong, you are simply IGNORANT!" accused Hertha. Her words stabbed deeply into what was left of my ego. "One is uneducated, and ignorant, unless he believes in evolution. All educated people now believe it."

That accusation came hot on the heels of this Sabbath challenge from my wife. Of course, Hertha was only about 19, and had had but her freshman year in college. She was yet immature enough to be a bit oversold on what had been presented to her as a mark of intellectual distinction. Nevertheless, her manner was cutting, and a bit sarcastic, and I accepted it as a challenge.

"Hertha," I responded, "I am just starting a study of the Bible. I intend to include in this research a thorough study of the Biblical account of creation. Since it is admittedly one of the two—evolution *or* special creation—I will include an in-depth study of evolution. I feel sure that a thorough study into both sides will show that it is *you* who are ignorant, and that you merely

293

studied one side of a two-sided question in freshman biology, and accepted what was funnelled into your mind without question. And if and when I do, *I'm going to make you EAT those words!"*

And so it developed that I now had a *double* challenge to go to work on—a *dual* subject involving both the Biblical claims for special creation, and also a more in-depth study than before into texts on biology, geology, paleontology, and the various works on the theory of evolution.

Actually, this is simply the study into the TWO possibilities of origins. It threw me directly into an in-depth research of what is perhaps the most BASIC of all knowledge—the very *starting point* in the acquisition of knowledge—the search for the correct *concept* through which to VIEW all facts.

The two subjects—or, rather, the two sides of the same subject of origins—*should* be unprejudicially and objectively studied together, *yet seldom are!*

Most believers in the Bible and in the existence of God have probably just grown up believing it, because they were reared in an atmosphere where it was believed. But perhaps few ever studied into it deeply enough to obtain irrefutable PROOF.

Likewise, the educated, who have gone on through college or university, have, in the main, been taught the theory of evolution as a BELIEF. They have accepted it, in all probability, without having given any serious or thorough study of the Biblical claims.

I had come to the point where I wanted THE TRUTH!

I now had the time on my hands. I was willing to pay the price of thorough and in-depth research to BE SURE!

The reader is reminded that I had chosen, instead

294

of the university, the process of self-education, selecting my own courses of study. I had studied diligently, after leaving high school at age 18, and continuously up to this incident in 1926. But I was now entering on a field of research in which previous study had been minimal.

I began this intensified study by obtaining everything I could find in the way of books, pamphlets and other literature both for and against what was often called "the Jewish Sabbath." I wanted, not only everything I could lay hands on, on the case for Sunday, and *against* the 7th-day Sabbath. I wanted, also, the arguments or proponents *for* it, which I hoped to be able honestly to refute.

At the same time, I found, in the Portland Public Library, many scientific works either directly on evolution, or as a teaching in textbooks on biology, paleontology and geology. Also I found books by scientists and doctors of philosophy puncturing many holes in the evolutionary hypothesis. Strangely, even the critics of evolution, being themselves scientific men, paradoxically accepted the very theory they so ably refuted.

But, reading first the works of Darwin, Haeckel, Spencer, Huxley, Vogt, and more recent and modern authorities, the evolutionary postulate began to become very convincing.

It became apparent early that the *real* and thorough-going evolutionists universally agreed that evolution excluded the possibility of the existence of God! While some of the lesser lights professed a sort of fence-straddling theistic evolution, I soon learned that the real dyed-in-the-wool evolutionists all were atheists. Evolution *could not* honestly be reconciled with the first chapter of Genesis!

295

Does God Exist?

And so it came about that, very early in this study of evolution and of the Bible, actual *doubts* came into my mind as to the existence of God!

In a very real sense, this was a good thing. I had always *assumed* the existence of God because I had been taught it from childhood. I had grown up in Sunday school. I simply took it for granted.

Now, suddenly, I realized I had never PROVED whether there is a God. Since the existence of God is the very first BASIS for religious belief and authority—and since the inspiration of the Bible *by* such a God as His revelation to mankind is the secondary and companion basis for faith and practice, I realized that the place to start was to PROVE whether God exists and whether the Holy Bible is His revelation of knowledge and information for mankind.

I had nothing but TIME on my hands. I rose early and STUDIED. Most mornings I was standing at the front entrance of the Public Library when its doors were opened. Most evenings I left the Library at 9 p.m., closing time. Most nights I continued study at home until my wife, at 1 a.m. or later, would waken from her sleep and urge me to break off and get to bed.

I delved into science. I learned the facts about radioactive elements. I learned how radioactivity proves there has been no past eternity of matter. There was a time when matter did not exist. Then there came a time when matter came into existence. This was CREATION, one of several proofs of GOD.

By the laws of science, including the law of biogenesis, that only LIFE can beget life—that dead matter cannot produce life—that the living cannot come from the not-living, by these laws came PROOF that God exists.

In the Bible I found one quoted, saying in the first person, "I am GOD." This God was quoted directly in Scriptures, *proved* to have been written hundreds of years before Christ, pronouncing the future fates of *every* major city and nation in the ancient world. I delved into HISTORY. I learned that these prophecies, in every instance (except in prophecies pertaining to a time yet future), had come to pass precisely as written!

Refuting Evolution

I studied the creation account in the Bible. It is not *all* in Genesis 1. I studied it *all!* I studied evolution. At first the evolutionary theory seemed very convincing—just as it does to freshmen students in most colleges and universities.

I noted evidences of comparative anatomy. But these evidences were not, in themselves, PROOF. They merely tended to make the theory appear more reasonable IF proved. I noted tests and discoveries of embryology. These, too, were not PROOF, but only supporting evidence IF evolution were proved.

I noticed that Lamarck's original theory of use and disuse, once accepted as science, had been laughed out of school. I learned that the once scientific spiral-nebular theory of the earth's existence had become the present-day laughing stock, supplanted by (in 1926) Professor Chamberlin's planetesimal hypothesis. I sought out the facts of Darwin's life. I learned the facts about his continual sickness—about his preconceived theory and inductive process of reasoning in searching for such facts and arguments as would sustain his theory.

I researched the facts about his tour on the good ship *Beagle.* I read of how he admitted there were perplexing problems in his theories and in what he had written, but that he nevertheless continued to promulgate evolution. I learned how his colleagues glossed over these perplexing problems and propagandized his theory into scientific acceptance.

Then I came to the matter of the human mind. As far back as 1926 I was concerned about the vast GULF between animal brain and human mind. Could that gulf have been bridged by evolution? It appeared that, even if the evolutionary process were possible, in reality the TIME required to bridge this gulf in intellectual development would have been millions of times longer than what geology and paleontology would indicate.

But, most important, I knew that I, with my mind, am superior to anything my mind can devise, and that I can make. Likewise, it became axiomatic that nothing *less* than the intelligence of my mind could have produced something SUPERIOR to itself—my mind! Of necessity, the very presence of human intellect necessitates a superior and greater Intellect to have designed, devised, and produced the human mind! It *could not* have been produced by natural causes, and resident forces, as evolution presupposes. Unintelligence could not produce intelligence superior to itself! Rational common sense demanded a Creator of SUPERIOR MIND!

I came to see that there was only one possible proof of evolution as a fact. That was the assumption that, in the study of paleontology, the most simple fossils were always in the *oldest strata,* laid down first; while, as we progress into strata of later deposition, the fossils found in them become gradually more complex, tending toward advancing intelligence.

That one claim, I finally determined, was the TRUNK of the tree of evolution. If the trunk stood, the theory

298

appeared proved. If I could chop down the trunk, the entire tree would fall with it.

I began a search to learn HOW these scientists determined the age of strata. I was months finding it. None of the texts I searched seemed to explain anything about it. This TRUNK of the tree was carelessly *assumed*—without proof.

Were the oldest strata always on the bottom—the next oldest next to the bottom, the most recent on the top? Finally I found it in a recognized text on geology authored by Prof. Thomas Chrowder Chamberlin. No, sometimes the most recent were actually *below* the most ancient strata. The age of strata was *not* determined by stages of depth. The depth of strata varied in different parts of the world.

How, then, was the age of strata determined? Why, I finally discovered in this very reputable authority, their age was determined by the FOSSILS found in them. Since the geologists *"knew"* their evolutionary theory was true, and since they had estimated how many millions of years ago a certain fossil specimen might have lived, that age determined the age of the strata!

In other words, they ASSUMED the age of the strata by the supposition that their theory of evolution was true. And they "PROVED" their theory was true by the *supposition* of the progressive ages of the strata in which fossil remains had been found! This was arguing in a circle!

The TRUNK of the evolutionary tree was chopped down. There WAS NO PROOF!

I wrote a short paper on this discovery. I showed it to the head librarian of the technical and science department of a very large library.

"Mr. Armstrong," she said, "you have an uncanny knack of getting right to the crux of a problem. Yes, I have to admit you have chopped down the trunk of the tree. You have robbed me of PROOF! But, Mr. Armstrong, I still have to go on *believing* in evolution. I have done graduate work at Columbia, at the University of Chicago, and other top-level institutions. I have spent my life in the atmosphere of science and in the company of scientific people. I am SO STEEPED in it that I could not root it from my mind!"

What a pitiful confession, from one so steeped in "the wisdom of this world."

The Creation MEMORIAL

I had *disproved* the theory of evolution. I had found PROOF of CREATION—PROOF of the existence of GOD—PROOF of the divine inspiration of the BIBLE.

Now I had a BASIS for belief. *Now* I had a solid FOUNDATION on which to build. The BIBLE had proved itself to contain AUTHORITY. I had now studied far enough to know that I must LIVE by it, and that I shall finally be JUDGED by it—not by men, nor by man's church denominations, theories, theologies, tenets, doctrines, or pronouncements. I would be judged by Almighty GOD finally, and according to the BIBLE!

So now I began to study further into this Sabbath question.

Of course I had procured all the pamphlets, books and booklets I could find in defense of Sunday observance, and purporting to refute the "Jewish Sabbath."

Especially I sought out eagerly everything claiming apostolic observance of Sunday as "the Christian Sabbath." Early in my study, I learned about the many Bible helps—the concordances, which list alphabetically all the words used in the Bible, showing where they are used, and what Greek, Hebrew or Aramaic word was

300

originally written—the Bible Dictionaries, the Bible encyclopedias, the commentaries, etc., etc.

From the exhaustive concordances I soon learned that the command I sought, "Thou shalt keep Sunday," was nowhere to be found in the Bible. In fact the word "Sunday" was not used in the Bible. That surprised me.

I really became excited, however, when I learned that there are eight places in the New Testament where the phrase "first day of the week" appears. And I read eagerly arguments in tracts or booklets claiming that these established that the original apostles were holding their weekly worship services on "the first day of the week"—which is Sunday.

But I became painfully disappointed on learning by more careful study, that there was not a single instance of a religious service being held on the hours we call Sunday—Saturday midnight to Sunday midnight. The Apostle Paul, after spending a "Saturday" Sabbath with the church at Troas, preached to them Saturday night until midnight. But although, in the Biblical manner of ending each day and beginning the next at sunset, that was—Biblically speaking—on "the first day of the week," it was *not Sunday,* but Saturday night, lasting *until* Sunday began at midnight.

I was further disappointed in this case, when I discovered on careful study, that on that Sunday Paul indulged in the labor of *walking* some 19 miles to Assos. The others of Paul's company had sailed, beginning sunset when the Sabbath ended, around the peninsula, some 65 miles to Assos. By walking the 19 miles straight across, on Sunday, Paul had gained the extra time to continue speaking to the people Saturday night.

So my effort to find a command to observe Sunday met with disappointment.

I found there is no command to observe Sunday. Sunday is nowhere called holy time, but to my chagrin, I found this "Jewish Sabbath" *is,* and is said to be holy to God. There was not even a single example of any religious meeting having been held on the hours called Sunday!

On the other hand, I had to learn, like it or not, that Jesus kept the Sabbath day "as His custom was," and the Apostle Paul kept it "as his manner was." Also Paul spent many Sabbath days preaching and holding weekly services, and in one instance the Gentiles waited a whole week in order to be able to come and hear Paul preach the same words on the following Sabbath!

I learned that CREATION is the very PROOF of GOD! A heathen comes along, pointing to an idol made by man's hands out of wood, stone or marble or gold.

"This idol is the real god," he says. "How can you prove your God is superior to this idol that I worship?"

"Why," I answer, "My God is the CREATOR. He *created* the wood, stone, marble or gold that your god is made of. He created MAN, and man, a *created* being, MADE that idol. Therefore my God is greater than your idol because it is only a particle of what my God MADE!"

Another comes along and says, "I worship the SUN. We get our light from the sun. It warms the earth and makes vegetation grow. I think the SUN is God."

"But," I reply, "the true God CREATED the sun. He created light. He created force, energy, and LIFE. He makes the sun shine on the earth. He CONTROLS the sun, because He *controls* all the forces of His creation. He is supreme RULER over His universe."

Then I began to see that on the very seventh day of creation week, God set that day aside from other days.

302

On that day He RESTED from all He had created by WORK. On that day he *created* the Sabbath, not by work, but by REST, putting His divine presence in it! He made it HOLY TIME. No man has authority to make future time holy. No group of men—no church! Only GOD is HOLY! Only GOD can make things HOLY. The Sabbath is a constantly recurring space of time, marked off by the setting of the sun. God made every recurring Sabbath HOLY, and commanded man (Exodus 20) to *keep* it holy.

WHY did He do it? WHY does it make any difference?

I found it in the SPECIAL SABBATH COVENANT in Exodus 31:12-18. He made it the SIGN between Him and His people. A SIGN is a mark of identity. First, it is a sign that GOD is the CREATOR, because it is a MEMORIAL OF CREATION—the CREATION is the PROOF of God—it identifies Him. No other space of time could be a memorial of CREATION. Thus God chose that very space of time for man to assemble for worship which KEEPS MAN IN THE KNOWLEDGE OF THE TRUE IDENTITY OF GOD AS THE CREATOR. Every nation which has NOT kept the Sabbath has worshipped the *created* rather than the Creator. It is a sign that identifies God's own people, because it is they who OBEY God in this commandment, while this is the very commandment which everyone else regards as the LEAST of the commandments—which they REBEL against obeying!

GOD is the one you OBEY. The word LORD means MASTER —the one you OBEY! This is the one point on which the largest number of people refuse to OBEY the true GOD, thus proving they are *not* His people!

Law and Grace

I studied carefully everything I could obtain which

attempted to *refute* the Sabbath. I wanted, more than anything on earth, to refute it—to prove that SUNDAY was the true Christian Sabbath, or "Lord's Day."

I read the arguments about "law or grace."

I was pointed to, and read, Romans 3:20: "Therefore by the deeds of the law there shall no flesh be justified in His sight."

But I looked into the BIBLE, and found the pamphlet had left out the rest of the verse which says: "for by the law is the knowledge of sin." That is true, because I read in I John 3:4 that the Bible definition of SIN is NOT man's conscience, or his church "DON'TS," but *"Sin is the transgression of the law."* Naturally, then, the KNOWLEDGE of sin comes by the LAW.

And I discovered the pamphlet forgot to quote the 31st verse:

"Do we then make void the law through faith? God forbid: yea, *we establish the law.*"

I read in a pamphlet, ". . . the law worketh WRATH" (Rom. 4:15).

I turned to my Bible and read the rest of the same verse: "for where no law is, there is no transgression." Of course! Because the law DEFINES sin. Sin is disobedience of the law!

I read in one of the pamphlets that the law was an evil thing, contrary to our best interests. But then I read in Romans 7: "Is the law sin? *God forbid!* Nay, I had not known sin, but by the law: for I had not known lust, except the law had said 'Thou shalt not covet.' " And "Wherefore the law is HOLY, and the commandment holy, and just, and good." And again, "For we know that the *law is spiritual*" (verses 7,12,14).

I learned that GRACE is PARDON, through the blood of Christ, for having *transgressed* the law. But if a human judge pardons a man for breaking a civil or

304

criminal law, that pardon does not repeal the law. The man is pardoned so that he may now OBEY the law. And GOD pardons only after we REPENT of sin!

The Bitter Pill

But do not suppose I quickly or easily came to admit my wife had been right, or to accept the seventh-day Sabbath as the truth of the Bible.

I spent a solid SIX MONTHS of virtual night-and-day, seven-day-a-week STUDY and research, in a determined effort to find just the opposite.

I searched IN VAIN for any authority in the Bible to establish SUNDAY as the day for Christian worship. I even studied Greek sufficiently to run down every possible questionable text in the original Greek.

I studied the Commentaries. I studied the Lexicons and *Robertsons's Grammar of the Greek New Testament*. Then I studied HISTORY. I delved into encyclopedias—the *Britannica*, the *Americana*, and several religious encyclopedias. I searched the *Jewish Encyclopedia*, and the *Catholic Encyclopedia*. I read Gibbon's *Decline and Fall of the Roman Empire*, especially his chapter 15 dealing with the religious history of the first four hundred years after Christ. And one of the most convincing evidences against Sunday was in the history of how and when it began.

I left no stone unturned.

I found clever arguments. I will confess that, so eager was I to overthrow this Sabbath belief of my wife, at one point in this intensive study I believed I might possibly have been able to use arguments to confuse and upset my wife on the Sabbath question. But there was no temptation to try to do it. I *knew* these arguments *were not honest!* I *could not* deliberately try to deceive my wife with dishonest arguments. The thought was immediately pushed aside. I know now she could not have been deceived.

Finally, after six months, the TRUTH had become crystal clear. At last I KNEW what was the truth. Once again, GOD had taken me to a licking!

It had been bewildering—utterly frustrating! It seemed as if some mysterious, invisible hand was disintegrating every business I started!

That was precisely what *was* happening! The hand of God was taking away every activity on which my heart had been set—the business success before whose shrine I had worshipped. This zeal to become important in the business world had become an idol. God was destroying the idol. He was knocking me down—again and again! He was puncturing the ego, deflating the vanity.

Midas in Reverse

At age 16 ambition had been aroused. I began to study constantly—to work at self-improvement—to prod and drive myself on and on. I had sought the jobs which would provide training and experience for the future. This had led to travel, to contacts with big and important men, multimillionaire executives.

At twenty-eight a publishers' representative business had been built in Chicago which produced an income equivalent to some $35,000 a year measured by today's dollar value. The flash depression of 1920 had swept it away. At age thirty, discouraged, broken in spirit, I was removed from it entirely.

Then, in Oregon, had come the advertising service for laundries. It was growing and multiplying rapidly. After one year, in the fall of 1926, the fees were grossing close to $1,000 per month. I saw visions of a personal net income mounting to from $300,000 to a half million a year with expansion to national proportions. Then an action by the Laundryowners National Association swept the laundry advertising business out from under my feet.

It seemed that I was King Midas in reverse. Every material money-making enterprise *I* started *promised* gold, but turned to *nothing!* They vanished like mirages on a desert.

Yes, God Almighty the Creator, was knocking me down—again and again. As often as I got back to my feet to fight, on starting another business or enterprise, another blow of utter and bitter defeat seemed to strike me from behind by an unseen hand. I was being "softened" for the final knock-out of material ambition.

Now came the greatest inner battle of my life.

To accept this truth meant—so I supposed—*to cut me off from all former friends, acquaintances and business associates.* I had come to meet some of the independent "Sabbath-keepers" down around Salem and the Willamette Valley. Some of them were what I then, in my pride and conceit, regarded as backwoods "hillbillies." None were of the financial and social position of those I had associated with.

My associations and pride had led me to "look down upon" this class of people. I had been ambitious to hobnob with the wealthy and the cultural.

I saw plainly what a decision was before me. To accept this truth meant to throw in my lot for life with a class of people I had always looked on as inferior. I learned later that God *looks on the heart,* and these humble people were the real salt of the earth. But I was then still looking on the outward appearance. It meant being cut off completely and forever from all to which I had aspired. It meant a total crushing of vanity. It meant a total *change of life!*

I counted the cost!

But then, I had been beaten down. I had been humiliated. I had been broken in spirit, frustrated. I had come to look on this formerly esteemed self as a failure. I now took another good look at myself.

And I acknowledged: "I'm nothing but a burned-out old hunk of junk."

I realized I had been a swellheaded egotistical jackass.

Finally, in desperation, I threw myself on God's mercy. I said to God that I knew, now, that I was nothing but a burned-out hunk of junk. My life was worth nothing more to ME. I said to God that I knew now I had nothing to offer HIM—but if He would forgive me—if He could have any use whatsoever for such a worthless dreg of humanity, that He could have my life; I knew it was worthless, but if He could do anything with it, He could have it—I was willing to give this worthless self to HIM—I wanted to accept Jesus Christ as personal Saviour!

I meant it! It was the toughest battle I ever fought. It was a battle for LIFE. I lost that battle, as I had been recently losing all battles. I realized Jesus Christ had bought and paid for my life. I gave in. I surrendered, unconditionally. I told Christ He could have what was left of me! I didn't think I was worth saving!

Jesus said, "Whosoever will save his life shall lose it: and whosoever will lose his life for my sake shall find it." I then and there gave up my life—not knowing that this was the ONLY way to really *find* it!

It was humiliating to have to admit my wife had been right, and I had been wrong. It was disillusioning to learn, on studying the BIBLE for the first time, that what I had been taught in Sunday school was, in so many basic instances, the very opposite of what the Bible plainly states. It was shocking to learn that "all these churches *were* wrong" after all!

But I did, later, have one satisfaction. I wrote up a long manuscript about the Sabbath, finally tying it up with evolution, and PROVING evolution false. I gave it to my sister-in-law, Mrs. Dillon. She read it unsuspectingly. Before she realized what she was reading, she had accepted the evidence and PROOF that evolution was false.

"You tricked me!" she exclaimed.

But she *did* have to "eat those words"!

17

At the Crossroads—and a Momentous Decision

I T WAS humiliating to have to admit my wife had been right, and I had been wrong, in the most serious argument that ever came between us.

Disillusionment

But to my utter disappointed astonishment, I found that much of the popular church teachings and practices were *not* based on the Bible. They had originated, as research in history had revealed, in paganism. Numerous Bible prophecies foretold it. The amazing, unbelievable TRUTH was, the SOURCE of these popular beliefs and practices of professing Christianity was, quite largely, paganism and human reasoning and custom, *NOT the Bible!*

I had first doubted, then searched for evidence, and found PROOF that God exists—that the Holy Bible is, literally, His divinely inspired revelation and instruc-

310

tion to mankind. I had learned that one's God is what a person OBEYS. The word "LORD" means MASTER—the *one* you OBEY! Most people, I had discovered, are obeying *false* gods, rebelling against the one true CREATOR who is the supreme RULER of the universe.

The argument was over a point of OBEDIENCE to GOD.

The opening of my eyes to the TRUTH brought me to the crossroads of my life. To accept it meant to throw in my lot with a class of humble and unpretentious people I had always looked upon as inferior. It meant being cut off from the high and the mighty and the wealthy of this world, to which I had aspired. It meant the final crushing of VANITY. It meant a total *change of life!*

Life and Death Struggle

It meant real REPENTANCE, for now I saw that I had been breaking God's Law. I had been rebelling against God. It meant turning around and going THE WAY OF GOD—the WAY of His BIBLE—living according to every word in the Bible, instead of according to the ways of society or the desires of the flesh and of vanity.

It was a matter of which WAY I would travel for the remainder of my life. I had certainly reached the CROSSROADS!

But I had been beaten down. God had brought that about—though I didn't realize it then. Repeated business reverses, failure after failure, had destroyed self-confidence. I was broken in spirit. The SELF in me didn't want to die. It wanted to try to get up from ignominious defeat and try once again to tread the broad and popular WAY of vanity and of this world. But now I knew *that* way was WRONG! I knew its ultimate penalty was DEATH. But I didn't want to die *now!*

It was truly a battle for LIFE—a life and death

struggle. In the end, I lost that battle, as I had been losing all worldly battles in recent years.

In final desperation, I threw myself on His mercy. If He could use my life, I would give it to *Him*—not in physical suicide, but as a *living* sacrifice, to use as He willed. It was worth nothing to me any longer.

Jesus Christ had bought and paid for my life by His death. It really *belonged* to Him, and now I told Him He could have it!

From then on, this defeated no-good life of mine was GOD's. I didn't see how it could be worth anything to Him. But it was His to use as His instrument, if He thought He could use it.

JOY in Defeat

This surrender to God—this REPENTANCE—this GIVING UP of the world, of friends and associates, and of everything—was the most bitter pill I ever swallowed. Yet it was the *only* medicine in all my life that ever brought a healing!

For I actually began to realize that I was finding joy beyond words to describe in this total defeat. I had actually found JOY in the study of the Bible—in the discovery of new TRUTHS, heretofore hidden from my consciousness. And in surrendering to GOD in complete repentance, I found unspeakable JOY in accepting JESUS CHRIST as personal Saviour and my present High Priest.

I began to see everything in a new and different light. *Why* should it have been a difficult and painful experience to surrender to my Maker and my God? *Why* was it painful to surrender to *obey* God's right ways? WHY? Now, I came to a new outlook on life.

Somehow I began to realize a NEW fellowship and friendship had come into my life. I began to be conscious

312

of a contact and fellowship with Christ, and with God the Father.

When I read and studied the Bible, God was talking to *me,* and now I loved to listen! I began to pray, and knew that in prayer I was talking with God. I was not yet very well acquainted with God. But one gets to be *better* acquainted with another by constant contact and continuous conversation.

A Doctrine at a Time

So I continued the study of the Bible. I began to write, in article form, the things I was learning. I did not then suppose these articles would ever be published. I wrote them for my own satisfaction. It was one way to learn more by the study.

I had been reared of Quaker stock. The Quakers do not believe in water baptism. But now I wanted to PROVE, by the Bible, whether I ought to be baptized. So I began to study about baptism—and receiving the Holy Spirit.

As this study of the Bible continued, I was forced to come out of the fog of religious babylon *a single doctrine at a time.* It was years later before I came to see the WHOLE picture—to understand God's PURPOSE being worked out here below, and why, and how, He is working it out. Like a jigsaw puzzle, the many single doctrinal parts ultimately fit together, and then, for the first time, the WHOLE picture burst joyfully into view.

It was like being so close to one tree at a time I could not see the forest. I had to examine every doctrinal tree in the religious forest. Many, as I had been brought up to believe them, were felled on close examination IN THE BIBLE. New doctrinal trees came into view. But finally, after years, I was able to see the whole forest of TRUTH, with dead doctrinal trees removed.

313

That is why students at Ambassador College today are able to learn the TRUTH much more rapidly than I could. That is why the readers of *The Plain Truth*, the regular listeners of *The World Tomorrow* program, and the students of the Ambassador College Correspondence Course are able to come to mature knowledge of the truth so quickly. The pioneer work has been done. The weeds have been removed. The very *trunks* of the trees of false doctrines have been chopped down and uprooted.

But I myself had to check carefully and test every doctrine, one at a time.

And so next, after repentance and surrender to God, came an intensive study of water baptism.

Disillusioned About Preachers

During my initial six months' study, I had studied not only the Bible, but every book, booklet or tract I could get on the religious subjects under study. On the Sabbath question, I had sought out eagerly and studied avidly everything I could find *against* the Sabbath and supporting Sunday as the "Lord's Day." But I had tried to be fair, and searched also the literature on the other side of the question. But always the BIBLE was the sole authority. Thus I became quite familiar with Seventh-Day Adventist literature.

Never, however, did I attend any Seventh-Day Adventist church service.

Also I checked over carefully the literature of the Church of God, with headquarters at Stanberry, Missouri.

Upon surrender to God, I had lost all sense of animosity toward Mrs. O. J. Runcorn, the elderly lady who had started my wife on the religious "fanaticism" which proved to be God's TRUTH. We even came to call

314

her and her husband our spiritual parents. Mrs. Armstrong and I visited with her frequently when in Salem at the home of my parents. Through her and her husband we became acquainted with a small group of "Church of God people" in Salem and near Jefferson, Oregon.

One day when we were in Salem we learned that a preacher of this Church of God had just arrived from Texas, an Elder Unzicker. He and his wife were staying at the home of a neighbor, member of the Church of God. Mrs. Armstrong and I walked across the street to this neighbor's house to see him. I wanted to ask him questions about water baptism.

Questioning Other Ministers

Next I went to a Baptist minister in Portland, to learn *why* Baptists believe in baptism. He was courteous and patient, glad to explain his church's teachings.

I went to a Seventh-Day Adventist minister. He, too, was courteous and glad to explain his belief, according to the Bible.

Then, finally, I went to see a minister of the Friends Church.

I asked him WHY the Quakers did not believe in water baptism. He explained the Quaker belief. They believe in *spiritual,* not water, baptism.

"Well, Herbert," he said finally, "I'll have to confess I can't honestly justify our church position by the Bible. This very thing bothered me a great deal when I first felt called into the ministry. At first, I felt I could not consistently become a minister in the Friends Church because this stand on water baptism really bothered me. But then, I looked at some of the great preachers of the church (naming several, including my own great-uncle Thomas Armstrong), and they all

315

seemed to be holy men of God. And so I decided that if such great and holy men could preach against water baptism, so could I."

To me, this was disillusioning and discouraging. It showed me that ministers are human, like other people, after all. As a boy, I had somehow come to assume that ministers of religion are *different* from other people. Preachers were HOLY. Other people were sinners. Other people had human nature. But preachers were *above* the temptation and weaknesses of mortal humans. They were a sort of special species, about half way between ordinary humans and God. I had looked on ministers of religion with a sort of embarrassed awe. I think many people think of the clergy in similar manner.

Of course I was not a minister, and at that time did not ever expect to be. In my Bible study up to this point I had become painfully aware that "the heart [human] is deceitful above all things, and desperately wicked" (Jeremiah 17:9). This is true of every human, and I had to realize it included me. But I had to come to see that clergymen are human also—and perhaps have even a harder fight against temptation than laymen.

My Experience Utterly Unique

Actually, though I didn't realize it then, I was, myself, being literally thrust into the Ministry of Christ, though not at all of my own seeking. And I know now that my experience was, in all probability, utterly UNIQUE! Most certainly the manner in which I was put into it was unlike any other I had heard of.

How does the average minister come to enter the clergy? I'm sure most choose the ministry in the same manner that other young men choose medicine, law, architecture or science as a life profession. So, naturally, they enter into whatever course of preparation is

316

provided by their particular religion, church or denomination. Probably they enter a theological seminary. There they are taught the doctrines of their particular religious organization.

But I did not belong to any particular religion, church or sect. I did not CHOOSE the clergy as a profession. Actually, that would have been the very *last* choice in my case. But, though it was not yet realized, the profession I *had* chosen, after thorough self-analysis and survey of professions and occupations—journalism and advertising—provided the very background, training and experience to fit me for what I was now being drawn into.

I did not enter the course of study of some particular religion or church. I was not being taught by MAN! I had entered on the in-depth study of the Bible to prove my wife was wrong in a new religious belief. Being challenged also on the theory of evolution, my research led me to question even the existence of God and the authority of the Bible. And I had accepted the reality of the existence of God, and the authority of the Bible, ONLY AFTER finding incontrovertible PROOF.

How do most people come to believe what they do? The philosopher C. E. Ayres commented that few indeed ever stop to inquire in retrospect HOW they come to believe what they do, or WHY they believe it. Most people believe whatever they have been taught, or what they have read, or heard, or whatever their particular group, religion, church, political party, or area of the world believes. They simply "GO ALONG." They carelessly ASSUME, because others do.

Our system of education encourages this. It fails abysmally to teach growing children to *think* for themselves, to question, to seek PROOF before believing. In school and college students are taught to accept and memorize whatever is in the textbook, or given in the lecture. They are graded on how well they have accepted and memorized what has been thus funneled into their unsuspecting minds. And I know of no seminary that departs from this process, or encourages students to thoroughly question *whether* their sectarian doctrines are true.

Of course, too, people usually believe what they WANT to believe. That is to say, they refuse to believe what they *don't* want to believe. But in my case I was forced, on thorough examination and research, to believe what, prior to that research, I had definitely and vigorously *not* wanted to believe. I was forced, to accept, on PROOF, that which I had started out to prove FALSE. I was forced to admit, under most humiliating circumstances, on PROOF, what I had hoped to disprove.

And what I was forced, on PROOF, to accept was probably the most *unpopular* belief, and the *hardest* for most people to accept. But I had, against my wishes, found it to be TRUE, and once proved TRUE, I did finally come to embrace it with gladness and JOY!

In no other manner, I believe, could the mind of anyone have been opened to see the most BASIC, VITAL truths of the revealed Message of God to mankind—the MOST IMPORTANT KNOWLEDGE OF ALL—utterly overlooked and unrealized by this world's religions, churches and sects.

It was in this UNIQUE manner that I was brought to discover THE MISSING DIMENSION IN EDUCATION—the truth as to WHY humanity was put on this earth—the true PURPOSE of human life—the CAUSE of all the world's unhappiness, unsolvable problems and evils—the difference between the TRUE VALUES and the false—THE WAY that can be the ONLY *CAUSE* of PEACE between nations, groups and individuals—the only CAUSE of true

318

success in life with happiness, peace, prosperity and abundance.

No, I know of no one who was thrust into the Ministry of Jesus Christ, untaught by MAN, but by the living Christ through His written Word, in the manner in which I was. I didn't realize it yet, but I was being brought into His Ministry by the living Christ in a manner UTTERLY UNIQUE, and totally unlike any other of which I know!

But back, now, to my study in regard to baptism.

Begotten of God

Finally the study of the subject of baptism was completed. There was no longer doubt. Peter had said: "REPENT, and BE BAPTIZED every one of you in the name of Jesus Christ for the remission of sins, and ye shall receive the gift of the Holy Spirit" (Acts 2:38). To Cornelius and his house, who already had received the Holy Spirit, Peter said: "Can any man forbid WATER, that these should not be baptized, *which* have received the Holy Spirit as well as we? And he COMMANDED them to be baptized in the name of the Lord" (Acts 10:47-48).

It was a command. There was no promise of receiving the Holy Spirit until after being baptized— although Cornelius, the exception to the rule, had been begotten by the Holy Spirit prior to baptism. Yet even he was *commanded* to be baptized IN WATER. What I had learned in this study on baptism is recounted in our free booklet *All About Water Baptism.*

And so I was baptized forthwith and without delay.

Immediately upon coming up out of the water, I definitely experienced a *change* in attitude and in mind generally. I had already repented and surrendered to

God's rule over my life. The natural carnal hostility to God and His Law already had gone.

Yet, now, for the first time, I felt CLEAN! I *knew,* now, that the terribly heavy load of sin had been taken off my shoulders. Christ had paid the penalty for me. All past sins were now blotted out by His blood. My conscience was clean and clear.

For the first time in my life I experienced *real inner PEACE of mind!* I realized, as never before, how futile and useless and foolish are the ways of this world, on which most people set so much store. There was a quiet, wonderful happiness of mind in the sure knowledge that now I was actually a begotten son of GOD! I could really call GOD *Father!*

There were no excitable *physical sensations* or exhilarating FEELINGS running up and down the spine. Nothing of the nervous system. That is physical—not spiritual. Nothing of the senses—nothing *sensual,* as some people, diabolically misled and deceived claim to experience. But there was a KNOWING! There was an unmistakable *renewing of the mind* (Romans 12:2).

For six months I had struggled night and day, with a carnal mind, to learn the truth about one single doctrine in the Bible. Prior to that my wife and I had read the Bible clear through—but *I had not understood a WORD of it!* Most of the time I asked my wife to do the reading, because she could read faster. We got through quicker. But it was like reading or listening to a foreign language. I simply *could not UNDERSTAND the BIBLE!*

But now, from this point of baptism on, a strange, wonderful, delightful new thing took place. I could read the Bible and UNDERSTAND what I read! Of course I could not understand the WHOLE Bible in five or ten minutes. I still had to study it a doctrine at a time. But it was

320

UNDERSTANDABLE! It MADE SENSE! Even though it took time, I was now getting some place. But I was comprehending and learning *so much faster* than during that initial six months' study!

It was like a miracle! And indeed, it *WAS* a MIRACLE! The very Holy Spirit of God had come into and *renewed* my mind. I had been *baptized* by the Holy Spirit *into* the true Body of Christ, the Church of God—but I did not realize that fact literally. I was still to search earnestly to find the one and only *true* Church which Jesus founded, before recognizing fully He had already placed me in it!

18

Learning Whether God Answers Prayers

WHERE *is* the one TRUE Church today? That is the question that still haunted my mind in the late spring and the summer of 1927.

During that six months' diligent research, I had run the gamut of disillusionment, doubt, confusion, frustration—and finally, the SURE knowledge, *proved*, that GOD EXISTS, and that the Holy Bible is His revealed Word.

Finally, sadly disillusioned about believing "all these churches couldn't be wrong," I began to ask, *"where is the one true Church today?"* I read in Matthew 16:18 where Jesus said: *"I will build my Church."*

Therefore I knew He *did* build it. He said the gates of the grave would never prevail against it. It had to be in existence still. But WHERE? Which church could it be?

I had been astounded to learn that the BIBLE teaches truths diametrically opposite to the teachings of the large and popular churches and denominations today. I saw in the Bible the real MISSION of God's true Church. But these churches, today, were *not* carrying on the real work and mission of Christ.

The SOURCE of their beliefs and practice was *not* the Bible, but paganism! There was no recognizable comparison between them and the original TRUE Church I found described in Acts and other New Testament books. Yet *somewhere there had to exist today* that spiritual organism in which Christ actually dwelt—a church empowered by His Spirit—acting as His instrument—carrying out His Commission.

But WHERE?

I was to be some years in finding the answer.

I still had to sift out the real truth *a doctrine at a time!*

Mrs. Armstrong and I began to attend many different churches. I wanted to check on each—compare it with the Bible. I continued almost daily study at the Portland Public Library.

Getting Relatives "Saved"

One must not assume, from what has been written about my surrender to God, and the *change* that came with God's Spirit, that I had reached spiritual maturity and perfection at one quick bound. No one ever does. A human baby must creep before it learns to walk. It must learn to walk before it can run. And it stumbles and falls many times. But it does not become discouraged and give up.

The newly converted are mere babes in Christ. I had not learned much, as yet. Vanity was far from being eradicated.

Upon surrendering to accept God's TRUTH—as far as I had then come to see it—my first impulse was to

share it with my family and relatives. Once the
natural-born hostility to God and His Law had been
crushed, the Bible TRUTH appeared as a glorious
light—the most WONDERFUL thing I had ever known. I
was suddenly filled with zeal to get this precious
knowledge to all who were close to my wife and me. I
wanted to get *them* converted.

Suddenly I began to feel so *un*selfish in this new
Christian experience that I felt my own final fate was
not important, if only I could get those related by blood
or marriage ties into God's Kingdom.

But sad disillusionment followed every overture. I
had absolutely no success whatsoever trying to cram
"my religion" down their throats.

Facing the Tobacco Question

Then, immediately I was baptized, the matter of
smoking had to be settled.

Of course the Quaker church, in which I had been
reared as a boy, taught that smoking was a sin. But I had
been unhappily disillusioned to see that in so many
basic points the Bible teaching is the very opposite of
what I had absorbed in Sunday school.

"I've got to see the answer to the tobacco question
IN THE BIBLE!" I said to myself.

Until I found the answer *in the Bible*, I decided I
would continue as before—smoking mildly.

I had continued to smoke lightly, averaging three or
four cigarettes a day, or one cigar a day. I had never been
a heavy smoker.

Now I had to face the question: Is smoking a SIN?

I wanted the BIBLE answer, for I had learned by this
time that Christ had said we must live by EVERY WORD OF
GOD. The BIBLE is our Instruction Book on right living.
We must find a BIBLE reason for everything we do.

I knew, of course, there is no specific command, "Thou shalt not smoke." *But the absence of a detailed prohibition did not mean God's approval.*

I had learned that GOD'S LAW is His WAY OF LIFE. It is a basic philosophy of life. The whole Law is summed up in the one word LOVE. I knew that *love* is the opposite of *lust*. Lust is *self*-desire—pleasing the *self* only. Love means loving *others*. Its direction is not inward toward self alone, but *outgoing*, toward *others*. I knew the Bible teaches that "lust of the flesh" is the way of SIN.

So now I began to apply the *principle* of God's Law.

I asked myself, "WHY do I smoke?" To please others—to help others—to serve or minister to or express love toward others—or only to satisfy and gratify a desire of the flesh within my own *self?*

The answer was instantaneously obvious. I had to be honest with it. My only reason for smoking was LUST OF THE FLESH, and lust of the flesh is, *according to the BIBLE, sin!*

I stopped smoking immediately. This beginning of overcoming was not too difficult, for it had not been a "big habit" with me. Once weaned, I was able to see it as it is—a dirty, filthy habit. And today we know it is a serious and major contributing cause of lung cancer!

God designed and created the human body. He designed the LUNGS to take in FRESH AIR to "fire" and oxidize the blood, and at the same time to filter out of the blood the impurities and waste matter the blood has picked up throughout the body. Befouled smoke, containing the poisons of nicotine and tars, reduces the efficiency of the operation of this vital organ.

The physical human body is, God says, the very TEMPLE of His Holy Spirit. If we defile this TEMPLE — this *physical* body—God says He will *destroy us!* God intended us, if we are to be COMPLETE, to live happy, healthy and abundant lives, and to gain eternal life, to *take in* HIS SPIRIT—*not* poisonous foreign substances like tobacco.

Mrs. Armstrong Stricken

I was now beginning to *grow* in Christ's *knowledge* and in His GRACE. His Holy Spirit had renewed my mind. I could now UNDERSTAND God's TRUTH as I studied His Word.

I had come to understand, *the hard way,* the truth about Law and Grace. I had come to understand the Bible teaching about water baptism. I had come to see that I could not help others unless I, myself, were obedient and practicing what I preached. I had come to see the truth about tobacco. Now God saw fit to teach my wife and me another most important and useful truth. He let us learn it through severe experience, coupled with Bible study.

Along about early August, 1927, a series of physical illnesses and injuries attacked Mrs. Armstrong.

First, she was bitten on the left arm by a dog. Before this healed over, she was driven to bed with tonsilitis. She got up from this too soon, and was stricken violently with a "backset." But meanwhile she had contracted blood poisoning as a result of being stuck with a rose thorn on the index finger of her right hand.

For two or three days her sister and I had to take turns, day and night, soaking her right hand in almost blistering hot epsom salts water, and covering her wrist and forearm with hot towels, always holding her right arm high.

The backset from the tonsilitis developed into quinsy. Her throat was swollen shut. It locked her jaw.

326

For three days and three nights she was unable to swallow a drop of water or a morsel of food. More serious, for three days and three nights she was unable to sleep a wink. She was nearing exhaustion. The red line of the blood poisoning, in spite of our constant hot epsom salts efforts, was streaking up her right arm, and had reached her shoulder on the way to the heart.

The doctor had told me privately that she could not last another twenty-four hours. This third sleepless, foodless and waterless day was a scorching hot summer day in early August.

Does God HEAL Today?

On this late morning, a neighbor lady came over to see my wife.

"Mr. Armstrong," she asked, out of hearing of my wife, "would you object if I ask a man and his wife to come and anoint and pray for your wife's healing?"

That sounded a little fanatical to me. Yet, somehow, I felt too embarrassed to object.

"Well, no, I suppose not," I replied, hesitantly.

About two hours later she returned, and said they would come at about seven in the evening.

I began to have misgivings, I began to regret having given consent.

"What if these people are some of these wild-fire shouters," I thought to myself. "Suppose they begin to shout and yell and scream like these 'holy roller' or 'pentecostal' fanatics do? *Oh my!* What would our neighbors think?"

Quickly I gathered courage to go to our neighbor who had asked them to come. I told her I had been thinking it over, and felt it better that these people did not come. She was very nice about it. She would start immediately, and ask them not to come. Then I learned she would have to walk over a mile to contact them. They were living in some rooms in the former Billy Sunday tabernacle that had been built for Billy Sunday's Portland campaign some years earlier. This tabernacle was out beyond 82nd Street, near Sandy Boulevard.

It was now in the heat of the day—the hottest day of the year. I began to feel quite ashamed to impose on this woman, by asking her to make a second long walk on that sweltering afternoon.

"I do hate to ask you to make a second trip out there," I said apologetically. "I didn't realize it was so far. But I was afraid these people might yell and shout, and create a neighborhood disturbance."

"Oh, they are very quiet people," she hastened to assure me. "They won't shout."

After that I decided not to impose on this neighbor who was only trying to help us.

"Let's let them come, then," I concluded.

The Meaning of FAITH

That evening this man and his wife came, about seven. He was rather tall. They were plain people, obviously not of high education, yet intelligent appearing.

"This is all rather new to me," I began, when they were seated beside my wife's bed. "Would you mind if I ask you a few questions, before you pray for my wife?"

He welcomed the questions. He had a Bible in his hands, and one by one he answered my every question and doubt by turning to a passage in his Bible and giving me the Bible answer.

By this time I had become sufficiently familiar with the Bible to recognize every passage he read—only I had never thought of these Biblical statements and promises and admonitions in this particular light before.

As these answers continued coming from the Bible, I began to understand, and to BELIEVE—and I knew the same assurance was forming in Mrs. Armstrong's mind.

Finally I was satisfied. I had the answer from the Bible. I believed. My wife believed. We knelt in prayer beside her bed. As he anointed my wife with oil from a vial he carried, he uttered a quiet, positive, very earnest and believing prayer which was utterly different from any prayer I had ever heard.

This man actually dared to talk directly to God, and to tell God what He had PROMISED *to do!* He quoted the promises of God to heal. He applied them to my wife. He literally held God to what he had *promised!* It was not because we, as mortal humans, deserved what he asked, but through the merits of Jesus Christ, and according to God's great mercy.

He merely claimed God's PROMISE to heal. He asked God to heal her completely, from the top of her head to the bottom of her feet.

"You have promised," he said to God, "and you have given us the right to hold you to your promise to *heal* by the power of your mighty Holy Spirit. I hold you to that promise! We *expect* to have the answer!"

Never had I heard anyone talk like *that* to God!

It was not a long prayer—perhaps a minute or two. But as he spoke I *knew* that as sure as there is a God in heaven, my wife *had to be healed!* Any other result would have made God out a liar. Any other result would have nullified the authority of the Scriptures. Complete assurance seized me—and also my wife. We simply *knew* that she was released from everything that had gripped her—she was *freed* from the sickness—she was *healed!* To have doubted would have been to doubt God—to doubt the Bible. It simply never occurred to us to doubt. We believed! We knew!

As we rose, the man's wife laid a hand on Mrs. Armstrong's shoulder. "You'll sleep soundly tonight," she smiled quietly.

I thanked them gratefully. As soon as they had left, Mrs. Armstrong asked me to bring her a robe. She arose, put it on, and I walked slowly with her out to the street sidewalk and back, my arm around her. Neither of us spoke a word. There was no need. We both understood. It was too solemn a moment to speak. We were too choked with gratitude.

She slept soundly until 11:00 a.m. next day. Then she arose and dressed as if she had never been ill. She had been healed of *everything,* including some long-standing internal maladjustments.

We had learned a new lesson in the meaning of faith. Faith is not only the *evidence* of that which we *do not see or feel*—it is not only the ASSURANCE of what we hope for—it is definite knowing that God will DO whatever He has *promised.* Faith is BASED on God's written PROMISES. The Bible is filled with thousands of God's promises. They are there for us to claim. They are SURE. God can't lie.

If there is any one attribute to God's character that is more outstanding than any other, it is God's *faithfulness*—the fact that HIS WORD IS GOOD! *Think* how hopeless we would be if God's *word* were not good! And if a man's word is not to be trusted, all his other good points go for naught—he is utterly lacking in right character.

A Dumbfounded Doctor

Shortly before Mrs. Armstrong had been confined to

330

bed in this illness, she had taken our elder daughter Beverly to the doctor with a felon on her finger. It had not been bandaged for some days.

The morning after her miraculous healing, my wife arose about eleven, ate a breakfast, and then took Beverly to the doctor's office to have the bandage removed. Incidentally this was the last time we have ever called a doctor for any illness in our family.

"WHAT are *you* doing *here!*" exclaimed the doctor, looking as if he had seen a ghost.

"Well," answered my wife, "do you believe in divine healing?"

"I don't believe Mary Baker Eddy has any more 'pull' with God Almighty than I have!" asserted the physician.

"But I don't mean that," Mrs. Armstrong explained, "I mean miraculous healing direct by God as a result of prayer."

"Well—*yes*—I—*do!*" replied the astonished doctor, slowly, incredulously. "But I never did before."

Studying a New Subject

This awe-inspiring experience brought a totally new subject before me for study. And remember, I had plenty of time on my hands for Bible study. Only one laundry client remained. We were now reduced to real poverty. Although I had been beaten down and had made a complete surrender to God, giving myself to Him, yet without realizing it much of the self-pride and vanity remained. Of course God knew this. He was yet to bring me down much lower. I was yet to be humiliated repeatedly and thoroughly chastened before God could use me.

In those days we were constantly behind with our house rent. When we had a little money for food we bought beans and such food as would provide the most bulk for the least money. Often we went hungry. Yet, looking back over those days, Mrs. Armstrong was remarking just the day before this was written that we were finding happiness despite the economic plight— and we did not complain or grumble. But we *did* suffer.

From the time of my conversion Mrs. Armstrong has always studied with me. We didn't realize it then, but God was calling us *together*. We were always a team, working together in unity.

And now came a new subject to study, and new enlightenment. We entered into it with vigor and joy. We searched out everything we could find in the Bible on the subject of physical healing. We discovered that God revealed Himself to ancient Israel, even before they reached Mt. Sinai, under His name "Yahweh-Ropha" which means "The Eternal our Healer," or "Our GOD-HEALER," or, as translated in the *Authorized Version*, "The LORD that healeth thee."

He revealed Himself as Healer through David: "Who forgiveth all thine iniquities; who HEALETH all thy *diseases*" (Psalm 103:3). And again: "Fools because of their transgression, and because of their iniquities, are afflicted. Their soul abhorreth all manner of food; they draw near unto the gates of death. Then they cry unto the Eternal in their trouble, and ... He sendeth His word, and HEALETH them" (Psalm 107:17-20).

Then I made a discovery I had not read in any of the tracts and literature we had been sending for and gathering on this subject. Healing is actually the *forgiveness* of transgressed *physical* laws just as salvation comes through forgiveness of transgressed *spiritual* law. It is the forgiveness of physical SIN. God forgives the physical sin because Jesus PAID THE PENALTY

332

we are suffering IN OUR STEAD. He was beaten with stripes *before* He was nailed to the cross.

Experience of the Crooked Spine

After we had made some little progress in gaining Biblical understanding of this subject of healing, Aimee Semple McPherson came to Portland.

She held an evangelistic campaign in the Portland Auditorium. My wife and I attended once, and then I went alone another time. We were "checking up" on many religious teachings and groups. Unable to gain entrance, because of packed attendance, I was told by an usher that I might be able to slip in at the rear stage door if I would hurry around. Walking, or running, around the block to the rear, I came upon a sorry spectacle.

A woman and child were trying to get a terribly crippled elderly man out of a car near the stage entrance. I went over to help them. The man had a badly twisted spine—whether from arthritis, or deformity from birth, or other disease I do not now remember. He was utterly helpless and a pitiful sight to look upon.

We managed to get him to the stage door. Actually, I should never have been admitted, had I not been helping to carry this cripple in. He had come to be healed by the famous lady evangelist.

We were unable to gain contact with Mrs. McPherson before the service. And we were equally unable, after the service. I helped get the disappointed cripple back into their car.

"If you really want to be healed," I said before they drove off, "I would be glad to come to your home and pray for you. Mrs. McPherson has no power within herself to heal anybody. I have none. Only GOD can heal. But I do know what He has promised to do, and I believe

333

God will hear me just as willingly as He will Mrs. McPherson—if only you will BELIEVE in what GOD has promised, and put your faith in HIM and not in the person who prays for you."

They gave me their address, just south of Foster Road. The next day I borrowed my brother Russell's car and drove out.

I had learned, in this study, that there are two conditions which God imposes. 1) we must *keep His commandments*, and do those things that are pleasing in His sight (I John 3:22); and 2) we must really BELIEVE (Matt. 9:29).

Of course I realized that many people might not have come into the understanding about keeping all of God's Commandments—he does look on the *heart*. It is the *spirit, and willingness* to obey. And therefore some who really BELIEVE are healed, even though they are not strictly "commandment keepers." But once the *knowledge of the truth* comes, they must OBEY. In this case I felt sure that God wanted me to open the minds of these people about His Commandments, and that SIN *is* the transgression of God's LAW.

Consequently, I first read the two scriptures quoted above, and then explained what I had been six months learning about God's Law—and particularly about God's Sabbath. I wanted to know whether this cripple and his wife had a spirit of WILLINGNESS to obey God.

They did not.

I found they were "pentecostal." They attended church for the "good time" they had there. They talked a good deal about the "good time" they enjoyed at church. They scoffed and sneered about having to obey God. I told them that, since they were unwilling to obey God and comply with God's written conditions for healing, I could not pray for him.

Was This an Angel?

This case had weighed heavily on my mind. I had been touched with deep compassion for this poor fellow. Yet his mind was not impaired, and I knew that God does not compromise with SIN.

Some weeks later I had borrowed my brother's car again, and happened to be driving out Foster Road. Actually at the time my mind was filled with another mission, and this deformed cripple was not on my mind at all. I was deep in thought about another matter.

Coming to the intersection of the street on which the cripple lived, however, I was reminded of him. Instantly the thought came as to whether I ought to pay them one more call—but at the same instant reason ruled it out. They had made light of, and actually ridiculed the idea of surrendering to *obey* God. Immediately I put them out of mind, and again was deep in thought about the present mission I was on.

Then a strange thing happened.

At the next intersection, the steering wheel of the car automatically turned to the right. I felt the wheel turning. I resisted it. It kept turning right. Instantly I applied all my strength to counteract it, and keep steering straight ahead. My strength was of no avail. Some unseen force was turning that steering wheel *against* all my strength. The car had turned to the right into the street one block east of the home of the cripple.

I was frightened. Never before had I experienced anything like this. I stopped the car by the curb. I didn't know what to make of it.

It was too late to back into traffic-heavy Foster Road.

"Well," I thought, "I'll drive to the end of this block

335

and turn left, and then back onto Foster Road."

But, a long block south on this street, it turned right *only*. There was no street turning east. In getting back onto Foster Road I was now compelled to drive past the home of the cripple.

"Could it possibly be that an angel *forced* the steering wheel to turn me in here?" I wondered, somewhat shaken by the experience. I decided I had better stop in at the cripple's home a moment, to be sure.

I found him stricken with blood poisoning. The red line was nearing his heart.

I told them what had happened.

"I know, now," I said, "that God sent an angel to turn me in here. I believe that God wants me to pray for you—that He will heal you of this blood poisoning to show you His power, and then give you one more chance to repent and be willing to obey Him. And if you will do that, then He will straighten out your twisted spine and heal you completely.

"So now, if you want me to do so, I will pray for you and ask God to heal you of this blood poisoning. But I will *not* ask God to heal your spine unless and until you repent and show willingness to obey whatever you yourself see God commands."

They were now desperate. He probably had about twelve hours to live. They were not joking and jesting lightly about the "good times" at "pentecostal meetin'." They wanted me to pray.

I was not an ordained minister, so I did not anoint with oil. I had never yet in my life prayed aloud before others. I explained this to them, and said I would simply lay hands on the man and pray silently, as I did not want any self-consciousness of praying aloud for the first time to interfere with real earnestness and faith. I did have

336

absolute faith he would be healed of the blood poisoning.

He was.

I returned the next day. The blood poisoning had left him immediately when I prayed. But, to my very great sorrow and disappointment, they were once again filled with levity, and sarcasm about God's Law. Again they were jestingly talking about having a "good time" at church.

There was no more I could do. It was one of the great disappointments of my life. I never saw or heard from any of them again.

19

Trying to Convert Relatives

IN ALL my experience since conversion
one oft-repeated incident has brought
sorrow and regret. Many times a certain
individual has been used to bring us light, or truth, or
help, or certain advancement or stimulus to the Work of
God, only to lose out spiritually and be discarded, once
his usefulness was over.

Resurrection Not on Sunday

It was about this time, summer, 1927, my wife and I had
learned an exciting, shocking truth. The resurrection of
Christ did not occur on Sunday morning!

The crucifixion was not on so-called "Good
Friday." These I had found to be mere traditions, totally
unsupported by any evidence, and completely refuted
by the sole historic record—the Bible.

I had learned—and found completely PROVED—that
Jesus was in the tomb of Joseph of Arimathaea *three*

days and three nights. Jesus Himself said so (Matthew 12:40). It was the *only SIGN* He gave as a miraculous PROOF of Messiahship.

The usual argument employed to discredit Jesus' statement, that this was an idiomatic expression in the original Greek meaning only three *parts* of days, or *either* a day or night, did not stand up. We had the same three days and three nights duration expressed in Jonah, inspired in Hebrew which knows no such idiomatic twist—or *idiotic* twist. Also many other passages verified the full 72-hour duration.

The crucifixion was on Wednesday. The resurrection of Jesus Christ from the dead was late Sabbath afternoon, prior to sunset. This is proved conclusively, not only by all the scriptures on the subject, which are many, but also by astronomy, and by the Hebrew calendar. In the year in which Jesus was crucified—A.D. 31—the Passover was on a Wednesday, not a Friday.

The reader, if not already familiar with this truth, is invited to write for the booklet titled *The Resurrection Was Not On Sunday,* and also, to learn the true origin and full truth about Easter, ask for the booklet titled *The Plain Truth About Easter.* Both are free, of course.

From the beginning of the new Spirit-led life, I wrote, in article form the thrilling new truths being unfolded in this continuous almost night-and-day study. This discovery of the true dates of the crucifixion and resurrection was written in an article captioned *"Foundation for Sunday Sacredness Crumbles."*

I had found that opponents of God's Sabbath can invent some fifty-seven varieties of arguments to explain why they *don't* keep the Sabbath. But they have only *one* argument for observing Sunday—the supposition of a Sunday morning resurrection.

Of course no scripture anywhere tells us to observe the day of the resurrection. That, too, is a man-made argument.

Actually, there is absolutely *NO* Bible *authority* for Sunday observance. The *only* authority for it is that of the Roman Catholic Church—a fact I believe any Catholic priest will confirm. Protestants, whether knowingly or not, acknowledge the *authority* of the Roman Catholic Church in observing Sunday.

With a Sunday resurrection illusion shattered, the last *supposed* foundation for Sunday observance had crumbled.

Disheartening Disappointment

This article, *"Foundation for Sunday Sacredness Crumbles,"* I believe, was never published. I did not write the articles, in those days, with the intention or expectation of having them published. I had been a trained advertising-copy and magazine-article writer. It simply came naturally to put into article form these intriguing, fascinating truths for my personal enjoyment and record.

But, exciting as these new truths were to me, I realized fully I was *new* in the truth—a novice spiritually—a "babe in Christ." I deemed it wise to have this newly discovered truth about the day of the resurrection verified by others more experienced in Biblical understanding than I.

It was but natural to look upon the man whose prayer God had so miraculously answered in healing my wife as a "man of God." So, even though I felt sure this truth was proved, I wanted to be doubly sure. Also I sincerely wanted to share this wonderful truth with the man whom God had used in sparing my wife's life. So I walked down to the old Billy Sunday tabernacle, out past 82nd Street, where this man was caretaker, one evening, very shortly after my wife's healing.

This "man of God" promised he would study my article and give me his opinion. Then a few nights later I returned to his living quarters in a corner of the giant tabernacle.

For several minutes other subjects occupied the conversation.

"But did you study into my article about the day of the resurrection?" I asked, since he avoided mentioning it.

"Well, yes, Brother," he replied, "I took it to our pastor and we went over it together."

"Well, did you find any error in what I wrote?" I persisted.

"Well, no, Brother," he admitted, "we couldn't find anything wrong with it. It does seem to be according to the Scriptures, but Brother, we feel that studying into *that* kind of subject is likely to be *dangerous*. It might get you all mixed up. We feel it would be better for you to just forget all about that—just get your mind clear off of that. There are *more* important things for you to think about and study into. It's best to just keep your mind on Christ."

"But," I rejoined, suddenly disillusioned, "if the resurrection was on the Sabbath, and not on Sunday, the only reason anyone has for Sunday observance is gone. Don't you think we might be breaking the commands of God and sinning, if we ignore such a truth?"

"Well, now, Brother," he tried to reassure me, "that's just the trouble. You see how it could get you all upset. All the churches observe Sunday. We can't start to fight all the churches. Now we are saved by GRACE, not of works. We think there are *more important* things in salvation than which *day* Christ rose on, or which *day* we keep. This could just get you all mixed up. It could be *dangerous*. Better just get your mind off of such things."

I walked back to our home on Klickitat Street in Portland, grieved and sorrowfully disillusioned. I had had a lot of confidence in this man. Now here he was, *admitting* I had brought him a new TRUTH, proved by the Bible, *yet rejecting* this LIGHT—and, more, advising a newly converted man who had confidence in him to reject THE WORD OF GOD!

Arriving home, I happened to turn to Hosea 4:6, where God says that because we have rejected His knowledge, He will reject us.

TRUTH, or Consequences

A week or two later I walked back out past 82nd Street to the huge old Billy Sunday tabernacle. This thing had weighed heavily on my mind. This tall, uneducated, plain and simple man had been an instrument in God's hands not only in saving my wife's life, but also in opening our eyes to the truth of God's healing power. I felt deeply grateful. I hoped that even yet I might help rescue this man from the consequences of rejecting God's revealed knowledge.

I found him in the big auditorium. He appeared dejected, downcast, worried.

"Brother," he said, on looking up and seeing me, "Brother, something terrible has come over me. God has left me. *He doesn't answer my prayers any more.* I don't understand what has happened."

Poor man! I understood what had happened.

He had been a trusting and deeply sincere, if simple, man. God had used this man. God used him to bring my wife and me the knowledge that God actually

342

performs miracles for those who trust Him—He heals—*if* we obey and *believe.* And how many other people God had helped through this man's prayers I did not know.

Evidently, until God used *me* to test him by bringing to him a new truth, he had not deliberately rejected truth nor disobeyed God's commands *knowingly.* God looks on the *heart,* and until this man followed his preacher in deliberately *rejecting* light and truth from God which he acknowledged to be truth and which led to wilful disobedience, his heart was honest and sincere in his simple way.

But he had rejected God's knowledge. And now God had rejected him!

His prayers were no longer answered.

He was now guilty of *disobedience* of God's Law. And God reveals through John that "whatsoever we ask, we receive of him, *because* we keep his *commandments,* and DO those things that are pleasing in HIS *sight*" (I John 3:22). This man no longer complied with the divine conditions. Yet, if ever I met a man who had the "gift of healing" spoken of in I Corinthians 12:9, this man had had it.

God had used him to bring to us a truth. We accepted it, and began to *walk* in it. Then God used me to take to him a truth. He acknowledged that it was the truth. He had seen it *proved.* Yet he rejected it, and walked in disobedience instead of in the light! God used this man no more.

Of course he had MUCH to learn, had he continued as an instrument in God's hands. True Christians must continually *overcome,* and GROW in grace and the *knowledge* of Jesus Christ.

The servant of God cannot stand still. Either he advances, and *grows* spiritually against opposition and obstacles, or he falls by the wayside to be rejected. It is not an easy road.

This incident just described is but one of many of its kind. Later I was to encounter many more whom God used to help me and His Work, only to see them endure but a while, and fall aside. Several of these have been among our closest and most loved personal friends. These experiences have provided our greatest suffering in God's service. They were pictured by Jesus' parable of the sower and the seed. It seems the majority who start out on this straight and narrow road of opposition, persecution, trial and test, self-restraint, continuous attitude of repentance, overcoming, growing, fail to endure until the end.

It has grieved Mrs. Armstrong and me deeply to see so many for whom we were grateful—who had helped us and God's Work—whom we learned to love so much, turn aside finally and drop out of the race for eternal life.

"Let him that thinketh he standeth *take heed,* lest he fall!" *How about YOU?*

Don't YOU Make THIS Mistake!

That year 1927 was a very eventful year in my life.

As soon as I swallowed my bitterest pill of rebellion, surrendered to *obey* and trust fully in the Mighty God through faith in the living Jesus Christ, this new Christian WAY became the most happy, joyful experience of my life. Studying the Bible became a passion and a joy. I plunged into it with concentrated zeal.

The all-day sessions at the Portland Public Library did not stop with my capitulation to the truth following the six months' angered study to end my wife's "fanaticism."

No longer was it an intensive study driven by anger

and determination to have my own way. Now it was an enthusiastic study of eager anticipation, literally *thrilling* to every new discovery of spiritual "light" and basic knowledge.

Now a passion swept over me to "get our families converted."

With the best intentions in the world, I set out on a vigorous campaign. To me, it was the loving and intense desire to *share* the wonders and glories of Bible knowledge with those we felt we loved most. But to most of them, it was an unwanted effort to "cram my crazy religion down their throats."

I did succeed, apparently, in talking one sister-in-law into a certain start. I had to learn later it was a false start. She was baptized, either when I was, or very shortly afterward. But, as too often happens when a high-pressure salesman talks one into something he doesn't really want, she turned against it all shortly afterward.

I had to learn, however, that, even though I had believed I was a pretty good salesman in my earlier business experience, I was unable utterly to "cram my religion down my relatives' throats." My efforts only aroused hostility. They said I was "crazy."

This is a universal mistake committed by the newly converted. Especially is this true where a husband or wife yields to God's truth without the other.

It actually threatened to break up our marriage—even though Mrs. Armstrong did NOT attempt to inject her new religious belief into me. In our case the marriage was saved because I accepted the challenge to study into it myself, confident I could prove she was wrong.

But most mates will not study into it. Most unconverted mates, especially if the converted one tries to talk the other into his or her religion, will break up the home instead.

In all the years since my conversion, I have known of many marriages that have ended in divorce *because the newly converted mate tried to talk the unconverted one into it.* I have never heard of a case where the unconverted mate was talked into accepting it.

Of all things evil and harmful a newly converted Christian can do, the very WORST is to try to talk your husband or wife into your religion. WHATEVER else you do, let me *plead* with every such reader, *NEVER* commit this tragic sin. If you love your husband or wife, *don't do it!!* If you love your Saviour who died for you, and now lives for you, *DON'T DO IT!!!*

Learning the Lesson

Remember these scriptures: "No man can come to me," said Jesus, "except the Father which hath sent me draw him" (John 6:44, 45). Again, Jesus said: "Think not that I am come to send peace on earth: I came *not* to send peace, but a sword. For I am come to set a man at variance against his father, and the daughter against her mother . . . and a man's foes shall be they of his own household. . . . He that loveth father or mother" . . . (or wife or husband) . . . "more than me is not worthy of me. . . . And he that taketh not his cross and followeth after me is not worthy of me" (Matt. 10:34-38).

God made every human a free moral agent. Thank God!—no one has power to force on *you* any unwanted religion.

Every individual makes his *own* decision. A religious difference between husband and wife is a serious handicap. The Bible *forbids* a converted person from marrying an unconverted.

But if such difference already exists, do not make

346

matters worse by *talking* religion to your mate. Do all your *talking* to God in prayer. Let your mate *see* your happy, pleasant, cheerful, joyful, loving WAY of life—not *hear* your arguments or nagging! Allow your mate complete religious latitude and freedom—whether to be converted, religious, irreligious, or atheistic!

I am glad I learned that lesson early. I have had to maintain certain business connections with many people, since being plunged into God's Work. I must maintain contacts with radio men, publishers, professional men. I get along splendidly with them. A big reason is that I never talk religion to them.

I never try to talk *anyone* into accepting Bible truth or being converted. I go *to* the world over the air, and in print, and everyone is free to listen, or read—or to dial out or not read. No one gets our literature unless he personally requests it. We try never to force God's precious truth on anyone. That's GOD's WAY!!

How NOT to "Witness for Christ"

Do you know how the Apostle Paul won individuals to Christ? Not the way people attempt to do it today. He said "I am made all things to all men, that I might by all means save *some.*" When he talked to an unconverted Jew, do you suppose he spoke as a Christian thinking he is "witnessing for Christ" would do today? Do you suppose Paul said to the unconverted Jew: "Have you received Christ as your personal Saviour?"

No, that is not the way Paul spoke to unconverted Jews. Paul said: "Unto the Jews I became *as a Jew*" (I Cor. 9:22, 20). Paul spoke to others *from their point of view!* He talked to a Jew just like *another Jew*—from the *Jewish viewpoint*—showing sympathy and understanding of the *Jews'* way of looking at Christianity. Paul did not arouse hostility—he put it down, so that

347

they were *sympathetic* toward him, not hostile. He became *as* a Jew, "that I might gain the Jews." Even so he gained only a small minority, yet it was a large number.

Perhaps you have had your eyes opened to the fact that sin is transgression of God's Law. Most professing Christians have been taught, and consequently sincerely believe, that "the Law is done away." Paul was inspired to write that the carnal mind is hostile to God and to God's Law; "it is not subject to the law of God, neither indeed can be" (Rom. 8:7). If you say to your unconverted mate who is hostile to God's Law, "You're just a rebellious *sinner,* and your church is just one of these false worldly churches," you have not only aroused hostility, you have yourself *been hostile,* and you probably have broken up your marriage.

How did Paul talk to such people? Listen: "To them that are without law, *as without law,* that I might gain them that are without law."

First Principle in Influencing Others

One of the first principles of successful advertising I learned early in my career is that to get results you must *first* learn the attitude of your reading audience toward whatever product or service you are advertising. You must not antagonize those whom you expect to persuade. You must approach them from *their* point of view—not from *yours,* especially if your viewpoint is contrary to theirs. To win them to *your* point of view, you must approach them from *their* viewpoint. Otherwise you only arouse hostility.

I know that these words are addressed to a very large number who have made this terrible mistake. That is why I have devoted so much space to this point.

If you believe God's truth, and your husband or

wife does not, NEVER TALK RELIGION to him or her. If your mate normally thinks and speaks only of material and worldly things, then you must speak of material things to your spouse.

If the *World Tomorrow* broadcast has, probably because of your own aggressiveness in trying to get your mate to listen, become a sore spot, go off to some private room to hear the program. Keep the volume turned down. *Make every effort NOT to antagonize* your husband or wife.

And again, when you *talk* about it, talk to God in prayer. Let your mate see your *good conduct,* in a manner that he or she will naturally approve. Avoid every hostility. Be *pleasant.* Keep *cheerful. Be happy.* Radiate JOY! Give LOVE and warm affection! Do everything to cause your husband or wife to *like* you! *THAT IS THE CHRISTIAN WAY!*

20

The First Sermon

THIS chapter of the Autobiography is being written in Rome. It dawns in my mind that there is intriguing significance in the fact that I should be here at the very time when this chapter must be written.

The Apostle Paul wrote some of the books of the Bible here in Rome. It was then the seat of the ancient pagan Roman Empire. It was world headquarters of the pagan religion.

Today it is world headquarters for the largest and most powerful professing Christian church.

We come now to the time, in recounting my life experiences, where I had been sadly disillusioned about organized traditional "Christianity." As earlier chapters have explained, my wife, in early fall of 1926, had begun to observe the seventh-day Sabbath. To me that was the most disgraceful fanaticism she could have embraced. But six months' intensive and determined night-

and-day study of the Bible had failed to find the authority for Sunday observance I had felt confident it contained.

"All these churches can't be wrong," I had contended. I felt certain that all their teachings whether Catholic or Protestant, had come directly from the Bible. I did not then realize that the Roman Catholic Church makes no such claim, but claims that church itself is the sole official and infallible authority. The various denominations, I supposed—just as millions still suppose—were just so many different parts of the one true Christian church.

Disillusioned—Perplexed

I have already told you repeatedly how rudely I was disillusioned. I had seen, with my own eyes, that the plain teachings of Christ—of Paul—of the Bible—were *not* the teachings of the traditional "Christianity" of our time. Nothing had ever been more shocking to discover. Incredible as it seemed, the beliefs and practices of the churches today, I found, were *far* astray from the teachings and customs of the TRUE Church as Christ organized it. In fact, in most essentials, the very antithesis!

This emphatically was not what I *wanted* to believe.

It had left my head swimming. I was stunned, perplexed!

I began to ask, "WHERE, then, is the real true Church which CHRIST founded?"

The True GOSPEL

My shocking, disappointing, eye-opening discovery, upon looking into the Bible for myself, had revealed in stark plainness that the teachings of traditional

351

Christianity were, in most basic points, the *very opposite* of the teachings of Christ, of Paul, and of the original true Church!

Could the original and only *true* Church have disintegrated and disappeared? Could it have ceased to exist? No, for I read where Jesus said the gates of the grave would never prevail against it. Also He had said to His disciples who formed His Church, "Lo, I am with you always."

Then I saw that the very PURPOSE of the Church was *to preach Christ's GOSPEL!* It is HIS BODY—His *instrument* by which HE carries on GOD'S WORK!

I looked carefully at that Gospel as Christ Himself preached it, and taught it to His first ministers. It is recorded in the four books of Matthew, Mark, Luke and John. At almost every point of teaching that Jesus enunciated, the teachings of traditional Christian bodies today are just the opposite.

THEY WERE NOT PREACHING THE SAME GOSPEL AT ALL, BUT A TOTALLY OPPOSITE MESSAGE! This was shocking—incredible—unbelievable! Yet I was compelled to see it was true!

Jesus *began* the work of preaching the very Gospel which GOD the Father had sent to mankind through Him. He commissioned His disciples—His Church—to carry this same Gospel to all the world. And He had said He would never drop the Work He had begun! But WHERE was it going on *today?*

Seeking an Obedient Church

I knew now that when I found the one and *only* true Church, I would find a Church *obedient to God*—keeping His commandments—having the testimony of Jesus Christ, which is the TRUTH of the Scriptures.

I had been much impressed by a description of the

true Church, as it is to be found in our time—just before the second coming of Christ. It is found in Revelation 12. It is the time when Satan is filled with wrath against God's Church, "because he knoweth that he hath but a short time" (Rev. 12:12). Satan is making war with "the *remnant* of her seed." The *"remnant"* means the very last generation in this age. The Church is definitely described. It is those *"which keep the commandments of God,* and have the testimony of Jesus Christ" (Rev. 12:17).

My intensive study had revealed one thing plainly: "the commandments of God" mean "Sabbath keeping" to most traditional denominations. They say, "The commandments are done away!" They reject "the commandments of God."

That automatically ruled out all churches observing Sunday. So far as I could learn, it reduced the search to three small groups—the Seventh-Day Adventists, the Seventh-Day Baptists, and a little, almost unheard-of church called the Church of God, which maintained a small publishing-house headquarters at Stanberry, Missouri.

So I examined Seventh-Day Adventist teachings— just as I did those of many other denominations. I obtained their magazines, their booklets and pamphlets, their large book of Bible readings, or Bible "home instructor."

The true Church is the one which lives by EVERY WORD OF GOD—the words of the BIBLE!

Never an Adventist

It seems necessary to add here that I have *never* been a member of the Seventh-Day Adventist denomination. False statements have appeared in various church or religious magazines, pamphlets or tracts that I am a former Seventh-Day Adventist. I did obtain much of their literature, *to compare with the Bible.* I did examine and study it with an open mind, and without prejudice. I was happy to find that, like most denominations, they do have certain points of truth. None is 100% in error.

But my familiarity with Adventist doctrines has come entirely through their published literature. *I have never attended a regular Sabbath church service of that denomination!*

Next, I looked into the teaching of the Seventh-Day Baptists. I found it to be virtually identical, except for observing a different day of the week, with other Protestant denominations—especially the Baptists.

But of these three churches to which the search had been narrowed, only *one* had the right NAME for the true Church. This was the small, little-heard-of Church of God whose headquarters were at Stanberry, Missouri.

The True NAME

Twelve times in the New Testament, I found the NAME of the Church which Christ established plainly stated as "The CHURCH OF GOD."

I looked into this word "church." It is the English word translated from the Greek word *ekklesia.* It merely means a congregation, an assembly, or group or crowd of people. I found that the word, by itself, had no divine or spiritual connotation whatever. For example, the name "Lutheran Church" or, as it might be otherwise stated "Church of Luther," means simply, Luther's congregation, or assembly of people. A name like "Wesleyan Church," means, simply, Wesley's group or congregation, without any religious or spiritual or holy implication whatever.

In Acts 19:23-41 is an account of an angry and

hostile uprising against the Apostle Paul instigated by Gentile pagans who profited in business from the sale of silver shrines to the goddess Diana. Three times in this passage the original inspired Greek language called this angry crowd of citizens an "ekklesia." It is here translated into the English word "assembly." In verse 39 it actually refers to a "legal assembly" (Moffatt translation) in a courtroom. It certainly was not a Christian CHURCH assembled for worship—nor was it holy.

The only thing that adds sacredness to the word "church" is the true name "Church of GOD." That is *not* any man's church—but GOD's congregation—those *owned*, and *governed* by GOD whom they worship and follow.

In Ephesians 3:15, speaking of the FATHER of our Lord Jesus Christ (verse 14), we read: ". . . of whom the whole family in heaven and earth is named."

Jesus Christ is the *Head* of the Church, but it is *named* after God the Father. Although Jesus is Head of the Church, "the head of Christ is GOD" (I Cor. 11:3).

In His last prayer for His Church, before being seized to be crucified, Jesus prayed: *"I have manifested THY NAME* unto the men which thou gavest me out of the world: thine they were, and thou gavest them me; and *they have kept thy word* . . . Holy Father, *keep through* THINE OWN NAME those whom thou hast given me, that they may be one, as we are . . . While I was with them in the world, *I kept them in THY NAME"* (John 17:6-12).

Those in the true Church are begotten *children of God.* They become the affianced Bride of Christ. Christ is the Son of God. It is a FAMILY. The family, is, properly, named after its Father. The 12 passages, aside from these Scriptures here quoted, which plainly call the true

Church "The Church of God," or, collectively as local congregations, "The Churches of God," establish the true NAME.

Could GOD'S Church Be Fruitless?

The only Church I had so far found which "kept the commandments of God, and the testimony of Jesus Christ," and at the same time bore the NAME of the original true Church, was this almost unknown little Church of God with its small publishing house in Stanberry, Missouri.

But this left me quite confused. For this was a *little* Church, especially compared to the Roman Catholic, the Methodist, the Baptist, the Presbyterian, the Lutheran, or other large churches numbering millions of members. Then I saw where Jesus called His Church the "little flock."

But still I was not completely satisfied. I was deeply concerned. I prayed a great deal over it. For here was a church, which, compared to the large-scale activities of the Catholic and big Protestant bodies, was ineffective. I could see that it was imperfect. It wielded no great power. Jesus had said: "ALL POWER is given unto me, in heaven and earth" (Matt. 28:18). I read how Jesus Christ was to be *IN* His Church! He guides it! He directs it! He EMPOWERS it! He said His Church was to RECEIVE POWER (Acts 1:8).

No person is even a member of the true Church unless he has received, and is filled and led by, the Holy Spirit—and the Holy Spirit is the Spirit of POWER! This little church seemed to be powerless—comparatively impotent! I failed to see where it was bearing much if any fruit! Could a fruitless church be the ONE AND ONLY true Church of GOD on earth?

I was deeply perplexed. Here was a little church,

with scattered members probably numbering less than 2,000—mostly in rural areas. Apparently, as nearly as I could learn, it had only a very limited number of local churches, none as large as 100 members. As I began to come in contact with some of its leaders, they seemed to be men of little education—no college degrees—its ministry could hardly be described as an educated ministry. Their preaching had a certain fire, yet seemed totally to lack the POWER that attracts sizable audiences, that *moves* people, *stirs* hearts, and changes lives. I could see no visible results.

Could *this* be God's one and only true Church on earth? The very question seemed preposterous!

... But, Where Else?

And yet—

Yes, and yet, small, powerless, resultless, impotent though it appeared to be, here was a church with the right name, "keeping the commandments of God and the testimony of Jesus Christ," and *closer,* in its doctrines and teachings, to what God had been opening my eyes to see plainly in His Word than any other church of which I knew! Small and impotent though it appeared, *it had more Bible TRUTH than any church I could find!*

At this time, God was opening my understanding to *some* Biblical TRUTHS which this church did not accept; and also to some errors, even though minor, which it *did* embrace. Plainly, it was *not perfect.* It merely appeared to be more nearly so, and less imperfect, in its beliefs and practice, than any other.

COULD such a church—imperfect, fruitless, feeble, lacking in any sizable accomplishment, be the TRUE Church of God? Could *this* be Christ's INSTRUMENT through whom He worked, in carrying on GOD'S WORK on earth? Jesus said, "By their fruits ye shall know them." Its fruits were not evil—it simply did not seem to produce fruit!

I was bewildered. I was unable to come to the answer then—or until many years later. The real answer to this perplexing question will come out in this Autobiography later, at the account of the time when I myself found the true answer. I will state here, however, that I did learn later that it was merely the remnant of a church that had been more alive many years before.

Meanwhile, what was I to do? I was not at all convinced this was the one and only true Church. Yet, if it was not, *which one was?* This one came *closer* to the Bible qualifications than any I knew.

Therefore, I began to fellowship with their scattered and few members in Oregon, while at the same time refraining from acknowledging membership.

We were living in Portland, Oregon, at the time. I knew of no members of this church in Portland, but there was a sprinkling of them through the Willamette Valley between Salem and Eugene, in Oregon—mostly farmers or truck gardeners. They welcomed the fellowship of myself and Mrs. Armstrong.

We found them to be simple, plain and humble people, hard working and industrious, and loving the Bible TRUTH—as much as they had—willing to suffer persecution for it.

And so it was, in this detached fellowship, that Mrs. Armstrong and I continued the first three and a half years of my ceaseless night-and-day STUDY of the Bible—of history, especially as connected with Biblical history and prophecy—and of pertinent allied subjects. These, too, were years of much and earnest prayer. Much of the Bible study done at home was done *on my knees,* combining study with prayer. Much time was

358

spent during these years, as it had been that first six months, at the public library. I delved into intensive research in the commentaries, Bible encyclopedias, Bible dictionaries, comparing various translations of the Bible, examining Greek and Hebrew texts of doubtful or questionable passages, checking with lexicons and *Robertson's Grammar of the Greek New Testament*. I made an intensive study of ancient history in connection with Biblical history and prophecy.

But, as mentioned before, all this study and research had to be approached *a single doctrine at a time*. I was to be some years in getting to the very TRUNK of the tree of the very PURPOSE of which mankind was placed on earth, and getting clearly straightened out with a right understanding of God's PLAN.

Nevertheless, as I've mentioned, having been a trained magazine and advertising copywriter, the results of these studies were written up, purely for my own benefit, in article form. My wife began showing these articles to some women members of this Church of God who lived in Salem. Soon they began to urge me to preach before them. But becoming a preacher was the very *last* thing I had ever wanted to do. I felt an instinctive aversion to the idea.

Meanwhile, on their urging, a few of these articles had been mailed in to *The Bible Advocate* in Stanberry, Missouri. These articles began appearing on the front page.

The Dual Test

Early in this three-and-a-half-year period, between 1927 and 1930, I decided to try a dual test to help settle the question of whether this was, in actual fact, the true Church of God.

The Church is merely the sum total of its members.

By the one Spirit of God we are each baptized, or *put into,* the true Church (I Cor. 12:13). Jesus promised that when we receive the Holy Spirit, His Spirit shall guide us into ALL TRUTH—not merely part of it (John 16:13).

But no person can receive ALL truth instantaneously. The human mind receives knowledge gradually. The child of God must GROW in the knowledge of our Lord (II Peter 3:18). Also he must have the spirit of REPENTANCE, always ready and willing to acknowledge error and to turn from it. The Scriptures are profitable for REPROOF and CORRECTION, as well as INSTRUCTION in knowledge new to us. And God CORRECTS every son He loves (Heb. 12:6).

Now it was a simple truism that if each individual member of the Church must be GROWING in the knowledge of God, constantly OVERCOMING, being corrected, and eliminating error, then all the members *together,* which form the CHURCH, must also be constantly willing to confess error and eliminate it, and to accept that which is "new light" from God's Word to the Church.

I knew of no church or sect or denomination that had ever publicly confessed error or embraced new truth. Yet, plainly, this would be a *test* of the true Church.

So, as the first step in this test, I wrote up an exposition of some 16 typewritten pages proving clearly, plainly, and beyond contradiction that a certain minor point of doctrine proclaimed by this church, based on an erroneous interpretation of a certain verse of Scripture, was in error. This was mailed to the Stanberry, Missouri, headquarters to see whether their leaders would confess error and change.

The answer came back from their head man, editor of their paper and president of their "General

360

Conference." He was forced to admit, in plain words, that their teaching on this point was false and in error. But, he explained, he feared that if any attempt was made to correct this false doctrine and publicly confess the truth, many of their members, especially those of older standing and heavy tithe payers, would be unable to accept it. He feared they would lose confidence in the Church if they found it had been in error on any point. He said he feared many would withdraw their financial support, and it might divide the Church. And therefore he felt the Church could do nothing but continue to teach and preach this doctrine which he *admitted in writing to be false.*

Naturally, this shook my confidence considerably. This church leader, if not the church itself, was looking to *people* as the SOURCE of belief, instead of to God! Yet, here was the *only* Church holding to the one greatest basic truth of the Commandments of God and the faith of Jesus, kept in the NAME of God, and in spite of this and a few other erroneous teachings, nevertheless being *closer* to the whole truth than any church I had found.

If *this* was not the true Church of God, *then where was it?*

The Second Test

A little later I tried the second test. After exhaustive study and research, I had found it PROVED that the so-called "Lost Ten Tribes" of Israel had migrated to western Europe, the British Isles, and later the United States—that the British were the descendants of Ephraim, younger son of Joseph, and the United States modern-day Manasseh, elder son of Joseph—and that we possessed the national wealth and resources of the Birthright which God had promised to Abraham through Isaac, Jacob and Joseph.

361

This truth was written in a lengthy manuscript of close to 300 typed pages, and mailed to this editor and leader of this church. I explained that although this new truth seemed to be proved beyond doubt, yet I was still comparatively new in Christ and Scriptural knowledge, and wished the judgment of one more mature and experienced in things Biblical.

I think it was some six months before the reply came. It was written on a train late at night. This church leader stated in his letter (which I still have) that *I was most certainly right*—that this was a wonderful new truth revealed by God, and that God surely had a special reason for revealing this new truth to me. However, he stated he did not know what use, if any, he could make of it at that time, but was sure I would hear more of it later.

Did this Church accept and proclaim this vital new truth—the KEY that unlocks the doors to all PROPHECY? Here was the KEY to understanding of one third of the whole Bible. But this Church refused then to accept it or preach it or publish it though their leader frankly confessed it was TRUTH and a revelation from GOD!

Yet here was the Church which appeared to have *more truth,* and *less error* than any other. It did "profess" the commandments of God, and have "the testimony of Jesus Christ." It *did* have the true NAME of the Church Christ built. Its members *did* love what truth they had and sacrificed for it! In spite of the fact this Church did not appear to be dynamically *alive* spiritually—in spite of its little or no accomplishment— still it came *closer* to the Biblical characteristics of Christ's true Church than any I knew!

Truly, this was bewildering!

My earnest and prayerful study continued. After some time, I made a discovery in the 31st chapter of

Exodus. At least I had found nothing in the published literature of this Church of God or of the Seventh-Day Adventists about it. It became very plain that in Exodus 31:12-18 was the account of a completely *different* and distinctive COVENANT God made with His people on earth. This covenant established God's Sabbath as binding FOREVER! It was entirely separate and apart from the "Old Covenant" made with Israel at Mt. Sinai.

My First "Sermon"

This was "new light" which I felt impelled to present before these church brethren we had come to know and love down in the Willamette Valley. Repeatedly they had urged me to preach for them. But preaching was the last thing I felt I wanted to do. I had continually refused.

Now, however, I was overcome with an urge to get this new knowledge before them. I was unable to refuse any longer to speak. It was arranged for me to speak, I believe, on the following Sabbath.

The meeting was held in a country store building, but we drove first, for lunch, to the farm home of one of the members south of Salem, near Jefferson. We were taken down by the Runcorns of Salem, who we now had begun to look upon as sort of "second parents." It was Mrs. Runcorn who had opened my wife's eyes to the truth of the Sabbath. I remember they drove a large Studebaker "President."

In the car, en route from Salem to the place of meeting, consternation suddenly seized me. We were to arrive by noon, and all were to have lunch outdoors under a large tree. The preaching service was to be held in the afternoon. Suddenly the terrifying realization dawned in my mind that I might be called upon to give

363

thanks over the food at the luncheon. I realized it would be customary to call on a visiting guest. I had never prayed aloud before others. The thought of doing so frightened me!

But by this time I had gone far enough in my Christian experience and study of the Bible to know what to do. I began praying silently, as we rode along, that, if called upon, God would put the words into my mouth and give me the help that I needed. The fear loosened its grip. I had been learning the lesson of faith. I knew that Christ would be with me and not forsake me, and all embarrassment over the anticipation left.

Sure enough, I was called on to ask the blessing over the food. I did have the help I needed. I don't believe that any there, except Mrs. Armstrong, knew that this was my first audible prayer in the presence of others—until I told some of them afterward.

The meeting was held in a vacant country store building, nearby. It was known as the old Dever Store. This meeting, I believe, was in the summer of 1928.

If that talk I gave, explaining this Sabbath covenant, could be called a sermon, it was my first. Mrs. Armstrong assured me it was far from being a powerful sermon. Yet it was enthusiastically received. *I did have a message,* and a sincere, earnest urge to present it.

I remember that one towering member, six feet four inches tall, who had moved to this Oregon Valley from Texas, and was somewhat of a leader among the members, rose to his feet after I concluded and said, "Brethren, I just want to say that I have heard nearly all of the leading ministers in the Church of God, but I have heard this afternoon the best sermon I ever heard in my life." This didn't quite coincide with my wife's evaluation, who said that the delivery was extremely amateurish and inexperienced—but, I suppose, the fact

364

that the message was *new* to them, and that I was enthusiastic and in earnest about this new "discovery" of truth, caused it to be so well received.

I was asked to speak before them again.

Opposition Begins

It has been related in previous chapters how my wife had been miraculously and astonishingly healed in the summer of 1927. Following this, I had plunged into a thorough study of the subject of healing in the Bible.

Consequently when, about a month later, I spoke again at a meeting of these people, at this same vacant Dever Store, my message was about God's power and promises to HEAL.

Apparently the ministers of this church had heard of my previous speaking to these people, and of their request for this second appearance before them. So this time one of the older ministers of the church in Idaho had been sent to Oregon to be on hand to counteract any influence I might have.

I had spoken first. When he followed, he devoted a good portion of his sermon to an effort to refute everything I had said. He warned the brethren that if they relied on God for healing, Christ would say to them, "Depart from me, ye workers of iniquity—I never knew you."

That was the beginning of years of continuous opposition from ministers. This also brings me to a stage in this history of events and experiences in my life which I have long dreaded to write.

It is simply the fact that from this point on—from the very second "sermon"—if those early talks could be called that—opposition from other ministers, both within this church and without, was met at every turn continually.

I Shall Not Hide the FACTS!

So I say candidly that I shall relate these events. I shall try to record truthfully what happened, without feeling of rancor—and I certainly harbor no resentment or bitterness against these ministers, whatever their intentions. I believe that, as these incidents and happenings are related in the coming several chapters, they will truly open the eyes of many who never knew the full truth about my contacts with, and efforts to work with and cooperate with, the ministers of that church.

For some little time, now, my articles had been appearing on the front page of *The Bible Advocate,* published by this Church of God in Stanberry, Missouri.

Up until this time, now 1928, there had been no minister of this church in Oregon, except for occasional visits by the minister from Idaho, and the one from Texas of whom I had inquired about water baptism during his visit to Oregon in 1927. But there were at that time perhaps 50 or 60 members of the church in Oregon, from Salem to Eugene.

And, with the beginning of my speaking before these people in Oregon—and with my articles being featured in their church paper—no time was lost in sending a minister to Oregon to take charge. He was a young man—I believe about 28 or younger—who, I believe, had come from Arkansas or Missouri. He came to see me in Portland. His attitude appeared cordial and friendly. But very soon after his arrival publication of my articles in the *Bible Advocate* was stopped.

Soon I learned the reason. Probably the most influential member in the state at the time was elderly G. A. Hobbs, of Oregon City. He was past 80 years of age, but very alert, aggressive and active. He had received a letter from the editor in Stanberry, Missouri, explaining that my articles were being discontinued at the request of the young minister newly arrived in Oregon. The grounds were that I was not a member of the Church and it was dangerous to give me this much standing and prestige before the brethren there. I might gain influence and become their leader and lead them astray.

This had aroused the fiery indignation of Mr. Hobbs. Immediately he sent a scorching letter back to Stanberry, a copy of which he let me read. It resulted in reinstating my articles for publication.

First Regular Preaching

As soon as I had heard of this Mr. Hobbs, and the little group at Oregon City, I had visited him a few days after my first "sermon." I found a very small group of brethren who met together in a little church building at the top of the hill, on the Molalla road, in Oregon City.

There were only around 8 to 12 of them, but they habitually met on Sabbath afternoons to study the "Sabbath-school lesson," using the "quarterlies" from the Stanberry publishing house.

On discovering this little group, I began going to Oregon City to meet with them regularly. Almost immediately they asked me to be their leader in the study of the lesson. And soon I was delivering them a "sermon" every Sabbath.

These were days of extreme financial hardship in our home. We often went hungry. Several times there was not enough carfare for my wife and family to accompany me to Oregon City—in fact it was seldom that they were able to go. At least three times, during the next couple of years or so, I had barely enough for carfare to Oregon City on the electric line—with no carfare to return home. I even lacked bus fare from downtown Oregon City out to the little church house at the top of the hill on the outskirts of town. It was probably two or three miles up a steep hill all the way, but I walked it, carrying my briefcase with Bibles, concordance, etc.

But in every instance when I had come without carfare to return home, someone would "happen" to hand me a dollar or two of tithe money. And, strangely, no one ever handed me any money on those Sabbaths when I had enough to get back to Portland. And, of course, I never made the need known. But God always had a way of supplying every NEED!

My First Son!

I believe I have recounted in earlier chapters that, following the birth of our second daughter, three doctors—one an eminent obstetrician of international reputation—had warned Mrs. Armstrong and me that she could never bear another child. They had said a pregnancy would mean the certain death of both mother and unborn child.

It is natural for every man to desire a son. Before the birth of our first child, neither Mrs. Armstrong nor I had cared whether it was a boy or a girl. Our second child was another daughter. When I was told we could never have another, I was *terribly* disappointed!

And now seven years had gone by—by 1927—without expectations of ever having a son.

But when, in the summer of 1927, Mrs. Armstrong had been miraculously healed of several things at once—and when we remembered that the man who had anointed and prayed for her had asked God to heal her *completely* of *everything* from the top of her head to the bottom of her feet, we had faith that whatever had made another childbirth impossible had *also* been healed. We planned, consequently, to have a son. And I had faith that God would at last give me a son.

And GOD *DID!!*

Our first son, named Richard David, was born October 13th, 1928. That day, I said then and for years afterward, was the happiest day of my life. I was simply filled to overflowing with gratitude to a merciful, loving God who so richly LAVISHES on us His grace and blessings completely beyond all we can anticipate or hope for—IF we yield our lives to Him and do those things that are pleasing in His sight—IF we seek *first* God's Kingdom and His righteousness!

We dedicated that son to God for His service.

During his college career, here at Ambassador College in Pasadena, California, which God was later to use me in founding in 1947, our son Dick, as we called him, was converted—his life *changed*—and he, himself, gave his life to God.

From that time it was used in God's service, with continually growing usefulness and accomplishment, until his sudden death in an auto accident in 1958. Dick worked hard on his own self, overcoming faults and weaknesses and habits which he freely confessed, repented of, and strove to overcome. He reached the high point of his spiritual growth and development, of overcoming and usefulness—having established the branch office of God's Work in London and becoming Director of all overseas operations.

God later gave us still another son, Garner Ted, only a year and four months younger than his brother Dick.

21

The "Million Dollar" Clay Business

E VEN IN 1928, the *lean years* were to continue quite a while longer.

But if these were the *lean years* financially, they were the fat years spiritually—years of coming into the *true* riches. Yet, I still had many lessons to learn. Jesus had said, regarding economic prosperity, "Seek ye *first* the kingdom of God, and his righteousness; and all these [physical] things shall be added unto you"! But God doesn't always add the material prosperity until after humans have been tried, tested and proved faithful.

Not only was there much more TRUTH to be discovered and dug out of God's spiritual gold mine—the Holy BIBLE—but there was much character to be developed through hard, cruel *experience*, the dearest teacher of all.

I should not have thought so at the time—but God *knew* that I needed much more humbling—much more

370

chastening at the hands of God!

I had been humbled! O yes! And still, I know now that had God allowed me to have prospered financially at that stage of spiritual experience, self-pride once more would have seized me and the humility would have fled! The lessons so far received by all this chastening would have been lost! I was to have to suffer much more—and my family to suffer it with me! The *material* blessings were withheld 28 years!

But do not infer from this that the material riches were my goal. No such idea even entered my mind. I had *given up* all idea and expectation of material prosperity.

At this time, during 1928, we were living on Klickitat Street in Portland, Oregon. We were falling dangerously behind in paying the rent. The real estate agent who collected the rent came very frequently to the front door. To others he was probably a kind and pleasant-looking man. He taught a Sunday-school class. But to us, he was a dark, foreboding, frightening, almost devilish-appearing man, when, of evenings, he so frequently stood at our front door, demanding in a deep, bass, stern tone: "Can I have the rent?"

We simply didn't *have* the rent! Whenever he came, we knew just how a whipped dog feels when his tail is between his legs. Actually, this man, who appeared to us almost as an enemy, was kind enough to pay our rent a number of times out of his own pocket.

At one time we were in darkness nights of involuntary necessity. The electricity was shut off because we were delinquent. My wife did her cooking on a small gas plate, and our gas was shut off. Only the water was left running. We were out of food, and out of fuel. Our heating stove was one my father had made, shaped something like an old covered wagon—with rounded top.

Uneatable Macaroni

The children were crying with hunger. My stomach gnawed with pain. Like old Mother Hubbard's, our cupboard was bare, save for a little macaroni. But there was no cheese or any of the ingredients used in baking macaroni. There was not even a grain of salt. AND, there was *no money* to buy any.

I decided to try to cook some macaroni, even without the accompanying ingredients. Without gas there was no oven to bake it in; so I boiled it. Patiently I tore up and crumpled pages of magazines, so I could set a fire in the rounded-top heating stove for heat. I balanced a pan of water and macaroni on top of the stove, and kept throwing in more crumpled magazine pages to keep the fire going.

I offered this "delicacy" to my wife and daughters. We all tried it.

That is all we did. We did not swallow it. We tried, but the slick, slithery, tasteless mess *simply would not go down!* You may laugh. I don't know why some Hollywood scenario writer never thought of this as a comedy idea. People love to laugh at the discomfiture of others in the movies. Movie actors pretend to suffer things like this to give audiences big amusement.

But to us it was not a bit funny!

It was about this time, while still living on Klickitat Street, that I learned what the Apostle Paul meant when he wrote to the Corinthians of how God "also hath made us able ministers of the new testament; not of the letter, but of the spirit" (II Cor. 3:6).

The SPIRIT of the Law

Most people, I had noticed, thought that the "letter" was done away, and that the ministration of the *spirit*

372

did away with the law and all obligation for OBEDIENCE to God.

I have told this many times in sermons, and on the air. But this experience occurred at this time, and I believe it belongs in this account.

Our eldest daughter, Beverly, then ten, had been in the habit of bringing books home from the school library. I had noticed they were always fiction. She was an inveterate "bookworm," and a rapid reader. We had noticed that she was beginning to have a little trouble with her eyes, and we attributed it, at least in part, to excessive reading habits. Besides, I had noticed that the constant reading of these fictitious, ready-made daydreams—which is precisely what fiction is—was causing her mind to drift and wander, rather than to think actively.

"Beverly," I said one day after my wife and I had discussed it, "Mother and I want you to stop taking these fiction books out of the library. You are injuring your eyes with too much reading."

Two days later, I observed Beverly in her usual slumped-over position in a chair, with a book opened near the middle.

"Let me see that book, Beverly," I demanded. "Isn't this another fiction story?"

"Yes, Daddy," she replied, handing it to me. Already she had read it half through.

"Beverly," I said sternly, "didn't I tell you to stop bringing these books home and rest your eyes?"

"Well, yes, Daddy," came the innocent reply, "but I didn't get this book at the library. *I borrowed it from Helen.*"

Beverly actually *obeyed* the literal *letter* of the law, but she completely disobeyed the SPIRIT of what I had told her! The *spirit* of the law goes much further than

373

the mere letter. It *includes* the letter, but also its obvious meaning, or intent.

That is the way WE must obey God—*not only* the "letter," but the SPIRIT or intended MEANING of the law as well! Jesus explained this in His sermon on the Mount (Matt. 5:17-28—especially verses 21-22, and 27-28).

My First Personal Healing

It was also while living here, during 1928, that I had perhaps my first experience in applying God's miraculous power of healing, as a personal experience in my own body.

For fuel we burned wood—when we were able to have it. One day in chopping wood, the axe slipped, and struck my left thumb in mid-air. It cut clear to the bone. I had to pull the sharpened axe out of the bone. It had cut quite a deep gash.

Instantly I prayed, asking God to prevent pain, and to heal it over rapidly, as I ran into the house to wrap and bandage it. At first such a cut often benumbs the nerves, as it did this time—but normally the pain soon follows. This time I felt no pain at all.

I made one slight mistake later, else I am convinced I should never have had so much as a scar. I left the bandage on for some three days. But I became over-anxious to look at it. When we trust God for healing, we need to keep our eyes and our minds on CHRIST—not on the physical part. I unwrapped it too soon. I experienced the only pain at any time from that severe cut in removing the wrapping to look at it, and pulling off a scab that had formed.

The result was that there is, to this day, just the slightest trace of a scar across the length of my left thumb. But, even so, it is so slight that one would never notice it unless pointed out. The cut was directly across the knuckle. I believe it could have robbed me of the use of the thumb. As it is, there is no impairment whatsoever.

Advertising Job — Rejected

It must also have been during this year of 1928 that another advertising job was offered me.

I mentioned, in connection with the advertising service for laundries, the soap builder used by laundries manufactured by the Cowles Detergent Company, of Cleveland, Ohio. This company was a subsidiary of the Aluminum Corporation of America. They manufactured an unusual product, unique and exclusive, so far as I know, in the laundry industry. I understood that this company was the largest operation in the laundry industry.

The Cowles Detergent Company had become familiar with the advertising I was writing and designing for laundry clients. Also they were familiar with the astonishing results. These ads had been building the volume of business of my clients in unprecedented fashion.

And so it was that, about this time, the sales manager of the Cowles company, a Mr. Fellows, came to Portland to interview me and offer the post of advertising manager of their company. Actually the job was to organize and establish a new advertising department! Up to that time, they had delegated all advertising preparation and placing to their advertising agency.

Bear in mind, I was not yet a minister. Although I had given a few talks that might by a stretch of the imagination have been called preaching, and had been speaking almost every Sabbath before the little group in Oregon City, I most assuredly did not think of myself as a minister. Nor did I expect, at this time, ever to be.

The laundries of the nation, through their national association, had gone into their five million dollar national campaign. This had pulled right out from under me—like a rug being jerked out from beneath one's feet—all my laundry clients, save one. I still had the account of the National Laundry, second largest in Portland. But, as I have mentioned before, this required only about 30 minutes a week of my time. It was our sole income—$50 per month. It was not enough to pay house rent, and keep us fed and alive.

If you will remember, in 1924 I was offered the job of advertising manager of the Des Moines *Register*— rated by many as one of the ten great newspapers of the United States. I had turned it down because I believed that I was not an executive. I believed I could not direct and supervise the work of others. I found it so distasteful to make out reports and keep records— which would have been a regular routine on such a job—that I felt I was simply not fitted for such an office.

I explained all this to Mr. Fellows. I told him frankly that one of my faults was that I worked in spurts. I felt I was moderately talented in certain directions, but this was offset by serious faults I had not yet been able to master and overcome. At times my performance would be brilliant. Results would be outstanding. But then I might go into a slump for a week or a month, during which I would accomplish little or nothing. What I did not tell him was that my wife and I had talked it over, and decided that in order to obey God and keep His Sabbath, I must reject the offer.

Lest any suspect that I went into the ministry to

■ *Miss Loma Dillon Armstrong, about 27, and the new three-weeks-old baby, Beverly, outside the store at Motor, Iowa, late May, 1918. She was on a visit to the family in her home town.*

■ *Above, Loma Armstrong with first daughter, Beverly, in the apartment area where the Armstrongs lived. Left, Herbert Armstrong, holding Beverly, and Loma Armstrong on a visit to the country in 1918.*

■ *Top left, Mr. Armstrong with Beverly, the age of nine months, in February 1919, Jackson Park, Chicago. Mrs. Armstrong with Beverly in November 1919. Left, with mother in Chicago during 1920. Russell Armstrong with Beverly, age two, in Chicago.*

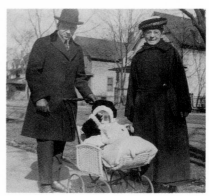

■ *Top, Herbert Armstrong at time of visit of his brother Russell to Chicago in 1920. Left, Walter Dillon, Mr. Armstrong's brother-in-law, during oratory contest. With his mother in Maywood shortly before second daughter was born.*

■ *Above, Mrs. Armstrong, about November, 1920, now the proud mother of two daughters—Dorothy Jane, age four months, and Beverly Lucile.*

■ *Far left top, the Armstrongs with their two daughters in an informal pose. Far left bottom, Walter Dillon with Herbert Armstrong and daughters. Mr. Armstrong played tennis till he was past 55. Top left, Herbert Armstrong with the Walter Dillons. Top right, Jessie Hole at 94 (he died at 98), brother of Elon Hole, father of Lydia Hole Armstrong, the grandmother of Herbert Armstrong. Bottom right, Loma Armstrong with daughter Beverly.*

■ *Top, en route west from Iowa to Oregon in a Model T Ford. Luggage loaded down the car between Iowa and Oregon. Center, roads were seldom paved and tire trouble was frequent. Another view, bottom, of the Model T.*

■ *Above, encamped at the ocean resort, Seaside, Oregon. The other car was Mr. Richard* *Talboy's 1924 Maxwell. Below, after arrival, en route for a weekend at Seaside, leading Oregon resort.* *Mr. Dillon is at the wheel, Mrs. Armstrong in rear seat.*

■ *Early twenties laundry ads by Herbert Armstrong. The brochure "A Frank Comparison" put in print the results of Mr. Armstrong's laundry survey.*

■ *An advertisement is reduced to almost one-third the original size as it appeared in the newspapers. These ads changed the thinking of thousands of women toward laundries —doubling their volume of business.*

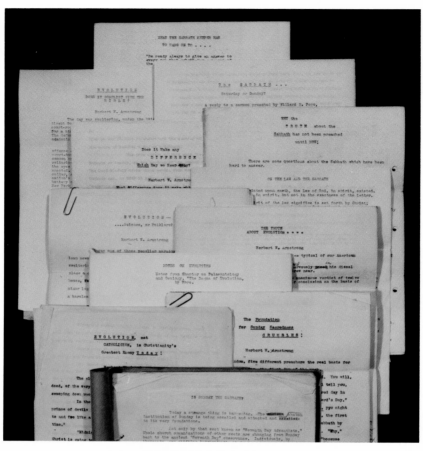

■ *Top, a display of typed manuscripts by Herbert Armstrong. He prepared these manuscripts on the Sabbath and evolution to better explain the issues to himself. Later they became the basis of his writings for others. Left, the clay project brochures.*

■ *Richard David Armstrong, the third child of Herbert and Loma Armstrong, at age six months. Even as a child Dick had beautiful light clear blue eyes and a happy spirit.*

On Train To Maridian, Miss.
Feb. 26, 1929.

Dear Brother Armstrong:

I presume you think I am very neglectful of duty in
not answering your letter before this, but it was a long
while before your manuscript reached me on the Third Angel's
Message and only the first installment has come to my
attention to this time. Likely the balance will be at the
office when I arrive home next week. If so I will get at it
just as soon as possible and write you again.

I have been very busy for the past three months especially
and in fact for the past six months I have been speaking about
every night. I just left Ala. yesterday where I spend nine days
and spoke sixteen times which with my other work you see is
heavy. I am only able to endure by the help of the Lord.

I feel that we are entering into a new era for the
message and that it is going to take on new life. In fact the
time for the message is now here which I have long contended it
would be when the events of the past few weeks came to pass.

With christian love to you and yours,
Your Brother in the one faith.

A. N. Dugger

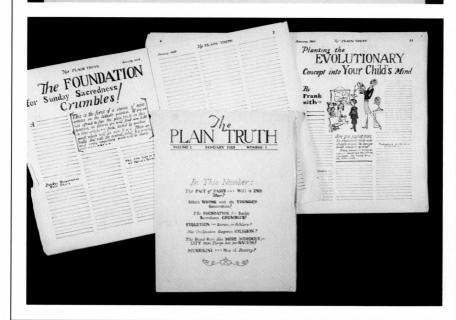

■ *Left, top, an important prophetic letter by church leader A.N. Dugger. Left, bottom, proposed* Plain Truth *in 1929. Top, old Dever store in Salem, Oregon. Mr. Armstrong gave his first sermon here in summer of 1928. Below, country schoolhouse in the Dever area where the Church at one time met.*

■ *Garner Ted Armstrong, the fourth child of Herbert and Loma Armstrong, when he was seven months.*

make money (and I suppose most could not realize one could have any other motive), I was rejecting a very flattering offer.

Mr. Fellows thanked me sincerely for my honesty in telling him of these shortcomings. He returned to Cleveland. I never heard whether he found the man he needed, and started his new advertising department.

Actually there may have been some providential guidance in my supposition that I could not become an executive. Had I accepted this job, which, as I remember, would have paid a salary of $8,000 a year in 1928 to start—the equivalent of a much larger figure in today's dollar value—and about $12,000 if I made good, I would have been snatched away from the calling God was drawing me into. I would probably be back in the world today.

Actually I was mistaken about not being able to become an executive. When God later began to build His Work around me, and the Work began to grow steadily and continuously at the rate of about a 30% increase each year over the year before—which rate of growth continued for 35 years—I *had* to become an executive! And with God's help and power, it was achieved, and the working in spurts was long ago overcome. For many years, now, I have had to work at the same steady pace day in and day out.

Cash Position Desperate!

Also it was about this time, late in 1928, that our position was so desperate that I prayed earnestly and asked God to open a door for some income that very day.

Having asked in faith, in the morning, I took the streetcar to downtown Portland, seeking the "open door" to a job, or something with some cash in it. All the circumstances have dimmed somewhat in my memory, but I believe that we had to have a certain amount of money by 5:30 that evening, or be evicted from our home. But I *knew* that if I did my part, God would provide the need.

All day long I sought open doors—but every door was closed and apparently locked tight. My faith was being tried. Then 5:00 p.m. came. Time had almost run out.

But I still relied on God.

At that moment it came to my mind to stop up at the office of a Mr. Davidson, manager of the Merchandising Service Department of the Portland *Oregonian.*

"Say," he exclaimed, "you're just the man I've been looking for. The advertising agency for the Bissell carpet sweeper people want a survey made in Portland on the relative opinions of women between the carpet sweeper and the vacuum cleaner. You are the only man I know with the experience to conduct such a survey. Can you take time to do it?"

I most certainly could!

It was going to pay just the exact amount I needed by 5:30 that evening to prevent being evicted. But the check would not be forthcoming until about 30 days, after the survey was completed.

With brisk step, after having been briefed on what the Bissell company wanted in the survey, I walked rapidly over to the offices of the mortgage company where the house payment had to be made, arriving right on the deadline, 5:30 p.m.!

I explained about the survey to be made immediately. I offered to simply endorse the check and hand it over for our house rent when it came, if the company would accept it some 30 days later.

378

My word was good with them. Since it was definitely sure, they agreed to accept this check 30 days later, on my promise to endorse it over.

And Now — 1929!

1928 ended. It had been a year of great progress in my life. Spiritually, that is—certainly not financially.

It had been a year of outstanding world events. Trotsky, Zinoviev and other Communists were exiled from Russia January 16th that year. The first all-talking motion picture was shown in New York that year on July 6th. This was preparing the way for our filming *The World Tomorrow* for television, beginning 1955. October 13th of that year God had blessed us with the birth of our first son, Richard David.

In the spring of 1929 we moved to a house on 75th Street, north of Sandy Boulevard. 1929 was to be a year of struggle, spiritual growth, and miraculous answers to prayer.

In world events, too, 1929 was an epochal year! The notorious "St. Valentine's Day massacre" in Chicago occurred February 14th. On June 7th that year, the Papal State, extinct since 1870, was revived as a state, or nation. The Kellogg Peace Treaty, known also as the Pact of Paris, outlawing WAR, was signed July 24th. Albert B. Fall, Secretary of the Interior, came to his terrific FALL November 1, when he was sentenced for accepting a $100,000 bribe. Commander Richard E. Byrd made the first flight over the south pole November 28. And, biggest event of all, the New York Stock Market crash occurred October 29th. 16,000,000 shares changed hands. The decline in value of stocks was estimated at 15 billion dollars by end of 1929. And stock losses, by 1931, were estimated at 50 billion, affecting directly 25 million people. It plunged America into its worst depression. It prevented me from making a million dollars!

Incident of the Mystery Woman

1929 not only *ended* as a depression year for us—as it did for millions of others—it *began* as just another of the *lean years!* For us, it was another year of desperation to keep ourselves alive.

Very shortly after moving into the house on 75th Street, we had reached another crisis of hunger and desperate need. Again I prayed earnestly for God to either send us some money or provide a way for me to earn it.

An hour or two later, a strange woman knocked on our front door. Mrs. Armstrong opened the door. There was something mysterious about the woman's appearance.

Who was she? She did not introduce herself. She gave no inkling of her identity.

"If your husband isn't too proud to do it," she said in a low, quiet voice, "there are two truckloads of wood he can throw in at this address. Jot it down." My wife jotted down the street and number.

The mysterious woman walked quickly away and disappeared.

People in Portland used wood for fuel. Portland is in the heart of the Oregon-Washington lumber country. Throwing wood into the woodshed, garage, or basement, was an odd-job customarily reserved for the bums who came along. Very few men in Portland threw in their own wood. To be seen doing it was to appear as a down-and-out bum.

We were totally perplexed as to the identity of this strange woman. How did *she* know we were in such desperate need? Who was she? We never knew.

But I did know I had just asked God to provide. And at once I recognized one fact. This woman was like the mischievous boys playing a trick on a poor widow. Her window had been open. She was praying aloud, asking God to send her some bread for her children. The little boys, playing just outside the window, overheard her prayer.

"Let's play a trick on her," said one of the boys. "Let's toss a loaf of bread through her window."

When they did, she knelt again and gave God thanks.

"Ah-ya-ya!" jeered the boys. "God didn't throw in that bread—we boys did."

"Well," answered the grateful widow, smiling, "Maybe the devil brought it, but just the same *GOD sent it!*"

No matter who this mysterious woman was, I knew *God sent her!* And I realized instantly that God was answering my prayer HIS way, and not mine. I knew He was giving me a test to see whether I would accept a humiliating job. I realized I had not yet been freed completely from ego and pride. I knew that God was giving me a lesson in humility at the same time He answered my prayer.

I walked immediately to the address the woman gave. It was about a mile from our house. There was a large pile of wood in front. I went to the door, asked for, and got the job of throwing the wood in the basement.

Realizing God was teaching me a lesson, I resolved to do it HIS WAY, which was to do the best job I could. A thing worth doing is worth doing *right!* Now that God allows me to be the employer of many men, I insist that they do their work in the *right* manner—or else tear it out and do it over.

I stacked the wood up as neatly and orderly as I

381

could. I worked rapidly, and did it as quickly as I could. Several people walked past the house. Every time one saw me, I winced. I knew they thought I was a down-and-out bum. Each passerby knocked off a little more of that vanity. But I just prayed silently to God about it, and thanked Him for the lesson, and asked Him to help me to be humble and industrious.

When the job was finished, the woman inspected the piled wood in her basement.

"Why, you've done that so neatly, and so fast, I'm going to pay you double," she said.

The satisfaction and inspiration this gave was a far bigger reward than the extra money.

Clay Mine a GOLD Mine?

About this time a clay mine was brought to my attention. It promised to become a million dollar "gold mine."

My former associate on *The Vancouver Evening Columbian,* who had been its Business Manager, Samuel T. Hopkins, brought it to me. He had encountered an elderly man who owned a farm on which a mysterious kind of clay was mined. It was located in the foothills of the Cascade Mountains, in Skamania County, Washington.

One day this farmer had cut a bad gash on the back of his hand on a rusty barbed wire fence. He had been digging rather deeply in the vicinity and had dug into a semisoft grayish blue-green clay. Without thinking much about *why* he did it, he reached down, scooped up a handful of the soft clay and slapped it over the back of the hand to cover the cut. Then he proceeded with his day's work. The clay dried in some 20 or 30 minutes.

That evening on removing the now dried and

hardened clay, he was surprised to discover that it had coagulated the blood, drawn the skin together from the wide gash, and virtually healed it over!

The farmer became curious. A member of his family was plagued with eczema. He experimented. This clay was placed over the portion of skin affected, and allowed to dry. There was noticeable improvement. A second and third application was applied. Soon the skin disease disappeared.

The farmer knew Sam Hopkins, and told him about it. Mr. Hopkins made a few experiments on cases of acne and eczema. Results were astonishing.

This clay contained a certain amount of fine sand and grit which proved somewhat harsh on women's skin. So he experimented with rubbing the clay through a very fine copper wire screen, removing most of the sand and grit.

Astonishing the Doctors

About this time he came to me with his discovery. He thought it contained great possibilities, but didn't know how to market it. He offered me a 50% partnership in whatever we might do with it. I was considerably intrigued. I took a sample to a well-known doctor in Portland who specialized in skin diseases.

"It is certainly a coincidence," said the doctor, "that you came at this psychological time. I have a stubborn skin disease case which has persisted six months. I'm not making any headway with it. I couldn't tell my patient, but I don't mind admitting to you that I am desperate enough to *try* this clay. Under other circumstances I'd be very reluctant to experiment with anything new."

I returned a week later. The doctor was very excited.

"There's something very mysterious about that clay," he said. "Why! a few applications cured that skin disease completely!"

We had noticed that it was 50% heavier than water. A pound-size jar of this clay weighed 24 ounces. He felt it might contain radium, or other radioactive substance. He suggested I take it to another Portland physician, then president of the Oregon-Washington Medical Association, who specialized in cancer and radium treatment. He called this doctor on the telephone and set up the conference for me.

I found this physician maintained a large suite of offices, or treating rooms, like a private hospital, with eight registered nurses in constant attendance.

He made a number of experiments, and became quite excited. It cured acne, eczema, psoriasis. One day he contacted me, requesting a large supply of the clay. He had a patient almost completely covered and his whole body swollen with poison oak—the most severe case he had ever seen—and the patient was in critical condition. After the first application of the clay, the painful itching was greatly relieved, and after the second it was stopped. This patient was kept in his private hospital quarters, and after several days the poison was completely gone!

This physician made a photographic test for radium—not a completely reliable or conclusive test, but he felt it would give some indication. The film, left overnight inside a metal case placed next to a jar of clay, had been exposed to light when developed. This indicated radium! But the doctor would not accept it as final, saying this was not a completely conclusive test.

Some four or five rooms down the hall his X-ray apparatus was located. He said it was barely possible that the film had been exposed by this machine, instead of by the clay. If this were true, I reasoned, then why were not all his X-ray films exposed by that apparatus, so he could never use any of them? But I was not a scientist, I discarded my reasoning as worthless.

Option on the Mine

This physician acquainted a friend of his, a leading corporation attorney, with the facts about this clay. This attorney had connections in the east with wealthy men and interests who had large sums to invest.

He advised us to tie up the clay mine at once on an option to buy.

"I'll tell you what I'll do," said the lawyer. "You men cannot afford to pay me the fee I would charge to handle this for you. But the doctor has told me enough to give me confidence in this thing. I'll make you this proposition: I'll handle the legal end of it, and give you whatever advice I can. I will do what I can to get it financed. You either have a million-dollar proposition or nothing. If it fails, you owe me nothing. If you succeed, I'll charge you a double fee, and in that event you'll be amply able to pay it."

We agreed.

He drew up an option contract, under which we were to be given *exclusive* right to all of the clay for one year, at a certain price per gallon. We were given one year to exercise the option and purchase the property. The purchase price was set at about three times the value of the property as a farm. The owner signed the option contract. We had one year to make our million dollars.

It was probably August or September, 1929, when we got the contract signed and were ready to start building our million dollar fortune out of the clay mine.

With the cooperation of this doctor, I immediately sought out the leading, most aggressive and the best-informed beauty shop operator in Portland. Many inquiries in the field led to one certain woman. Since this clay seemed to quickly rid women of acne, eczema, and other common skin diseases, we decided the biggest single market possibility was through the beauty shops.

This woman made experiments. The results were the same. It cleared up splotched faces after a reasonable number of applications. But, she discovered, it had a drawing power too severe for many women. Applied as a face masque, or a "mud-pack," it seemed to hold the face in a stiff vise. Its drawing power was exceedingly strong.

"For use as a mud-pack facial," this beauty shop owner advised, "I recommend cutting down the severe drawing power by mixing a certain facial oil in it. And it must be perfumed."

"We'd better have the advice and cooperation of a top-flight chemist," I said. I went to the chief chemist of the largest wholesale drug house in Portland. He agreed to help. Between him, the beauty shop expert, and the physician, we worked out a formula which the beautician pronounced perfect, the doctor and chemist pronounced safe and harmless, which had the most delightful fragrance, and which, after many tests, we found to have the same powers of eradicating embarrassing face blotches—except that it required perhaps one or two more treatments than before.

Selling Mud Packs

But, just as we were getting everything ready to approach one of the largest cosmetics concerns on a deal to sell them our formula and the raw supply of the

386

clay—just as we were devising various *other* possible uses and markets—that fateful October 29th, 1929, rolled around.

The stock market crashed. The nation was plunged into the worst economic depression of its history.

It became utterly impossible to finance a new business, or sell a new product to a cosmetic firm.

Once again, as if some unseen supernatural hand were taking every business opportunity away from me, another promising business of million-dollar possibilities was swept away by powers and forces beyond my control!

I began to call myself King Midas in reverse! Everything *I* touched turned—well, this time—to CLAY! It was certainly not a gold mine. It was only a clay mine, after all.

By this time I had no means of keeping my family alive, except to try to sell this clay. I had to explain to beauty shop owners that they could not sell these facial masques as a means of healing, or curing a facial disease. They could be prosecuted for practicing medicine without a license if they did. But they could recommend these treatments to customers as the finest of all facials, and suggest that if, incidentally, they found that the acne disappeared, that would be very nice!

I also worked out a formula for poison oak. I called it P.O.P.—Poison Oak Paste. A certain amount of distribution for this was developed through local Portland drug stores. All who bought it reported astonishing results.

The facial masque, or clay-pack, I named Marvé. This I began to sell in "booth-size" pound jars to beauty shops. But each jar actually weighed 1½ pounds! Before long, many of the Portland shops were using it, and gradually resales increased.

I found a way to dilute the clay until it became a soupy liquid. All the sand and grit would sink to the bottom. Then I siphoned off the top. Straining it through fine copper-wire screens did not remove all the fine grit. My new way left it soft and utterly smooth. Our kitchen on 75th Street became virtually a clay factory. After the siphoning process, I boiled the clay down to the consistency I wanted it. This boiling did no harm to its curative powers, and made it more sanitary.

"Here's Your Breakfast!"

Shortly after we moved into the house on 75th Street, a Mr. and Mrs. Charlie Beck moved into the corner house next door. Helen Beck was one of the most cheerful women we ever knew. She seemed full of sunshine and good cheer within and without. She was quite religiously inclined, even emotionally so. She learned and accepted quite a little Biblical truth through us, but seemed unable to see quite *all* of the truth. Nevertheless she appeared to walk in all the truth she really grasped—and if I ministered to some extent to her in spiritual matters, she ministered to us in a material way.

She learned that we often did not have enough to eat. When we did get in a little money, we went to the markets and loaded up on beans and food that "went the farthest and cost the leastest."

But often when we were out of food, she would come to our back door with her cheery "Good morning, folks, here's your breakfast," carrying a tray full of steaming hot breakfast. Prior to the bust of 1920 it would have cut my pride unbearably to have received this kind of "charity" from a next-door neighbor. But hers was the kind spoken of in I Corinthians 13, where it says that though you may speak with the tongues of

388

angels, understand all knowledge, have all faith, "and have not charity," you are NOTHING!

Actually this cheerful "good morning" act of charity profited both ourselves and Helen Beck. It *is* more blessed to give than to receive. She reaped that greater blessing. But I reaped the spiritual blessing of being humbled a little further—having to swallow more pride, and see the hand of God in it!

And so the year 1929 had come and gone. 1930 was to be another of the "lean years"—as indeed were several others to follow. We were at rock bottom financially. We had learned what it is to go hungry. But these were, nevertheless, years of spiritual growth.

These were the years in which Jesus Christ, the *living* Head of His Church, was instructing me in His Word, preparing me for His ministry, humbling me, rooting out the *self*-confidence, the cocky conceit, the vanity and egotism.

But he was replacing these *self*-trusting attributes with reliance and dependence on GOD. Instead of self-confidence, He was giving me painful but valuable lessons in FAITH. He was granting us a few miraculous answers to prayer. Some far more astonishing answers to prayer were to follow in the year 1930.

22

Astounding Answers to Prayer

NEVER in my life have I faced a more serious problem than the situation that confronted us at the beginning of the year 1930. Not only were we confronted with another lean year *economically*—with our own personal financial condition at rock bottom—with the whole nation plunging on down, *down, DOWN,* into the depths of depression—but it seemed as if we were destitute of faith in God as well.

We were within six weeks of the birth of our fourth child. My wife, who had been so miraculously healed in 1927, was now in an alarming condition. She was anemic. Her blood was lacking in iron. Her strength appeared depleted. The doctor was definitely alarmed. He was afraid of complications at the time of delivery, due to her weakened condition. He insisted she go to the hospital where every emergency facility would be available in event of trouble.

The Lesson of Fasting and Prayer

But we had been in such financial depths that the hospital bill for our first son's birth had not been paid. The hospital would not admit my wife again until the previous bill was paid—or else we paid in advance.

I had prayed for Mrs. Armstrong's healing. But she had not been healed. I had prayed again. And *again!* But there had been no improvement, and time was running out. We were becoming desperate.

What was wrong? I had learned that God does heal. We had experienced almost incredible miracles. My wife had been healed before. But *why not now?*

Obviously God had not changed—He is the *same* from eternity to eternity. He has *promised* to heal, and His Word is SURE! The fault could not be with God. I knew it had to be with me. But where? I "searched my heart." One condition to receiving miraculous healing is that we OBEY God.

"Whatsoever we ask, we receive of him BECAUSE *we keep his commandments*" (I John 3:22).

But I had surrendered to obey God's commandments three years before. FAITH is the second condition. But I *believed,* as firmly as when God first healed my wife.

There was no more time to lose. I *had* to find the answer. I knew of only one way. *Fasting* and prayer! It was the last-ditch resort. I didn't know how one ought to fast and pray—I had never done it before. But when Jesus' disciples were unable to cast out a demon, Jesus said such a result came only by fasting and prayer. So I began to fast.

The fasting was begun on a Sabbath morning. That morning I ate no breakfast. Not knowing *how* one ought to go about fasting and prayer, I first prayed and asked

391

God to show me the way—to open my understanding. Then, since God speaks to us through His written Word, I began to search the Bible for instruction about fasting. For one hour with the aid of a concordance I studied passages of Scripture on the subject of fasting and praying, much of the time on my knees.

Then for one hour I sat in thought and contemplation. I turned over in my mind the scriptures I had read. I reflected on my own life in recent months. I tried to compare it with God's way, as revealed in the Scriptures. Then I spent the next hour in talking to God—in prayer.

And so I decided to continue in this order—one hour in Scripture study, one in contemplation, and one in prayer. I did not once ask God to heal my wife—as yet. I had been doing that for weeks, without result. I was fasting and praying, not for the purpose of bringing pressure on God to force Him to obey my will and give what was asked—but to find out *what was wrong with me!* I realized we did not need to nag at God. *NEVER* fast *as a means of inducing God to answer!*

I read of Elijah's prayer, in presence of all the priests of Baal, when God answered and the fire came down from heaven. I timed that prayer. It was very short—only about 20 seconds. But the awe-inspiring answer came crashing from heaven instantly! Elijah did not need to talk God into it by a long prayer, or by repeated prayers. But I knew that Elijah at that moment was *close to God*—that he *had previously* been spending *hours* in long prayers to be *in contact* and close communion with His Maker! And he naturally *knew* His Maker would answer!

Gradually the truth began to pierce through the fog in my mind. Gradually, as this process of fasting and prayer continued all day, and into the afternoon of

392

Sunday—as I became more and more hungry—but closer and closer to God, the realization came that I had been keeping my mind more and more fully on this clay project.

Finding the Trouble

This experience in fasting and prayer, and the overwhelming result, has been broadcast over the air, and probably related previously in *The Plain Truth*. But it is one of the outstanding experiences in my life and properly belongs in this present account, even though a repetition for numerous readers.

This process of self-examination, in the order of one hour of Bible study, followed by an hour of reflection and contemplation, and then an hour of prayer, under the unpleasant weakness of fasting, continued until the middle of Sunday afternoon.

Suddenly I heard one of our daughters cry out: "Here comes Grandpa and Grandma!"

My father and mother were driving their Ford 2-door sedan up our driveway. At the moment I was lying on the bed in our bedroom, in an hour of thinking and reflecting. By this time *I KNEW* where the trouble had been. I realized fully that I had gotten so wrapped up in this clay project—the development of formulas—devising plans for marketing—and selling enough of it to beauty shops to keep us from starving, that I had unconsciously been drifting farther from the previously close relationship with God.

I had not stopped Bible study or prayer. I had not even realized that I had been diminishing it. But now I realized that I had actually become *closer* to this clay project than I was to God. It was fast becoming *first* in my mind, my interest, and my time. And God will not play second fiddle to *anything!*

393

I wonder, as I write, how many of my readers are more wrapped up, in their interest, and in their hearts, in some material business, project, or other interest, than they are in GOD! Probably *most* of you who are reading this need what God had brought me to do.

I realized now that God had mercifully, in His wisdom and His love for me and my family, refused to answer my prayers to *force* me to fast and pray and come to see where I was unconsciously drifting.

But in a flash, as I heard my father's car drive past the bedroom window, the realization came that the mission of the fasting was accomplished! No need to continue it, now! I must end it, and go out and greet my parents.

And so, in a brief prayer not much longer than Elijah's, but in deep earnestness and absolute faith, I now—for the first time during this fast—asked God to heal my wife and put iron in her blood and give her needed strength. Like a flash it came to mind that we were completely out of food—out of wood for fuel to keep warm (in January)—so I asked Him to send us food and fuel. I asked Him to send money for the hospital bill for the delivery of the baby. Quickly I thought of my winter topcoat—it had a big hole at the rear of one hip, which was embarrassing and a handicap in my work—and asked God for a new coat.

Asking God for these five things had taken less than a minute. But by now my parents were alighting from the car, and I wanted to go out to meet them. Two scriptures flashed to my mind:

"Your Father knoweth what things ye have need of, *before ye ask him*" (Matt. 6:8).

"My God shall supply *all your need* according to his riches in glory by Christ Jesus" (Philippians 4:19).

So quickly I ended my prayer, saying, "Father in

heaven, you know what I need, *before* I ask—and you have *promised* to supply every need—so I ask you to supply whatever else I need." Then I quickly thanked God for it, rose and ran to greet my parents.

. . . and the ASTOUNDING Answers Came!

Dad was just handing Mother a big covered roaster out of the car, and then gathering up an armload of wood. He had removed the back seat before leaving Salem, and piled into the entire rear part of the car a large supply of wood.

We soon had a fire going in the kitchen cook stove, and Mother reheated an entire big dinner she had brought in the roaster. Dad had managed to pile about a week's supply of wood into his car. So here, even as I was asking for it, was the answer to two of my prayer requests—the immediate fuel and food.

Arising Monday morning, my wife's cheeks were rosy red! When the doctor saw her, he exclaimed:

"What in the world has happened to *you!*" He could not understand how her anemia had so suddenly disappeared. She had her old zip and pep and strength. (Mrs. Armstrong always was an energetic person—as recorded earlier, her brothers had nicknamed her variously "Shebang," and "Cyclone" as a little girl.)

The very first mail delivery after my prayer request, on that Monday morning, brought a letter from one of my wife's uncles in Iowa containing, most unexpectedly, a settlement from her mother's will, in the exact amount of the hospital bill! My wife's mother had died when she was twelve.

You may be sure that Mrs. Armstrong and I were overwhelmed with gratitude. Our prayers that morning were all of thanksgiving to a God who is REAL, and near to every one of us—*if* we will be near to Him!

But Monday was another business day in downtown Portland, and it was necessary to make the rounds of some of the beauty parlors once again to sell more clay. Arriving in the lobby of an office building I would remove my topcoat, and carefully fold it so as to hide the big hole in the side, carry it on my arm, and then enter the shops or offices where I had to call.

About eleven that morning I found myself across the street from the building of the gas company, where my brother Russell was an information clerk. So I crossed over. We chatted for a couple of moments.

"Herb," exclaimed Russell suddenly, eyeing the hole in my coat, "You've got to have a new overcoat. Meir & Frank are having a big sale on overcoats. Today is January 20th. I have a charge account at Meier & Frank's, and anything charged beginning today is not billed until the March 1st statement, and I will have until March 10th to pay and keep my credit good. You go over now, and select an overcoat, and I'll meet you over there at noon and have it charged."

"Oh, no, Russ" I remonstrated, "I couldn't let you do that."

But suddenly, as I continued to protest, it seemed as if a still, small voice within said to me: "Didn't you ask God to give you a new overcoat? Are you willing to receive it *the way* God gives it, or not?"

It is human nature to rebel against God's *way*. We want to do things in a different *way* than God commands. We want to live a different *way* than God's Law. I broke off the remonstrance immediately.

"O.K., Russ," I smiled humbly, and gratefully, "I'll go select a coat—and thanks a million!"—as my eyes began to water.

It was humiliating to me to take this coat from my brother. I felt he could not afford it. But I realized it was

God's answer, coming *the way* God had chosen to answer my prayer. He was still humbling me. But this was good for me, and actually, giving the coat was good for my brother. It just did not seem so, *humanly.*

On Tuesday or Wednesday of that week my other brother, Dwight, drove over to our house in his Ford.

"I got to thinking, Herb," said Dwight, "You may have to rush Loma to the hospital at any unexpected hour of day or night. I've brought my car over for you. I'm going to leave it until you go to the hospital. And in the meantime, just use it as if it were your own."

I think it was on Thursday afternoon Mrs. Armstrong and I were sitting in our living room reviewing what had happened, and thanking God. It was about three o'clock.

"You know, I never should have thought of needing a car for a sudden emergency trip to the hospital," I said. "But I asked God to send whatever else we needed, besides what I asked for specifically—and He sent it."

"There is only one thing more that I can think of," mused my wife. "I never thought of this before, but I do not have a robe or slippers to wear in the hospital. If I had those, every need would be complete."

We dismissed it from our minds.

But that evening, my sister's husband drove her over to our house. She seemed highly embarrassed, and a little flustered.

"Loma," she said, "I don't understand this at all—and you may think I'm crazy. But this afternoon, about three o'clock, something strange came over me—an insistent urge to go to my bedroom and pray. And while I was praying something put it in my mind—just like a voice saying: 'Take your robe and slippers to Loma! Take your robe and slippers to Loma!' I didn't understand it! I never had any experience like

397

that before. You may think I'm crazy, but I simply *had* to bring these to you."

We then explained how God had answered my prayer, and how, at that precise time that afternoon we had been in conversation about that very remaining need—the robe and slippers.

Truly, God does move in mysterious ways, His wonders to perform!

Garner Ted Is Born

It was just a little over two weeks later that the loan of Dwight's car was justified, and I rushed my wife to the hospital.

On the 9th day of February, a Sunday, my second son was born.

My wife named him Garner Ted. The name Garner had been a family name in her family and her mother's family for generations. Her maternal grandmother was a Garner before marriage. Several men in the family had been given the name Garner as a first name.

Mrs. Armstrong had known an intelligent young man in college in Iowa by the name of Ted, whom she greatly admired. The name seemed, she said, "so short and simple and direct."

He was our fourth child.

For eleven years of married life I had been denied a son. After Mrs. Armstrong's first miraculous healing, in 1927, I knew that, despite warnings from three doctors, we could have another child without fear of fatal consequences. God had blessed us with our first son, Richard David, on October 13th, 1928. That day was the happiest day of my life. I was filled to overflowing with gratitude for a SON after all those years—a gift from God.

But now, a year and four months later, God blessed

398

us with a second son. And Ted, too, was born as a result of an almost incredible miracle of healing only three weeks before his birth!

23

Prelude to Ministry

IHAVE related previously how my wife nearly died of toxemia eclampsia shortly before our second daughter was born. Three physicians had warned us that my wife could never have another child. We did not know the reason then. It was many years later that we learned we had the opposite RH blood factor—she being negative, and I positive. This was unknown to the doctors who said Mrs. Armstrong could not bear another child. It probably was not the cause. This, however, was undoubtedly the cause of Ted having been born with yellow jaundice.

This, as nearly as we can remember now, was one of the reasons it was necessary to supplement the new baby's breast milk. Another reason was the fact that Mrs. Armstrong did not have enough to eat. She simply was not able to supply sufficient milk.

One day a few months after Ted was born— probably early summer, 1930—I arrived home from the beauty shop rounds in midafternoon. The baby was crying lustily. "Hurry!" exclaimed my wife, "Go to the store and get a quart of milk. The baby has missed one feeding, and it's a whole hour past his second feeding, and I haven't a bit of milk for him."

Asking God for a Dime

"Well, I'm broke. Give me a dime," I said. Milk was then ten cents a quart—*think of that!*

"But if I had a dime, I'd have sent Beverly after the milk long ago," she replied. "I've been waiting for you—praying for God to hurry you home. I thought you'd have at least a dime."

The baby howled louder than ever. We had never established credit at any store.

"There's only one thing to do," I said. "We're helpless, of ourselves. There's no human to help us. We'll have to rely on God. He has *promised* to supply all our NEED—and this is a need."

Jesus said we should enter into our closet, or small room, and pray to our Father in heaven in secret, and He will reward us openly. The only small room of absolute privacy in our home was the bathroom. I locked the bathroom door and knelt beside the bathtub. God had *promised* to supply our every need, "according to His riches in glory by Christ Jesus." I believed Him.

But we had to have the answer immediately. I had learned that sometimes God does not answer at once—He sometimes tries our faith in order to develop patience in us. But right now it seemed that little Garner Ted needed his milk more urgently than I needed patience.

I felt there was not time—or need—of a long prayer. Instantly the 70th Psalm flashed into my mind.

401

God by His Holy Spirit inspired David to record, as part of the very Word of God, David's prayer wherein he asked God to "Make haste, O God, to deliver me; *make haste* to help me, O Lord . . . I am poor and needy: *make haste* unto me . . . O Lord, make no tarrying." I knew that prayer would not be in God's Word unless it was God's will to ANSWER that same prayer for me. So I asked God boldly to MAKE HASTE!

I arose, unlocked the door, and walked back toward the kitchen. Before I even reached the kitchen, one of our girls cried out from the living-room window:

"Oh Mother, here comes the old rag and bottle man!"

"Well, quick! Beverly," called out my wife, "run and stop him! We have a lot of old things in the basement we can sell him!"

The only entrance to our basement, I remember, was from the outside at the rear of the house. In eager anticipation we led the rag and bottle man down the basement stairs. My wife showed him all kinds of things. We expected to get at least a dollar from him.

He only shook his head.

"No. Nothing here I want," he said, starting back up the stairs.

Our hearts sank. Halfway up the steps he stopped, glanced at a high stack of old magazines beside the stairs. Slowly he turned and retraced his steps, examining the stack of magazines.

"I'll give you a dime for these," he said. "This is all I want."

I had asked God to *send to us a dime*—immediately—in haste! When God sent it, within the very minute I asked, we tried to increase it to a dollar or more. But the immediate NEED was a dime for milk. God has not promised to supply our *wants*—only our NEED.

The need I had asked was a dime—ten cents! That is what God sent—immediately!

We had learned another lesson!

We gratefully gave God thanks, as I ran all the way to the store and then back with the milk.

Jesus said: "What things soever ye desire, when ye pray, *believe* that ye receive them, and YE SHALL HAVE THEM!" I know that is true. Do YOU?

This incident has been made public before—over the air and in *The Plain Truth*—but it properly belongs here in the Autobiography, so I relate it again.

A New Job

A family by the name of Melson lived on 74th Street in Portland at this time. Their house and ours were opposite, back to back. Some years later this family became nationally famous. A feature article about them on "How America Lives" appeared in one of America's leading mass-circulation magazines. We can remember that they had three little girls, Anna Lou, Marilyn, and Joyce. Little Dickie, our older boy, called Anna Lou "Ah-woo."

One evening Mr. Melson came over and asked me if I would accept a job with the Wear-Ever Aluminum Company. He was a salesman with that company, selling to retail stores. The job open to me was selling the heavy "New Method" utensils direct to consumers.

The sale of the clay to beauty shops was not providing a living. This aluminum job was the straw a drowning man would grab. We were in such down-and-out financial circumstances we were grateful for anything that promised enough food to eat.

I went to their office. I found this company had developed a type of salesmanship with which I was not experienced—and they had reduced it to a virtual science. They sold this particular line of utensils, not through stores, but direct to consumers by a system of "demonstration dinners," which they called "dems." First, to see what it was like, I attended one.

A woman was offered a valuable utensil prize if she would invite a number of married couples to a dinner in her home. The prize was in accordance with the number who came. They had to be couples—husbands and wives. The salesman supplied all the food and ingredients and cooked the dinner. It had to be the most delicious dinner the guests had ever eaten, and of natural foods—no concoctions.

After the dinner, he gave a lecture on health, and the causes of sickness and disease. I observed that the salesman giving this "dem" seemed to know more about the causes of sickness and disease than the physician who was a guest with his wife—and he kept quoting nationally known physicians and surgeons for his statements, and then asking the local guest physician if he agreed. Of course he did—for the statements were all medically correct, and the guest doctor would be disagreeing with outstanding national or international authorities unless he endorsed everything the salesman said.

Before he was through, the guests were impressed that this salesman-lecturer knew more about the minor ailments in their families than their family doctor. Enough of these common ailments had been mentioned—colds, fevers, constipation, rheumatism, tooth troubles, stomach troubles, digestive disturbances, etc., etc., that every family present was sure to be affected. Then the salesman made appointments to call at each home at a time when both husband and wife would be present, in order to give private and confidential counsel about how to prevent these ailments by proper diet and method of preparing food.

404

Every couple present willingly made the appointment. I could see that most of them were actually eager to make it. They had never heard a lecture of this type before. It had been sparkling with interest, and had opened up facts about common ailments they never knew before.

I was intrigued. I saw that this job offered me the opportunity to make an intensive study of the causes of sickness and disease, and of nutrition and the part diet plays in health or illness. I had already been doing enough preaching to have had some little experience in giving these lectures. Also, the lectures would provide experience for more effective preaching.

One thing that appealed to me was the fact that a salesman, in this rather unique work, could be doing a great deal of good. I learned, during the following years, that many of these salesmen were conscientious and used their work only for the good of the customer.

Lecturing on Health

My first "dem" was a very large cooperative one, held in a public hall in Oregon City. Several of the men out of the Portland district headquarters participated, a more experienced one delivering the lecture. Actual participation gave me initial experience.

The district supervisor, a Mr. Peach, gave me a list of several books, whose authors were nationally famous physicians and surgeons, on the subject of diet, causes of common ailments, sickness and disease.

At the library and bookstores I searched out other books beside these he recommended. I plunged into an intensive study in this fascinating field. Mr. Peach also gave me mimeographed material, data, and facts which his office had condensed from many qualified authorities—including many shocking figures and statistics on

405

existing national health conditions. The office also supplied me with large charts, illustrated, showing many of these little-known facts. The charts were used in the lectures.

I obtained pamphlets from the U.S. Department of Agriculture, showing results of scientific government tests made, I believe, at the University of Wisconsin. These tests showed the percentage of mineral elements and vitamins lost from various kinds of foods by cooking at or over the boiling temperature. These figures were astounding. They showed that excessive temperatures, in cooking, rob foods of from 23% to 78% of these vital health elements.

I learned of what the human body is constituted—primarily 16 elements of matter, 12 of which are alkaline-reacting mineral elements, and 4 of which are acid-reacting carbohydrates. I learned that, while the human body requires for health that the diet be composed of a large majority of the alkaline mineral elements, the average American meal is in fact a dietetic horror—consisting of an overwhelming preponderance of the starches, sugars, and greases—the carbohydrate acid-reacting elements which cause numerous ailments and diseases.

Most natural foods are rendered harmful by sauces, gravies and dressings. I learned that leading physicians—that is, the very few who have studied foods, or the *causes* of sickness and disease—estimate variously that from 85% to 95% of all sickness and disease which is not of mental origin is caused by faulty diet, and the small remaining percent from all other causes combined.

Soon I had an eye-opening, interest-compelling lecture outlined. Of course the study was continued intensively—along with continued Bible study for the

406

next year, and the lecture progressively altered and supplemented.

The details are now dim in memory—this is being written almost 30 years later—but it seems that I teamed with another more experienced man in the next one or two "dems."

Then I must have been transferred to the territory around Salem, Oregon. Also it seems this move was influenced by the fact that I had not yet gotten sufficiently established in this aluminum selling to have been able to pay our house rent, and my father was having to pay it for us. Apparently he felt it would be less burden on him for us to move back into the parental home in Salem.

Our First Automobile

About the time I was getting started in this new work, we acquired the first automobile we ever owned. I had learned to drive a car when I was Assistant Secretary of the Chamber of Commerce at South Bend, Indiana, when I was 23. I had driven cars a great deal. Often I had borrowed my brother Russell's car, and also my brother Dwight's. But it was impossible to hold these "dems" without a car.

So an arrangement had been made with my father whereby I received his car—a two-door Ford sedan—and he acquired a better car. Just what the three-cornered deal was is too cloudy in mind to recall.

So, along about October, 1930, we left the house on 75th Street in Portland, and once again moved in with my parents on Highland Avenue in Salem.

The religious interest did not diminish. Rather, this new study of the causes of ill health and disease, and these "dems" with their health lectures, only supplemented my continued study of the Bible.

I learned quite a little about fasting as a means of eliminating toxins and poisons from the body. Always the people I visited after a "dem," had in the family some of these common ailments or diseases. Never before had most of them heard any explanation of *why* they had these sicknesses.

Most people seemed to suppose it is natural for our bodies to get sick. But sickness is *not* natural. Sickness comes only from broken physical laws within our bodies. Most of the time it comes from excess of carbohydrates. Part of the time from malnutrition—a *lack* of essential elements. Under fasting the body naturally eliminates stored up toxins and poisons.

Many on whom I called were, by fasting followed by right diet, relieved of rheumatism, constipation, colds, and many other chronic ailments or diseases.

Of course most doctors do *not* recommend fasting. Many M.D.'s refer to fasting as a "starvation diet." At that time some doctors seemed to feel that if a patient missed a single meal or two he or she would starve. No matter what the sickness or disease, if one were admitted to a hospital, one very probably was fed, even if intravenously.

Actually, if people would fast more, as animals do by instinct when sick, and eat more carefully, it might just be that the *doctors* would starve, not the patients!

But those doctors wanted to stay in business. They did not often recommend fasting.

On the other hand, one should not fast for more than three to five days unless he is under the care of a physician who *does* understand and believe in fasting, or someone equally experienced. And one kind of fasting is required to rid one of constipation, and another kind is indicated for other situations.

It is regrettable that medical "science" was so

narrow that it tried to make a cure-all of one thing
—medicine; or, in some cases, of surgery. One doctor
confided to his elderly mother that if all drugs were
dumped into the ocean, it would be so much better for
humanity, and so much worse for the fish. But such was
the "science" of man that all too often it is, as the Word
of God says plainly, "science falsely so called." The day
will come when the whole world will wake up to that sad
fact!

I never did, on these calls, ask people if I could pray
for their healing. God's instruction is, "Is any sick
among you; *let him call for* the elders of the church"
(James 5:14-15). They are told to ASK FOR IT. And I was
not then an elder. I was not then ordained.

However, when the subject of God's truth did come
up—as it frequently did—if I found the people I was
visiting were believers, and they asked me to pray for
their healing, I always did. This happened a number of
times, and several were healed. But I had learned never
to force religion on any one, and the approach to the
subject had to come from them. This is God's way.

What I learned during this year of study and
lecturing on sickness and disease was actually an
important part of the preparation God was taking me
through for His ministry.

The Near Fight at a Meeting

Along in November of 1930 the Runcorns, neighbors of
my parents, asked me to go with them to a business
meeting of brethren of the Church of God, being held in
the home of Mrs. Ira Curtis, near Jefferson, Oregon.

Although I was a guest—I had never become a
member of this church, whose headquarters was at
Stanberry, Missouri—they asked me to act as secretary
and take down the minutes of the meeting. I learned that

409

the meeting was called for the purpose of organizing these Oregon members into an Oregon Conference.

I sensed immediately there was a feeling of division among them. Elder A. N. Dugger was the real leader of the church at Stanberry. He was editor of the church's weekly paper sent to members. He either was, or had been, president of their General Conference. I learned that they were organized as a General Conference, with elections of officers held biannually. Most of the Oregon members lived in the Willamette Valley in the vicinity of Jefferson. Most of them were in attendance at this business meeting.

About half of them were opposed to Elder Dugger. They wanted to organize a State Conference. Some of the other states had state conferences. The purpose of this Oregon State Conference was to hold the tithes and church funds contributed by Oregon members in Oregon.

But actually, it was born of opposition to and dissatisfaction with the Stanberry membership and state conference. The other half were just as verbal in their loyalty and support of Elder Dugger and the Stanberry regime.

The dispute over Stanberry politics and Elder Dugger's personal fitness and integrity waxed more and more heated. One tall man who weighed considerably over 200, and was a leader, spoke of "dirty politics" and called Elder Dugger a "ward-heeler." An equally vociferous man on the other side of the dispute rose to defend the honor of Mr. Dugger. Words flamed hotter and hotter. Each side was sincere and in roused earnest. Under the tense pressure tempers were flaring. I became afraid it was going to be settled (or unsettled) by fists.

At that instant I rose, and in a loud but calm voice

410

asked if I might say a word. Since I was a guest, they didn't refuse.

"Brethren," I said, "you all know how, as recorded in the first chapter of Job, when the sons of God came together, *Satan came also.* You also know how, in the 12th chapter of Revelation we are told that the people Satan is most angry with are those who keep the Commandments of God and have the testimony of Jesus Christ. That means us. Satan is here. He is stirring up rage and anger in your hearts. I am going to drop to my knees right now, and ask God Almighty to cast Satan out of this house! All of you who wish may kneel with me and pray silently."

Without another word, I quickly dropped to my knees beside my chair, and began asking God to rebuke Satan and this controversial spirit that was rousing these men to anger, and to drive Satan from our presence, and to give us peace and love.

When I rose there were some wet eyes, but there were no angry voices. These people were sincere. They simply believed what they believed and had allowed themselves to be caught off guard, and roused to anger.

Asked to Conduct Campaign

The state conference was agreed to and formed. The concept of church government seemed to be that lay members should be in the offices of authority. Ministers were to be employed, and under orders from the lay members. This is essentially the concept of what we call democracy: government from the bottom up. Those being governed dictate who shall be their rulers and *how* their rulers shall rule them.

The most perplexing subject in all the Bible to me was this matter of church government. I never did come

411

to clear understanding of the BIBLE teaching on the subject until after Ambassador College was formed and well on its way.

I believe that elderly G. A. Hobbs of Oregon City, previously mentioned, was made the first president of this state Conference, and that O. J. Runcorn, with whom I had come to this meeting, was president the second year. I have in my old files my Ministerial License Certificate, which is reproduced in this autobiography, dated March 2, 1932, and signed by O. J. Runcorn as President, and Mrs. I. E. Curtis as Secretary. This was almost a year after I was ordained— probably my second certificate.

At the close of this business meeting, the newly elected officers caused me great embarrassment.

They asked me if I would hold an evangelistic campaign for them in the church building they rented in Harrisburg. I had never preached before the public. Only before these brethren in the Willamette Valley and at Oregon City. As I have stated before, becoming a preacher was the very *last* thing I should ever have wanted to do. I had been literally *drawn into* what little preaching had been done before these few brethren. Most certainly I had never pushed myself in.

But to hold a public evangelistic campaign! Consternation seized me! By nature, I shrank from the idea. Yet here were these simple, Bible-loving people, looking to me for leadership. It was as if they were sheep needing a shepherd. They wanted to get the Gospel out. It seemed impossible to refuse. If I was severely embarrassed at the thought of doing it, it would be even more embarrassing to refuse. More and more I was being *drawn into* the ministry by some power greater than I.

Inexperienced though I still was in the Gospel area, I had come to realize that the success of any campaign

412

depended more on the amount and earnestness of *prayer* behind such a campaign, than on the oratory or eloquence of the speaker. One thing I knew—if GOD was in it—if I were merely an instrument and GOD was really conducting the campaign, it was bound to bear fruit.

Embarrassment on the Other Foot

All these things flashed through my mind in a few seconds.

"Well, brethren," I replied, "I have never preached before a public audience in my life. All the revivals and evangelistic services I have attended have wound up in altar calls. I'll tell you the truth—I simply could not do this without a lot of help from God. And I know that results will depend more on the PRAYER back of the meetings than on my preaching. In fact, the effectiveness of the preaching will depend on prayer and the extent to which I can allow God to speak through me. This would really be a very hard assignment for me. But I'll make you brethren a proposition. If every one of you here at this meeting will *pledge* yourselves right now to devote *not less than one hour every day* to earnest and believing and prevailing PRAYER for the success of these meetings—for God to help me and speak through me—for God to cause the ones He is calling and drawing to attend—and for God to convict the ones He is calling—and if you will solemnly pledge to keep up this hour or more a day of prayer, beginning now, and until the last night of the meetings—then I will undertake this campaign. I could do it at the end of December. Our company does not work from December 20th until after New Year's day. I could start the campaign on Sunday night, December 21st, and eleven nights right up to the end of the year. The Wear Ever company has a convention in Seattle the first week in January and I must be there. But I will have these eleven nights free."

And now, it was *their* turn to be embarrassed. Perhaps some had been spending an hour a day in prayer—but I was sure most of them had not. Their tempers would not have boiled over into a near fistfight if they had. But, as I had been too embarrassed to refuse their offer, they were too embarrassed to refuse mine. To refuse to devote an hour a day on their knees would be very un-Christian! Yes, that would have been more embarrassing than to go through with it!

They agreed. They pledged themselves to this intensive prayer.

I agreed. I was brought one step closer to the ministry of Christ!

These brethren realized that the Stanberry church was not getting the Gospel to the world with power. In this area the church was virtually impotent. The Oregon brethren were anxious to "get the Work going." Although I had been greatly humbled by business reverses not of my making, and by conversion, they were aware of my past experience in the business world.

And actually, from the time of this business meeting, the brethren in Oregon looked to me for the leadership that would revitalize the work of the Gospel. There had been no minister of the church resident in Oregon. But from this time ministers were to be sent there to counteract the favor these Oregon brethren were showing toward me. Always I was to meet opposition from the ministers.

The First Public Preaching

You may be sure that I, too, practiced what I demanded of them. In fact, I was afraid not to. If ever I had needed the help of God it was now.

414

I designed a good-sized circular. This was the first time my 20 years of advertising experience was used in God's Work. I did not have the money to have the handbills printed, but the new conference officials agreed to pay all expenses for the meetings. I had the circular printed at the job printing department of the Salem *Statesman.* I do not remember how they were distributed, but I think church brethren living near Harrisburg must have volunteered to do it. The handbills were distributed to every house in Harrisburg and for some five miles around.

Even before conversion I had attended two or three evangelistic campaigns. A businessman, a prosperous and successful owner of a factory in southeastern Iowa, had conducted a big tent campaign in Indianola, Iowa, during the summer of 1923. At that time I was working with my brother-in-law, Walter Dillon, on his college oratory, and also conducting a merchandising survey for an Indianola weekly paper.

I had attended several of these meetings. The businessman was a vigorous speaker, somewhat of the Billy Sunday style. He had a very effective song leader and team—much as Billy Graham was to do later on a much larger scale. Always there were altar calls—the traditional "sawdust trail." Workers urged people of the audience to go forward.

In my inexperience, I took these traditional methods for granted. In these beginning years of my ministry I went along with many of these religious practices—and even some doctrines—commonly accepted by the evangelical denominations, and which I later had to UN-learn.

I had to learn one doctrine, and one truth, at a time.

The little church building in the little town of

415

Harrisburg, then about 500 population, had seating capacity of perhaps 150. On the first Sunday night we had about 100 or more in attendance.

I think the attendance dropped a little after the first night, but it held up not far under a hundred. Our little group of church brethren assembled in the church about an hour and a half early each evening, and had their hour of prayer together in the church.

We did not have droves of hundreds or thousands "hitting the sawdust trail," but God did give us four who were converted in the meetings.

However, we knew that the greatest good done was the spiritual revival that took place in the church brethren as a result of that hour a day spent in solid prayer!

They were a changed people! They were happy. They were closer to God—and this was evidenced by their manner, their conversation, their lives!

WHO Should Baptize?

The subject of water baptism had been the very first I had studied in the Bible, after my original surrender to Christ. Now I had four new converts to be baptized. One of those was my own brother, Dwight Armstrong.

But WHO was to baptize them? I was not an ordained minister.

A young minister of the Church of God who had been sent out from Stanberry, Missouri, headquarters, had been in an automobile accident in Harrisburg. He was confined to bed with a broken leg at the time. I consulted him. It was a problem neither of us had confronted before.

We looked at Matthew 28:19-20.

"Go ye," said Jesus in His Great Commission, "therefore, and teach all nations, baptizing them . . ." It

416

appeared that whoever taught those who repented and accepted Christ was to do the baptizing. Nothing was said about being ordained.

We examined Acts 2:37-41—the initial New Testament experience on the day of Pentecost. Three thousand were baptized. It was evident that the twelve disciples of Jesus could hardly have baptized this vast number.

In Acts 8, Philip, a deacon, and apparently not yet at that time an ordained evangelist, baptized those to whom he preached at Samaria, and later the Ethiopian eunuch.

We decided that I had the authority of God to baptize those converted during my first public preaching.

I baptized them.

This brought stern criticism from "authorities" higher up in the church. There was criticism because the Conference paid expenses when I was not even a member. In fact, from this time I was to meet continued criticism, opposition, persecution, and political maneuvering by ministers. But the lay members looked more and more to me for leadership.

24

Ordained to Christ's Ministry

THE YEAR 1931 dawned for Mrs. Armstrong and me, like those preceding, with dark and overcast skies. It was one more of the economically *lean* years. It was an exceedingly high-point year in my life. It was the year in which I was ordained as a minister of Christ's Gospel, plunged full time into the ministry. Yet this very ordination was to foment multiplied opposition and persecution from the Stanberry ministers.

God did not induct me into His service as an imposing figure impressing others as a man of importance, wisdom and distinction.

Rather, the Eternal put me into His ministry a good deal like the Apostle Paul, who wrote: "And I, brethren, when I came to you, came not with excellency of speech or of wisdom . . . and I was with you in weakness, and in fear, and in much trembling" (I Cor. 2:1-3).

418

Greenhorn Tail-End Minister

I was no VIP entering the ministry. There was no red-carpet welcome—no pomp and ceremony—no spectacular acclaim. It would not have been God's doing, had it started out auspiciously. Everything God does through human instruments must start with a humble beginning, the very smallest. God brings down low and to naught the proud and the lofty. The Eternal is able to exalt in His own due time those He first humbles.

Every person has his IDOL. GOD cannot receive and convert a human life until his idol has been smashed or torn from him. My idol had been an egotistical sense of self-importance—a cocky self-assurance—a passion to become successful—to attain STATUS—in the eyes of the material world. God is creating in those He calls a righteous character which can be developed only through *experience;* and experience requires TIME. God has a lot of time—He is Eternal—He has always existed—He always will.

It took *time* to eradicate from my heart the love of the praise of men. God gave me, instead, the false accusations, the unwarranted oppositions, the scheming persecutions of jealous, competitive-minded ministers. It required *time* to bring me to a place where I no longer set my heart on material possessions and the finer things of this material world.

This process required not one or two years—not seven—but *four sevens!* For 28 financially lean and humiliating years out of *the very prime of life,* God continued to root out of my life and character this vain idolatry!

From the first, and for some time, I was treated *by the ministers* as the green-horn tail-ender among them.

They used every practice and device constantly to humiliate me and belittle me in the eyes of the brethren. *I needed this*—and I knew God knew I needed it! Aware of my need of humility, I felt, myself, that I was the "least of the ministers." However, the brethren *loved me* and continued looking to me for leadership. The *only* "fruit" being borne resulted from my efforts. This, naturally, was the very reason for the opposition and persecution.

And so the year 1931 dawned.

The Convention at Seattle

The first evangelistic campaign was over. It was just a short 11-night campaign in the little rented church building in Harrisburg, Oregon. Attendance had been good for such a small town—around 100. I had not known better than to follow the Protestant evangelical method of giving "altar calls," for repentant sinners accepting Christ to come up to the altar and kneel. Four had come, and been baptized.

The pastor of one of the churches in the neighboring larger town, Junction City, asked me to hold a campaign in his church. I do not remember which church, but I believe it was the Baptist.

I was still dependent on my job with the Wear Ever Aluminum Company, giving dinner "dems" with health lectures and selling their "new method" heavy aluminum utensils. It was necessary that I attend the annual convention of their Pacific Northwest sales force in Seattle, beginning at or after the first week in January.

This prevented any extended campaign at the church in Junction City. However, it was arranged that I should hold three special services there—on Saturday night, and on Sunday afternoon, and Sunday night—

420

with the pastor himself holding his usual Sunday morning service.

I shall never forget the thrill of accomplishment and thankfulness I experienced as I rode with the Runcorns back to Salem after the Harrisburg meetings. It was a deeper and far more intense sensation than I had ever experienced at a football game.

The Wear Ever district convention was held at the New Richmond Hotel in Seattle. There I met all of the top-ranking salesmen of the district—some of whom were of the high-pressure type and extremely successful, earning large incomes.

However, this convention was somewhat disillusioning. Actual appointments in homes, with a husband and wife who ostensibly were attending a "dem" lecture, were acted out. The entire district sales force saw these top-ranking salesmen in simulated action. I came to realize that these men who were in the big money used high-pressure methods which I, as a Christian, could not employ. It became apparent that I could never get into the big-money bracket on this kind of a job. I was not making enough to meet the actual *needs* of my family—just enough to keep us from starving.

I did, however, learn things I had not known about health, nutrition and diet, causes of disease, etc. One thing I learned which seemed important—the reason *why* "One man's meat is another man's poison."

Different individuals are of varying chemical types. One person would be classified as the potassium type. The element potassium is somewhat dominating in his physical constitution. These people are said to be the outdoor type, usually extroverts loving to be with other people.

The salesmen analyzed and classified one another

421

as to chemical types. I gave the most "expert" among them considerable difficulty. I seemed to be a mixture of several types, but they finally agreed that calcium was the dominating chemical constituency in my makeup. This must be true, because I require more calcium than most people. Calcium is found in largest quantities in milk and milk products. I seem to crave and need a goodly amount of milk, cheese, and butter.

The First Funeral

We were still living, at this time, with my parents in Salem.

Shortly after returning to Salem from the convention in Seattle, a death occurred in the family of a young couple, Mr. and Mrs. Milas C. Helms, who lived near Jefferson. Parents of both of them were members of the Church of God. Their baby son, Richard Leon, born November 23, 1930, had died on Monday, January 12, 1931.

I was contacted and asked to conduct the funeral. This was a new and frightening experience for me. The dread and fear of it grew.

As the day of the funeral dawned, this dread had almost driven me berserk.

"I can't do it!" I kept saying. "I just can't go through with it! I WON'T! *I won't do it!*" I finally shouted.

Not many times in my life did my father's powerful bass voice speak sharply and with authority to me. This was one of those few times.

"Herbert!" Dad's voice cracked like a sudden thunderclap, in unmistakable authority, *"snap out of that instantly!* WAKE UP! *Come to your senses!* Those people are stricken with grief! They are depending on you! You can't let them down! You are going to sit right

down and prepare this funeral sermon. Then you are going down there and fulfill this obligation!"

If I had been almost out of my senses, this brought me back instantly. It was like a sudden awakening from a nightmare.

"Yes, Dad," I said. "Thanks for waking me up. I'll ask God to help me, and I will do it."

I had attended very few funerals. I did not know what customary funeral sermons were like. I did not want to know. I felt it would only be a pagan ceremony. I merely prayed and asked God to direct me through His Word. Soon I had a short sermon worked out from the Scriptures, reading certain basic scriptures on the subject of death and the resurrection, with a few brief comments expounding them.

It turned out that only a graveside service had been planned. When the moment came for me to officiate, my prayer for God's help was answered, and I was calm, sympathetic, and in sincere earnest.

That brief sermon from the Scriptures, together with the grief of losing their little son, deeply affected and moved Mike and Pearl Helms, and resulted in bringing them to repentance and conversion through Christ as their Saviour.

It was the beginning of a very close friendship, and Christian fellowship between us for several years to come. I have always had a very special warm spot in my heart for Mike Helms, and I feel sure it is mutual. We were to go through many rough experiences together in God's Work—experiences which brought us together like two close brothers.

Mike was a vegetable gardener, and a very successful one. He was a natural leader. Inevitably, you will read quite a lot about him if you continue reading this story of my life, for he became closely connected with it and the many experiences I must relate from this point on.

We Move Again

Through the first half of the year 1931 the study and lectures on the *causes* of sickness and disease continued. Enough of the heavy aluminum was sold to keep the family alive—but no more.

Two or three cases during that time come back to memory. One man in Salem was troubled with chronic constipation, and with rheumatism. After my first visit to his home he went on a ten-day fast, followed by a diet of natural vegetables and fruits, lean meats and whole grains—a diet free of starches, fats and white sugar. Both the rheumatism and the constipation disappeared. Another case was a man who had ulcers of the stomach. He could not even drink milk and hold it down. Yet a milk diet, with nothing else for many weeks, was his logical corrective. I squeezed a half lemon into a glass of milk, stirred it, and had him drink it. Of course it curdled slightly. He held it in his stomach, and was started on his milk diet. His stomach healed over naturally after several weeks.

Because I thoroughly believed in what I was doing, I held "dems" for the church brethren in the Jefferson area. Most of them purchased the heavy aluminum, and began eating *natural* foods.

In the spring of 1931 my father bought a small farm about fifteen miles south of Oregon City, trading their home in Salem for the farm. Of course my brother Russell had been married several years and was living in Portland, and my sister also was married and living in Portland. My youngest brother, Dwight, went with the "folks" to the farm.

At that time we moved to a house on East State

Street in Salem. A number of events were to happen to us in that house—among others, little Garner Ted being miraculously given his voice. When Ted had been about six months old he had fallen out of his crib, landing on his head on the floor. From that time he had been dumb, and he never learned to speak a word until he was past two years old. But that is getting ahead of our story. He was about 14 months when we first moved to the State Street house.

R. L. Taylor Arrives

In early summer of that year a former S.D.A. minister, a Robert L. Taylor, came to Oregon from California. It was practice among these Church of God people to hold all-day meetings about once a month. It was at one of these meetings that Mr. Taylor preached. We were all quite impressed.

"He's a better preacher than any of the leading ministers from Stanberry," seemed to be the common exclamation. Indeed we were all rather "swept off our feet" by his preaching.

After a few weeks, the brethren of this "Oregon Conference," which had been formed the preceding November, wanted to team Elder Taylor with me to hold an evangelistic campaign. They were becoming anxious to see a little "life" in the work of the Church.

They found Elder Taylor very receptive to the idea. By this time a modest balance had accumulated in the new Conference treasury. You will remember that the object in forming this State Conference was to create a local state treasury and keep their tithes and offerings in the state, instead of being sent to Stanberry, Missouri. These were days of rapidly descending economic depression, but several of these brethren were vegetable gardeners. They were doing very well financially.

425

Elder Taylor said he would be glad to undertake this campaign with me, suggesting it be held in Eugene—for reasons I was to learn later. We decided to speak on alternate nights, the one not speaking to lead in the song service.

This made it necessary that the Oregon Conference ordain me to the ministry.

ORDAINED Christ's Minister

Being ordained and entering the ministry full time meant a complete change in my life. In former years the idea of becoming a minister was the very *last* thing I should have wanted to do. But by June, 1931, I had been preaching a great deal for three and a half years. By this time my whole heart was in it.

I had come to see, at the Seattle salesmen's convention, that this aluminum sales job was not permanently compatible with the Christian life. I was unable to adopt some of the high pressure methods—in the interest of the salesman's commission, but not in the customers' interest—which the top-ranking salesmen employed. I knew I could never make more than a bare existence for my family. And anyway, by this time I think I recognized that God had called me to His ministry.

I had remained in this aluminum selling only because I realized I was acquiring valuable knowledge about food and diet, and the causes of sickness and disease. But now I had devoted a year to this study. There was no point in continuing.

The decision was not difficult. God had now brought me to the place where I really "heard" the voice of Christ as if He were saying, "Come, and follow me, and I will make you a fisher of men."

It was decided by the officers of the Conference

426

that on the next all-day meeting I was to be ordained.

I shall never forget that moment of my ordination.

The meeting was being held outdoors. I do not remember where—except it was in the general rural area of Jefferson. I do not remember other circumstances.

But I do remember the ordination itself. It was one of those once-in-a-lifetime experiences like being married, and being baptized. Only this seemed to me to be the most momentous event of my entire life.

All the brethren—as many as could get their hands through to my head—laid their hands on me—on my head, my shoulders, my chest and my back.

I am sure it was the weight of the *experience,* from a spiritual and emotional standpoint, rather than the physical weight of hands and arms—but it seemed I was entirely weighted down with the heaviest load I had ever stood up under.

To me this was symbolic of the tremendous responsibility that now came down on my head and shoulders.

And let it be made plain here: I was ordained by, and under the authority of, the Oregon Conference of The Church of God, separately incorporated; *not* by the Stanberry, Missouri, headquarters.

Coincidence? — or DESIGN!

This brings us to a series of almost incredible facts. Whether strange coincidence or planned acts of God I cannot now say. But these are FACTS, nonetheless.

I never recognized these facts until just a few months before the writing of this present chapter. Certainly this strange chain of occurrences was not of my planning.

Here, then, are the actual *facts:*

First, Jesus Christ began His earthly ministry at about age 30. God took away my business, moved me from Chicago, started bringing me to repentance and conversion preparatory to inducting me into His ministry, *when I was 30!*

Second, Jesus began the actual *teaching and training* of His original disciples for carrying HIS GOSPEL to the world in the year A.D. 27. *Precisely* 100 *time-cycles later,* in 1927, He began my intensive study and training for carrying HIS SAME GOSPEL to all nations of today's world.

100 Time-Cycles

It is important that we realize the significance of 100 time-cycles!

God set the earth, sun, and moon in their orbits to mark off divisions of *time* on the earth. One revolution of the earth is a *day*. One revolution of the moon around the earth is a lunar *month* (according to God's sacred calendar). One revolution of the earth around the sun is a solar *year*. But the earth, the sun, and the moon come into almost exact conjunction only *once in 19 years*. Thus 19 years mark off one complete time-cycle!

Now consider further facts—whether strange coincidence, or providential design.

The actual ordination, or completing of the ordination and enduement of power for sending out the original disciples into the ministry occurred after 3½ years of intensive instruction and experience. It was on the Day of Pentecost. And the year was A.D. 31.

Exactly 100 time-cycles later, after 3½ years of intensive study and training, Christ ordained me to preach this *same* Gospel of the Kingdom in all the world as a witness to all nations (Matt. 24:14). *This ordination took place at, or very near, the Day of Pentecost, 1931.*

I do not remember the exact day of the month of this ordination. No special significance was attached to the date then. Most of those who participated are now dead. But the date was June, 1931.

But *that is not all!* Consider further!

More Amazing Parallels!

Christ started out His original apostles preaching the *very* Gospel of the Kingdom which God had *sent by Him,* and *which He had taught the apostles,* in the year A.D. 31. For exactly one 19-year time-cycle this preaching was confined to the continent where it started—Asia. After *precisely one 19-year time-cycle,* A.D. 50, Christ *opened a door* for the Apostle Paul to carry the same Gospel to EUROPE! This was A.D. 50. Before A.D. 70, Roman armies besieged Jerusalem. From that time the Roman government stamped out the organized mass spreading of the Gospel of Christ. Soon a *different* gospel was being tolerated, *later* endorsed and then enforced by Roman government. It was Roman paganism now being palmed off under the new name "Christianity."

For nearly 19 centuries the world has been rendered spiritually drunk on the wine of *this counterfeit gospel!* As prophecy foretold, ALL nations have been deceived. But looking into *our time,* just before the END of this age (Matt. 24:14), Jesus foretold that *His same original Gospel of the Kingdom of God* was to be preached and published (Mark 13:10) in all the world as a witness to ALL NATIONS! This was to immediately precede HIS SECOND COMING!

TODAY THIS IS BEING DONE! Now consider *this* amazing parallel!

God first *opened a door*—that of radio and the printing press—for the mass proclaiming of HIS

429

ORIGINAL TRUE GOSPEL *the first week in 1934!* The exact date was January 7, 1934. *Exactly one time-cycle later,* January 7, 1953, God opened wide the massive door of the most powerful commercial radio station on earth, and RADIO LUXEMBOURG began broadcasting Christ's Gospel to EUROPE and Britain!

What startling coincidences!—or *are* they mere coincidences?

My First Extended Campaign

My ordination ended the "dems" and selling of aluminum. The state Conference employed Mr. Taylor and me as evangelists at salaries of $20 per week. Remember this was 1931. The country was undergoing rapid deflation.

Immediately Mr. Taylor and I went to Eugene. The Conference owned a small tent. With a small platform across the front, we were able to set up 50 folding chairs—that is all—50!

This tent was pitched on a vacant lot in Eugene on West 10th Avenue. I rented a room with a small kitchenette on the second floor of a house across the street, within the same block. Mr. Taylor and his wife had moved to a small chicken ranch on the outskirts of Eugene. They had a car. I must have left mine in Salem. It probably died of old age at that time, or shortly later.

I do not remember about preliminary advertising, but we must have had some. I was entirely too advertising-conscious after my long years in that profession to have started without it.

I opened the first Sunday night's meeting as MC and song leader. Elder Taylor preached. The tent was full—50 people.

On Monday night he opened the song service, and I

preached. Thus we continued for the six weeks, alternating each night. Services were held six nights a week—none on Saturday nights.

In Portland I had gained some little experience with "pentecostal people." I had been somewhat overawed by their "speaking in tongues," and their glib "testimony." I had not yet at that time fully understood it. But I had noticed that most of these people refused to obey God's commandments; almost none had any real sound understanding of the Bible; they customarily had a wide knowledge of certain scattered texts—verses or partial verses—which they usually misapplied, entirely out of context, putting only a meaning of pseudo-spirituality on them. They spoke in what was supposed to be spiritual-sounding language. They loved to show off—to brag, especially about their own spirituality which usually consisted of sentimentality and emotion.

The "brethren" in the Willamette Valley had been decidedly antagonistic toward "tongues" speaking and "pentecostalism" in general. Elder Taylor had also appeared to be opposed to it.

But a couple families of "pentecostal" people began attending our tent meetings in Eugene. Soon I noticed that Mr. Taylor was especially friendly to them. He welcomed, and gradually began to encourage their loud "amens" and "hallelujahs" and "Praise the Lord" expressions during his preaching.

But, for the first few weeks I thought little of it.

Sole "Fruit" Borne

This was my first ministerial experience teaming with another man. Jesus sent His disciples out two and two together. The teaming of two ministers together certainly has Biblical precedence and approval. But if God refuses to use either member of the team, no

431

spiritual results can be produced by the team. This lesson I was to learn.

I was surprised, somewhat incredulous, somewhat discouraged, as our meetings wore on, to notice that no "fruit" was being borne. I could not understand it.

Then one night the lone exception occurred.

It was an exceedingly stormy night. Mr. Taylor and I went over to our tent to loosen slightly the ropes, so the shrinkage from soaking would not up-stake them, and also to drive down the stakes more securely. It was a nasty night. We did not expect anyone to come. While we were there, one couple who had attended regularly drove up in the storm. I had noticed this couple. I had felt sorry for them. I supposed they were very poor people—why, I didn't know, except that he was as far from being handsome as Abraham Lincoln had been, and she had no "beauty" of the worldly sort. Later I was to be much surprised to find that they were very successful and prosperous, though thrifty, farmers—leaders in their community.

I had not, up to this stormy evening, become acquainted with them further than shaking hands with them at the tent entrance.

No one else came that night. No service could have been held in the tent.

"It would simply be a dirty shame for you to have come all the way into town on such a terrible night, and then be deprived of a service," I said sympathetically. "Why not come on over to my room, and we can at least have a Bible study together?"

"That would be splendid," smiled Mrs. Fisher. I had never known their names before.

"Well count me out," answered Mr. Taylor. "It's too stormy to stay around here. I'm going home."

This was my first shock of disappointment in Mr.

Taylor. He had been my "ideal" as a minister. But one incident like this could not cause me to lose confidence in him.

Over in my room, Mrs. Fisher said:

"I wonder if you would mind giving us a Bible study on the question of which day is the Sabbath of the New Testament. My husband believes the only Bible Sabbath is Saturday. But it never seemed possible to me that all these churches could be wrong. I'd like to have you explain just what the Word of GOD says."

"Why," I replied in some surprise, "that is exactly the way I felt when my wife began keeping the Sabbath. That is the very thing that started me studying the Bible—to prove that 'all these churches can't be wrong.' I'll be very happy to open the Bible and show you what I was forced to see for myself. This is the very question that resulted in my conversion."

After my opening up the Scriptures, and having Mrs. Fisher read them for herself—and after answering her rather sharp questions later, and explaining some vague passages she brought up, she smiled and said:

"I thank you, Brudder Armstrong"—she was Swedish, and talked just a trifle brokenly, "it is all clear now. My husband and I will keep the Sabbath together from now on."

And that was the sum total of the tangible results produced by this entire six weeks' campaign!

But God was to use Mr. Elmer Fisher, and Mrs. Margaret Fisher, in a most important way in raising up this very work which now thunders the true Gospel of Christ worldwide, into every continent on earth! You will read much of them, later!

Suspicious Incidents

As our tent campaign progressed, a few little incidents

began more and more to disturb me in regard to "Brother Taylor."

I began to notice that he was becoming much more "chummy" with the two "pentecostal" families than others who were attending. Finally he asked me to attend an all-night "tarry meeting" they were going to have out at his place following our evening meeting.

"You need a deeper spiritual experience," he said to me. "You need to pray, and agonize, and 'tarry' until you receive your 'baptism of the Holy Ghost'," he said.

"Brother Taylor," I answered, "I know I need a deeper spiritual experience. I do want a still closer fellowship and contact with God. But I prefer to seek it the way Jesus attained it—by going out to a solitary place—perhaps up on a mountain—or, at least as Jesus commanded, to enter into 'a closet' or small room, *alone with God,* and pray."

I shall never forget his astonishing answer.

"You'll never get your 'baptism' that way, brother!" he said sharply, with emphasis.

I was shocked—and disappointed.

"I'm sorry," I replied firmly. "But if this 'baptism' is something I can't get the way Jesus taught and commanded—if it is something I have to get from *men* and cannot receive from God while *alone* with Him, *then it is something I do not want!"*

Prior to this, Mr. Taylor had come to me and said:

"Brother Armstrong, our people"—referring to the "brethren" of the Oregon Conference—"are not spiritual enough. We need to seek a closer walk with God." To this I had agreed.

Now it began to dawn on me that Mr. Taylor was, little by little, attempting to lead the church into the very thing he had told them, in his sermons, he was "against"—this "wild-fire pentecostalism." When he had first heard that the brethren were "against" it, he assured them he was also against it. But now, by careful and adroit methods, he was gradually beginning to try to introduce this very thing.

Was he, himself, just beginning to believe he had been wrong? Had he been honest and sincere? Was he now honest in claiming God was opening his eyes to see that we were not "spiritual" enough?

"Why, didn't you know?" later exclaimed a man who had known Mr. Taylor much longer than we had, "Taylor has always been 'pentecostal.' He just pretended he wasn't, in order to get in with the church."

But from the moment I turned down his "tarry meeting" invitation, his attitude toward me became coldly courteous, and I sensed repressed hostility.

Correcting a Member

During this tent campaign in Eugene, we attended Sabbath services with brethren at the church building in Harrisburg. One elderly "brother" whose name was "Rough" as nearly as I remember (pronounced "Row") had been, in his deep sincerity and zeal for a certain contention, stirring up a "row" at nearly every service.

He lived out east of Eugene on the Mackenzie Highway.

He contended the church was in error on one scripture. He could shout his antagonism like a lion's roar. The brethren wanted Mr. Taylor and me to visit him and see if we could not change his mind or at least quiet him.

I had just read, some time previous, an article in the old *American Magazine* on "how to win an argument."

The idea was to make your opponent first state his case fully. Ask him questions. Make him state every detail. Exhaust him, till he has nothing more to say. Just listen—do not reply to any of his arguments—until you have made him state them all. Then summarize his entire position briefly, showing you fully *understand* his argument. State it even more clearly than he did, if possible.

Then AGREE with him on those points where you find you actually are in agreement. Then, finally, tear apart his remaining arguments, disproving them— leaving him without anything to come back with.

We decided to use this method. In our morning session, before noon dinner, we just listened to his reasons. We asked questions, but gave no answers. We drew him out exhaustively.

Mrs. Rough had prepared a delicious chicken dinner. I think this was my first experience with the custom of serving chicken when the minister is the guest. I never understood the reason for it. But I was to eat a great deal of chicken from that time on.

After dinner, we questioned old Brother Rough some more, until he simply had to drift into silence for want of anything more to say.

Then we summarized his arguments, and got him to agree we thoroughly understood his reasons—which he had always claimed the church was not willing to understand. Next we *agreed* on certain points.

But, finally, we riddled his whole conclusion by scriptures he had not considered, which totally reversed his whole argument. It left him without any answer or comeback. The "lion's roar" had been reduced to "a kitten's meow." There were no more explosive eruptions from that time on to disturb "Sabbath-School" or church services—and he remained friendly.

Building a Church

As our campaign neared its close, Mr. Taylor was promoting with the church brethren the idea of building a church building in Eugene. Actually, there were no members in Eugene. Some lived a few miles north, but most of them lived north of Junction City or Harrisburg—although two families lived out east of Eugene on the Mackenzie Highway.

The Eugene campaign added only the Fishers, and, I believe, one other man who continued only for a while.

It was planned that I was to leave Eugene and put on a campaign up in St. Helens, Oregon, 25 miles north of Portland, with a minister by the name of Roy Dailey, who had just returned from Stanberry or points in the Middle West. The Conference had just employed him. There were now three of us on the payroll at $20 per week. At this rate the Conference treasury was soon going to be empty.

But Elder Taylor was to remain at Eugene, superintending the new building. Many events were to take place in that little church building.

25

Evangelistic Campaigns in Full Swing

M Y FIRST full-length evangelistic campaign with Elder Robert L. Taylor in Eugene, Oregon, came to its almost fruitless end. Mr. and Mrs. Elmer E. Fisher, who lived seven miles west of Eugene, were the only ones added to the church by this campaign. And they had been brought in by a private Bible study in my room—not in a preaching service.

Mr. Taylor had induced the Oregon Conference members to build a church building in Eugene. He felt sure he could build up a good congregation there.

It turned out that Mr. Taylor had, for some little time previous to our campaign, been in the retail lumber business in Eugene. He had apparently failed, and salvaged out of it only a small amount of lumber. This lumber, although not enough to build it, was put into the new little church building. The money for the remaining lumber, and all other expenses, were

438

contributed by the church members. The members purchased a 50-foot lot just outside city limits on West 8th Street.

However, because of the lumber he donated, Mr. Taylor managed to have the entire property deeded in his name personally. Before leaving Eugene I attended one service in the new church building. It was entirely unfinished. The siding had not been put on the outside. Slabs of plaster wallboard had been nailed up on inside walls, but the cracks had not been filled in, nor had it been painted. Folding chairs were brought in for seats. A small speaker's stand substituted for a pulpit. Actually, that was as far as Mr. Taylor was to proceed in finishing the church.

The St. Helens "Campaign"

The officers of the Conference decided to team me up with Mr. Dailey, since Mr. Taylor was staying on in Eugene to try to build up a congregation for the new church building, still to be completed. Actually, he never added a single member.

We were assigned to go to St. Helens, Oregon, 25 miles north of Portland, on the west bank of the Columbia River. In West St. Helens, sometimes called "Houlton," lived a very zealous member of the church, Mrs. Mary Tompkins. She was filled with zeal and a spirit of love—although we were to learn that she had more love and zeal than wisdom. Mary Tompkins was a "worker." She "witnessed for Christ" in a most active way. She had for a long time pleaded with the Conference to send evangelists for a campaign in St. Helens. She assured them there was a tremendous "interest" there. So the Conference sent us.

Arriving in St. Helens, we first sought out a hall for meetings and rented a second-floor hall. I do not

remember whether it was the old K.P. Hall or the old
Masonic Hall. Whichever lodge, it had built a new one.
However this old hall was reasonably attractive, and
appeared quite desirable.

Next we went directly to the newspaper and placed
a half-page advertisement, ordering a few thousand
reprints to be distributed as circulars.

Then while we awaited the first Sunday night
service, I spent some three or four days going from house
to house, inviting people personally to come, and leaving
a circular. I was surprised at two things. Practically
everybody I invited, except those Mary Tompkins had
talked to, promised to attend. Elder Dailey and I saw
visions of having to hang out the SRO (Standing Room
Only) sign. But I was even more surprised to find, at the
many homes where Mrs. Tompkins had visited, that the
people were hostile, and regarded this dear, well-
meaning lady as a pest.

Sunday night came. But the expected crowds did
not! To our utter dismay, not a soul showed up!

We couldn't understand it. On Monday, I went to
the newspaper office to see if they had an explanation.
They had.

"Of course nobody came," the man grinned. "That
hall has been condemned as a fire-trap. Everybody knew
that but you."

"And you took our half-page ad, and our money
—and also our money for all those reprints, and didn't
tell us a word!" I exploded.

He only grinned.

I felt he really *needed* some of our fiery gospel
preaching!

But we didn't give up immediately. We returned to
the hall on Monday night. One couple came. I then
heard something I had never heard before in my life.

440

Mr. Dailey mounted the platform, walked behind the pulpit, and preached an entire sermon. And I mean *"preached"!* His style had a bit of the old "preachy-tone"—and he preached, full volume, just as if the hall were packed with people. And to only two people! That was a new experience for me!

"Well, we know now," Mr. Dailey said as we went back to our room after this 'meeting,' "that we are not going to have a crowd here. But I know a place where we *can* draw a crowd—over in Umapine. It's in eastern Oregon, near Walla Walla, Washington. I have visited one of our members there, Bennie Preston. We can stay at his house and save room rent, and we can draw enough people there to make it worth while."

Next morning, early, he started out in his car for Jefferson, Oregon, to get permission from the Conference Board for this switch to Umapine, and a little additional expense money.

On Tuesday night, left in St. Helens alone, I went again to the hall. Two couples of young people came. I did not preach. Instead I sat down with them and had an informal Bible study, letting them ask questions, and answering them.

On our long trek in Mr. Dailey's car over to Umapine, we exchanged views on a lot of things. I was especially puzzled over the matter of church organization. Not yet having come to see and understand the plain and clear Bible teaching, I had gone along with the Oregon Conference in its idea of government by the lay members. In this Conference the governing board was composed solely of lay members. They hired and fired the ministers.

"If we were to have the ideal organization," opined Mr. Dailey, "all the officers would be ministers—not laymen." This sounded strange to me at the time. But

441

the question of church organization and government was to keep coming up in my mind for years, before it was finally to become clear. Remember, I still was driven by the persistent question: "WHERE is the one *true* Church—the same one Jesus founded?" This Church of God, with national headquarters at Stanberry, Missouri, seemed to be closer to the understanding of Bible truth than any—yet I was unable to reconcile myself that such a small, and especially such a *fruitless* church, could be that dynamic fruit-bearing spiritual organism in which, and through which CHRIST was working. Surely the instrument Christ was using would be more alive—more productive! Yet I had not found it!

The Meeting at Umapine

We were welcomed by Bennie Preston and his wife, and given a room where Roy Dailey and I slept in the same bed. We quickly rented a hall on the main street, ground floor.

Here, as Mr. Dailey had promised, results were different. We certainly did not have a crowd of thousands, but attendance, as I remember, ran between 35 and 50 which, at the time, we considered satisfactory. We had no local church to swell attendance. We were unknown, locally. None of the factors that produce great crowds was present.

One little event I shall never forget. Bennie Preston raised some sheep. He decided to butcher one for us. He had impressed me as a man filled with true Christian love.

"I should hate to kill this tame, loving little sheep," he said, "if it were not true that God created sheep to produce wool and meat for man. That is their only purpose in existence. Man has a different and far greater purpose—to become sons of God."

442

Still, Mr. Preston loved that helpless little sheep, now about to give its life for food for us. He led it to a spot in his backyard. He lovingly caressed it first. Then he hit it a hard, stunning blow on top of the head with the sharp edge of a small sledge hammer, and quickly slit its throat to drain out the blood. The sheep suffered no pain. The sharp, quick blow rendered it instantly unconscious.

We Separate

After about two weeks of our Umapine meetings, a letter from Mrs. Florence Curtis, secretary of the State Conference, informed us that a business meeting of the board had been called for only two or three days after our receipt of the letter.

"I know what this meeting is all about," said Mr. Dailey. "It means the conference treasury is running out of funds. They are going to have to lay off at least two of us three ministers. If we don't go back there and protect our interests, at this meeting, they will be sure to let you and me out, and keep Elder Taylor on. We're going to start back to the Willamette Valley at 5:30 tomorrow morning."

"But Roy," I protested, "we are only halfway through our meetings here!"

"Aw, we won't accomplish anything by staying here."

"Whatever we accomplish is in God's hands," I replied. "We are merely His instruments. God has sent us here to preach His Gospel. We have people coming. The interest is increasing, and so is the attendance. I'm going to let God protect my personal interests at that Conference Board meeting, Roy; but I'm going to stay right on the job where He has put me, and continue those meetings."

Elder Dailey was now becoming a little nettled and disgusted with me.

"I told you I'm starting for the valley at 5:30 in the morning," he returned. "If you don't go with me, you'll force the Conference to have to pay your bus fare to get you back home. They won't like that."

But I was just as firm as he.

"Regardless of what the men on the Board like, I know GOD would not like it if I desert, while I'm here on duty. To me it would be like deserting an army, and running away, in the thick of battle in a war. This is God's battle. He put me here, and I am staying right here on the spiritual firing line until the campaign is over!"

Why must men always consider only their own personal interests—and cater to what *men* will like?

I know Mr. Dailey thought I was wrong. He sincerely believed I was wrong most of the time from then on. But to me it was a matter of duty, and a matter of principle, and a matter of obeying God.

At precisely 5:30 next morning, Mr. and Mrs. Preston and I bade Elder Dailey goodbye, and he started alone, giving me final warning that "the brethren" were not going to like my remaining behind and costing them extra bus fare to get home.

As it turned out, the special business meeting was called off, and Mr. Dailey had raced back to the Valley for naught. But later, just as he anticipated, both he and I were laid off and Elder Taylor kept on—but not until after I had returned from completing the campaign.

Left Alone — Fruit Borne

I continued the meetings alone.

Interest continued to pick up at the meetings in the hall. Results were not great—but *there were results!*

444

Details are rather hazy in memory, now. I am not sure whether Mrs. Preston had already been converted and baptized, or whether she was converted by these meetings.

In any event, we had a total of five by the close of the meetings. There were three or four to be baptized. I learned that a son of our Conference president, the elderly G. A. Hobbs, was a local elder in the Seventh-Day Adventist Church. I went to this younger Mr. Hobbs, and through him arranged for the use of the baptistry in the church.

Before leaving, I organized the five members into a local Sabbath school, to meet at the home of Bennie Preston, appointing Mr. Preston as superintendent and teacher. This should have grown. But there was no minister to feed the flock and protect it from "wolves in sheep's clothing." Bennie Preston was a substantial and upright man, but he lacked the leadership and qualifications of a minister.

This tiny flock endured for a while. But some little time later, Mrs. Preston died. I am not sure whether this was the cause of the disintegration of the little Sabbath school, but Mr. Preston was hit a demoralizing blow by her death. Some years later he moved to the Willamette Valley. He had remarried by then.

This Umapine experience was one more in which no fruit could be borne as long as I teamed with one of the ministers of this church, connected with, or springing from the Stanberry, Missouri, political center.

Years later, still in my search for the one *true* church, still questioning whether this could be that church, still not having found it elsewhere, I asked Mrs. Runcorn (whom Mrs. Armstrong and I looked upon as our "spiritual mother") if she could point out a single real bonafide convert, brought in from the outside, resulting from the ministry of any of the preachers affiliated with "Stanberry." She thought seriously for quite a while. Then she slowly shook her head. She knew of none. I asked several others who had been in the church for years. Their answers were the same.

My first evangelistic effort was conducted alone, at the end of 1930, in Harrisburg. There were conversions. In 1931 I was teamed with Elder Taylor, who had arrived from California. There were no results, except for the night it stormed the meeting out, and in a private Bible study in my room Mrs. Elmer Fisher had accepted the truth. I was teamed with Elder Roy Dailey. There were no results. He left Umapine. I continued alone, and *there were conversions.* Results then were small— indeed it was a small beginning, compared to the mounting worldwide harvest of today—but God was using me, and producing "fruit."

I have always noted, in my years of experience since, that if even one member of a two-man team is not a true instrument of God, there will be none of the kind of "fruit" borne which is produced only by GOD through human instruments. This very undeviating method of God, verified by experience, is the source of great inspiration and encouragement today. For in God's Church today, without exception, every minister or team of ministers is used of God, and God really *does things* through them! "By their fruits ye shall know them," said Jesus.

A Thrill and a Jolt

I remember distinctly the all night bus ride back to the Valley from Eastern Oregon. Arriving home, on East State Street in Salem, I learned that the State Conference board had run low on funds, and, unable to continue paying three salaries each of $20 per week in the descending depths of the great depression, had decided to retain Mr. Taylor, and release Elder Dailey and me until funds revived.

Also, a few days after arriving home, happy over "success" in the campaign, this sense of elation was rudely jolted by a stern letter from old Mr. Hobbs. He had heard from his son. He wanted to know what a young whipper snapper like me meant, using the prestige of his name with his son, and baptizing people in Umapine without "authority," or special consent from the Board? Shortly following the first evangelistic experience at Harrisburg, Mr. Hobbs had sternly called me on the carpet, asking me what authority I had for baptizing those converted in the meetings. I had answered that I had GOD's authority — that of Matthew 28:19—where those who do the "teaching" resulting in conversions are commanded to baptize those taught. This rather stumped him, at the time.

But elderly Mr. G. A. Hobbs was a stern, fiery little old man—a stickler for proper form and system, and proper "authority" for everything. He had been an Adventist since a young man—probably beginning somewhere around 1870, or perhaps earlier. Adventists during those earlier years were very strict, legalistic, and exacting. Mr. Hobbs had left the Adventists rather late in life when he saw clearly, in the Bible, that the Millennium will be spent on earth and not in heaven. But he retained his strict disciplinary teaching to his death.

But if old Mr. Hobbs was one of my strictest and sternest critics, he was also one of my staunchest supporters to the day of his death. He defended me against *other* critics with the same fiery zeal with which he criticized me to my face. His sharp criticism for baptizing the converts God gave me at Umapine, plus

447

the sudden, though not unexpected loss of salary, did dull somewhat the spirit of rejoicing over the results God granted at Umapine.

But having my salary cut off caused no worry. By this time I had learned to trust God. Already we had experienced many miraculous answers to prayer. I knew God has promised to supply all our need, "according to his riches in glory by Christ Jesus" (Phil. 4:19).

So, in perfect faith, I prayed and told God of our need, and asked Him to supply it, and use me wherever He willed.

But I had *not yet learned* that everything that happens is not, necessarily, from God. I had not learned to "try the spirits, whether they are of GOD" (I John 4:1). While this scripture is speaking of *spirits*—angels or demons—yet we must learn also to test *experiences,* and *happenings,* whether *they* be of GOD.

It was now late November.

Back Into Advertising!

In serene confidence, I was expectantly awaiting God's answer to supply our financial need. Not more than two or three days later, my former newspaper associate, Samuel T. Hopkins, who had been Business Manager of the *Vancouver Evening Columbian,* appeared at our door.

He had left the *Columbian,* and now was Editor and Manager of a new morning newspaper in Astoria, Oregon, the *Morning Messenger.* He and two Astoria associates, a physician, and the superintendent of a salmon cannery, had started a new newspaper in Astoria. But they were in deep trouble. They had started a brand-new daily newspaper in the depths of the national depression, and without adequate capital.

"Herb, you've just got to come out to Astoria and

help us," pleaded Sam Hopkins. "You are the only man I know with the specialized advertising and selling experience who can put this thing over for us. I know you can do it. Right now I'm not even in position to guarantee you any regular cash salary. Actually I'm depending on you to get in the business to make even your own salary possible. But once we put this over, we'll give you a large chunk of the stock in the company—*anything*, if only you'll come on out to Astoria and inject the life we need into this paper. I want you to come as Advertising Manager. We'll set your salary at $25 a week at the start, and hope we can pay it. But as we get the paper on its feet, the sky's the limit. You'll have a big salary, and a large chunk of stock."

"But Sam," I answered, "I'm in the ministry now. I can't go back into the newspaper business."

He would not give up. He kept pleading. It was a matter of life and death to him. I began to think of how I had prayed for God to supply our new financial need. In my inexperience, this did seem to be the answer. I did not then realize this was not GOD'S answer. This was not GOD'S *WAY* of answering.

I did realize that I could not accept this job as a permanent thing. I knew I had been called to the ministry. I had been ordained. I had been successful in a small way. Everything I had ever touched in business, since age 30 in Chicago, had turned to nothing. But in the ministry, everything I did was, in the small way of a small *beginning,* successful. Yet, this did appear to me, in my inexperience, to be God's answer to my prayer. Since I could not go back into the advertising business, and *leave* the ministry, permanently, I *reasoned* this solution:

"Tell you what I might do," I finally said to Mr.

449

Hopkins. "I know I have been called to the ministry. I've been ordained. But my salary is temporarily cut off. It seems to me this is God's answer as a temporary fill-in for our financial need. I'll come on out to Astoria *just for one month only*. Then I'll have to return here."

How many times, since, have I quoted the scriptures: "Lean not unto *thine own* understanding," and "There is a way that seemeth right to a man, but the end thereof are the ways of death." Human reason is usually faulty. But this did *seem* like the right decision. I was to pay a high price over the next 15 months to learn that lesson.

I was to have to learn two basic requirements of God, before He can use one for an important commission in His great Master Plan working out His Purpose here below: 1) Not only must God's instrument "preach THE WORD faithfully," but having been plunged by Christ into God's Work, he must never turn back (Luke 9:62). And 2) he must rely on GOD, and not man, for his NEED—*in*, not *out* of God's Work. The *REAL WORK* started only *after* I learned these lessons!

How I found myself caught in a trap of unforeseen circumstance, forced to break all precedent in methods of selling advertising space; and how, after 15 long and almost sleepless months I finally got back into the ministry, is related in the next chapter.

26

Caught in Newspaper Business Trap

GETTING back into the newspaper business was a tragic mistake. A too dear price now had to be paid to learn an important lesson: when God once truly calls a man into His ministry, he must "keep at it, in season and out of season" (II Tim. 4:2).

And if he attempts, like Jonah, to run away from the mission, God will first teach him a stern lesson and then yank him back to perform what God called him to perform!

Arriving in Astoria, I made a disillusioning discovery. Immediately I made preliminary get-acquainted calls on the leading merchants. It was then, for the first time, that I learned the true state of affairs. It was far worse than Mr. Hopkins had told me. Every merchant told me our situation was hopeless. We faced a predicament unprecedented, as far as I know, in the newspaper business.

451

Caught in a Trap

It called for desperate and unprecedented measures for solution. And before I realized it, I was caught in a trap of circumstances from which I was unable to extricate myself for fifteen months.

This was the unheard-of situation: Only months before, the opposition newspaper had purchased the old established morning paper, *The Astorian,* for $50,000. But the opposition publisher had also signed up all local stores which advertised on five-year contracts in which they agreed *not* to advertise in any other Astoria English-language paper. (There was, in Astoria, a Finnish language daily paper not harmed by the contracts.)

Apparently this publisher and the merchants had assumed the rather general concept of those in smaller cities, viewing advertising in terms of obligatory "support" of the newspaper, rather than as an effective means of selling goods, lowering costs, and increasing profits. This publisher offered to save the merchants from having to "support" *two* newspapers by buying out and thus eliminating his competitor—provided the merchants would sign up on these five-year contracts. Every store in town which was a regular advertiser, with the single exception of the J. C. Penney store, had signed.

"But," I protested, "that kind of contract is illegal! It is in restraint of trade!"

"We know that," came the answer, "but there is more to it than mere legality. You just don't know your opposition publisher. Maybe you don't realize what he could do to us in retaliation, if we broke our contracts. He could print things harmful to us, slanting the news so as to reflect against us, or assassinate our character right

452

on the front page. I for one am afraid to try to break my agreement—and I think the other merchants are as afraid as I am. We just won't take this chance!"

A few days later I learned what he meant. Our news editor handed me a clipping from the teletype. It was a dispatch from Oregon City, Oregon, reporting an automobile accident involving one of Astoria's leading merchants. It exposed also the fact he was having a clandestine "affair" with an attractive woman, who was with him in his car. The press service had sent it along as a nice "juicy scandal" for Astoria papers.

But *The Messenger* did not print it. Neither did the opposition. I took the teletype strip personally to the merchant involved. His face reddened.

"Thanks!" he exclaimed in extreme embarrassment. "Man! This could have ruined me if you had printed it! It would have broken up my home, and ruined my business. You see, Mr. Armstrong, *this* sort of thing is the reason none of the merchants dares try to break his contract with your competitor by advertising with you."

Yes, I understood, now, only too well!

Our plight was utterly frustrating. Our newspaper was new. The opposition paper was old, well established. The evening paper had the dominant circulation. It was well financed. The morning *Messenger,* on the other hand, did not have the capital to do those things necessary to build a better paper, or, for that matter, even to keep it on its wobbly feet. And every retail advertiser in town, save one, actually by agreement and by *fear* was prohibited from advertising with us.

It Means Something to YOU!

I am going to relate what was done in this predicament,

because the experience has a direct connection with the lives of all my readers.

You probably shall never run into this specific *kind* of problem. But nearly all people *do,* more than once in a lifetime, find themselves in some frustrating, apparently hopeless trouble.

One of the seven basic laws of success in life is *resourcefulness.* Resourcefulness is the ability and determination to *find a way* to solve every problem, trouble or obstacle. It accepts and acts on the old adage: "where there's a will, *there's a way!"* Another of the seven principles of success is *endurance.* Nine out of ten who have every other ingredient for success finally give up and quit, when just a little more "stick-to-it-iveness" mixed with resourcefulness would have turned apparent hopeless defeat into glorious success. Of course there *is* a time to get out and leave whatever you are in: if it is *wrong,* or if it really *is* totally *dead.* But usually it only appears dead.

The seventh and most important rule of success is contact with God, and the guidance, wisdom, and help that can be received from Him.

In this desperate situation, I did invoke these three recourses. I do believe I had made a costly mistake in supposing this call to the newspaper business in Astoria came from God. Yet, once in it, I did call on God for guidance and help. And a way *was* found to break those five-year contracts, and fill our newspaper with advertising! I think the account of how it was done may be interesting, informative, and—if you will apply the principles to your own problems—helpful.

"Inside Facts" About Advertising

This unprecedented situation, I knew, called for a totally unprecedented solution. Most people are absolutely *bound* by precedent. They are slaves of habit. They are conformists. They must do just what society does—the *way* society does it. I have never been afraid to break precedent, or to go counter to established procedures, if such action is both right and necessary.

Advertising space in newspapers and magazines had always been sold on the basis of a certain price per column inch, or per page. The rate is set according to volume and class of circulation, being influenced also by competition and general circumstances.

So now let me give you a few "inside facts" not known by most of the general public. Full-page advertising space in large mass-circulation magazines costs tens of thousands of dollars.

"Do you mean for just *one time?*" many will ask incredulously.

Yes, for one page in just one issue. But that is *not* expensive. It is, actually, one of the *least* costly ways to get a message to people!

The magazine may have a circulation of *one million copies,* often actually read by two or three million people! Now suppose you try to get just a very brief message to one million homes by inexpensive post cards. You would have to pay not only the costly postage but also for the blank cards. You probably never realized that before. Then figure what you would pay to have your message printed one million times on a million cards. Add the cost of hiring enough people to write names and addresses of one million people on the cards. I think you will decide it would be much less costly to pay for a *whole page* of space, as large as a news magazine-sized page, which *includes* the cost of the paper, of the printing, of the postage for mailing, and of the stamping on of the names and addresses. And, more than this, in every home where your message is received,

455

the recipient *asked for* the magazine to come, and (except for *The Plain Truth)* actually *paid* to receive it. If you were to spend money to print and mail out a million post cards, they would be uninvited, and probably unwanted in most homes.

So you see, magazine and newspaper advertising is not expensive.

You probably have heard that advertising forces up the price of a commodity or service to the consumer. Many people believe that if they can purchase a non-advertised brand they save money. They suppose the merchant or manufacturer who advertises must add the cost of the advertising to the price.

Do You Pay More for Advertised Goods?

Let me tell you the true "inside facts"—*The Plain Truth* about this supposition. Truly, people as a whole are DECEIVED today, not only about God's truth, but even facts about business.

Actually, *if* the advertising is intelligently and effectively used, *it reduces the price to the consumer!* I think it may be interesting to you to know how it works:

Suppose a certain comparatively small store sells $100,000 worth of men's clothing and haberdashery in one year. This store spent nothing for advertising. But it did pay, shall we say, $70,000 for the merchandise to the manufacturers. And it also had to pay, shall we say, $15,000 for clerk hire, and $10,000 for store rent, heat, light, water, wrapping paper—all other expenses. So you see that for every dollar of goods bought by a customer, the merchant had to pay, over and above the cost of the merchandise, 25¢ which is 25% as a cost of doing business. He had 5¢—or 5% of sales—left for himself. This merchant, then, based on sales price, had

456

a cost of 70% for merchandise, and 25% as cost of doing business, with 5% profit for all his own time, hard work, worry, and return on his capital investment.

Now suppose this merchant tries advertising the next year. This is, approximately, what *did* happen in a similar interesting case in Astoria, as I shall relate. I am assuming this merchant's advertising is effective.

So the following year this merchant spends $4,500 in advertising. It is effective, and brings in new customers. This year his sales increased to $150,000. But because in the preceding year his salesmen did not have enough customers to keep them busy, he does not need to hire additional clerks. He still pays the same rent, public utilities, and similar expenses—a total of $25,000, the same as the year before.

But here is the big difference. That $25,000 was a 25% cost of doing business the year he sold $100,000 worth of goods. But now, with sales of $150,000, it is only 16⅔%. But he did have one increase in business expense—his $4,500 advertising. But even so, his $29,500 cost of doing business is only 19⅔%. This merchant passes this saving in total cost of his business expense, per dollar of sales, to his customers, still taking for himself the same 5% of sales for profit.

Lowering Prices

Now see where this leaves the customers, and what it makes for the merchant. You may think the customers were the *only* ones who benefitted, since the merchant still took only 5% profit. But the merchant actually made half again more for himself—because his 5% profit now is taken from $150,000 sales, instead of $100,000. So the merchant did all right for himself! He made $7,500 this year instead of only $5,000. But what about prices to the customers? The same item—or number of items—that sold for $100 the nonadvertising year are now priced at only $92.92. It is simple to figure. The merchant still paid $70 for this amount of merchandise. But his business expense now was only 19⅔%, and profit 5%—total 24⅔% instead of 30% the year before. This is $24.67 in expenses per $100 in sales. Add the $70 wholesale price to this $24.67, and the new sale price is $94.67, a savings of over $5 to the customer.

So what actually happened? The merchant saved his customers more than 5 cents on the dollar—or $5.33 on each $100 of purchases. So his advertising *reduced the cost of goods to the customer!* At the same time, this merchant made $7,500 for his own year's work, which was $2,500 more than he made the year before he advertised.

You might ask, didn't the advertising cost anything? Of course. It cost $4,500—or 3% of his year's sales. Then HOW did it save the customers money, and make more money for the merchant? The answer is that it does cost money to run a store. It does cost money for us who are customers to have a merchant take all of his time, and all of his salesmen's time, to gather in merchandise from New York, from Chicago, from London, from Los Angeles, and assemble it all in one store for the convenience of us customers. But could *we* go to the clothing manufacturer in New York, the shirt manufacturer in Utica, New York, and the shoe manufacturer in Boston or St. Louis to buy our goods, without spending money over and above the factory cost? Of course not. And if we all did this individually, the manufacturer would have to charge us more, because it would add to *his* expenses to have to deal with so many people. When the factory sells enough suits, or

458

shoes, or hats for 200 people, or 500 people or more to just one store, he can sell for much less than he could by making 500 different transactions with 500 individual customers. So actually the local merchant renders us a pretty valuable service, far cheaper than we could do it ourselves.

In so doing, he has a cost of doing business. And, as the experience of thousands and thousands of retail stores shows, that cost is reduced by spending about 3% or 4% in advertising, because then he spends *less,* per dollar of sales, on such other expenses as rent, salaries, public utilities, etc. His *total* expenses of operating his store are less, per dollar of sales.

That is how it works. Why your local merchants do not use a little of their advertising to just explain these simple but interesting facts to their public, I do not know. But I have spent years of my life as an advertising and merchandising specialist, and I thought that these *facts* about the price you pay for goods you buy every day—whether at the grocery store, the clothing store, the dry-goods store, or wherever, might prove interesting. You come in direct contact with this very merchandising operation at least every week of your life.

Now let me relate to you the rather exciting story of an experience with one store in Astoria.

Breaking All Precedent

There were four retail clothing (men's) stores in Astoria. Three advertised, and were signed up on these five-year contracts. The second largest, Krohn & Carson, had never spent its first dime in advertising. I checked financial ratings in Dunn & Bradstreet. Krohn & Carson had the highest financial rating of the four.

So I went immediately to Krohn & Carson. I found

them as firmly set against advertising as a 50-foot-thick stone wall. Apparently it was even more impossible to crack their stone-wall resistance against advertising than to break these five-year contracts. Yet I did have a will, and I did find a way!

I mentioned above that newspaper and magazine advertising has always been sold by the column inch or by the page. *The Messenger* rate was 25¢ per inch. The larger evening paper charged 50 cents per inch. But now I deliberately shattered all precedent in newspaper advertising practice.

I proposed an entirely new, completely revolutionary plan to Krohn & Carson. I explained to them what I have explained to you, above, how effective advertising works. The clothing stores in Astoria were each selling only about 40% as much merchandise as they had sold before the depression.

"But," I explained, "for every $100 that men used to spend in these four stores, they still spend $40. Now if we can show Astoria men and their wives that you can save them money in this depression, a *larger portion* of that $40 will come to you. I can show you how you can still *double* your business, and your own profits, and at the same time save your customers money by lowering prices!"

It sounded fantastic, preposterous! But it cost them nothing to listen to my plan.

"First," I proposed, "you will put on a big price-reducing sale. Your shelves are loaded with goods that are not moving. Retail success depends more on *turnover*—keeping your goods moving—than on big margins of profit. You have capital tied up in all these goods. Put on a sale. Sell it for less money—get your money back out of the merchandise, plus a *small* margin to cover business expenses—reinvest that money in more goods—keep it moving. Better make 12 profits a year of only 1 cent on a dollar of sales, than a 10 cent profit once in two years. This way you take 12% on your investment. The way you are doing now you make only 5¢ per dollar.

"Now, here is how we will make this sale a success, and double your business. Harvard Bureau of Business Research figures show that the retail clothing stores which spend 4% of sales in advertising have the *lowest* cost of doing business, and the highest turnover. To spend less than 4% in advertising means to spend higher percentages in salaries, rent, utilities, and other expenses. To spend more than 4% does not bring enough additional increase in sales to pay. So this is what I propose. It is a new plan. It is *unheard of* in newspaper advertising! *You pay us just 3% of your sales.* That is one fourth less spent on advertising than most successful stores spend. Then we will give you *absolutely unlimited space* in *The Messenger.* I will give you my own personal service in writing all your advertising. Your competitors cannot afford to bring specially trained professional advertising writers to Astoria—and they do not know how to write ads that can compete with what I will write for you.

"We will start out with *four full pages,* announcing this sale. We will make it a BIG sale—and we will make it *look* big! We will reprint the four pages in our job printing department as a big handbill, and you can hire boys to distribute those to every house within the entire Astoria trade territory. We will charge you nothing extra for the circulars, but you hire them distributed. We will follow this up with two-page ads as long as the sale lasts. It will be an Astoria sensation.

"Now that people can spend only 40% as much for clothing as they did before the depression, they have to

461

try to save every penny. They are price conscious. These lower prices will bring in crowds of customers from miles around."

How Could WE Afford It?

"But, Mr. Armstrong," protested the younger partner, Mr. Krohn, who was Mr. Carson's son-in-law, "how can you afford to give us four whole pages, and then repeated double pages, at no increase in cost to us—just this 3%?"

"Two reasons," I explained, smiling. "First, because I know this policy and this big space will greatly increase your sales. If we double your sales, we double what you pay us. It makes us a partner in your business, in a way. We get paid according to the results we bring you. If we don't bring more customers, you don't pay more. Then there is a second reason why we can afford to do this. We have to print eight pages every day—never less. The paper now has very little advertising. I am going to write these ads and design them with great, large display type. It will cost us far less to set a page, or two pages of these big-type ads than for our linotype operators to have set all pages in small news type."

Mr. Krohn persuaded Mr. Carson to accept my offer.

The sale drew crowds. Sales soared.

During the sale an opportunity came to the store to double its floor space, and still reduce rent. The store occupied a corner location. The landlord had not reduced rent in proportion to reduced business during the depression. A ladies' ready-to-wear store which had occupied a middle-of-the-block location with twice as much space as Krohn & Carson, and with four times as much front window display space, had failed and closed up. The landlord of this storeroom, faced with a *no*-rent

462

prospect for the duration of the depression, offered this to Krohn & Carson for half the rent they had been paying in their corner location.

I advised taking it. Then I recommended a new merchandising policy.

"If you double the size of your store, you will have to also double the volume of business, or such a big store space will look rather foolish," I said. "Now, you are *reducing* your expenses, by lower rent, not adding to them. If you will be willing to try out a new merchandising policy, I think my ads will convince the men of Astoria, and make it work. My idea is that you now keep these special reduced sales prices in effect right along. If you have doubled the sales volume—or keep up what you are doing in this special sale—without increasing your expenses, you can make at least as much profit—perhaps more, and win the good will of the customers—help the public by reduced prices—and, as the depression begins to end and prosperity comes again, you'll be the largest and best liked store in town."

They agreed. As soon as the sale ended, and they moved to the new larger store, I began running full-page, "editorial"-style advertisements. They were of the nature of a straight "Man-to-Man Talk" with the men of Astoria and vicinity.

I told the men that, if they would keep up the sales volume, this store believed it would be able to keep these reduced special sale prices in effect every day in the year. I told them of the reduced rent. I told them of Krohn & Carson's well-known financial capital—how they were able to take cash discounts, and buy for less—and were willing to pass these savings on to customers, if customers in turn would keep up the sales volume. I explained, as I have above for you, how

463

increased sales volume, if it does not increase expenses, can lower the price to the consumer.

The ads were sensational in policy—dignified in appearance—and they had a ring of sincerity that rang true. The men of Astoria responded.

"Breaking" the Opposition

I am taking space to explain in some detail this experience for one reason. I hope many readers may get from it the lesson of a valuable principle: *there is always a WAY where there is a WILL!*

Would *you* have quit, thrown up your hands, and said, *"It can't be done"?*

And let me explain, here, another principle I always followed in my business experience—especially in advertising and selling. It was never to sell anything, unless I was convinced it benefitted the other fellow, as well as myself.

"Be an expert *adviser* in your customers' interests" was a slogan I tried to follow. "Know your stuff" was another—in the advertising man's vernacular. Always educate yourself in your field. Know more about it than your competitors, or your customer. Know how to *help* your customer. If you are profitable to him, he will stay with you. Another adage I followed was: "A *customer* is more valuable than a *sale.*" The one-time sales to customers who feel they were talked into something unprofitable costs more to make than it is worth. I have always wondered why more businessmen do not understand these principles. Honesty *is* the best policy!

But back to our story.

As I said, the men of Astoria responded. Soon Krohn & Carson was doing more than half of all the clothing and haberdashery business in town. The ones my work did *not* benefit—and for this reason I would never do this again—were the competitors.

In this experience I learned a few things about Jewish people. Both Mr. Krohn and Mr. Carson were Jewish. So was their chief competitor, who had previously had the biggest business, across the street. In business, these men were bitter enemies. But after business hours—well, that was different. Then they were friends. At the synagogue they were friends. But in the store—there they looked across the street at the competitive store with intense rivalry.

It's the same in many other businesses or professions. I certainly do not waste time watching prizefights on television. But who can avoid seeing a few seconds of one occasionally, turning the dial from one channel to another? Have you ever noticed the end of such a fight? Men who have fought viciously, unmercifully, with the "killer-instinct" trying to knock each other unconscious, will dance to their "enemy" of a second ago, after the final bell, and throw their arms around each other in loving embrace—and it makes no difference if one is white and the other black! Lawyers who will fight each other angrily in a courtroom during the heat of a trial, will go out to lunch together after it's over, as the best of friends! I've seen bankers who have been bitter rivals forget it completely, and call each other by their first names, "buddy, buddy" fashion, at national bankers' conventions.

But, in business Krohn & Carson's Jewish rival across the street was bitter and now getting more and more bitter!

In desperation, as his customers flocked over to Krohn & Carson's, he ran a half-page ad in the "opposition" paper. It cost him twice as much per inch as our regular inch rate. In it he advertised a

465

price-slashing sale. Mr. Krohn called me to the store.

"Look at this!" he exclaimed, worried. "Now maybe *he* will get the business, and our new plan will fail after all."

"Oh no," I laughed. "This only means it's time for you and me to get busy. I want you to take that ad, and mark your own prices, cut STILL LOWER, on every item—item for item—listed in his 'ad.' Tomorrow morning we will run a TWO-PAGE ad, listing exactly the same items, every one priced LOWER—and once again reminding the men that Krohn & Carson SAVE THEM MONEY. We'll run a special sale tomorrow, also, on these same items."

Mr. Krohn looked at me and shook his head in amazement, and then began to grin, as he went to work marking lower prices.

Next day all the special sale customers filed into Krohn & Carson's—the biggest day in some time, while their rival across the street looked more discouraged than ever in his empty store.

Later that day, he telephoned *The Messenger* office, and asked if I would come to the store to see him.

"Look here," he stormed, "you are breaking my business. I can't afford to run many half-page ads in the evening paper at their high rates—and even when I do you come out with a bigger one for Krohn & Carson, and they get all the business from my ad as well as their own! You have brought me to the place where I am willing now to take a chance on the evening paper doing anything if I break my agreement not to advertise with you. I want you to make me the same deal you did Krohn & Carson—and I am willing to sign up right now!"

"I'm sorry," I replied, "but you and all the other

466

merchants turned me down cold when I first came to Astoria. You presented me with a kind of unfair competition such as I never heard of. You forced me to break all precedent to develop new advertisers out of non-advertising merchants. That plan was offered to only ONE merchant in each line. You said you were bound and could not advertise with us. Now WE are bound, and can't give you this same deal of unlimited space on a percent of sales."

"Well, then," he countered, "can I buy space with you at your regular price by the inch?"

"Oh yes, of course" was the answer.

"But that is not enough," he continued. "It is the way you write these ads that is bringing the business to Krohn & Carson's. Will you write my ads, as well as theirs? If you will, I will start advertising with you, and quit with the evening paper."

I had not bound myself to exclusive ad-writing service, so I was free to agree. Next morning, his first ad, about a third of a page, appeared.

When I walked into the Krohn & Carson store that day, Mr. Carson was like a wild man.

"LOOK at this!" he shouted. "Anyone would know *you* wrote that ad. You cancel our advertising immediately, and don't ever come in this store again."

"All right, Mr. Carson, if that's what you really want to do," I said. "But first, I want you to calm down and listen to me just one moment. I never offered you my advertising-writing services exclusively. I have *not* given your competitor the unlimited space on a percent-of-sales basis at all. He has to pay the regular rate by the inch. Mr. Carson, I have doubled your business for you in the midst of this terrible depression. I have worked hard for you, and made you money. But I am advertising manager of *The Messenger,* and when

467

my plan begins to really *work,* and break down these unethical and illegal contracts our 'opposition paper' holds over these other merchants, that is the real reason I evolved this unprecedented system that has doubled your business, and made you the LEADER in Astoria, instead of second-fiddle like you were. Now, if you didn't appreciate that, and want to cancel—O.K.! I'll walk out of this store, and never come back again—and now you free me to give this whole plan to your competitor across the street!"

I began to walk out rapidly.

Mr. Carson showed surprising and amazing athletic ability in scampering behind the counters to the front door before I could get there! He darted into the doorway, blocked it, holding up both hands.

"Wait! *Wait!*" he exclaimed. "Don't you walk out of here! Don't you cancel our agreement!"

He came up and threw his arms around me, and cried like a child.

"Mr. Armstrong," he said, embracing me, "I have loved you like a son. I didn't mean what I said. I want you to still be my advertising manager and adviser— even if you do write ads for that fellow across the street."

Even though dollars were at stake, Mr. Carson spoke from the heart. He was filled with emotion, now. He was really sincere—he *did* really feel a deep love for me. It was not only because of the business success our relationship had brought—our close personal association had brought about mutual affection. He was a businessman—he was very conscious of *dollars,* and had acquired his share of them — but underneath was a real warm heart capable of real friendship.

Our radio listeners have heard me say that I bear no hatred toward Jews—I love them, as I love all people.

Some, allowing themselves to become "hooked" on the insidious, poisonous "drug" of anti-Semitism, and hatred for Jews, have never learned all there is to know about Jewish people. Sure, many of them, despised and hated and persecuted by race prejudice, have developed a keen sense of "dollar consciousness," but who among us is so free from faults and sins he can throw the first stone? I have learned that many Jews also have very warm hearts of friendship. We have all been carnal, weighted with human nature, until converted and filled with God's Holy Spirit of LOVE, and TOLERANCE!

Unable to Leave

I have been getting ahead of my story. I have carried this one experience with this one advertising client on to its conclusion, over a period of many months. But I wanted to complete this one case history, as a typical example of the Astoria newspaper experience.

Back, now to December, 1931.

In Astoria was one of the two leading hardware stores not tied up on those 5-year contracts, besides the J. C. Penney store, one of the "movies" and several restaurants. I induced most of the restaurants to take out advertising *in trade* for meal checks for our employees, and the Penney store and the hardware store accepted my unlimited space on a percentage-of-sales basis.

But by December 31, I found I was caught in a trap. We had 23 men employed. If I left then, the paper would have folded and these men would have been out of work. There still was no money in the Oregon Conference church treasury to bring me back into the ministry. I was stuck in Astoria. God intended for me to learn a lesson. It seems that most of the time I have had to learn these lessons the HARD WAY, through experience, and suffering. This was to be no exception. It was not until the end of February, 1933, that my prayers to be relieved of these newspaper responsibilities, and to be allowed to return to God's ministry, were answered.

27

Stuck in Astoria

A FTER the Krohn & Carson experience forced their main clothing-store
competitor to break its 5-year con-
tract, other stores gradually began cautiously to put a
limited amount of advertising in *The Messenger*. This
drove our opposition publisher to adopt a new type of
competition. Now the going became rougher than
before.

Competition Gets Rough

Both the evening paper, and ours, maintained
job-printing departments. There was, besides, one
independent job-printing establishment. But the evening newspaper job department did more than half of all
the printing. With this and the newspaper combined,
the opposition newspaper employed more than half the
employees in all three unions involved—the typographical, the pressmen's and the stereotypers' unions.

The depression, by spring of 1932, had descended to such depths that if a man lost his job he had small chance of finding another. At union meetings, the evening paper employees had a majority vote.

So we had the unheard-of spectacle of our competitor's employees being forced by their employer, on threat of losing their jobs, to vote *our* employees out of their jobs on strike, while all our employees voted desperately against the strike. It meant the loss of their jobs. They knew they would be unable to obtain employment elsewhere.

Actually, our competitor's employees did have a technical violation to charge us with. Our employees were not receiving their full wages *in cash*. Our paper simply did not have the money. One reason I had felt obligated to remain on in Astoria after December, 1931, was the responsibility of keeping our 23 employees from starving. I had traded advertising space for meal tickets in local restaurants. I had traded advertising space for rooms in hotels and small apartments in large apartment houses. I had taken most of the Krohn & Carson 3% compensation in clothes for our men. Thus we had managed to keep them clothed, fed, and sheltered. We had paid them small amounts of cash for other expenses, but the balance of their wages was being paid them in stock in the paper. Thus they were part owners. If and when the paper got on a paying basis, they would then receive their wages with interest.

When the strike was first voted against us, Mr. Hopkins and, I believe, our city editor, took a quick trip to Seattle to appeal to the district union chief, a Mr. Pelkey. We awaited their return anxiously. Their smiling faces told us, on their return, they had succeeded. Mr. Pelkey had called off the strike. He realized the desperate competitive situation. But this was a reprieve—not the end of the matter.

A month or two later, our opposition employees again voted our employees out on strike. Again Mr. Hopkins raced to Seattle. Again Mr. Pelkey rescinded the strike vote. During the summer our competitor's employees did it again. A third time Mr. Pelkey vetoed the strike.

But our opposition simply wore down Mr. Pelkey. A fourth time the opposition men voted ours out on strike. This time Mr. Pelkey said he was getting "fed up" with this Astoria quarrel, and he let the strike become official.

The Strike STRUCK!

The date was Labor Day, 1932. Our employees had to face the problem of whether to defy the strike vote, stay on the job, and thus be put out of the unions—in which case their entire future in the printing business was ruined—or lose their jobs with no prospect of finding others. The men, however, decided that their futures, after the depression had subsided, meant more to them than the immediate job.

Mr. Hopkins immediately brought a few non-union printers from Portland to Astoria. But they were unskilled, and totally unsatisfactory as workmen—and they were too few. I had never operated a linotype machine, although I had been around composing rooms for 20 years. Now I had to work all night long with a "hunt and peck" effort to set the type.

Also I set ads in display type. After 36 hours without sleep, we finally got out the paper, in the evening of Labor Day.

Our *morning* paper came out *after* the *evening* paper of the same day. But we got it out! Otherwise we should have been put out of business altogether!

For three days and three nights Mr. Hopkins and I and a few of the newsmen worked straight through without sleep. We literally lived that 72 hours on coffee. There was an all-night cafe across the street. We kept them constantly making coffee!

The day following Labor Day we got the paper "to bed" in mid-afternoon. The next day by about noon. Gradually we gained an hour or two each day, and within a week we were getting the papers on the street by early morning. But it was indeed a sorry looking newspaper! It came out full of typographical errors, bad typesetting. But we were fighting to keep it alive.

Even before this 72-hour stretch without *any* sleep, I had been consistently losing sleep in Astoria. For the entire 15 months on this newspaper job I *averaged* about 5½ hours sleep per night. I *need* a minimum of seven. This continuous loss of sleep proved a real handicap after I did finally get back into the ministry in 1933.

Two Awe-Inspiring Miracles

During the 15 months of this stay in Astoria, God blessed us with two amazing miracles. For the first seven months, still hoping from week to week to be able to wind up this newspaper detour and get back on the main road of God's ministry, Mrs. Armstrong and our children remained in the house on East State Street in Salem. During that time I managed to take frequent weekend trips home to be with my family.

Finally, by early July 1932, we decided to move the family to Astoria. This resulted from my wife calling long distance late one afternoon asking me to rush home. Little Garner Ted was stricken with pneumonia! I drove *The Messenger* coupe down to Salem, arriving

474

late that night. The children were asleep. Mrs. Armstrong was still up, beside little Ted's sofa, on which he was lying. Immediately, we both knelt beside our sick baby. Little Garner Ted was then two years and five months.

And I must explain here that he had been, to that time, dumb—unable to talk. While somewhere between six months and a year old, he had fallen out of his crib-bed headfirst onto the hard wood floor. We attributed his inability to talk to this fall, landing on his head. He would point to whatever he wanted to tell us about, making motions, and grunting "Ugh! Ugh!" But he was unable to speak a single word. We were becoming much concerned.

I anointed Ted and began to claim God's promises to rebuke the fever and heal him. As I was praying, Mrs. Armstrong silently prayed, asking God that, if it was His will to heal our baby of this dumbness at that time, to put it in my mind to ask for this, as well as healing from the pneumonia.

I did also have this in mind—or God put it in my mind—for the very instant she had asked for this, I began asking God to restore Ted's power of speech.

His fever left quickly. The very next day he was able to say a number of single words. In about three days he was talking in whole sentences.

After this experience, my wife and I decided to move the family immediately to Astoria. I remained a few days to help pack our goods.

After everything was packed, I crowded our two daughters and Dickey (we called our boys "Dickey" and "Teddy" until the day they entered Junior High School) into the coupe and drove to Astoria. Mrs. Armstrong followed with Teddy on the train. Little Teddy was so frightened by the train that my wife had some difficulty in getting him aboard. But once on, and relaxed and reassured, he began talking.

"Here we go," said Teddy cheerfully, "to see Daddy, see Ba-wee (Beverly), see Dorsee (Dorothy), see Dickey!" That was a 12-word sentence, gushing out only about three days after I had prayed for his healing!

I had arranged for one of the members of the Church, who lived near Jefferson, to haul our furniture and things to Astoria. We went first to the hotel in Astoria. Mr. Hopkins and I had lived there, trading advertising for rooms.

Soon we rented a house, high up on an embankment above a street overlooking the mile-wide Columbia River. We were only ten miles from the ocean at that point, and the mighty Columbia widens to a very great river at its mouth. From our house there was an unobstructed view straight out the river to the ocean.

About that time I managed to obtain a portable radio by trading advertising space, and taking it as part of my salary. This small portable radio would receive stations from great distances—much farther than even large and expensive modern sets today. After our strike finally did *strike,* I was kept at the newspaper office until midnight or later about six nights every week.

Arriving home at midnight or 1:00 a.m., I often turned on the radio in order to "unwind" my nerves a bit from the tense business day before retiring. Any night at that hour, which was around 6:00 p.m. in Japan, I was able to get Radio Tokyo *on standard wave* direct. There was no obstruction between the aerial atop our house and Japan—just the mile-wide mouth of the Columbia, and straight across the ocean.

Also, at the time, I was able to "bring in" clearly such stations as WLS, Chicago, WLW, Cincinnati,

476

WSM, Nashville, WHO, Des Moines—all of which I was later to have the privilege of broadcasting over.

Hunting for Bear

My son Garner Ted loves to hunt and fish. He may not remember when the excitement of hunting was first implanted within him, and he may read this now, along with all our readers.

As soon as God gave us our first son, for whom my wife and I had waited eleven years, I wanted to be a pal to him. I had begun calling little Dickey, as soon as he could talk, my "Pal." But now, as soon as little Teddy began to talk, on hearing me call his elder brother "pal," he exclaimed, "Well, I'm your *pal, too,* Daddy."

From that moment Teddy became "Pal Two," and Dickey "Pal One."

One of the very first things I did, after we moved into the house in Astoria, was to take my two "pals" "bear hunting." I have explained that our house sat on an embankment high above the sidewalk below. This hill ran up steeply from the great river below, and continued on uphill behind our house, thickly wooded. I took my two sons, armed with wooden sticks for guns, on frequent "hunting trips" up this steep heavily wooded slope, "hunting for bear." The boys would growl like a bear, and confidently expected to get a shot at one any second.

The basement of our Astoria house was on the ground level in front, but basement level at the rear. In Astoria, as well as when we lived in Salem and Eugene, we burned wood for fuel. My sons helped me carry chopped wood up the basement stairs into the kitchen. Although Teddy was speaking whole sentences three days after his speech was restored, he did not pronounce all his words like an adult immediately.

I shall never forget his rapping on the basement door, three or four sticks of wood across his outstretched arms, yelling:

"Open d' doagm—open d' doagm—here tums dreat bid mans!"

Our younger daughter Dorothy got in Teddy's hair on occasion. On one of these occasions, in the kitchen, little Teddy became exasperated and started for his tormenting sister with clenched fists.

In fear Dorothy ran through the hallway, and up the stairs to the second floor like a frightened deer, with little Teddy scampering after her in red-hot anger, shouting,

"Boy, oh boy! I'll hap your hace!"

Apparently Dorothy found refuge in a bedroom and locked the door.

I suppose we have had quite the same experience rearing children that most parents have. Most of the time our two daughters, only two years and two months apart, have been the best of chums and buddies, but they had their share of quarreling over the things most sisters quarrel over—whose turn it was to do the dishes—or when one girl had put on the other girl's clothes. But our two sons seldom quarreled, and surely no two brothers could have gotten along better together, or been closer to each other. Their fights were usually with older sisters!

Another typical experience many fathers should understand. Early in the Christmas shopping season, 1932, I managed to obtain for my boys an electric train, with quite a lot of track and accessories—by trading advertising space for it. The price of the train was charged at the newspaper, of course, as part of my salary since only a small part of salaries could be paid in cash. Mrs. Armstrong said smilingly that I got the electric train for the boys, so I could play with it! I wonder how many fathers have done the same thing!

The Second Miraculous Healing

It was during the midst of the winter, December 1932 or January 1933, that Milas Helms appeared in Astoria one night. He finally located me at one of the "movie" offices, where I was picking up an "ad" at around 10:00 p.m. His little son, James, was stricken with a most serious case of pneumonia, and was in extremely critical condition. Mike had driven his pickup truck all the way from his farm, southwest of Jefferson. He asked me if I would not drop everything and go with him to anoint and pray for his boy's healing.

We drove through the night around the icy sharp mountain curves of the only highway in those days, through a driving snow-storm blizzard, on to Portland, and then some 75 miles more to his farm.

We arrived there around 5:00 a.m. The oil lamps were still burning, and Mike's wife, Pearl, was still up. Little James was gasping for breath, with an extremely high temperature, but still alive. Immediately we knelt beside his bed, and I anointed him and claimed God's promises to heal him. Almost immediately the boy sank into a sleep, and then all of us laid down to get some overdue rest and sleep.

We awakened at 10:00 a.m. Little James awakened, too, at about the same time, and immediately scampered out of bed and began playing around the room. His temperature was normal. He had been completely healed. I returned to Astoria.

An END of Going Hungry

I have mentioned repeatedly how God had brought me down, reduced us to poverty and want, and how much

479

we had suffered hunger through those years. Much of the time in Astoria, up until about the time of this emergency trip to the Helms' farm, we had not had enough to eat.

I have explained in past chapters how, after conversion, I had to come to learn and understand one doctrine at a time. The truth was not acquired all at once. I had known that the Bible had quite a little to say about tithing one's income. Yet somehow it had never become completely clear.

At about this time, in the little time I had from my work at the newspaper for Bible study and prayer, I had made a special and thorough study of this matter of tithing. We saw the mistake we had been making, and started a definite practice of strict tithing. We had only a very little on hand, but we sent a tenth of it, plus an offering, to the Oregon Conference treasurer.

That very day, the way opened for us to be able to stock up at home with a reasonable abundance of food. For one thing, we had a large thick steak. My wife cooked it at low heat with the utensils we had acquired when I had devoted a year to selling them. I shall never forget that steak! It was way and by far the best steak I have ever tasted!

Although we still were required to live another 14 years in the barest and most modest financial circumstances, we have never from that day had to be actually hungry, and miss meals, because of financial poverty! We have since heard of scores and scores of case-histories of the experiences of others who were immediately prospered, once they began tithing. But we, ourselves, lived through this same experience. I am very grateful to have been privileged to have been instrumental in bringing countless others into this same divine *blessing!* My wife and I had to learn it the HARD WAY!

"Dickey" Becomes Lost

One day in August or September, 1932, shortly before Dickey was four years old, he became "lost," and his mother became frantic. I was not home at the time.

When Mrs. Armstrong discovered he was missing, and was nowhere to be found around the house or yard, she started an immediate worried search. Neighbor children had seen him going east. A little farther along the street two little children said he had asked them to go with him to a children's playground in Rose City Park, to play on the swings and slides.

Rose City Park was in Portland, more than a hundred miles away! After running, out of breath, some distance past the end of our street, and onto the highway to Portland, not finding him, she turned back. He had not been gone long enough to have gotten farther on the highway. Now the terrifying thought gripped my wife:

"What if little Dickey had wandered down to the river bank, and had fallen in the river!"

She retraced her steps back, and, half running, half walking breathlessly, began following the river bank westward. Finally she found him, trying to walk back home along the river bank. When the two children had refused to go to Rose City Park with him, he had decided he didn't want to go alone, and had started back home—by way of the river bank! He had supposed he could soon walk to Rose City Park!

I have often wondered how any of the millions of us men on earth ever survived the dangers of growing boyhood, and lived to be men—unless indeed God *has* assigned an angel to watch invisibly over every boy, and keep him from physical harm and tragedy!

While we were in Astoria, I received a letter from

Elder Taylor. Just one letter, in that year and a quarter. It told me "we have lost the little church" in Eugene. The brethren, he said, had been unable to keep up payments. When I finally got back to the Valley I learned how WE really had lost it. Mr. Taylor had traded it for a more saleable house and lot next door. Then he had traded that, with another place he had acquired, for an island farm. But more of that at the proper time, later.

Our Prayers Finally Answered

One day, late in February, 1933, Mike Helms drove his pickup truck up to our house. He had come to take us back to the Valley. The church Conference had now accumulated a small balance. Mike was now president of the conference. He said they would be able to pay us only $3 per week, but farmer brethren would supply us with vegetables, and the members would buy other food for us.

Behind him, he said, was coming one of the men from the Valley with a large truck to haul our small amount of furniture and furnishings back to the Valley.

At last God had answered our prayers to allow me to be put back into His ministry! Mrs. Armstrong got into the truck with Mr. Helms, and they drove downtown in search of me. I was overjoyed at the news.

We were nearly all night getting packed and ready for the tedious trip back to the Valley. The next day we left.

All of the newspaper employees I had felt a responsibility for keeping alive, except Mr. Hopkins and two or three newsmen, had long since left, anyway. I felt no obligation to remain another day.

482

A couple months or less after our departure I heard that *The Morning Messenger,* which had come to be dubbed the *"Morning Mess,"* had gone out of business. I had kept it alive for 15 months. I had learned a valuable lesson, and collected some valuable experience.

28

Back into the Ministry

WE SOON LEARNED there was a reason why Mike Helms had come for us when he did. The former president of the California conference, A. J. Ray, had moved to Oregon, near Jefferson. A very small balance had accumulated in the conference treasury, and small amounts of tithes from members once again were beginning to trickle into it. Mr. Ray learned of the Oregon Conference's plans to bring me back into the ministry as soon as funds permitted. He had moved swiftly to forestall that, by sending for a close friend—I believe he was a former Seventh-Day Adventist minister—Sven (Sam) Oberg, whom *he* wanted as the Oregon minister.

The Plots Begin

Apparently Mike had known of Mr. Oberg's imminent arrival, and drove immediately to Astoria to bring me back. We both arrived about the same time.

484

Now the newly arrived Mr. Ray raised the question of whether to employ Mr. Oberg, or me. A business meeting was called. I believe it was held at the church building in Harrisburg.

Mr. Oberg was a man of 53. He kept himself in vigorous physical condition by strenuous calisthenic exercises every morning, including about 100 "push-ups." If Robert L. Taylor had swept the members off their feet, impressing them with his "spirituality" and preaching power in 1931, Sam Oberg did much more!

In fact, he appeared to be so *perfect,* so spiritual, my wife and I thought of Hebrews 13:2, stating that a stranger *might* be an angel being entertained unawares! He seemed too perfect to be human. He was strict in punctuality, spiritual in language and phraseology, immaculate in appearance, glib of speech, powerful in preaching delivery.

Yet, in spite of his almost awe-inspiring effect on the members, they had all liked and loved me, and still looked to me for the leadership to get the gospel going out. I had been ordained by them and employed by them before. I do not remember the details now, but I was employed instead of Mr. Oberg.

$3 per Week Salary

The condition of the conference treasury allowed them to pay me only $3 per week salary. However, most of the members were farmers, and they promised to supply us with vegetables and such foodstuffs as they raised. Also, they paid our house rent—I believe $5 or $7 per month, and purchased for us a certain amount of food. This consisted of 100-pound sacks of whole wheat flour, large sacks of beans, large bags of raw sugar—the kind of food that supplied "the mostest for the leastest."

The $3 cash salary per week, then, was to cover

butter, milk, water and light and clothes—if any. We were moved into a small house on Hall Street, not far from the state Fairgrounds. There were two fireplaces and the kitchen stove to supply heat. We burned wood altogether.

But I was to be disillusioned, and to learn that a person who first appears to be TOO good to be true *usually isn't!* Both Mr. Ray and Mr. Oberg schemed constantly to discredit me and get that $3 per week for Mr. Oberg. More of that as we go along.

Starting the Salem Meetings

However, I was still looking on Mr. Oberg with a sort of awe, feeling I had never met a person so perfect and so righteous and so powerful in preaching. True, I had behind me a most unusual wealth of experience, as these Oregon members were aware. But my still comparatively new Christian experience had humbled me to virtual unawareness of that fact and I was trying to efface self. But I did have vision.

I suggested that we try to hold a big city-wide campaign, with Mr. Oberg doing all the preaching— since I felt I was not worthy—as a minister of Christ—to team up with so great a man. My suggestion was that I use my advertising experience to be the public relations man, prepare circulars and newspaper advertising, and draw in the crowds. I had suggested we try to hire the big armory in downtown Salem. I felt that with an evangelist of Mr. Oberg's power, I could really pack in a big crowd.

My suggestions, as became usual with the other ministers, were turned down by Mr. Oberg. I was slightly disillusioned to learn that Mr. Oberg did not think BIG. He wanted to hold a small campaign in a small empty store building out in the "Hollywood" suburb of

Salem—just a small local neighborhood campaign. And he wanted to share it with me, speaking on alternate evenings.

There were many vacant store buildings. We were now at the very *bottom* of the great economic depression. We were able to hire a vacant storeroom for $10 per month.

We worked hard making preparations. Mr. Oberg was not lazy. He was a hard worker. I believe we rented folding chairs. I had handbills printed and distributed over that general part of Salem.

The opening night arrived. Immediately I was greatly alarmed—as also, it appeared, was Mr. Ray. Already I had seen quite a little of that type of religious people who call themselves "pentecostal." I had learned that they had no UNDERSTANDING of the Bible, although they glibly quoted certain verses, or partial sentences, usually misapplied and entirely out of context.

Those I had known had never surrendered their rebellious spirit against *obedience* to God and His written commands. They were always SEEKING—not to serve, share, or obey, but for those emotional and supposedly "spiritual" things that would glorify the self and its vanity and please the senses.

Mr. R. L. Taylor, with whom I held my first evangelistic campaign in Eugene in 1931, had started a series of meetings in this same north end of Salem, following our Eugene campaign. The "pentecostal" people had come, and he had encouraged them. They would keep reasonably quiet until Mr. Taylor, after two or three weeks of preaching, had a few unconverted and non-"pentecostal" people brought close to repentance and conversion—and then they would begin to "take over" with their loud-shouting "hallelujah's" and ridiculous demonstrations. This immediately discour-

487

aged those near conversion, chilled them completely, and they dropped out and quit coming. After this, Mr. Taylor went around that end of town, inviting new people to come, and in a few nights had a new small crowd. The experience was repeated —until he finally had to quit with no results whatever for his efforts.

In Portland, at "pentecostal" camp meetings, I had heard women wail and then shriek like a fire siren, audible for three or four blocks.

Our Problem

When we saw about 25 or 30 of these same "pentecostal" people who had ruined Mr. Taylor's meetings coming into our little hall, Mr. Ray and Mr. Oberg and I went into a quick huddle. Mr. Ray purported to be completely opposed to this brand of "pentecostalism."

"What shall we do about this?" he asked. "We've got to get rid of these people, or they will simply take over the meetings and there will be no results."

"Just leave the situation to me," said Mr. Oberg. "I know how to handle these people."

We were reassured.

But by the second or third night, we began to realize that Mr. Oberg, far from discouraging or "handling" these people, was deliberately catering to them. Gradually we began to realize that Mr. Oberg was "pentecostal" himself—a fact he had carefully concealed. Indeed, he had deliberately led us to believe he was opposed to it. Soon I realized these people were definitely "IN" and firmly established. It was too late to change it.

For the first few nights Mr. Oberg and I alternated, each speaking every second night. But it became apparent that the "pentecostal" people, now more than 90% of the attendance, warmed up much more to Mr.

488

Oberg's preaching. He encouraged them. He invited their loud amens just as "pentecostal" preachers do constantly, getting them stirred up to an emotional and excitable pitch. So after about a week, I suggested that Mr. Oberg do all the preaching, and I preached to our own members who came up from the Valley for the Sabbath services.

About the end of the first week word came from the manager of a lumber yard situated very close to our hall, asking if I would stop in and see him. He had attended the first five or six meetings, then dropped out.

"Mr. Armstrong," he said, "I just wanted to explain to you why I stopped attending your meetings. I was really quite interested in hearing *your* sermons, but this man Oberg's constant succession of stories, and whooping up those 'holy rollers' into shouting and emotional frenzy and foolishness is more than I can take. I think you were wise in just letting this other man take over the meetings. Not many who are seeking the real truth that *you* preach will be attending from now on, anyway. I would have continued attending, if you had been conducting the services alone—but I can't tolerate that senseless wildfire."

My Father's Death

Along about the 20th or 21st of April in that year of 1933 word came that my father was very ill. I asked Mr. Oberg to accompany me, and we hastened to his farm, between Oregon City and Molalla. Apparently we asked Mr. Ray to take the service till we returned.

Dad had suffered an acute attack of indigestion. We anointed and prayed for him. He seemed to recover at once. He also had called for us because he wanted to be baptized.

My father, as I may have stated before, had always

489

been a *good* man. He had been jolly, friendly with everybody. He never smoked, drank, swore, or indulged in any such vices. He never opposed or harmed a soul, but always was willing to help. He had, as I recounted earlier, a marvelous deep bass voice. Dad had attended church regularly all his life, and had been active —especially in singing.

But my father was actually *so good,* humanly speaking, and so void of vices and any of the commonly accepted "sins" that he was actually in the same category as Job. Job was so righteous that even Satan could not find anything of which to accuse him. Actually Job's one great sin was his own righteousness. It blinded him to his HUMANITY, the actual NATURE of sin in every human. Job was the most difficult man on record for God to convert. Finally, God brought Job to the place where he *did REPENT,* and come to completely ABHOR himself!

My father had come to that same place. He came to realize that mere human goodness and uprightness is not, after all, the true RIGHTEOUSNESS of GOD, which is received only from God's Holy Spirit after the painful and suffering *experience* of repentance. But now he had repented. And now he had come to recognize his real NEED of Jesus Christ as personal Saviour. He had thrown himself on God's mercy, in faith believing.

That afternoon, his acute indigestion healed, but still needing rest and sleep to recover strength, we planned to go down to the river at the edge of his farm and baptize him the next day.

Late that afternoon, we all sang "Praise Him! Praise Him!" with my father's deep melodic bass voice ringing out. It was to be the last time he ever sang.

When we finished, he had tears in his eyes, and his face literally *illuminated* in a happy smile.

490

"It's just wonderful!" he exclaimed. "It's absolutely *WONDERFUL!*"

"What do you mean, Dad?" I asked.

"That God at last has forgiven all my sins!" he exclaimed. "It seems like a load of many tons has been rolled off of my shoulders—and I don't have to carry that weight of guilt around any longer!"

We left him to rest.

A while later we were called back into the room. He had sunken into a coma, not from indigestion, but a heart attack. We anointed and prayed for him again. We put him to bed in an adjoining bedroom. We noticed his feet were swelling. He did not come out of the coma. We kept up an all-night vigil of prayer. The swelling continued up his legs.

Dawn came. We continued praying. I know that I continued *believing.* By this time we had been granted many miraculous answers to prayer, and I felt I never had more faith in my life.

Yet, at 9:40 that morning, the day after he entered his 70th year, my father died. I was stunned. This I could *not* believe!

Suddenly I was confused, bewildered. I knew that God had given His written PROMISE to heal. Always before, since learning this truth, God had healed all in our family. I realized that there are two conditions— obedience, and faith. But I had surrendered fully and unconditionally to God's commandments, given my life to Him and His service. And I had believed with positive conviction. There had been no wavering—no doubt— just calm ASSURANCE.

For three days I was in a mental fog. Not that I began to lose faith in God, or the reality of Biblical promises. Not that doubts began to be entertained. I was still quite a *"babe* in Christ" in the new Christian

491

life, but we had been put through enough experiences—
and I had studied and PROVED the Scriptures
sufficiently—that I did not allow *doubts* to begin to
arise. When one permits DOUBTS to enter his thoughts
and reasonings, he is on dangerous ground. He is
thinking negatively. Whoever DOUBTS is damned. I want
the reader to learn that lesson.

If one is not certain—if he has not PROVED a
doctrine or a fact—then the teaching of God is, with
open mind free from prejudice, to seek *all* the facts—to
PROVE it. This is not negative, but positive thinking and
procedure. Doubting is not proving. Doubting is not
intelligent! It is negative thinking about something one
does not know enough about to warrant this form of
unfounded disbelief.

Strengthening FAITH

I *knew* that God could not break a promise. I *knew* God
has promised to HEAL—that Jesus took the penalty of
physical sickness and infirmities and paid it for us by
having His perfect physical body broken by being
beaten with stripes!

But WHY, then, did my father die? Through James
God instructs us that if any lack wisdom, he shall ask of
GOD asking in FAITH, not wavering or doubting—and
God promises wisdom shall be given. I prayed earnestly.
I asked God for UNDERSTANDING.

And I searched the Scriptures for the explanation. I
did not doubt—but I *did* seek an explanation. Faith
must be based on UNDERSTANDING, and I knew there was
something I had not yet come to understand. Naturally I
soon came, in this search, to the "faith chapter"—the
11th of Hebrews. Then the answer became plain.

God gives us many examples of faith in that
wonderful chapter. I noticed the example of Abraham—

492

the *father* of the faithful. He, with Isaac and Jacob and Sarah "all died, *not having received the PROMISES.*" My father, like them, died, not having received God's promise of healing—*AS YET!* Did the death of Abraham, *before* he received what God had unconditionally PROMISED, nullify that promise? Did his death mean that God failed—that God's promise was worthless, not to be kept? NOT AT ALL!

No, it simply meant that, for God's own reason and purpose, the fulfilling of the promise is delayed UNTIL THE RESURRECTION!

In like manner, I could now understand that God has PROMISED to heal—but He has *not* promised how immediately, or by what manner, He will do it. I knew, now, that my father's healing is still absolutely SURE. He will be resurrected—HEALED! I saw, now, that our days are indeed numbered. God has not promised that we shall live in this mortal existence eternally. It is appointed to men once to DIE—and after this the resurrection. I read how the TRIAL of our faith is allowed to work PATIENCE.

God, then, does give us tests of faith. Faith is the EVIDENCE of that NOT seen, NOT felt. Once we FEEL and SEE that we are healed, we no longer need the invisible spiritual evidence of faith. Faith, then, is our evidence—our PROOF of the healing—which God gives us to be exercised and utilized BETWEEN the time we ask, and the time the physical evidence is granted.

We should not *go* to God, asking, unless we have FAITH that God *will* do what He has promised, and what we are ready to ask. Then, after we ask, we should *still* have faith—just as before—that God WILL do as He has promised.

Now I understood!

Some people, in the clutch of fatal DOUBTS in their

493

faulty reasoning, will try to REASON that unless God heals instantaneously, either God has not kept His promise—or that the one who asked is guilty of such sin that God will not hear him. Such people are wresting the plain teaching of God to their own destruction.

The net result of this shocking experience of my father's death was a great strengthening of FAITH. I hope sincerely that the recording of this experience will strengthen the faith of many readers. God's very purpose in giving us this temporary physical existence is to build righteous spiritual character, *through EXPE-RIENCE.* In the Bible God gives us many EXPERIENCES of those He has dealt with, that we may learn by reading of their experiences. The only reason I am continuing with this autobiography is the hope that many readers may learn lessons God intends them to learn, through these recorded experiences.

Was It GOD's Spirit?

As the meetings in Salem continued on, after the first week or so, almost the only people coming were these "pentecostal" people. Their antics drove away most others. Though it is rare among this type of people, many, or most, of them were "Sabbath keepers." But, aside from the fourth commandment, there did not appear to be any desire to obey God, or to "live by every Word of God." Their whole desire was a "good time" during meetings. They came for the temporary thrill and enjoyment of going on an emotional spree of excitement, shouting, and bragging in "testimony meeting" about how glad they were they "had their baptism," and how much better they were than others, for precisely the same purpose that other people attend a football game to shout and yell, and work up sensations of excitement.

494

They were definitely *not* SEEKING "the KINGDOM OF GOD AND HIS RIGHTEOUSNESS," but they were continually SEEKING physical and sensual pleasure and thrills and excitement, under the deceptive illusion that all this was pleasing to God. One of these women, some months later, after the close of the meetings, who had "received her baptism" as they term it, became disgusted with it and told my wife in private that what she and they all got from it was what she termed "sublimated sex thrills." She said frankly it was plain lust of the flesh. Yet the people in it are deceived into sincerely believing that they are *seeking,* and receiving, the Holy Spirit of God!

One night while Mr. Oberg was preaching, one very fat woman, who must have weighed 250 pounds, arose and with short, jerky, staccato steps, slowly waddled up front to the piano, shaking her fat hips at each jerky step. She sat down on the piano bench and began to hit the keys with the palms of both hands in a discordant jumbled manner about like a one-year-old baby might do. There was no chord, harmony, tune—no regularity of beat or rhythm—just a spasmodic discordant POUNDING in utter CONFUSION.

As she began, the one other big fat woman in the hall, of equal horizontal proportions, arose and began a sort of awkward dancing jig, her arms floundering around, uncontrolled, overhead, her very fat hips waddling and shimmying. For some two to five minutes these two women continued their unrefined duet.

Mr. Oberg stopped his preaching, with expressions of "Praise the Lord! Glory Hallelujah! Praise you, Jesus!"—to which the whole "pentecostal" attendance immediately joined in until the place was a bedlam of din and confusion.

As we were walking home that night after the

service, our elder daughter, Beverly, then of junior high school age, asked:

"Daddy, was that the Holy Spirit making those women do those things?"

I was well familiar with Christ's saying that the blasphemy against the Holy Spirit—accusing the work of the Holy Spirit of being the work of the devil—was the unpardonable sin. Although I was by that time quite aware that these practices of "pentecostal" people were *not* in conformity with either the teaching or example found in God's Word, nevertheless I was afraid to take any slight chance of committing the unpardonable sin.

"I just can't answer that, Beverly," I replied. "I suppose those women were sincere in *believing* they were being moved by God's Spirit. Most people are deceived, today. But I don't want to try to judge."

A few paragraphs back, I quoted the lumberyard manager as referring to Mr. Oberg's succession of stories. We soon learned that his preaching consisted more of telling various stories than of expounding the Scriptures. He was one who believed Jesus spoke in parables in order to make his meaning more clear. Actually, Jesus Himself said He used parables for precisely the opposite reason—to HIDE the true meaning, so they could *not* understand. Mr. Oberg had made it a practice to memorize just about every story he ever heard—or could read.

He constantly used stories to illustrate his points. He had stories in his memory by the thousands. As he himself claimed, he had stories to produce laughter, stories of pathos, tear-jerkers to make his audience weep—and these especially he told with great acting ability. He continually urged me to acquire a large stock of stories. But, as Will Rogers might have said, I just couldn't see it that way. That is not the way the original apostles preached.

NO Fruit Borne!

When the meetings came to the end of the planned duration, and absolutely NO "fruit" had been borne, except for the nightly emotional jamboree, Mr. Oberg was reluctant to stop.

Sam Oberg and his young 25-year-old wife had been living with Mr. and Mrs. O. J. Runcorn. I believe it was Mr. Runcorn who put up the $10 for one more month's hall rent. The total duration of the meetings ran either three or four months.

But even after the extended month, there were no conversions—no members added to the Church—absolutely no visible results. The "pentecostals" had been enjoying a continuous nightly show. There was nothing else to show for it.

I have stated before, that never once, when I was working *with* any of these other ministers, were any results apparent. Never, in all those years, did I know of a single conversion resulting from the work or preaching of any of those ministers! Yet *never* did God fail to grant good results, with people converted and baptized, when I was working alone. I do not say this with any joy—for while I do rejoice and am grateful for the harvest God has produced through my efforts, I have sorrowed and *not* found any pleasure or rejoicing in the lack of fruit borne by the others. That has truly been one of the disappointments we have had to suffer.

However, God has now changed all that. Today, as I write, thirty-nine years later, God is *abundantly* blessing ALL His ministers whom He now graciously has added to His Church, with conversions, changed lives, healings, and continuous blessings. God's Church TODAY is going forward in constantly accelerating POWER—the true power of GOD!

The Plots Progress

All through this campaign in Salem, personal relations between Mr. Oberg and Mr. Ray and me were, on the surface, very friendly and cooperative. At least that was my attitude of heart. But, under cover, their plots began to thicken.

After my father had died, at his farm north of Molalla, in April of 1933, my wife had gone to the farm for a visit with my mother. I do not remember the exact month, but I believe it must have been along in late May or early June.

One night she was disturbed and frightened to be awakened from a startling dream, in which it seemed an angel was telling her! "Go to Salem at once! Go to Salem at once! Enemies are plotting against your husband."

She was so alarmed that she was afraid to chance the dream possibly meaning nothing. She came immediately that day to Salem. At the same time, Mike Helms had come to tell me that Mr. Oberg and Mr. Ray had gone around to a number of the brethren in the valley, and set up an accusation against me, in a secret plot to get me out of the ministry. They wanted the $3 weekly cash salary, and the benefit of the other money being spent for our house rent and beans and flour, etc.

They had brought enough pressure to force Milas Helms, as president of the Conference, to call a business meeting for the following Sunday at the church in Harrisburg.

"They plan to discredit you," explained Mr. Helms, "by charging that your wife is not a neat housekeeper— and then turning to the Biblical qualifications for an Elder, for ruling well his own household. Since they will

498

claim that you are not ruling your wife sternly enough to be a better housekeeper, they will claim that you are not Scripturally fit to be a minister, and must be put out of the ministry."

This came as a shocking surprise! Their accusation was *false*. My wife was a good housekeeper, and I *did* rule my own family and household, and have my children in subjection. But these men knew that most members did not *know* all about our private family life, and would believe their lie.

These men had been so very friendly—*to my face!* I had not realized they were enemies, speaking lies about me and my wife behind my back! Mike saw that I was deeply hurt.

"The only thing I know that I can possibly do to help you," continued Mr. Helms, "is to give you the opportunity to speak first, if that will be any benefit. I will be chairman of the meeting, and I can give you the chance to speak before they do."

I accepted the offer. You may be sure I prayed a great deal over it. Actually, Mrs. Armstrong has always been a very clean housekeeper, and a very neat one, with the exception that, during the years when we had four growing children in the house—and at this time the youngest was 3, and the eldest 15—children *did* leave a few things misplaced, on occasion, of course. But the charge Mr. Oberg planned to make was simply *an outrageous LIE!*

Defending My Wife!

Sam Oberg made a fetish of stern neatness, punctuality, and certain OUTWARD mannerisms designed to lead others to think him righteous. Actually, although he was unreasonably *stern* with his little 3-year-old daughter, he knew about as *little* of proper child rearing as anyone

I ever knew. He went to the extreme on stern demands for certain mannerisms of decorum, and punished his child with over-severity, while at the same time he completely neglected her in most other ways, failed to properly teach and train her, and allowed her to do other things that should not have been done.

There have been times, since I have been *changed* by God's Spirit, that righteous indignation arose instantly to white-hot heat. This was one of them.

But I prayed, and God helped me to put down anger. Also it came to mind what to do. You may not think God put it there, but I do.

At Harrisburg on Sunday, Mr. Helms, after opening the meeting with prayer, gave me the floor first. I think this was a surprise to Messrs. Oberg and Ray. I told the Board members and other brethren assembled that I understood this meeting had been called as an inquisition, to crucify me by false charges. I told them I did not wish to defend myself. I told them I knew I was full of faults and weaknesses, the same as each of them. I told them I had been striving, and with God's help, overcoming many of these human frailties and weaknesses and habits since my conversion, some six years before—but I had not yet reached perfection. I felt that each of them—and Messrs. Oberg and Ray—lived in glass houses, also, in case any had a hating spirit of wishing to throw stones.

I stood there and confessed many specific faults and weaknesses, and asked them if they would PRAY for me that I might have help in overcoming them. Their eyes began to fill with tears—all but Oberg and Ray.

Then I quickly ended by saying that Mr. Oberg and Mr. Ray might say anything they wished against me—but that I understood they planned to accuse my wife falsely, and I then told them with all the power I had that God made me my wife's defender, and that if either of them dared to utter one word against my wife, I would—if need be—CLOSE their mouths before they could finish the first sentence. I did not specify the means. This was said with blazing eyes, and a sharp voice!

I sat down.

Mr. Helms then called on Oberg and Ray. I do not remember what they said—if anything. I do know that there was NOTHING left for them to say against ME—for I had said it all myself before them. And they somehow must have known that *I MEANT IT* when I said I would defend my wife's honor. They were *silent* about her.

I do know the result. Their plot backfired! I was not discharged. Rather, the brethren were still looking to me for leadership. But Mr. Oberg and Mr. Ray were not through gunning for me. There was much more to come later!

Chopping Wood

I began to realize that Messrs. Oberg and Ray were secretly carrying on a propaganda campaign against me. In talking privately to church brethren they would drop little suggestions implying, at least indirectly, anything possible against my character.

One day Milas Helms came to me with the offer to give me a very large tree on his farm if I would chop it down, saw it up and split it for our winter's fuel supply. This tree was six feet in diameter at the trunk—a huge fir.

"Some of the brethren," he said, "are getting the idea from Mr. Oberg and Mr. Ray, that *they* have to do hard physical work on their farms, but that *you* have it pretty soft merely preaching, visiting members and prospective members, holding Bible studies, getting out the news bulletin. If you will spend the next several days splitting up a year's wood supply, I will see that the word gets around about how energetically you are working. This will counteract this propaganda better than a million words of denial."

Somehow, it never seemed to dawn on the brethren, who listened to these subtle innuendoes suggesting I was lazy, that Mr. Oberg devoted his time, also, to the ministry and had no time for hard manual labor.

Gladly I accepted the offer, happy of the opportunity to provide fuel for my family. I counted the rings on the tree. That tree was growing there when George Washington was a boy! I was glad of the chance for the exercise and the fresh country air, as well as the wood.

Again, the plot was foiled.

Cackling Hens

During the course of the Salem meetings Milas Helms brought us a number of eggs one day—perhaps a dozen or so. "We have decided to start tithing our eggs, as well as money income," he said to us.

It was the off-laying season. This incident has been reported before in *The Plain Truth*, but it properly belongs at this point in the *Autobiography*. Even though it was out of season for Mike's hens, they immediately went on an egg-laying campaign. Never, it seemed, had they laid so many eggs.

After this incident was reported in *The Plain Truth*, one reader wrote that she had begun to tithe her eggs and received the same result. Experience repeatedly proves it *pays* to tithe!

Blessings in Disguise

Very shortly after our return from Astoria—possibly even before the meetings began in Salem, or very soon after they started, the Santiam River—on whose banks bordered the farms of Mike Helms and his brother-in-law, Yancy McGill—went on a rampage, overflowing its banks in a complete flood.

It happened on a Friday or Friday night. Mike told me of it when he came for church on the Sabbath. In fact, we attended a meeting with other brethren at some town west of Salem that day. En route, Mike told me of the calamity. His crops had been all planted. They were all under the water.

The reader can understand by this time that I felt a very deep affection for Mike Helms. I felt as badly about this as if it had been my own fields. I continued to express my deep concern and regret and sympathy.

"Mr. Armstrong," said Mike in what seemed like a half gentle rebuke, "you seem to be taking this a lot harder than I am. God says *everything* works together for GOOD, to them that love the Lord. I love the Lord, and I try to serve Him and obey Him and *I BELIEVE* Him. I am faithful in paying tithes. Right now I can't see how a thing like this can work together for my good. But I don't need to see how. I know God means what He says, and, in a way I can't see right now, this is going to work for my GOOD. I'm just praising the Lord for it!"

I hope that God used me in teaching Mike many valuable lessons, but this was a time when God used Mike to teach me a lesson I shall never forget. Perhaps, in this way through *The Plain Truth*, Mike can be used to teach many thousands of our readers a valuable lesson today, more than a quarter of a century later.

After the flood subsided a very strange thing became apparent. On adjoining farmland, without even a fence between, the crops were completely ruined. But the damage *stopped* at the very line of Mike Helms' and Yancy McGill's farms—all except one small patch of

Mike's land, which it was not too late to replant. And because the floodwaters had ruined the crops of so many vegetable gardeners, Mike's and Yancy's crops brought a higher-than-usual price that year! And *THAT* is *how* this calamity worked for GOOD!

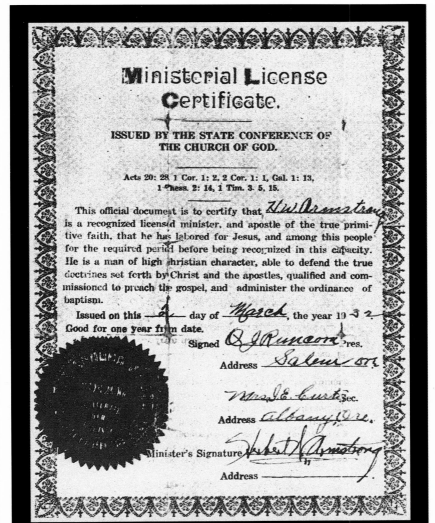

Ministerial License Certificate.

ISSUED BY THE STATE CONFERENCE OF THE CHURCH OF GOD.

Acts 20: 28 1 Cor. 1: 2, 2 Cor. 1: 1, Gal. 1: 13, 1 Thess. 2: 14, 1 Tim. 3. 5, 15.

This official document is to certify that _H. W. Armstrong_ is a recognized licensed minister, and apostle of the true primitive faith, that he has labored for Jesus, and among this people for the required period before being recognized in this capacity. He is a man of high christian character, able to defend the true doctrines set forth by Christ and the apostles, qualified and commissioned to preach the gospel, and administer the ordinance of baptism.

Issued on this _2_ day of _March_, the year 19 _32_. Good for one year from date.

Signed _O. J. Runcorn_ Pres.

Address _Salem Ore._

Mrs. J. E. Curtis Sec.

Address _Albany, Ore._

Minister's Signature _Herbert W. Armstrong_

Address ——————.

■ *The second ordination certificate issued to Herbert W. Armstrong in 1932. It was then custom to renew the certificates annually. The document is signed by O.J. Runcorn, husband of the woman who first enlightened Loma Armstrong about the Sabbath day.*

■ *The Jeans schoolhouse, 12 miles west of Eugene, Oregon, where Mr. Armstrong held evangelistic campaign in 1933. The Hampton Building, corner 6th and Willamette, in Eugene. Here in the small, inside one-room office,* The Plain Truth *was published. Right, the earliest issue of the fledgling magazine.*

The PLAIN TRUTH

VOL. I NO. I   *My Word is TRUTH*   February, 1934

Is a
World Dictator
About to Appear?

WE Live today in the most strenuous, anxious, momentous hours of earth's history.

Today we stand on the very threshold of colossal events that will stagger the mind of mortal man. Just now it is like the lull before a great and devastating storm. Everyone senses it!

The Lust for World Power

Ever since the Pharaohs ruled in Egypt---on down thru ancient Assyria, Babylon, Persia, Greece, and Rome---on to Napolian, and then the Kaiser---there has been a lust for power to rule the world.

Today at least three major world powers seek to rule the world.

Soviet Russia admits the theory of Communism cannot be proven until all opposition is wiped out, and the whole world is under its sway.

The amazing Tanaka Memorial of 1927, recently discovered and exposed, outlines a most astounding program of Japanese expansion, involving the defeat in war of the United States, and Russia, and then of the whole world. This program raises Japanese imperialism to the height of insane megalomania! Yet Japan's policies and actions during the past two years supply irrefutable proof of preparation to carry out the aims of this document.

It is commonly known today

WILL It be Mussolini, Stalin, or Roosevelt?

Everybody senses that something is WRONG with the world . . . that some mighty event is about to occur.

What is it? Bible prophecy tells! Here is a solemn warning . . . and it is the plain truth!

that Mussolini's whole aim is to restore the ancient Roman Empire in all its former splendor, power, and glory---and Rome ruled the world!

Today Prime Minister MacDonald of Great Britain and President Roosevelt are striving frantically to avert, or postpone, the impending next world war---while the nations prepare even more feverishly for WAR!

Three or four short years ago many laughed and scoffed when we said there would be another world war in five to seven years. They do not laugh and scoff today. Everyone KNOWS the next world war is coming, and SOON. Every move for peace has failed?

What is Going to Happen?

Will some super-man now emerge? Will the nations get together and appoint a world dictator?

Mortal man cannot prophesy the turns and trends of coming events. Only God knows the end from the beginning.

In words written, some nineteen hundred, some twenty-five hundred years ago, the Bible prophesies every outstanding phase of present world conditions---the depression, the unemployment, its causes, the hoarding of gold, the topsy-turvy political conditions thruout the world, the modern church conditions, and present social conditions. It

■ *Above, a Neostyle, trade name of a mimeograph. The first issues of* The Plain Truth *were mimeographed on a Neostyle similar to this model. The stencils were cut on a Corona typewriter by Herbert Armstrong himself.*

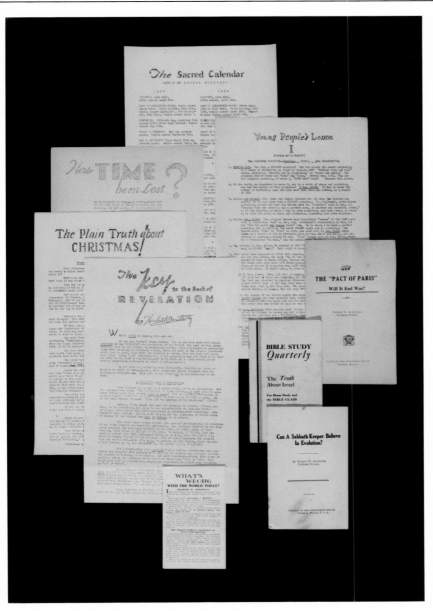

■ *Several early publications of the Church of God, Eugene, Oregon. Though at first* *mimeographed, publications were later printed in the same advertising format that Herbert Armstrong used in* *his ads in the years before his conversion.*

■ *The Bulletin of the Church of God in Oregon provides a history of the early development of Herbert W.* Armstrong's duties, including his appointment in 1933.

Credentials of Discipleship

Jerusalem, Palestine,
~~January 1, 1931,~~
October 1, 1934

BE IT KNOWN by this official document of the "Church of God," with headquarters at Jerusalem, Palestine; that *Herbert W. Armstrong* whose address is *460 W. 7th St., Eugene, Ore.* has been duly chosen according to the good hand of God to take part of the ministry and discipleship which the <u>seventy</u> noble disciples laid down in death as martyrs or otherwise.

With pleasure the Church endorses him as their duly qualified representative, and he is herein recommended as a man of the highest Christian character, worthy of your confidence and trust. By this document he is authorized to perform all the duties devolved upon the clergy and to share with the other ____seventy____ the spiritual duties devolved upon the ministry according to the gospel commission.

These credentials remain good so long as the life of the holder conforms to the standard set by Jesus and taught by the Church of God, in morals and doctrine. He herein agrees that in the event he is not able to see eye to eye with the Church in belief as well as to live according to the divine standard, that he will, without controversy or trouble of any kind, cheerfully return this epistle of commendation to the proper church authorities.

Signed:

General Secretary.

General Officer.

■ *After the Churches of God became divided over the matter of Church government in the early 1930s, Mr. Armstrong was sent a ministerial certificate signed by A.N. Dugger and C.O. Dodd, leaders of one of the divisions. Below, playing with three of his children.*

■ *Herbert Armstrong at the microphone in the earlier years of broadcasting. Left, receipts from radio stations KORE, KSLM, and KXL in Oregon. The weekly costs are unbelievable by today's standards. But those were the days of the Great Depression.*

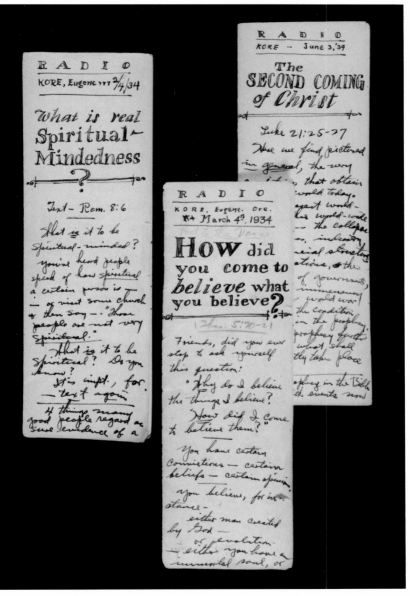

The handwritten radio scripts shown read:

RADIO
KORE, Eugene ··· 2/4/34
What is real
Spiritual-
Mindedness
?
Text – Rom. 8:6
What *is* it to be
Spiritual-minded?
you've heard people
speak of how spiritual
a certain person is –
– or visit some church
+ then say –: "Those
people are not very
Spiritual."
What is it to be
Spiritual? Do you
know?
It's impt., for.
– text again
4 things many
good people regard as
sure evidence of a

RADIO
KORE, Eugene. Ore.
★ · March 4th, 1934
HOW did
you come to
believe what
you believe?
[1 Thes. 5:10-21]
Friends, did you ever
stop to ask yourself
this question:
"Why do I believe
the things I believe?
How did I come
to believe them?"
You have certain
convictions – certain
beliefs – certain opinions
you believe, for in-
stance –
either man created
by God –
or evolution
– either you have a
immortal soul, or

RADIO
KORE – June 3, '34
The
SECOND COMING
of Christ
Luke 21:25-27
Here we find pictured
in general, the very
conditions that obtain
world today.
......

A selection of
early broadcast
scripts in Herbert W.
Armstrong's files.
They were
all written out in
longhand and,
though no one else
read them, they
reflect advertising
skills in their
headlines. Each script
is dated.

■ *Evangelistic campaign flyers, mimeographed, announce meetings and subjects to be delivered. In an age without television, these meetings were a major source of reaching new hearers.*

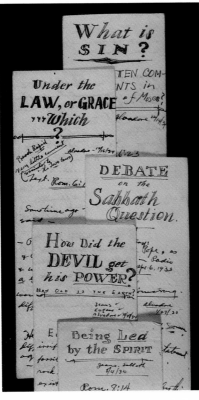

What is SIN?

Under the LAW, or GRACE ... Which?

TEN COM-... NTS in ... of Moses?

DEBATE on the Sabbath Question.

How Did the DEVIL get his POWER?

Being Led by the SPIRIT

Rom. 8:14

■ *A 1935 tent meeting, one of a few pictures that were taken during these financially stressed years. Left, evangelistic campaign sermon notes expounding such basic doctrines as law and grace, sin, the Sabbath, the origin of the devil, and conversion.*

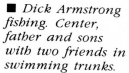

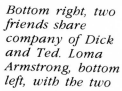

■ *Dick Armstrong fishing. Center, father and sons with two friends in swimming trunks.*

Bottom right, two friends share company of Dick and Ted. Loma Armstrong, bottom left, with the two

boys. Right, the four Armstrong children in about 1936.

■ *A collection of family photos of the later 1930s. Dick Armstrong and his mother, top far left. Herbert Armstrong in a beach pose, top far right. Below, far left, wading on Oregon beach. Above, son Dick with bicycle. Left, viewing the beach.*

■ *Herbert W. Armstrong with his brother Russell at a point in time in which volume one closes. Herbert Armstrong often spoke admiringly of his brother Russell to friends who never were able to meet him. Mr. Armstrong always had a sense of good photography, which was reflected in his perception of magazine covers and layout.*

29

The Real Beginning of Present Work

THE MEETINGS held by Elder S. A. Oberg and me in the "Hollywood" district of Salem, Oregon, ended on July 1st, 1933. Just prior to this date I received an invitation that was to result in the start of the great worldwide Work of today.

This invitation came from Mr. and Mrs. Elmer E. Fisher. They were the couple who had been brought into the church by our private Bible study in my room, the night the storm prevented the meeting, during the tent campaign in Eugene, in the summer of 1931. The Fishers were successful farmers, living seven miles west of Eugene. Mr. Fisher was a member of the school board of the one-room Firbutte school, eight miles west of Eugene on the old Elmira road. The Fishers asked me to hold meetings in this country schoolhouse, inviting me to be their guest in their farm home during the meetings.

Organizing Another Church

But I was still in the employ of the Oregon Conference of the Church of God. The salary, as stated in the preceding chapter, was $3 per week. The Conference was to have paid our house rent in Salem, and they supplied us with bulk foods—whole wheat flour, raw sugar, beans. Farmer members supplied us with vegetables and fruits. However, part of the time the Conference was unable to pay our house rent, which was $7 per month, and my wife had to make up the deficit by doing the washings for our landlady. In addition to this, I raised a vegetable garden on our lot that summer.

Decision about the Firbutte school meetings near Eugene required a special Conference Board meeting. About the same time the Fishers' invitation came, the way opened also for a series of meetings to be held in the little church building we had rented in Harrisburg. The Board wanted to decide which assignment was to go to me, and which to Elder Oberg.

But since the Harrisburg church seated about 150 people, and was located in a town, while the Firbutte schoolhouse seated only 35, and was located 8 miles from town, in a sparsely settled rural district where farmhouses were a half-mile apart, the Board readily agreed to assign me to the country schoolhouse. Elder Oberg was assigned to the church building in Harrisburg, at his urgent request.

Meanwhile, the Salem meetings, after three months, ended on July 1st, 1933, with no results. Mr. Oberg left immediately to make preparations for his Harrisburg meetings.

After he left, Mrs. Armstrong and I visited a number of the people who had attended regularly. They had not come into the church because of a few doctrinal differences. Mr. Oberg, as explained earlier, had done nearly all the preaching after the first week. The meetings had become altogether "pentecostal"—or, as some might have stated it, "inspirational." These doctrinal differences had not been explained. I felt that I could explain them. As a result of nearly a week's work with these people in their homes, a number of them did accept the truth. We thereupon accepted them into fellowship as members of the Church.

During these four or five days I rented a church building in the same general part of Salem, at 17th and Chemeketa, for Sabbath services, and Thursday night prayer meetings. After conference with the Board, it was arranged for Mr. A. J. Ray to act as pastor of the new church at Salem. The members from the Jefferson area agreed to attend at Salem, and this formed a church of around 30 or 35 members.

The church there lasted only a few months. The new "pentecostal" members apparently dropped out after a few weeks, and the older members around the Jefferson area went back to meeting in a country schoolhouse southwest of Jefferson.

The START of the Present Work

As soon as arrangements were completed for starting the new church at Salem, I hurried on down to the Fisher farm to start the new campaign west of Eugene.

Mr. Oberg was starting his new meetings in Harrisburg on Sunday night, July 9. The Fishers and I decided to start the meetings at the Firbutte school the same night. I arrived at the Fisher farm, leaving my wife and children at our home in Salem, about July 5th or 6th.

This was the small—actually infinitesimal—*start* of what was destined to grow to a major worldwide

Gospel Work reaching multiple millions of people every week.

But if small, it started with a burst of energy and inspiration. First, it started with intensive and earnest private prayer. To the rear of the Fisher farm home was a fair-sized hill. Running over this hilltop for exercise I discovered a rock about 14 inches high. It was in a secluded spot. It came to mind how Jesus had dismissed the multitudes, and gone up into a mountain *"apart"* to pray—alone with God. I dropped to my knees before this rock, which seemed just the right height to kneel before, and began praying earnestly for the success of the meetings. It became sort of a daily pilgrimage, during my stay at Fishers', to this, which became my "prayer rock." I'm sure that I drank in much energy, spiritual strength and inspiration at that prayer rock.

Preparing for the meetings, I borrowed a typewriter. I think the Fishers arranged this for me through one of their relatives. With carbon paper, I typed out some thirty notices, announcing the meetings, and the topics of the sermons for the first week or ten days.

There was no local newspaper in that localized school district. We could not have afforded to purchase advertising space to announce the meetings, had there been one. We could not afford to have handbills printed. But I took these typed notices, and part of the time walking, part of the time with Mr. Fisher driving me, and part of the time driving his car which he let me use, I visited all the homes for some five miles around— farther, toward the west—telling the people about the meetings, inviting them to attend, and leaving the typed announcements.

Then we anxiously awaited Sunday night. Would the people come?

Twenty-seven people filled 27 of the 35 seats that first night. I spoke on prophecy.

The second night attendance dropped to 19. But that night we had a bit of excitement. An event occurred that greatly stimulated interest.

Heckled — Put on the Spot

In this neighborhood, near the schoolhouse, lived an elderly "Bible scholar" with quite a reputation in the community. His name was Belshaw. He owned the most extensive theological library in the district—probably the only one. The neighbors regarded him as something of a Bible authority.

Mr. and Mrs. Fisher had warned me of one of his habits which was traditional in the neighborhood. In Eugene, adjoining the University of Oregon campus, is a theological seminary. Frequently advanced students were sent to one of these country schoolhouses to hold a short series of meetings as part of their training. It was Mr. Belshaw's custom to attend one of the first two meetings, and to put the speaker on the spot by heckling with a trick question.

It was Mr. Belshaw's contention that these young men did not really have a thorough knowledge of the Bible. He was sure that he did. He was adept at asking questions the answer to which he was pretty sure the young preacher, or preacher-to-be, did not know. If he could tangle the speaker up and expose his ignorance, the neighbors would have a good laugh—and then fail to attend any further meetings.

"If Mr. Belshaw can trap you with a trick question, no one will attend your meetings after that," warned Mr. Fisher. "He nearly always has a question these young men can't answer. But if you can answer him, or turn the tables on him, the news will spread

509

all over the neighborhood and the attendance will increase."

Mr. Belshaw had not put in an appearance the first night. Apparently he had decided to first see whether I had a good crowd. But the second night, he was one of the 19 present.

He interrupted my sermon.

"Mr. Armstrong," he called out, "May I ask you a question?"

"Yes Sir, Mr. Belshaw," I replied, "you may."

"Have you been saved yet?"

Instantly I knew what his trap was. He expected me to say that I had been, of course. Then he would have asked me if I did not know what Jesus said in Matthew 24:13. So I immediately quoted this scripture to him.

"Jesus said, in Matthew 24:13, that he that shall endure unto the end, the same *shall be saved*. And in the very next verse, Jesus also said that HIS gospel of the KINGDOM—which is the RULE of God—the keeping of His commandments—shall be preached in all the world as a witness. That is what I am doing here tonight. Why do you not OBEY the Commandments, as Jesus said, Mr. Belshaw?"

I knew that Mr. Belshaw argued against the Ten Commandments.

"I would, if I could see any LOVE in them," he replied.

"Then you must be spiritually blind," I said. "The Ten Commandments are merely the ten *points* of the great Law of LOVE. The first four tell you *how* to love God; the last six *how* to love thy neighbor. The Bible says LOVE is the fulfilling of the Law. The Commandments came from God, and God *is Love*. He gave the Commandments. Do you think God ever did anything that was not done in LOVE?"

510

Mr. Belshaw had no answer. He was silenced for the night. But he was not through. He tried to trap me with the Scriptures three more times, in later meetings.

The news did spread.

Tuesday night 36 were in attendance—one having to stand through the service. Thursday night 35 came—every seat filled. Our highest attendance was 64—with 29 standing in the crowded little room. Attendance for the six weeks averaged 36—one more than seating capacity.

Heckled Again — and Again!

The final Sunday night, beginning the last week of the meetings, a young minister who also fought against God's Law came as a visitor. It was the custom to ask visiting ministers to lead in prayer—a custom from which I have long since learned to depart. I asked him to lead in prayer.

My sermon topic had been announced. He knew I was going to speak on the subject of God's Sabbath. In his prayer this young preacher did his best to belittle me, discredit everything he thought I could say in my sermon, and give the impression I was not preaching the gospel.

"I thank Thee, O Lord," he prayed in a strong voice, "that we have a CHRIST to worship, and not a *day!* Help us, O Lord, to preach CHRIST, and Him crucified—not about days and laws. Help us to be like the Apostle Paul, who said, 'I am determined to know nothing among you, save Jesus Christ, and Him crucified.' "

As he prayed, I realized he was trying to knock my sermon into some kind of a cocked hat before I could start preaching it—and that unless I had the right answer his prayer would cause many to be prejudiced,

511

and to reject everything I would say. As he prayed, I *prayed desperately,* asking God to put the right answer in my mind. God did! Instantly I knew what to say.

This is another incident that has been mentioned before, on the air and in *The Plain Truth*—but it properly belongs at this point in the Autobiography. After his prayer I said to the audience:

"I am glad to know that Mr. . . . (I don't remember his name) says he is determined to know nothing but Jesus Christ, and Him crucified, for I, too, am of the same determination. I am going to PREACH Jesus Christ, and Him crucified tonight! But to do that, one must first know WHY Jesus Christ had to be crucified!

"I have just received a letter from my wife in Salem," I continued. "She wrote me that our elder little son, Richard David, 5 years old, has just preached his first sermon. He, too, preached Christ crucified. He and another little boy were playing by the side of our house. The window was open, and my wife overheard the conversation. The other little boy had been using a lot of slang. Our Dickey was exasperated. He picked up two sticks, crossing the longer with the shorter one.

" 'Now you look here, Donald,' said Dickey with flashing indignation. 'Do you know what this is?'

" 'No,' answered Donald.

" 'Well, this here is a cross. And they had to put Jesus Christ up on a cross, and drive nails through his hands and his feet, and nail him to that cross so he would die, just because you have been saying gosh and darn and gee-whiz! Don't you say those words any more!'

"And I wonder," I continued, "if people realize that SIN is the transgression of God's LAW—and that Jesus Christ was CRUCIFIED *because you people have been transgressing His holy Sabbath!* DON'T YOU PROFANE

512

WHAT IS HOLY TO GOD ANY MORE! And now I propose to preach to you Christ CRUCIFIED tonight—and WHY He was crucified!"

My young preacher guest, in white-hot anger, stomped out of the schoolhouse, to the accompaniment of the laughter of the audience, all of whom apparently delighted to see the tables turned on one who took a hostile advantage of a friendly invitation to lead in prayer.

He had merely provided me with the most effective possible introduction for my sermon.

Belshaw's Last Stand

The elderly Mr. Belshaw tried twice more, during those meetings, to entrap me with the Scriptures. But each time, God through His Spirit put the correct answer in my mind, and the right scriptures with which to reply.

Much later, after the meetings had closed, and we were holding meetings three times a week at the next schoolhouse, 4 miles farther west—the Jeans school—he made one final attempt. He staked everything on this, his last stand.

He waited until after the close of my sermon. He accosted me in the rear of the schoolroom just as people were starting to leave.

"Mr. Armstrong," he said in a loud voice, "May I ask you a question?"

This acted like an electric shock on everyone present. Mr. Belshaw's question had stirred much excitement. The two or three who already had gone out the door rushed back in. All circled around Mr. Belshaw and me.

"Yes sir, Mr. Belshaw—you most certainly may try once again," I responded, and by this time with a confident smile.

513

"Well, Mr. Armstrong, have I not heard you mention the scriptures stating that the Apostle Paul told the Gentile converts that he had not shunned to declare unto them the *whole gospel*—and that he had not held anything back that was profitable to them?"

"That is correct," I smiled.

"And have you not also said that *no nation* ever kept the Sabbath, except the Israelites—that is, that these Gentiles had not been Sabbath keepers *before* Paul taught them?"

"That is also correct!"

"All right," pursued Mr. Belshaw confidently. He was sure he had the best of me this time. *"IF* the Sabbath law is binding on us today, then it was binding on those Gentiles as soon as they became Christians. They were never Sabbath keepers *prior* to conversion. *IF* it is binding on us, then it was necessary for Paul to teach them to keep it. Now can you show me any scripture where the Apostle Paul ever taught or commanded the Gentiles to keep the Sabbath?" He felt he had delivered a telling blow—unanswerable, that would finally discredit me and what I preached once and for all! He was shocked at my answer.

"Yes sir, Mr. Belshaw!" I answered without any hesitation. "I certainly can! But before I do, I will now ask *you* a question: If I do show you where the Apostle Paul commanded the Gentile converts to keep the Sabbath, then that is irrefutable proof that YOU are commanded to keep it today. Now before I show you this command, I demand to know this: IF I show where Paul commanded the Gentiles to keep the Sabbath, WILL YOU NOW GIVE UP YOUR REBELLION, AND SURRENDER TO KEEP IT ALSO?"

He looked at me completely dumbfounded. He had been sure there was no command in the New Testament from Paul to Gentiles to keep the Sabbath. My answer caused him to back up, so startled, he almost fell over backward. It literally staggered him. Now he was not so sure of himself. I appeared very confident. He wasn't sure whether I was bluffing. But he was afraid to take the chance.

"NO, I WON'T!" he snapped, and angrily stomped out of the schoolhouse.

I do hasten to add, however, that aside from these four skirmishes where Mr. Belshaw, as was his custom with all preachers coming to the neighborhood, tried to trap me, he was most friendly toward me. He respected me. He refused to agree, but he did respect me. We had many friendly visits together. Mr. Fisher and I called on him three or four times, but, much as he liked to argue Scripture, he usually avoided the subject when we came around.

After he left I did show the rest of the people present where Paul did command the gentiles to keep the Sabbath. My challenge to Mr. Belshaw was not a bluff.

30

The World Tomorrow Broadcast Begins

THE IDEA of a literal, yet invisible devil of supernatural powers is looked upon askance by the "liberal" clergy, and by most of the so-called "educated" of today. But you can PROVE that the Holy BIBLE is in actual fact the inspired very WORD of the Eternal God and Creator. And the Bible reveals that there is an existent devil! It reveals also that he is, in these last days, exceedingly angry and stirred to action against the true servants of God, who keep God's commandments, and have the faith of Jesus Christ (Rev. 12:12, 17).

An Angry Devil

It is also revealed that Satan's method is *to deceive,* and that he and his demons have power to put thoughts, suggestions, or impulses into unsuspecting human minds—unless we are alertly on guard against it.

The unseen Master Competitor had instilled into

516

the hearts of associated ministers a spirit of competition against me, even before the actual start of this present Work of God in that little Firbutte schoolhouse.

The very second time in my life I ever "preached"—if those early efforts could be called that—an opposing minister had appeared, and devoted most of his sermon to an effort to tear down what I had preached in the first sermon of the day, just before his sermon. Another minister had tried to prevent my articles from appearing further in *The Bible Advocate* organ of The Church of God. A plot had been hatched by two ministers, during the Salem, Oregon, meetings, by false accusations, to discredit me and get me off the payroll of the Oregon Conference of this church.

And now, at the very start of what was to continue steadily expanding into a worldwide force directed and empowered by God, Satan tried, more viciously than ever, to stop this Work while it was still small. Surely no activity could have started smaller. The things of God, when the Eternal works through human instruments, must start the very smallest—like the grain of mustard seed. But they grow. No power, no grouping of power, whether satanic or human, can stop or prevent God's PURPOSE! Satan may be far more powerful than man. But God is incomparably more powerful than Satan, and the devil can do no more than God allows.

I suppose these opposing ministers *thought* they were doing right. There is a way that seems right to a man. God says these ways are wrong, and end in death. But a deceived man cannot comprehend that. I do not wish to impute motives. I could not read these men's hearts. But I do know that, regardless of intent, their actions sought at every turn to DESTROY what has proved, by its fruits, to be the true WORK OF GOD!

517

Today, far more powerful and formidable human powers are being marshalled against it. Today, just as the Pharisees and Sadducees *hated* the Gospel Jesus was preaching, so modern organized churchianity *hates* that same identical Gospel now pouring like an avalanche over every continent on earth, preparing the way before Christ's coming to RULE all nations with GOD'S LAWS.

Thus prophecy is being fulfilled!

The "Pork" Obsession

The opposition through the spring and summer of 1933 had come through the two ministers who had moved up to Oregon from California, Elders Sven (Sam) A. Oberg, and A. J. Ray. Mr. Ray was developing, through the summer, a sort of obsession against the eating of "unclean" meats—pork, ham, bacon, seafoods, and those labelled "unclean" in Leviticus 11. The emphasis he continually put on this doctrine, almost with vehemence, rather gave the impression that, in his eyes, the eating of pork, which came in for his greatest condemnation, was the greatest of sins.

About the time the Firbutte school meeting started, July 9, 1933, Mr. Ray began aiming his "anti-pork" guns directly at me. He demanded that I state definitely my stand on this question. I had written him a Biblical exposition of the subject, showing that it was a physical FOOD question, rather than a spiritual or Gospel subject. Unless a man broke the tenth commandment by lusting after it, the eating of pork did not violate the Ten Commandments, which constitute a SPIRITUAL law.

I quoted Mark 7:15-23, where Jesus explained that sin is a spiritual principle—that which is *coming out* of the heart of a man—evil thoughts leading to actions of adultery, murder, theft, deceit, blasphemy, pride—

518

violations of the Ten Commandments; but that *nothing from without, entering in* his mouth, defiles the man *spiritually*. Jesus was speaking of SPIRITUAL principles, and SIN as a *spiritual* offense.

I explained that I was well aware that the unclean animals were unclean even before the Flood—not suddenly pronounced so by Moses. I also explained that I was well aware of the fact they are still unclean, and unfit for the physical digestive process; that Peter's vision of the sheet was given, *not* to cleanse unclean animals, but to show Peter that he should not regard a Gentile MAN as unclean (Acts 10:28).

Also that I well understood that I Timothy 4:1-5 did not make unclean foods digestible and healthful, but only those which are "creatures of God," and "sanctified" which means SET APART "by the Word of God and prayer." The Word of God does NOT sanctify the flesh of swine, or set it apart for holy use—but rather forbids its use for food. Undoubtedly millions of people have contracted disease from eating unclean meats.

But, I pointed out, it still was a PHYSICAL violation, not a spiritual sin. The Kingdom of God (Rom. 14:17) is NOT meat and drink; but righteousness, and peace, and joy in the Holy Spirit—SPIRITUAL things.

And, I explained, I was commissioned to preach to the outside world *The Kingdom of God,* which is NOT preaching meat and drink. I explained that neither I nor any of my family ate unclean meats; that I taught all converts not to eat unclean meats, as a matter of good health. But I asked him if he could show me by the Bible where I was in error, or any Scriptural commission to preach sermons to the unconverted on the eating of pork. I told him I refused to make this food question a subject for sermons to the unconverted, unless he could show me Scriptural grounds for so doing.

He was unable to reply. Instead, he set out with renewed zeal to discredit me and get me ousted from the ministry.

There was a ministers' meeting one Sunday afternoon, about four weeks after the Firbutte school meetings had started, at the Jeans schoolhouse, four miles west of Firbutte. Both Mr. Ray and Mr. Oberg came to talk to me. They were not friendly. Mr. Ray, especially, was wrathful.

Hatching Another Plot

Then a general business meeting of the state Conference was called for the following Sunday, at the church building in Harrisburg. I was instructed not to let the Fishers or any of the people in the Firbutte or Eugene district know about it.

I well knew the purpose of the meeting. I was having, in the one-room country schoolhouse out in this sparsely settled rural district, a larger attendance than Mr. Oberg was having in the larger church building in the town of Harrisburg. I already had three or four conversions, he had none.

At this meeting with Mr. Ray and Mr. Oberg, they strenuously objected to my baptizing new converts *before* I had preached to them against pork, and had evidence they had given it up. I knew that Messrs. Oberg and Ray intended to use this against me in the business meeting, as their latest try to get me ousted from the payroll.

I must repeat that I was receiving a salary of $3 per week! The farmer members provided my family in Salem with a certain amount of food, in addition to the salary.

I have not mentioned it before, but in April, 1933, during the Salem meetings, I had started the issuing of a monthly *Bulletin* for members of the conference. It was

520

mimeographed. At Salem, I had hired the *Bulletin* printed at the local mimeograph shop. At the Fisher home, after starting the Firbutte school meetings, I had borrowed a typewriter, and the Eugene mimeograph dealer permitted me to use one of his mimeographs without charge—though I had to buy the stencils and paper. These costs were paid by the Conference treasury.

After we started the meetings west of Eugene, some people in that area had begun giving me small amounts of money occasionally, which I began to use for the expenses and mailing of this conference *Bulletin*.

A Letter to My Wife

During this week, between the conference with the two ministers and the business meeting at Harrisburg, I wrote a letter to my wife. I was temporarily discouraged, and I was exasperated and indignant at the tactics of these ministers, professing to be the ministers of Jesus Christ. I simply felt I had to blow off the steam of righteous indignation. Some of the human nature asserted itself.

I really "got it off my chest" in a 6-page single-spaced letter I typed to my wife on this borrowed typewriter. Then, after "getting it out of my system" I folded up the letter. But I did not mail it. I must have neglected to destroy it, for I have run across the letter in an old dusty file. I had refrained from sending it to my wife, for I knew she would reprove me for "griping." I felt I had "murmured" like the grumbling children of Israel being led out of Egypt under Moses.

Nevertheless, although some of this letter reflects a humanness of which I was ashamed, it does give an account, written at the moment, of the very *feeling* of the situation.

I did go up the hill to my prayer rock, and get the complaining out of my heart. There it came to my mind that I should prepare a *written* defense of my action in baptizing the four so far converted at Firbutte.

But the truth is, God *did* prosper the work started in the Eugene area. With the Church then being raised up at Eugene, He DID start a work through us which He could, AND DID, PROSPER! He is still prospering it in a mighty way!

The "All-Day Wrangle"

Mr. Fisher drove me to the business meeting at Harrisburg on Sunday morning. But he, being excluded, returned home.

Both Mr. Ray and Mr. Oberg had their fighting tempers on. This time they were determined to have me put out of the Conference. One of them preached an hour and a half or two hours in the morning—until noon—in one long tirade against me. The other followed in the afternoon session, with another two-hour denunciation of my baptizing people on repentance and faith, *before* they had been given a complete education about God's Law, and before they had been instructed against eating pork. As usual, not much Scripture was given—but emotional arguments based on human reasoning, and worked up to a high pitch.

I knew they had swayed some of the brethren into believing I had done wrong in baptizing these people according to the Bible teaching.

I then asked to be allowed to defend myself, and present the Scriptural reason why I baptized as I did, according to SCRIPTURAL TEACHING. Immediately Messrs. Oberg and Ray were on their feet in protest.

"If Brother Armstrong is allowed to speak, he will take up too much time," they argued.

"I anticipated that," I replied. "I have my reply to these long speeches by Brother Ray and Brother Oberg typewritten. I have timed it. It takes exactly 15 minutes to read it. Are you going to allow these men *hours*—all morning and afternoon—to accuse me, and then refuse me even 15 minutes to answer their accusations, and show BY THE SCRIPTURES, who is right?"

On promise I would not take up more than 15 minutes' time, I was allowed to read my defense.

In brief it was this: The natural, unconverted mind cannot understand the Bible, and is not subject to the Law of God, neither indeed can be. There is no *promise* in the Bible God will give His Holy Spirit to anyone prior to baptism—even though He did in the case of Cornelius (Acts 10:44-48). God's order is, 1) REPENT, 2) BE BAPTIZED as a symbol of FAITH in Christ, and 3) receive the Holy Spirit. Repentance means unconditional SURRENDER to God, and to God's will and His way, or whatever He commands. It means having the rebellion in the human heart against obedience to God BROKEN. It means utter submission to GOD, and *to whatever* He instructs in His Word. Those I had baptized had REPENTED.

In Matthew 28:19-20, God's order is 1) go and preach the Gospel (compare with Mark's version, same words of Jesus, Mark 16:15); 2) baptize those who REPENT and BELIEVE; then, after that, 3) teach them to observe the COMMANDMENTS. Since people cannot fully comprehend the truth of the Commandments and the teaching of the Bible until AFTER they receive the Holy Spirit, and since there is no promise God will give the Holy Spirit until after baptism, therefore I baptized them after repentance and faith, just as the Bible instructs—and *then,* after laying on hands with prayer

523

for their receiving of the Holy Spirit (Acts 8:12, 14-17; Acts 19:5-6; I Tim. 4:14; II Tim. 1:6, etc.), I taught them God's Commandments, and not to eat unclean meats, etc. Every convert I had ever baptized had obeyed all the truths as soon as I taught them. They were submissive, teachable, yielded to God, hungry for His truth. The KNOWLEDGE of the Lord is something to teach *converted* people whose minds are opened by God's Spirit. We must continually GROW in this knowledge.

The Double Cross

As soon as I finished, Mr. Fisher's car had arrived to take me back to the Firbutte schoolhouse for the evening meeting. I was forced to leave immediately. Under the circumstances, I asked the Board members and ministers if they would postpone any action until another meeting when I could be present. To this they agreed.

About half of the brethren present were very plainly on my side. As I left the church, this half rose and walked outside to assure me of their sympathy, and that they would resist any action against me.

But as soon as I and all who would support me had gone outside, Messrs. Ray and Oberg broke their word! They immediately offered a resolution that I be required, if I remained in the conference, to baptize people their way instead of the Scriptural way, and those remaining inside the church building were swayed into voting for it.

As soon as I heard of the action taken, I immediately wrote a letter cancelling the $3 per week salary, and suggesting they give it to Messrs. Oberg and Ray. I did not resign from the Conference. But I refused further salary.

My wife was in complete accord with me.

"As for me and my house," I then said firmly, "we shall serve the Eternal our God, and Him ONLY shall we serve. If MEN pay us a salary—even as small as $3 per week—we have now learned we must preach only what MEN order us to preach. If we are to WORK FOR GOD we must look to God as our EMPLOYER, AND TRUST HIM TO SUPPLY OUR EVERY MATERIAL NEED. And then," I added, "if we fail to serve Him as HE commands, He will stop our income." I wrote my wife to this effect.

It may seem like a step that required great courage to give up even a $3-a-week income, when that was all we had. Of course, a few offerings were by this time being handed to me personally—but they were usually a dollar or less, and averaged less than the $3 weekly salary. But it really did not require any real courage. My wife and I *knew* we were obeying and serving God. We *knew* He was using us. The FRUITS being borne were loud testimony of this. God had prepared us for relying solely on Him by many miraculous answers to prayer. Therefore we *knew,* in perfect faith, God would supply our need.

The Crucial Test

Actually this was the turning point of my whole life—far more crucial than I realized at the time.

This was the crossroads—the final pivotal, crucial test before the living Christ began opening the doors of mass communication through which GOD'S WORK at last could *come to life* after centuries of sleeping, and go forth in mighty power to all the world, preparing the way before Christ's return to earth as Ruler over all nations.

I did not fully realize, then, that this was a crucial turning point in the history of the Church of God. My wife and I did not leave the Church. This was God's Church. Of that I was not, then, completely sure. They

525

came *closer* to Biblical truth than any other—but I was seriously disturbed by their lack of power and accomplishment.

What actually was happening, though we did not understand it then, was that a NEW ERA was dawning in the history of the Church of God. The words of Christ are quoted in the 2nd and 3rd chapters of the Book of Revelation, foretelling the history of God's Church in seven successive eras, or phases. Events since that time have revealed this to be the era in which Christ's message is to go worldwide just before the end of this age.

Mrs. Armstrong and I continued to fellowship with these brethren. I continued to work with them, and with their ministers, as far as that was possible. The lay brethren continued to look to me for the leadership for getting the Work of God going to the world. But from that "all-day wrangle" I was independent of them and their ministers, financially. From that time I was dependent, solely, on God. We did not ask or solicit financial contributions from any except those who voluntarily became financial co-workers with us. And that has been the policy ever since.

But, from that moment when we began to rely solely on God for financial support not only, but also for guidance, direction, and results, the Work began a phenomenal yearly increase of nearly 30% for the next 35 years. It doubled in size, scope and power on the average of every 2⅔ years. It multiplied eight times every eight years—64 times in 16 years. Today it is an immensely larger and greater Work than then.

WHY has this Work leaped from virtually *nothing* to worldwide power and scope, multiplying itself continually over and over again?

Certainly I had not the ability, the resources within

myself, to have planned, directed, and accomplished anything remotely like the phenomenal development into the worldwide enterprises that is reality today.

In my twenties I had been ambitious, self-confident—conceited, *supposing* I would be doing great things. But that SELF-inflation had been punctured and utterly deflated. I had been brought down to earth with a sickening thud. I had been forced to realize, in retrospect, that I had been merely "running around in circles," unable to develop any organization or take an executive job requiring the management and supervision over others. I had come to see myself as "a hunk of burned-out junk," unworthy to be cast aside on the scrap pile.

Conversion had deflated ego and replaced SELF-assurance with the CONFIDENCE that is FAITH IN GOD!

And *this* crisis was the *turning point* when my wife and I actually, in practice, began RELYING SOLELY ON GOD—no longer on either self or MEN!

Until those two milestones had been hurdled, God could not OPEN THE BIG DOORS! The DIFFERENCE between *THIS* Work of GOD and others is *just that*—this is the Work of *GOD* and not of MEN. It started, and continued, to rely on GOD, not on MAN.

I had been changed; I had seven years of intensive Bible study and growth in Biblical KNOWLEDGE behind me. I had five years of experience in preaching. I had become quite experienced in relying on God, instead of on self or on humans. Yet, notwithstanding, as long as I was EMPLOYED by men who were over me, and who had proved to be susceptible of being influenced and swayed by false ministers, into acting *contrary* to God's Word, I was not yet free to RELY ON GOD ALONE, and to be completely FAITHFUL to His Word!

The living Christ simply *could not* start *opening*

the doors for HIS WORK, until I was free to RELY SOLELY ON HIM!

I was now FREE! This final crucial test had proved that I would be FAITHFUL to God and His Word, even at cost of giving up *everything!*

I know of evangelists who probably are sincere in supposing they are serving God—and who would *like* to be free to proclaim many truths they now hold back. They reason something like this: "If I go farther, and preach those things, I'll lose all my support. I'd be cut off from the ministry altogether. Then I could preach NOTHING. Better serve God by preaching *as much* of the Biblical truth as possible, than to be prevented from preaching anything."

They are relying on the financial support of MEN, or of organizations of men. Anyone in that predicament is the SERVANT OF MEN, and NOT OF GOD, whether he realizes it or not.

A man accosted me as I was walking along the gravel country road, between the Firbutte School and the Jeans School in the fall of 1933.

"You won't get far," he said. "You're preaching the straight truth of the Bible. That offends people. The Bible is like a sharp two-edged sword. It cuts—it reproves, corrects, rebukes—people won't support that kind of preaching! You won't get far."

But I was not relying on the support of PEOPLE. If PEOPLE paid me, I would have to *serve* people. If I were to serve GOD, I would have to look solely to GOD for support!

Of course God does work through human instruments. But I had to rely on GOD to lay it on the hearts of people to support the kind of preaching that obeys Isaiah 58:1 by crying ALOUD—lifting up my voice and showing the people their SINS!

NEVER was a more important decision made than that decision to cut loose entirely from relying on MEN, and instead, relying solely on God—not only for truth, and for direction, but also for SUPPORT! That's why we never solicit the public for contributions.

Very quickly after *that* decision the living Christ began opening doors! Very small ones at first. Then additional small ones—then a BIG door—then more and more of them!

And, to finance what He opened before me, He added, slowly, gradually, but consistently to the little family of Co-Workers who voluntarily *wanted* to have a part in GOD'S WORK—in changing hearts, changing human nature, preparing for Christ's coming to CHANGE AND *SAVE* THE *WORLD!* But I could not *invite* people to become Co-Workers. I could *welcome* them with gratitude when GOD caused them voluntarily to become Co-Workers with Christ—but until *they* took the initiative I could not ask them. No other activity on earth is operated like this—and perhaps none has grown so surely.

The First Broadcast

The six weeks' meetings in the one-room Firbutte schoolhouse came to a close on Sunday night, August 20, 1933. A total of more than 20 had come with us—but this apparently included the ten members of the Fisher and Ellis families, members of the Church before the meetings started.

The October 1, 1933 *Bulletin* carries the report that "with the Fisher and Ellis families, more than 20 signified their desire to establish a new Sabbath-keeping Church of God in this district."

In September—*very* soon after rejecting a salary and being controlled and muzzled by MEN, the living

529

Christ began opening doors for the MASS-proclaiming of His Gospel. It was then that someone brought to my attention the fact that the local radio station at Eugene, KORE, then the very smallest minimum-power of 100 watts, had a morning devotional program scheduled, but that they were having difficulty getting local ministers to conduct the program. It was free time, carried by the station as a public service sustaining program of 15 minutes, 7:45 to 8:00 a.m.

Immediately I went to the radio station. A woman secretary told me she felt sure they would be glad to have me take the program for a week. I was to call back later for the exact date.

On my second call I was assigned the week of October 9th.

October 9th was surely a great big day in my life—the day of my very first experience before a microphone, *ON THE AIR!*

I took this opportunity very seriously. It was an opportunity to speak to several HUNDRED people at once! I had never spoken to that many before.

I spent the preceding week preparing rather extensive notes and script. I might never again have such an opportunity, so I decided to strike directly at the very heart of the Gospel of the Kingdom of God. Since the Kingdom of God is based on the promises made to Abraham, I began, on Monday morning's program with the PROMISES made to Abraham.

Mike-Fright

I had heard a lot about everybody getting mike-fright the very first time on the air. I wondered if I would experience this. It was probably the most exciting adventure of my life.

On Monday morning, I arrived at the radio studio

early. The announcer did not come into the studio until ten or fifteen seconds before 7:45.

Mike-fright? Why, I thought to myself, I'm calm and cool as a cucumber!

"Listen!" I said quietly but quickly to the announcer. "I've never been on the air before. If you have any instructions, you'd better give them to me in a hurry. We have only 10 seconds!"

He looked at me disdainfully, and a little bored.

"Just stand up there in front of the mike, and start talking as soon as I announce you," he replied.

About three seconds later he announced me. While he was giving this very brief announcement on the air, I thought, "Well I don't have any mike-fright. I'm sure glad of that!"

Then, for the first time in my life, I said into the microphone:

"GREETINGS, friends!"

But suddenly something had happened! Before those two words were finished, something had hit me like a jolt! Something had started my heart pounding like a sledge-hammer! I felt myself gasping for breath! During those opening two words, MIKE-FRIGHT had seized me!

I struggled with all my might to control my hard breathing so it would not be audible over the air. It was agony, but I concentrated my mind with all the strength I had on two things—to carefully say the words of my typed script as naturally as I could, and to control my hard breathing so it did not sound.

After two or three minutes I was making good progress in gaining control. After some five minutes my breathing had returned to normal, and I was so absorbed in getting this vital message over to the largest audience of my life—even though that audience was invisible— that I forgot all about the mike-fright.

The Surprising Response

The second morning there was no mike-fright. I was beginning to gain assurance, and able to speak a little more naturally.

It must have been about Thursday morning that the announcer told me the station owner, Mr. Frank Hill, wanted to see me in his office later in the morning.

He had received several letters and telephone calls from listeners, requesting copies of my talks. I had offered no literature of any kind. I had invited no mail response.

"This is rather surprising," said Mr. Hill. "We never had any response of any kind, before, from this morning devotional program. They told me you had not invited any. Yet it has been coming. I listened in on you this morning to see what was causing it. You have an excellent radio voice, and a way of delivering your message that arouses interest and holds an audience.

"Now, Mr. Armstrong," he continued, "I want to suggest that you work out a regular Sunday morning Church service, condensed into a half hour. I'd like to put that on as a regular sustaining program—free time—but I can't do that without offering equal time to every church in town. However I will sell you the time at less than bare cost of operation, $2.50 per half hour."

And THAT suggestion from Mr. Frank Hill is what put the idea of the WORLD TOMORROW program in my mind!

Altogether 14 letters and telephone calls came in to the radio station requesting copies of the messages I had broadcast.

I thanked him, and told him I would see what I could do.

But, $2.50 every week! *WOW!* That was almost as much as my entire salary had been! And I had just previously renounced even that small salary!

Today, $2.50 per half-hour broadcast seems incredibly small. We have to pay far more than that per minute on stations today! But it seemed like an insurmountable barrier then.

Yet I knew this was GOD'S WORK, not mine. I was only an instrument. God had promised to supply every need.

God had OPENED THE DOOR OF MASS EVANGELISM! I knew He wanted us to walk through that door. I knew He would somehow supply that $2.50 every week. I knew also that we had to do our part, not lie down, do nothing, and expect God to do it without any effort from us.

I was continuing to hold meetings at the Firbutte schoolhouse, twice weekly—Sabbath afternoons and Thursday evenings.

Then, on October 21st, at the home of Mr. and Mrs. Ed Smith, just across the road from the Jeans school, 4 miles west of Firbutte, a new Church of God was organized, with Mr. E. E. Fisher as deacon, and myself as Pastor. Meetings continued from that date, three times a week, Tuesday and Thursday evenings, and Sabbath afternoons. Attendance was averaging 22. A first action of the new Church was the decision of whether to go ahead with the broadcast. These new members and the lay brethren of the Oregon Conference all approved it joyfully as an effective evangelistic activity of the Church.

So I sent out a letter to the small mailing list of members we had for *The Bulletin*. I asked for pledges from brethren to help raise this $2.50 per week. But I asked this *only* of God's people —brethren in Christ — NOT OF THE PUBLIC! In due time pledges came back for just HALF enough—about $1.35 per week! We decided we would trust God in faith for the other $1.15 per week!

It was arranged with Mr. Hill to start the new half-hour program every Sunday, in the new year, 1934.

31

The Plain Truth Is Published

S URELY NOTHING could have started
smaller. Born in adversity in the very
depths of the Depression, this Work of
God was destined to grow to worldwide power.

But I did not realize its destiny then. There were no
illusions of grandeur. It was not through any planning of
mine that the little three-point campaign then being
launched was to expand into its present global scope and
influence.

Divinely Planned

Most people are conscious only of what they see—of
that which is material. They fail to see the invisible
Hand of GOD in the working out of things.

All I had in mind, as *The World Tomorrow*
program was being planned late in 1933, was to serve
God faithfully wherever He should lead in that local
territory of Lane County, Oregon.

It is true that "where there is no vision, the people perish." But few people realize that the source of true vision is GOD. *There has been vision* behind the planning and phenomenal growth of this great work. But this is the WORK OF GOD, not of man; and the vision and the planning has been that of Jesus Christ, the active, living HEAD of this Work, not of man.

Even in earlier business experience, I had always looked ahead. It had become habitual with me to think of expanding. I had envisioned my laundry advertising service becoming national in scope. I did have a vision of this broadcasting being expanded.

But, I most certainly did not sit down, in the fall of 1933, and lay out detailed plans in my human mind for a great, powerful, earth-encircling program to reach and influence the millions in every nation. There was no thought, then, of a gigantic radio program, and a publishing enterprise, starting in Eugene, Oregon, but soon expanding to every inhabited continent; there certainly was no thought of the massive television program of today (television was virtually unheard of until some 12 years later, after the end of World War II); nor was there the remotest idea that we should, at the proper time along the way, organize and build a college for training the personnel for a rapidly growing organization.

No, this Work, in the sense of the magnitude to which it has developed, was not of *my* planning or vision. This is THE VERY WORK OF *GOD,* and the vision behind it has been that of Jesus Christ—the planning HIS! I was merely His instrument.

A Powerful DOOR Opens

What actually was happening has been written for almost 1900 years. Of course no one—least of all

536

myself—had the remotest realization of it then. Jesus Christ said: "I will build my Church." He built it for a purpose—to become God's *instrument* in carrying on GOD'S WORK fulfilling His PURPOSE here below.

God *began* the Work of His Church through Christ. Jesus said that *He Himself was powerless*—it was the POWER of God's Holy Spirit working in *His personal human body* which really did the work.

But after His ascension to heaven, that same WORK OF GOD was carried on through the Spirit of God working in the *collective body* of God's CHURCH. That is why the true Church is called "the BODY of Christ" (Eph. 1:22-23).

God sent His Message—the GOOD NEWS of His Kingdom—of His REIGN—His GOVERNMENT—His divine FAMILY—to mankind by Jesus Christ. Jesus taught this Message to His disciples, who became the apostolic leaders of His Church as it started out.

This Message from God—Christ's GOSPEL—was also recorded in the Scriptures of the New Testament. A few accepted that Message, and it *changed their lives*.

But men generally rejected the Gospel—they crucified Jesus for teaching it! Those who preached it were persecuted—martyred!

During the first 19-year time cycle of the preaching of the Gospel—A.D. 31 to A.D. 50—the Gospel was being preached primarily to Jews. The Jews had understood about the Kingdom of God. They were familiar with the prophecies of Isaiah 9:6-7, of how the Messiah would come to set up the Kingdom and government of God over all the world. What the Jews did not understand was that Jesus' First Coming, as a babe born of the virgin Mary, was to qualify, by resisting and conquering Satan, to replace Satan on the throne of the earth as well as to announce that Kingdom to appear some 1,900

537

years later. And to pay with his own life's blood for the penalty of human sins.

Consequently, the twelve apostles devoted their preaching to the Jews primarily to proving that Jesus was the prophesied Messiah. The opposition against the spread of the Church was almost wholly from within the Jewish community, denying the messiahship of Jesus. The twelve apostles were eyewitnesses to the fact that Jesus was the true Messiah. They had been with him continually for some three and a half years before His crucifixion and forty days after His crucifixion until His ascension to God's throne in heaven.

But the preaching of the Apostle Paul and other apostles to the people of the Gentile world was the very gospel Jesus Himself had proclaimed—the good news of the future coming of the Kingdom of God and world rulership of Christ. The Gentiles had not heard of the Kingdom of God before.

Somewhere around the middle of the first century, a violent controversy had begun to develop as to whether the gospel to be preached was merely a gospel about Christ—of His Messiahship and death as our Savior—or the very message God sent by Jesus as the divine messenger with the message of the true gospel (good news) of the coming Kingdom of God.

Evidence of this is the letter the Apostle Paul wrote about this time to the churches in Galatia, in which he warned that they had already turned to a different gospel (Gal. 1:6-7).

At that time a most amazing thing occurred. The history regarding the Church—its Gospel and its development—seems almost totally to have disappeared. It was as if a curtain had been rung down on all historic accounts of church history until about A.D. 150. When this curtain was lifted after that lost century, in

538

the records of church history, an altogether different gospel was being preached—merely the so-called gospel of men about the Christ, the Messenger, but not proclaiming His message.

Except for the one true Church, persecuted, falsely accused, condemned, subjected to martyrdom over the centuries by the rising great false church (Rev. 17:5), the true gospel—the good news of the coming Kingdom of God was not preached to the world for 100 19-year time-cycles. Then, in 1953, God miraculously opened the door before me of the most powerful radio station on earth—reaching all Europe and Britain, Radio Luxembourg.

Christ foretold that, *just before* the END of *this* world—*this* age—*this* man-built society rejecting the laws and ways of GOD—HIS very *same* Gospel of God's KINGDOM "shall be preached" (Matt. 24:14) and also *published* (Mark 13:10) "in all the world for a witness unto all nations."

In the light of fast-developing, world-encircling events, it became apparent that what was actually happening in 1934 was precisely this: Jesus Christ was opening the gigantic mass-media DOOR of radio and the printing press for the proclaiming of His same original GOSPEL to all the world!

On that tiny-powered radio station KORE—in that infant mimeographed *Plain Truth*—was going out an *astonishing* Message! Just as the public, 1,900 years before, had been *astonished* at Christ's Gospel (Mark 1:14-15,22), so were those who began to hear this SAME GOSPEL in 1934. It was *so utterly different* from what had been palmed off as "Christianity."

The "Three-Point" Campaign

And so it was, that when Mr. Frank Hill, owner of

KORE, urged me to produce a half-hour Sunday program, consisting of a regular church service condensed into a half hour, using radio techniques, that I went to work on the idea with zest and enthusiasm.

This seemed BIG, compared to past activities. I saw in it immediately an opportunity to reach many more people with God's TRUTH.

Not only did I set out with a will to produce the radio program, but I realized there must be follow-up (and I do not mean a money-soliciting follow-up) if this new effort were to be resultful.

Immediately the idea came of realizing, at last, the dream I had cherished since 1927—the publication of a magazine, to be called *The Plain Truth*. Back in 1927 I had made up an entire "dummy" of this proposed magazine. I had even written articles for it. I even had a professional letter artist design a front cover idea in 1927—and I had tried designing one myself. But we had never had the "wherewithal" to start publishing a magazine.

This ambition to publish *The Plain Truth* was the natural outgrowth of earlier business experience. Much of my 20 years of advertising experience had been spent in the class magazine field.

Now, at last, I realized that this magazine was a *"must"* as a follow-up for the radio broadcast. Yet we were no more able, financially, than we had been in 1927.

Necessity is the mother of invention. If we could not afford to publish a high-quality, professional-appearing magazine, I would simply convert the mimeographed "BULLETIN" I had been issuing for our scattered church brethren in the Willamette Valley into *The Plain Truth*.

My idea for this magazine, from the start, had been

to publish a magazine, *not* for church members, but for the general public —the unconverted and unchurched— an evangelistic-type publication to bring to the world God's TRUTH—making it PLAIN!

So now, even if it had to start with about 250 copies done by hand on a mimeograph, I would start it! Like the grain of mustard seed, it started, very possibly, the smallest of magazines. But it has grown into a professional-appearing 32-page magazine of over 8,000,000 circulation.

Also I saw at once that the broadcasts should be followed up by continued public evangelistic services.

Therefore, I wrote to the small number of members on the mailing list I had—perhaps less than 50—the news of the forthcoming THREE-POINT CAMPAIGN: (1) The half-hour Sunday radio program; (2) the new mimeographed magazine for interested listeners, *The Plain Truth,* and (3) personal public meetings.

The broadcast, and idea of the Three-Point Campaign, had been completely approved, of course, by the brethren of the Church.

"ON THE AIR!"

On the first Sunday morning in the new year, 1934, precisely at 10 a.m., we were ON THE AIR. The program has been continuously on the air, without missing a single week, ever since.

Mr. Hill had suggested that we produce a regular Sunday morning church service, condensed into 30 minutes. I had planned it according to his suggestion. In our new local church, then meeting out at the Jeans school house, 12 miles west of Eugene, we had a young couple, Claude and Velma Ellis. Claude was a very good tenor. His wife Velma sang alto. They sang duets. They supplied the music.

I do not remember the exact format of the program, as it started, during those first few months. Very soon the duet was replaced with a mixed quartette, with our daughter Beverly singing soprano, Mrs. Armstrong alto, Claude Ellis tenor, and Alfred Freeze bass, with Mrs. Ellis at the piano.

As the program started out it was called the "Radio Church of God." It was, indeed, a church service on the air. There has been a gradual evolution in the format of the program. We were to learn, later, that an abbreviated church service appeals only to a very few church-going people, who may want to listen in on a church service—or to "attend church" without leaving their homes. It attracts only what is called the "religious audience." Through the years the program changed, until it became a program pointed toward the NON-churchgoing public—people who are not religious and may never attend church.

Gradually, we learned that it was the MESSAGE which attracted listeners. Radio station managers began to tell us that we really had a SPEECH-type program, and a Message and type of speech which would attract and hold a bigger audience than music.

But back, now, to January, 1934.

The Plain Truth's Modest Bow

Just as the 15-minute morning devotional programs had brought an unexpected mail response, so did the half-hour regular program of our own. Only it now brought a larger response. I began with the first broadcast, that first Sunday in 1934, inviting listeners to write in for the new magazine, *The Plain Truth.*

At the same time I began work on producing Volume I and Number 1 of this magazine of my dreams. I did not even have a "scope" for hand-lettering the

542

headlines. I was still living with the Fishers on their farm seven miles west of Eugene—my wife and children still at the Hall Street house in Salem. I had to hold the mimeograph stencils up against a window, and try to cut the headlines with my right hand while I tried to hold the stencil without slipping against the window pane with my left. The headlines were a little shaky. That first issue of *The Plain Truth* was somewhat amateurish, and homemade looking. Probably no one but myself would have dignified it by calling it a "magazine."

No publication could have had a more humble, or a smaller start. But it was a start. It grew. It was improved, as scanty funds permitted. It took years before we were able to have it printed on a printing press. But through the years it has been instrumental in making drastic *changes* in thousands of lives!

It was some time later, in 1934, that a few special offerings made it possible for us to purchase a very old, used, outdated Neostyle. It was predecessor to the mimeograph. It was entirely hand operated. The sheets of paper had to be fed into it one at a time by hand. There was *nothing* automatic about it. It cost $10. We had also finally been able, before or shortly after the first issue of *The Plain Truth*, to raise enough money to purchase a secondhand typewriter for $10.

And so finally *The Plain Truth*, homemade at Fishers' farm on the mimeograph I was permitted to use at the office of the local mimeograph dealer, but containing priceless plain TRUTH, made its humble bow to the world February 1, 1934. I have no record of the exact "press run" of that first edition, but it was in the neighborhood of 250 copies. I think we still have one copy somewhere in some old files.

Looking back now, we are a little amazed to see how

far the broadcast and *The Plain Truth* have gone since then. That "grain of mustard seed" is multiplying mightily under the guiding power of God!

32

Campaign Gets Under Way—Despite Opposition

"YOU'LL never get far, Mr. Armstrong," said a resident of the Jeans neighborhood whom I met on the roadside one day. It was during the time I was holding three meetings a week at the Jeans school house, 12 miles west of Eugene, Oregon. This followed the six weeks' meetings at Firbutte school and formation of the new local Church of God which met at the Jeans school.

"Why do you say that?" I asked.

"Because you are preaching exactly what the Bible says. The Bible corrects and reproves people. People don't want to be told they are wrong. People don't like correction. What you preach is too strong for them. People will never support it."

I smiled.

"If I looked to *people* for support, I would have to preach what people want to hear," I replied. "I have learned that by experience. But I was not called to this ministry by *people*. I was not taught the Gospel I preach by people. *People* did not put me in the ministry—Jesus Christ did. I am not employed by *people,* or any organization of men. I have been called, and sent with His Gospel, by Jesus Christ. He is my employer. I rely on HIM for support. He has given me the written promise that He will supply all my NEED. I believe He is able, and will do it!"

The man stared at me incredulously. He was speechless.

But now, nearly 40 years later, I can report that Jesus Christ *did* support His work through His servant. He did supply its needs (almost infinitesimal at first, increasing gradually, yet always increasing). True, God works through human instruments. He has moved on the hearts of those He could make willing to become Co-Workers with Him and with me in this work, now grown great and world-encompassing.

Eugene Campaign Starts

During the July-August meetings at the Firbutte school, and on through the winter with the new local church continuing meetings at the Jeans school house, 12 miles west of Eugene, my wife and children had remained in Salem. I had lived with the Elmer Fishers on their farm seven miles west of Eugene.

But by late March I had rented a house on West 4th. I think the rent was about $7 per month. I had arranged for meetings to start in the Old Masonic Temple on Seventh Avenue. Then one evening my wife and children arrived in Eugene with our household furniture and furnishings on Ed Smith's truck. That night we arranged for my family to sleep on mattresses on the second floor of the Old Masonic Hall.

The year and three months spent in Astoria,

averaging perhaps less than five hours sleep per night—with one ordeal of three days and three nights with no sleep—had left me in a condition which made it difficult to get to sleep at night. On this particular night, I had procured barbiturate sleeping pills, desperate for a full night's sound sleep. At this time these sleeping pills did not require a doctor's prescription. I shall never forget the experience. It was my first and last with the sleeping pills.

I had a good full night's sleep, all right. But it was a peculiar sensation. It was not a *natural*, but an induced sleep. It left me frightened. As I had sworn off chewing tobacco at age five, I now swore off barbiturate sleep-inducing forever.

A few busy days followed, cleaning up this virtually abandoned Old Masonic Temple auditorium. Beside my wife and children, Mr. and Mrs. Fisher, and one or two others in the Church joined in the cleanup.

The "Three-Point Campaign" was ready to leap ahead on all three points. The broadcast had started the first Sunday in January, 1934. *The Plain Truth*, mimeographed, made its first appearance February 1st. And now, the first of April, the meetings were started in downtown Eugene, in the old Masonic Temple.

As mentioned before, meetings still were being held three times a week out at Jeans school house—Tuesday and Thursday nights and Sabbath mornings. Consequently the meetings in downtown Eugene were held on Sunday, Wednesday and Friday nights. This was our first experiment in holding public evangelistic meetings three times a week. These meetings were carried on for five and a half months.

We learned by this experience that meetings held only three times a week are not as fruitful as meetings held consecutively six times a week.

Later, we were to learn that the same is true in broadcasting. A once-a-week broadcast, or even three times a week, does not produce results comparable to daily broadcasting six or seven times a week.

For this Eugene campaign I mimeographed handbills and announced it on the radio program. An attendance of approximately 100 was maintained up until the final two weeks. But this was much lower than later campaigns with consecutive six-nights-a-week services.

Here, as in the Salem meetings with Elder Oberg, the whooping, shouting, aggressive "pentecostal" people were much in evidence at the beginning. But by this time I had learned that they were primarily concerned with working up an emotional demonstration. They were not interested in learning Biblical TRUTH, obeying God's commands, and yielding their lives to be *changed* and transformed according to God's Word by a living Christ who does His saving work within us. A few vigorous sermons on *obedience* to God, and on overcoming, and living by every Word of God soon discouraged them. Most of them stopped coming.

"Pentecostal" Incidents

A large "pentecostal" church carried a full hour and a half broadcast on KORE of their Sunday night service. During one of these broadcasted services, their pastor said that if any of their members desired to visit any other church it would be quite all right, with the exception of the services I was holding. But he warned them against attending our meetings.

Shortly after we had moved into the house on West Fourth Avenue, three of the "pentecostal" people who had attended the tent meetings held in 1931 by Elder

Taylor and me came to our home. They were a middle-aged husband and wife and the sister of one of them. One of the women claimed to have a disease or sickness of some kind. They asked me to anoint this woman and pray for her healing.

I invited them into the house.

"Why," I asked, "when you people claim to have the baptism of the Holy Spirit and say that I have not—when you claim to be on a much higher spiritual plane than I—when your pastor and your church denounce me, and say I am not God's minister—when you claim that your 'pentecostal' preacher has God's spirit and power and that I have not—WHY do you come to me for anointing and healing instead of your own pastor?"

"Hmm!" they snorted, "who'd we go to over *there?*"

"Well," I pursued a little further, "in I John 3:22 God says that whatever we ask we receive of Him *because* we keep His commandments and do those things that are pleasing in His sight. This obedience to God's commandments is a distinct *condition* to being healed. You people do *not* obey God's commandments, although you attended our tent meetings in 1931 almost every night for six weeks, and you heard the truth about this made very plain. Now either you are deliberatly rebelling, and refusing to obey God, or else you have been so blinded in your carnality that somehow the truth never really got through to you although we made it very plain—and you just never did really *see* it. Which is it?"

"I guess we just didn't see it, brother," came the answer.

"All right," I said. "I can't read your mind and heart as God can. I have to take you at your word. Since you claim you have not come to consciously understand the truth, and have not knowingly rebelled and disobeyed, I will anoint you."

The minute I began to pray all three, true to "pentecostal" heathen and unscriptural custom, began to try to drown out my voice by their loud expressions of "O praise you, Jesus! HALLELUJAH! Glory to God!" etc. etc., in a babylon of noisy confusion. Then immediately the woman I was anointing went into a wild, loud, uncontrolled laugh. This seemed to be a new fad at the time among "pentecostals" in Oregon. They called it "the holy laugh."

Instantly I put my hands on her head, and in a loud voice called on God, by authority of Jesus Christ, to SILENCE this work of Satan, and cast the demon spirits out of my home!

Instantly, as if struck by a bolt of lightning, the woman's hysterical unnatural laughter was silenced, as were the shoutings of the other two. All was quiet.

They rose to their feet.

"Well, anyway," sneered the supposedly "ill" woman. "I'm healed, *so there!*" And quickly they left the house.

On another occasion a member of this "pentecostal" church came running up to me on a Eugene street one Sunday morning.

"We've had a dozen men out looking everywhere for you," he gasped breathlessly. "Please come quick! Our pastor's wife fell over backward 'under the power' during prayer, and she's unconscious, and we can't revive her. Our pastor sent us out scouring the town to find you. Please come and pray for her, that she will revive. We're afraid she is dying!"

I hurried over to this "pentecostal" church. There they were, probably four or five hundred of them, wringing their hands in despair, all crying out in confusion for God to revive the stricken woman.

I called out in a loud voice of authority for them all to be quiet. Then in very brief and few words I asked God to have mercy on their foolish heathenism, and revive this woman. I leaned down, laid my hands on her, and she revived. I took her by the hand and lifted her up, and then strode out of their church while an awed silence reigned.

I have never been quite able to figure out why so many, through the years, who have denounced me and claimed to be spiritually superior themselves, have come to me for prayer when they needed someone close enough to God that a prayer would be answered.

Visiting Jail

During the meetings in the old Masonic Temple, someone told me of a man in the county jail who requested that I visit him. The prisoner was the "black sheep" brother of a very respectable man.

This prisoner seemed to welcome my visit. He was scheduled to be released from jail in a couple of days, and promised to attend the services. Two nights later he came to the meeting, with a girl he introduced as his wife.

As I believe has been mentioned previously, in those days I followed the evangelistic custom of giving "altar calls." It was one of those things I thoughtlessly took for granted without checking for proof of any Biblical or divine origin. All of us have carelessly *assumed*, taken for granted, accepted and followed more customs, ideas and ways than we realize. As the years have raced by, I have learned to be much more careful to check and *prove* all beliefs and practices. Later, when I researched again over the ministry of Jesus, of Peter,

551

Paul, and the other apostles and evangelists of the New Testament, it became clear that they never practiced or instituted any such custom. So we dropped it immediately.

But at this time I was still learning, and giving the usual evangelical altar calls. And this young man and woman both came up. They appeared quite repentant. I spent some time with them afterward. They exhibited a spirit of willingness to obey God completely, and to embark on a new life of overcoming through faith in Christ, living by every word of the Bible. Next day I baptized them.

But I learned a serious lesson through this experience. Later we discovered that these two were not married. Actually they had gone through a ceremony of marriage, but it was bigamy. The girl had previously married another man in another state, from whom she had not been divorced. She had a little two- or three-year-old daughter whose father was a third man to whom she had never been married. From that time we have been very careful to check the marriage, divorce, and remarriage status of all candidates for baptism. God intended that we learn by experience, beside direct instruction.

I told this girl she would have to leave this man.

"Well," she replied, "I will, then, as soon as I can get a job."

"No," I said firmly, "you must leave him *now!*"

"But I can't leave him now," she protested. "I have no other place to go."

"You come along with us, then," I insisted. "Mrs. Armstrong will put you in our spare bedroom for tonight, and tomorrow we will help you make permanent arrangements."

She was a weakling, and so was this man. So she

gave in to our firm insistence. Next morning Mrs. Armstrong went into her room to call her to breakfast. The bed was empty. The window was open. The girl had climbed out the window and gone back to "her man."

However, they were soon forcibly separated again. They had bought furniture and furnishings for a cheap rented house on contract at a local furniture store. This young man had then sold much of it for cash, and failed to pay his installments at the store.

Helping a Weakling

This fellow was in jail again. He called to me for help. On visiting him again in jail I learned what had happened. He promised to be good this time, if only I'd get him out. The furniture merchant said he understood the fellow had a brother of some means.

"If you will go to his brother and get him to pay up the furniture bill, we will withdraw the charges," said the furniture merchant. "We don't want to be hard on the boy. We are business men. We only want our money."

I had no automobile in those days, but I traveled some distance to see the fellow's brother.

"Mr. Armstrong," he said after I explained the situation, "you may think I am a hardhearted brother, but I'm not. I'm going to do what I know is best for my brother's own good. If I pay this and get him out of jail, it wouldn't be thirty days until he would be back in jail again. My brother hasn't had enough punishment to learn his lesson yet. I think he needs this thirty days in jail to think it over."

He did think it over, and managed to keep out of jail for a year or so, after which I lost contact with him. But he and the girl were too weak to remain apart. They quarreled and fought when together, but they could not resist being together.

Rejecting all advice and counsel from me, the girl obtained a divorce from her first husband, and then had a justice-of-the-peace second wedding with this ne'er-do-well fellow, which at least legalized their adulterous living in the sight of man's law.

Whatever finally became of them I do not know. Mrs. Armstrong and I spent a lot of time trying to help them get straightened out, but they were the type Jesus spoke of in Luke 8:13 in the parable of the sower. They listened to and received the Word of God gladly, but had no "root" or backbone of character, and as soon as temptation came along were too weak to resist.

The quotation "God helps them that help themselves" is not found in the Bible, as many believe, but is a saying of Benjamin Franklin. Yet it does express a Christian principle. Long ago I learned that I cannot carry others into the Kingdom of God on my shoulders, or drag them in. I can only point the way, proclaim the truth, give counsel and advice, aid in many material ways, and pray for others. I can give aid and help—but each must stand on his own feet before God, and by strong motivation yield to allow God to transform him and mold him into God's own holy character. God does it by the power of His Holy Spirit. But we also have our part in denying ourselves, in overcoming, and in DOING! It is the DOERS, not those who hear only, who shall enter finally into His Kingdom (Rom. 2:13).

Nevertheless, this experience I have just related did cause a deal of reflection and study of the Bible to inquire *how* God is going to deal with human weaklings such as these. We find the answer in the parable of the pounds, and the parable of the talents.

In the parable of the pounds all ten of Christ's servants appear to have had equal ability, and each was given an equal portion from God at the start. The one

554

who by overcoming and growth in grace and knowledge of our Lord multiplied what he started with ten times was given the reward of ruling over ten cities. He who multiplied five times, over five cities.

But in the parable of the talents (Matthew 25:14-30) God gave to each, at the start of his Christian life, *according to his natural ability.* To one He gave five talents, to another two, and to another only one—according to the natural ability of each. The man with five talents doubled his spiritual stock-in-trade. Likewise, although the man with two produced less in number than the one with five, he also *doubled* what he started with. He did as well, *in proportion to his ability!*

Consequently we find it revealed that to whom much is given, much is required. To whom little is given, less is required. In other words, God judges each individual *according to how well he overcomes, yields, develops and grows, according to what he has to do with!*

This unfortunate couple of weaklings were not born with as much intelligence and strength of character (potentially) as many others. Consequently God does not require as much of them. But He *does* require of them as much effort *in proportion* to ability! We do have our part in the developing of the Christian life and character.

So-Called "Bible Organization"

During these late winter and spring months of 1934 the opposition of Elders Ray and Oberg did not cease. I had rejected receiving further the $3 weekly "salary" from the Oregon State Conference after the memorable "All-Day Wrangle" meeting in early August, 1933. But this alone did not appease their wrath against me.

At the biannual General Conference meeting of the Church at Stanberry, Missouri, which probably was held in August, 1933, Elder Andrew N. Dugger had lost his previous iron control of the church by one vote. Thereupon Mr. Dugger promptly bolted the Conference and organized a competing "Church of God" under what he termed "the Bible form of organization."

He managed to induce half or more of the ministers in the church to join him in this new "Organization," on the argument that they were now re-establishing the Bible form of organization. Among those joining with him were Elder C. O. Dodd of Salem, West Virginia, an Elder McMicken, Elder Alexander of Kansas, Elder Severson, and Otto Haeber of Hawthorne, California whom I knew as a good friend. Mr. Haeber had not, I believe, up to this time been ordained as an elder but was an influential member.

Mr. Dugger had been accused of dictatorship, bossism, and even crookedness. I had not as yet met him, and did not judge. Nevertheless his new form of organization tended to divert criticism. He claimed the original Twelve Apostles were intended to form the top governing permanent Board of the Church as Christ organized it. He called this Board "the Twelve." Mr. Alexander, Mr. Haeber, and Mr. McMicken, I believe, were put on the "Board of the Twelve" (although there never were twelve). But Mr. Dugger kept his own name off of that supposedly governing Board, thus avoiding the accusation that he was "running things" as the head.

Next, taking the "seventy" which Jesus appointed for a one-time special mission (Luke 10), Mr. Dugger, with Mr. Dodd and Mr. McMicken, set up "The Board of the Seventy" leading ministers. On this Board they appointed as many names as they could. There never were seventy, however. On this Board they had placed my name, and also those of Elders Oberg and Ray of Oregon. Elder Severson was, I believe, also on that "Board."

Finally, noting that the early apostles had appointed seven deacons to take care of the "business" of waiting on tables and serving proselyte widows (Acts 6:1-4), Mr. Dugger devised a Board of Seven to handle the BUSINESS of the Church, making himself Chairman of that Board. The difference was that the early Apostles' seven deacons merely relieved the Apostles from the physical "business" of waiting on tables, serving food, and otherwise serving physical needs of widows; while Mr. Dugger's "Board of Seven" handled all Church *income and finances!* Therefore it actually carried all the real power to govern. Mr. Dugger had control over the salaries of "the Twelve." The word "business" appears in the King James translation. But both the RSV and Moffatt translations have "duty."

Persecution Continues

This "Bible form of Organization" appealed to most of our brethren in the Willamette Valley of Oregon. There were still two factions in the valley—one of them still loyal to "Stanberry" as it was called, the other—which had incorporated as the Oregon Conference—being somewhat enamored of the new "Organization."

Mr. Dugger claimed "World Headquarters" as Jerusalem, Palestine, with United States Headquarters at Salem, West Virginia. Thus this became known as the "Salem church."

In those days one Biblical subject I was completely befogged on was the matter of church organization and government. I *knew* the "Stanberry" pattern of a General Conference was not scriptural. I *knew* that voting by human preference was unscriptural. I saw plainly that Christ *chose* His Apostles—that they and the evangelists, in turn, chose and ordained elders in local churches. Consequently in the church now meeting at Jeans school house, since I was the evangelist God used in raising up this church, I chose and appointed Mr. Elmer E. Fisher as deacon, remaining as Pastor myself.

But just what truly was the Biblical form of organization I did *not* at that time see clearly. I was really confused on the question. I had grave misgivings about Mr. Dugger's professed "Bible form" of organization. I talked it over with Mr. and Mrs. Fisher, Mr. Claude Ellis, and others of our Church at Jeans. Mr. Fisher was not "sold" on it, either. He advised going slow.

Meanwhile Messrs. Ray and Oberg were exerting every effort to urge the Oregon Conference to go in with, and to keep me out of, the new "Organization." One of the basic doctrinal points of the "Salem" organization was abstaining from "pork" and observing rigidly the food law of the "clean and unclean" of Leviticus 11. Mr. Ray now tried to discredit me with the new "Organization" with his anti-pork argument.

Consequently, Mr. Fisher, Mr. Ellis, the other members at Jeans and I decided we would simply leave the answer in God's hands. We would pray and ask God to show us in this manner: If the "Salem" re-organization did accept me as "one of the 70" in spite of the opposition of Messrs. Ray and Oberg, we would go in. Otherwise we would remain independent.

The Test

For some months the status quo remained. Neither acceptance nor rejection came from "Salem." Then one

558

day Otto Haeber came to the office I had set up in an anteroom in the old Masonic Temple, accompanied by Elder Alexander from Kansas.

I had never met Mr. Alexander before. But since I had heard a great deal about him, and read much about him in the Church paper, the *Bible Advocate,* I was happy to meet him. I was steering the conversation along the general lines of getting acquainted, asking about the work in Kansas and general conversation.

Suddenly Mr. Haeber interrupted, rather sternly.

"Mr. Armstrong," he said abruptly, "apparently you do not quite grasp the importance of this meeting. *Mr. Alexander is one of 'the Twelve!'* Mr. Alexander is a very important man! His time shouldn't be wasted by mere friendly conversation. Mr. Alexander is the man who has the power to bring about your acceptance on the Board of the Seventy, if you can satisfy him about your stand on the 'clean and the unclean' meat question."

I had known many important men in the business world, and I had not sensed anything in Mr. Alexander's appearance or personality that was overawing.

"Well!" I exclaimed. "I had not realized! I beg your pardon for wasting your valuable time. I will tell you my stand on this question in one or two minutes.

"Point number one: I read in Scripture that *sin* is the transgression of the Law. In Romans 7 Paul says the law it is sin to transgress is *spiritual*—a spiritual, not a physical law. Point two: Jesus Christ, speaking of spiritual defilement in Mark 7, says that physical food entering a man's stomach from without cannot defile him *spiritually,* but that which comes from within, out of the heart—adulteries, murders, thefts, covetousness—*transgressions of the Ten Commandments*—defile the man *spiritually.* Point three: The 'clean and

559

unclean' laws of Leviticus 11 are *physical,* not spiritual laws.

"Point four: Christ preached the Gospel of the Kingdom of God. He commanded the Apostles, and us today, to preach the KINGDOM *of God.* That is the GOSPEL I am commanded to preach. Point five: Paul says plainly in Romans 14 that the Kingdom of God is *not* meat and drink, but righteousness, which is obedience to God's Law.

"Point six: Therefore I do not *preach* to the unconverted meat and drink because it is not the Gospel. *But,* on the other hand, the physical body *is* the 'temple of the Holy Spirit,' and we are taught not to defile it, even *physically.*

"Finally, point seven: I realize fully that there were both the clean and unclean animals long before Mosaic Law—even prior to the Flood—and therefore from creation. God did not create the unclean animals for food. Just as many plants and weeds are poison and not food, so unclean animals were not made to digest properly or nourish the human body. They are not "creatures of God" intended for food. They are not sanctified—or set apart—by the Word of God. Peter's vision of the unclean animals in the sheet was given, it is distinctly stated in Acts 10, to show him that he should not call any *man* unclean—not to make unclean animals clean. Therefore I do *teach* every convert and every church member that they should not eat the unclean meats. We do not eat them in our home. Not one of our church members—not one of my converts—is eating unclean meats. But I teach it as a *physical* matter of health, not as a spiritual matter of the true Gospel.

"That, in few words, Elder Alexander, is what God's Word *says* and teaches and what I believe. Now

560

I'm very sorry I wasted your valuable time, and since it is so valuable, I shall not take up more of it. Good day, gentlemen."

And I opened the door.

Actually, I snapped out this explanation of my stand probably at a faster pace than most readers have been able to read it. It left Mr. Alexander a little bewildered. But he could not deny, refute, nor question a word of my explanation.

"Well, Mr. Armstrong," he managed to say as they were leaving, "it seems to me you believe the same way the church does, only you may have a little different way of stating it."

A short time later, I learned that they did consider me as one of "the Seventy."

Co-Operating — Not Joining

Thus we of the Church of God meeting at the Jeans school-house, along with our brethren of the Oregon Conference, decided to go along with it in co-operation, but we of the new local church near Eugene did not "join" in the sense of becoming an integral part of it.

I then began to send in regular minister's reports. We co-operated fully as brethren in Christ. But I did not accept salary or expense money from them. None in our local church put himself under their authority. We kept ourselves free to obey God as set forth in the Scriptures, should any differences come up. And they did later come up!

After the experience of being ordered to baptize contrary to the Scriptures and the renouncing of the $3 weekly "salary," we were firm never again to be placed in a position where we might have to obey men rather than God.

561

Result of Eugene Meetings

The meetings continued for two months in the second-floor hall of the Old Masonic Temple, just off the main street, Willamette, on West Seventh Avenue. But Mr. Chambers, owner of the building, had made arrangements for remodeling and permanent occupancy of the hall beginning June 1st. I managed to rent a hall on the second floor, on the east side of Willamette Street between Seventh and Eighth, beginning June 1st. Meetings continued there for three and a half months, closing the middle of September.

The downtown meetings had continued in Eugene five and a half months. Results actually were less than in other five or six weeks' campaigns where services were held six nights a week. Definitely we learned that holding meetings three times a week on non-consecutive nights does not build up or sustain an interest comparable to every-night services. This was an important lesson.

Nevertheless, there was a harvest. There always was a harvest. That was the main reason for the opposition from the other ministers. No one in the Church of whom I could inquire knew of any "fruit" whatsoever having been borne at any time by any of the other ministers then in the Church. Their jealousy, antagonism, competitive spirit, opposition against the only work God was blessing, eloquently testified to the reason—carnality—lack of real conversion and yieldedness to God. God can use only those who have surrendered to become instruments in His Hands.

I do not remember now how many had appeared to have repented, and believed, and how many had been baptized during and at the end of these meetings. It seems it was around ten to fifteen. But several of these were of the type Jesus referred to in His parable of the sower: the largest number compared to the wayside. Jesus Christ sowed the "seed"—the Word of God—by my voice. There were the ones who came and heard, but did not understand nor believe; and Satan took the truths they heard out of their hearts, *lest* they should believe and be saved (Luke 8:12). Those stopped attending before the close of the meetings. Some compared to the stony ground, including the young man and woman already mentioned. They received Christ's Gospel with gladness and joy—but had no depth of character, and endured only for a while. Others compared to the ground covered with thorns—the cares of this world and desire for worldly amusements caused them to drop out.

Nevertheless, even though few of those brought in during those meetings proved to be the "good ground" which endured, there were some ten or fifteen additional ones making the start of a Christian life. A new Sabbath School was organized for these, meeting at our home on West Fourth Avenue on Sabbath afternoons. The Sabbath morning services continued out at Jeans School house. Often several from there came in to Eugene for the afternoon class at our home.

33

Early Evangelistic Campaigns—the Trials and Tests

THE ACTIVITY that was destined to expand steadily into worldwide power and scope was now fast getting under way. No activity could have started smaller. None could have had a more humble and unpromising beginning.

But, with an insignificant $1.35 per week pledge for the radio broadcast, and what appeared then as a monumental additional $1.15 per week to be received purely on faith, The Radio Church of God had started on the air the first Sunday in 1934. It was the very bottom of the great depression.

Faith was rewarded, however, and the other $1.15 per week always came, sometimes only a half hour before broadcast time.

I had devoted some years to experience on newspapers and national publications. Now, at last, my dreams of a "magazine of understanding" making PLAIN the revealed TRUTH of the Bible—to be made available to all who requested it without price to them—had become a reality. Promptly on February 1, 1934, Volume I and Number 1 of *The Plain Truth* was published, or should I say "published"?

No publication ever made a more humble entrance before the public.

After the first issue had been mimeographed, through courtesy of the local A. B. Dick Company dealer on one of his mimeographs, we had managed to purchase—for $10, I believe—an old second-hand "neostyle"—ancestor of the mimeograph. It was entirely hand-operated, hand-cranked, hand-fed. Surely it was the most humble of printing presses! For the next few years *The Plain Truth* was to be run off on this ancient neostyle, before we could afford a secondhand mimeograph—and then some time longer before we could afford to have it printed.

The "Three-Point Campaign" had at last gotten fully under way with the downtown Eugene evangelistic meetings. These meetings had continued five and one-half months until mid-September.

Now, mid-September, plans were under way for another campaign.

Alvadore Next

Some 12 to 15 miles northwest of Eugene was a little community of Alvadore. It was not even a village. There was probably only one full general store. But there was a two-story school house. The Alvadore school consisted of two classrooms on the ground floor, and an assembly hall upstairs.

Mr. Elmer Fisher and I felt this was the site for the next campaign. We were able to engage the use of the assembly hall—practically without cost.

565

I do not now remember whether these meetings were conducted over a period of six, or eight, weeks. The only record now immediately available to me affirms that the campaign started in November, 1934, and ended in January, 1935. Probably we started in late November and finished in early or mid-January.

At any rate we had learned the sober lesson about holding services three times a week. In Alvadore we were back on the six-nights-a-week schedule.

Attendance was good. Interest was very good. By this time I was gaining in speaking ability due to the experience of speaking virtually six to eight times a week since July, 1933.

Learning to Speak Publicly

One learns to speak before the public by speaking. I remember how one asked Elbert Hubbard how he learned to write. He replied that he learned to write by writing. A pianist learns to play the piano by playing the piano—eight hours a day, *if* one is to become a concert pianist.

If there was anything I had never expected to become, it was a preacher or an evangelist. I have explained early in this autobiography how at age 18 I had put myself through a self-analysis with the book titled *Choosing a Vocation*. This self-conducted test indicated that I had an analytical mind, an intellectual curiosity, a desire to UNDERSTAND, and some natural aptitude for writing. The test pointed to the advertising profession. Those years of experience in advertising and news-gathering, editorial writing, and the writing of magazine articles, had prepared me for the calling to God's ministry.

But it was two or three years after conversion before I realized I was called to preach. I have just come across a carbon copy of a letter that I had written, dated July 11, 1928—even before our first son was born—to Mr. A. N. Dugger, at that time principal leader of the Church of God, at Stanberry, Missouri. It shows that at that time a little more than a year after my conversion, I did apparently realize that God was calling me for some definite mission, for which I was being prepared. I did not know what it was to be. I realized I was not yet ready. And I supposed, at that time, that it would be in the field of writing, not speaking. I feel that many who are reading this life history may find a few excerpts from that letter interesting.

Elder Dugger had invited me to join their church. I have explained previously that I never did formally join it. Here are portions of that letter:

"I appreciate your kind invitation to affiliate actively with the Church of God organization. Elder Stith approached me on the subject, also. . . .

"However, for the immediate present, until further developments, I do not feel led to join any organization, and feel that I should not take matters into my own hands, or rush, or hurry. I believe the Lord is dealing with me, preparing me for a very active and definite calling and mission, and that until matters have developed further I should do as Jesus commanded the Apostles—tarrying until I have received full preparation and power. . . . I feel it is absolutely necessary that we should permit ourselves to be led by the Holy Spirit, and not try to launch into something half prepared, by taking matters into our own hands before we are *sure* it is the will of the Lord. I do not know exactly, yet, what my mission or calling is to be, or what the method of carrying it out is to be. Unquestionably it will require organized effort, rather than attempting to carry out the mission alone and unaided.

Writing — Not Speaking

"I can say this much—I feel that it is along the line of writing rather than oral speaking or preaching.

"I believe the Lord bestows gifts and callings upon men mightily according to their natural talents and experience, giving spiritual gifts along these same lines. . . .

"My whole business experience has been along the lines of investigating, analyzing, and gaining an understanding of business problems and rectifying the situations, and in writing. Whatever natural talent I have is along those lines. I know something about public speaking, for I have studied textbooks on it, had contacts with professors of public speaking at the Universities of Illinois and Michigan, who are authors of the texts used in most colleges, and coached a brother-in-law into winning a big oratorical contest. . . . But he had the voice, and other necessary personal attributes for public speaking.

"If I am being given any of the gifts, it is that of UNDERSTANDING of the truth of scripture. . . . But I am not fully prepared as yet."

Little did I realize then that God could, and would, use my voice to reach worldwide audiences of multiple millions every week. But I did "sense," somehow, that God was preparing me for some definite mission and He had given me sufficient insight to realize that I did not yet know what it was and that I was not yet prepared or ready, and that I should not rush in until it became certain that GOD was leading the way. I knew I must not take things into my own hands.

Actually, my first "sermon," Mrs. Armstrong has assured me, was not preaching—but just a kind of talk. It did meet enthusiastic response, not because of any speaking ability, for there was none—but because I *did* have something vital to say. It was three years after the above letter was written before I was ordained a minister.

Even then I did not speak with any "drive" or "fire" or power. I still more or less just "talked." But there was, always, a vital message. After all, the MESSAGE, which comes from God, is the thing! Not the speaker or even oratory. I remember that it was either during, or shortly after, the first Firbutte campaign in late 1933, that the message began to pour forth with some power. It was during one of those all-day meetings held about once a month at the little church house in Harrisburg, Oregon (long since torn down). I was probably more surprised than the congregation that day. I did have a burning message—and I did *feel* it intensely—and suddenly the message began to pour forth in power. I did not "put it on"—rather I had to try to hold it in check. They told me afterward that for the first time I gestured with my hands and arms. I didn't realize it. My mind was on the audience and the message I knew they sorely needed.

Today I try to teach young future ministers to be natural—to quit thinking of themselves, their gesturing, their oratory or speaking ability. I tell them *never* to try to turn on the power—but wait until after the experience when dynamic power is there naturally.

Heckled Again

In this Alvadore neighborhood were three or four families of Seventh Day Adventists. They attended the meetings. I soon learned that one of them was coming for the sole purpose of learning what I was preaching, so he could visit the others in the daytime and try to refute everything I was saying. He didn't seem to be succeeding very well. The others continued to come with increasing interest.

Then there was Elder Day of the Christian Church and his wife and two late teen-age children. Elder Day was then about 84. He was a quiet, soft-spoken, rather scholarly gentleman. After two or three nights, he smiled as he shook hands with me at the door, and said, "Well, I have learned something new tonight."

This continued through the rest of the meetings. My heart surely went out to elderly Brother Day. When a man well advanced into his 80's is "learning something NEW" every night, he is a rare and precious individual, indeed. Always his face lighted up happily in this new knowledge!

But as we came into the final two weeks of the meeting, the one Seventh Day Adventist finally became vocal. I was just beginning the sermon one evening, speaking on the truth that Jesus was three days and three nights, exactly as He said, in the tomb after crucifixion—and then, therefore, the crucifixion was *not* on "Good Friday" and the resurrection was *not* on Sunday morning!

Now it so happened that, since their Mrs. White had a dream or vision in which she claimed the resurrection did occur on Sunday morning, Seventh Day Adventist doctrine cannot accept anything contrary.

I had hardly begun the service when this ill-advised man arose and began to heckle.

"That passage in Matthew 12 verses 38 to 40 does not mean that Jesus was in the tomb," he said. "It means he was in the hands of the Roman soldiers three days and three nights. Besides, the Bible plainly *says* Jesus ROSE early in the morning on the first day of the week!"

I immediately accepted his challenge.

570

"You mean you think the expression 'in the heart of the earth' means 'in the hands of Roman soldiers'?" I asked.

"Yes, it does!" he lashed back.

"And you say the Bible plainly states that Jesus actually ROSE early on Sunday morning?"

"Yes, it does," he affirmed.

"Well," I said. "Now I'll tell you what we'll do. You just be seated until the close of the sermon, and start hunting for that passage in your Bible. You won't need to listen to the sermon, because you won't believe a thing I say anyway, and you only listen in order to go around the neighborhood trying to confuse others and to refute everything I am preaching. Now I strongly advise you to utilize every single minute between now and the end of the sermon hunting that text—because you are going to need a lot more time than that to find what simply isn't there. Then at the close of the sermon, I am going to call on you to stand up again and to read to us out of the Bible where it says that Christ actually ROSE on Sunday morning."

At the close of the sermon, I called on my heckler and bade him to rise, and to read his text. He arose, and began thumbing through the New Testament of his Bible.

I had become a little provoked by this man's persistent opposition and determined to make an example of him and end any influence he possibly might have once for all.

"Come, now!" I said. "I noticed you did not heed my advice to devote all the time of the sermon hunting for the text that is not there. You should have been searching, then you wouldn't keep us all waiting like this. Come, now! Read it! Read where the Bible says Christ ROSE on Sunday morning."

He merely stood there, confused, flushed in the face.

"We are waiting!" I prodded.

I let at least three minutes of dead silence elapse. It seemed more like an hour. I purposely let it become embarrassing, to let the truth of this scripture sink deep in the audience.

Finally, I said, "Well, while this man stands there and hunts for the scripture that isn't there, let's look now at what he said about 'in the heart of the earth' meaning 'in the hands of the Roman soldiers.' Notice, this scripture says: . . . 'for *as* Jonas was three days and three nights in the whale's belly; *so* shall the Son of man be three days and three nights in the heart of the earth.' Now see how Jonah was a type of Christ. In the great fish's belly, Jonah says (Jonah 2:2): 'I cried by reason of mine affliction unto the Lord, and he heard me; out of the belly of hell [margin, Heb., *sheol*—the GRAVE] cried I.'

"Now, Jonah was in this GRAVE—for had he not been vomited up, it was a grave of DEATH—three days and three nights, after which he was supernaturally resurrected by being vomited up—to become the human saviour from physical destruction of the city of Nineveh. Likewise, Christ was in a tomb hewn back into the heart of the earth, three days and three nights, after which He was resurrected to become the spiritual Saviour of all mankind. The analogy is plain. The meaning is plain and simple. Christ was resurrected from the TOMB in the heart of the earth—He was not resurrected from the hands of the Roman soldiers!

"Now," I continued, "how many of you in the audience believe 'in the heart of the earth' means the TOMB from which Christ was resurrected? Let me see your hands!"

572

Every hand, except that of the very confused man standing, went up!

"Well," I said to him. "It sort of looks like we are all out of step but you. Have you found that scripture that isn't there, yet?"

He merely looked helplessly confused. Everyone was laughing at him. It was well-deserved and ought to have been profitable punishment.

"We can't wait longer," I said. "I do hope this will be a good lesson to you. You may sit down."

This was the only time I have ever made a laughing stock out of any man before others, to my knowledge. But this man had been spending weeks trying to discredit me and God's truth, and I felt it was the way to defend the truth for the good of all.

Meeting More Opposition

One family attending the Alvadore meetings regularly, and accepting the truths taught, was the W. E. Conns. Mr. Conn was a farmer in the neighborhood, doing quite a dairy business. One truth which seemed of tremendous importance to them was the fact the resurrection was on late Saturday afternoon, and not Sunday morning.

The following Sunday after preaching on that subject, Mrs. Armstrong and I were invited to their home for dinner. After dinner two men called. One was a preacher—apparently an independent, or of some small local sect, who had been serving as pastor to the Conns sometime before when they had lived in Salem, Oregon. The other was a man, also from Salem, who appeared to be associated with the preacher religiously. They had heard that the Conns had accepted the truth of God's Sabbath, being influenced primarily by the fact that the resurrection was not on Sunday. This knocked out from under Sunday observance the only prop which human tradition used to support it.

This preacher apparently came for a fight. He was angry. He was ready to get tough.

"The Bible says Christ rose from the dead on Sunday morning," he snapped, angrily.

I handed him a Bible.

"Read it to me," I said, simply.

He turned, as I knew he would, to Mark 16:9. But to my utter surprise, he did not read it as it is printed. He MIS-read:

"Now when Jesus *rose* early the first day of the week."

"My dear sir, you did not read that as it is written. Will you read it once again, and this time, read exactly what it says?" I demanded.

"Now when Jesus *ROSE* early the first day of the week," he repeated with heavy emphasis on the word "rose" which does not appear in the text.

I saw he was going to persist. I decided to maneuver this dishonest man, intent on deliberately deceiving, into a trap.

"The expression 'the first day of the week' is merely describing *when* Christ appeared first to Mary Magdalene," I said. "Punctuation was not inspired, but added by uninspired men long after the Bible was written. This was translated from the Greek. The comma belongs after the word 'risen,'" I said deliberately appearing to argue.

He took the bait, hook, line and sinker!

"Oh, no, you don't," he exclaimed angrily. "You can't go changing it."

"Do you mean we must accept the King James, or Authorized Version, just as it is, without changing a single comma, or any translation?" I inquired.

"I do!" he snapped. "You can't change a thing."

"Well, then, why don't *you* read it as it is, without changing it? Now I want you to read Matthew 28, verse 1."

He turned to read it. His face grew red with anger. It reads: "In the end of the sabbath, as it began to dawn toward the first day of the week, came Mary Magdalene and the other Mary to see the sepulchre."

"Yes, now read verses 5 and 6, and remember, this is in the end of or late on the Sabbath—NOT SUNDAY MORNING."

"I know that ye seek Jesus, which was crucified," he read. "He is not here: for he is risen, as he said."

"Yes," I added, "while it was still late in the end of the Sabbath, which ended at sunset."

"Oh," he began to explain. "But that is a mistranslation. It doesn't mean in the end of the Sabbath, but dawn Sunday morning."

"Didn't you just say that you cannot *change* the King James translation? Didn't you just say that I have to take it as it is, without changing or retranslating a thing?"

He was beginning to lose face. He had no answer.

"Now," I said, "turn back to Mark 16:9, and let's see whether you are honest enough to read it honestly."

"Now when Jesus *ROSE* early the first day of the week," he shouted.

I turned to Mr. Conn.

"I dislike to do this," I said, "but I had to show you how dishonest this man is, and how he had been deliberately deceiving you these past few years as to what the Bible says. Now, Mr. Conn, this passage tells what *state* Jesus was in early the first day of the week. It tells whether He was rising, or whether He already *was risen,* because He had risen the evening before. I want you, Mr. Conn, to read this. Does it say Jesus ROSE—or, early the first day of the week, that He already WAS RISEN?"

I handed the Bible to Mr. Conn. His hands trembled until he could hardly hold it. He was extremely nervous.

He read, "Now when Jesus *was risen* early the first day of the week."

The preacher and his companion strode angrily from the room, picked up their coats and hats and went out the front door without a word. Mrs. Conn broke down weeping.

"I hope I was not too harsh with those men," I said apologetically.

"Oh, you were not," sobbed Mrs. Conn. "They were harsh with you. But I tell you it *hurts,* to have to completely lose confidence in men you have looked up to as almost holy, and representing God, all these years. To see them show that they are deliberately dishonest and trying to deceive us is a terrible blow."

Another New Church

The Alvadore campaign ended. Fifteen had come with us, including the Days and the Conns. A new local church was organized, to meet in the Alvadore school auditorium Sabbath mornings. I ordained Elder J. M. Day as Elder, and W. E. Conn as Deacon.

Now I was forced to alternate between Alvadore and Jeans, every other Sabbath morning at each one, and Sabbath afternoon at our home in Eugene.

34

Steady Growth of Work at Eugene

I T WAS now spring, 1935. Holding Sabbath morning services alternately at the Jeans school, twelve miles west of Eugene, and at the Alvadore school fifteen miles northwest of Eugene, and Sabbath afternoon services at our house in Eugene soon became untenable.

Purchase of Church Building

Usually, members at Jeans would drive over to Alvadore, or attend at our home in Eugene, on the odd sabbaths after I was unable to preach at Jeans. Likewise, Alvadore members usually drove to either Jeans or Eugene when I was not at their school. But this situation was not very satisfactory.

The need of a church home in Eugene to combine these three small groups focused our attention on the place that our people had built in 1931.

The building of this little church house had begun

immediately following the close of the tent campaign held in Eugene in the summer of 1931 by Elder R. L. Taylor and myself.

Mr. Taylor had, prior to this campaign, owned a small retail lumber business in Eugene. Apparently, he had failed in business, but came out of it with a small amount of lumber on hand. He now proposed to "donate" that lumber toward the erection of a small church house in Eugene. He only had part of the needed amount of lumber, however. So church brethren were induced to contribute funds for most of the construction costs. A few donated labor, including a carpenter and an electrician.

They had never completed the construction. Siding had not been put on the outside, and plain slabs of wallboard had been nailed up inside, with quarter-inch spaces unfilled between slabs. And there were no seats or pulpit or furnishings of any kind.

While I was at Astoria in the newspaper business, in my final "detour" from my life's real calling, Mr. Taylor had written me that "we had lost the church building."

He was correct in saying that "we"—the church members—had lost it. But *HE* had not. He had traded it and a small piece of land he owned to a Mr. Powell who lived next door to the little church, for Mr. Powell's house. This, in turn, he had traded for a small island in the Willamette River opposite Eugene.

Because of the partial amount of lumber he had "donated" to the church house, Mr. Taylor had insisted on holding the deed to the property in his own name. Although church brethren had contributed much more than he, they had allowed it to be held in his name. He had "sold them down the river," and come out with a little island in the river for himself.

Late in May, 1935, Mr. Powell was living in the little unfinished church house. Mr. Elmer Fisher, Mr. W. E. Conn and I approached him about the purchase of the place. The purchase was made, for $500. Mr. Fisher put in the first $100 to bind the deal. Various church members put in, later, another $100 or slightly more, and most of the balance was contributed by elderly Mrs. S. A. Croffoot.

Now came the question of how the new property was to be deeded. Mr. Taylor's action had given church members cause to question the honesty of a minister who had the church property deeded in his name. I was determined that no such suspicion should have grounds for being directed toward me. I insisted that my name should not be connected in any way with the deed to this property.

In this particular case, as subsequent events proved, it would have been safer for the church if control of the property had been in my hands. But I said, then, "If we can't trust such men as Mr. Day, Elmer Fisher, and Mr. Conn, then nobody can be trusted." Perhaps I didn't realize as thoroughly as I do today that God says we can trust no man.

On my own recommendation, the property was deeded to "J. M. Day, Elmer E. Fisher, and W. E. Conn, as trustees for the Church of God at Eugene, Oregon." Actually, as I learned from attorneys later, this was a loose and unsafe way to protect the property of the church, legally. Anyway, the purchase was made late in May, 1935, after some four months of the unhandy functioning of those three little separate churches.

Completing the Building

Immediately we set out to put the building in shape for holding services. I asked the members to contribute special offerings to purchase necessary lumber and paint. We purchased the siding lumber, which was put on by volunteer labor. I filled in the quarter-inch spaces between plaster boards with the proper plaster cement, myself, then the inside walls were painted and the outside also.

I looked into other church buildings for ideas about the seating. The most economical way proved to be to build our own seating in the form of benches, with a center aisle and two narrow outside aisles down the side walls. I designed the pattern after observing various more costly benches in larger church buildings. I sat in various ones, to determine what design would give the most comfort. Then, with some of the men of the church helping, we built the seats. They were comfortable with contoured backs the entire length of each bench.

Mrs. Armstrong and Elmer Fisher painted those church seats in an attractive brown color while I worked on other things. In the new church at Alvadore, one of the members was a cabinet maker by profession. He built the pulpit and an altar rail around the front of the rostrum.

On June first, 1935, The Church of God at Eugene, Oregon, held its first service in the new building, consolidating the three groups into one church.

Convincing Atheist Communists

Soon after occupying the new little church building, I began holding every-night evangelistic services there. We mimeographed handbills and had them delivered to front porches all over town. We called it "The Little Church at the end of West Eighth Avenue." Its location, then, was a half block beyond the city limits.

While these meetings did not attract thousands, the little church house was usually fairly well filled.

One night my subject was the prophecy of Daniel 11—the longest prophecy in the Bible. It begins with events of Daniel's time, in the first year of King Darius. It foretells the swift conquering flight of Alexander the Great, his sudden death, the division of the Empire into four divisions. Then the prophecy carried along the events of the King of Egypt and the King of Syria or the Seleucidae—as "King of the South" and "King of the North."

One ancient history covers the details of those events and those following in this long prophecy. That night I read a verse of the prophecy, then a paragraph showing its fulfillment from *Rawlinson's Ancient History,* carrying straight through to the time of Christ, the early Apostles, and on to our present, and the immediate future.

At the close of the service a young lady who had come for the first time, with two companions, waited to speak to Mrs. Armstrong. Her friends went on out. She asked if she could make an appointment to talk to Mrs. Armstrong and me.

"I'm an atheist," she said. "Or at least I thought I was when I came here tonight. But now I feel myself slipping. To tell the truth we three girls thought it would be good sport to come out here and laugh at the ignorant medieval religious superstition we expected to hear. I've always believed religion is a silly superstition—the 'opium of the people.' But tonight we couldn't laugh. I never heard anything like this. I have to admit no human writer could have written that long prophecy and made it come to pass, step by step, over so many years. What I heard tonight makes sense. It is not like any religious teaching I ever heard. I want to ask you some questions."

Mrs. Armstrong arranged a private talk with her for

the next afternoon. She jabbed sharp questions and pointed questions at us, but they were all promptly answered. She continued to attend the meetings, and after a couple of weeks she believed, repented, and was baptized. We learned that she was the secretary of the local Communist Party! She resigned from the Communist Party forthwith.

This young lady was jeered and ridiculed for taking up with "medieval superstition," of course.

One day she walked into the small front room of the old Masonic Temple which I was still using, rent free, for an office. She was actually leading a half-reluctant man by the arm.

"Mr. Armstrong," she said, "this man is a Communist—one of my former associates in the Party. He's an atheist. He says he *knows* there is no God. We encountered each other across the street just now. He said he would like to meet that weak-brained idiot of a preacher that hypnotized me into believing foolish superstitions. He said that he would *prove* that evolution is true and there is no God by making a monkey out of you. So I grabbed his arm and said, 'Come right along. Mr. Armstrong's office is just across the street.' I have marched him over here, and I have come along to laugh at the show, as he proceeds to make a monkey out of you."

At the moment I had a Bible in front of me. I pushed it aside.

This was a challenge that inspired fast thinking. I gave a quick silent prayer for guidance.

"Sit down!" I said to the man in a commanding voice, and taking immediately the initiative before he had a chance to utter a word. "So you're going to make a monkey out of me by proving there is no God. First, I'll shove this Bible out of the way because you couldn't

582

believe anything it says, anyway. Now *you* must be a
very highly educated man, with a brilliant intellect. I
want to find out just how bright you really are, and how
much you know about some of the laws of science. Do
you know something about radioactivity and radioactive
elements?"

"Well, yes," he stuttered. Evidently my fast and
sharp attack caught him by surprise and he was on the
defensive before he could recover.

I asked him if he agreed with certain laws of
science. Of course he had to answer that he did. I
followed up the attack, snapping questions at him
forcing him to answer and commit himself. Before he
realized what was happening he had admitted that
science proved there had been no past eternity of
matter—that there was a time when radioactive
elements did not exist—and then a time when they did
exist. He had also admitted that life could come only
from life, and not from the not-living. Before he realized
it he had admitted there had to be a First Cause,
possessing LIFE, able to impart life to all living
organisms.

"Now," I pursued, "you're a real intelligent man.
I'm sure you won't deny that! You have a MIND. With it
you can think, imagine, reason, plan. You can make
things. But *you cannot make anything that is superior
to your mind!* Do you agree to that, or can you show me
that you can originate and produce something superior
to your mind?"

He was getting more confused by the minute. Of
course he could not demonstrate that he could produce
something superior to his own mind, so he was forced to
admit it.

"Then you have admitted that whatever can be
produced must be devised, planned, and produced by an

583

intelligence GREATER and SUPERIOR to whatever is produced. Do you know of *anything* that is more intelligent, and superior, than your mind?"

I knew his vanity could never admit of anything superior to his mind.

"I guess not," he admitted weakly.

"And yet you acknowledge that something less intelligent than your mind could never have produced your mind and that it must of necessity have been devised and produced by an Intelligence GREATER than your mind. So you see you have admitted a First Cause having LIFE, and of intelligence superior to the most intelligent thing you know, in order to bring YOU and YOUR MIND into existence. Look at all the forms of LIFE on this planet—the way each is constructed—the way each functions—the way each needs certain things like water, food, sunshine, and a certain range of temperature, in order to function and exist. Could YOU, without any pattern to go by, think out, design, produce, set in motion, and impart a functioning LIFE to all these life forms of the fauna and flora of the earth? Or do you think it took a GREATER POWER, a SUPERIOR INTELLIGENCE, a LIVING CREATOR, to design, plan, and create and sustain this earth and the entire vast universe?"

He could take no more. "W— W— Well," he stammered pitifully, "I won't worship God even if you DO make me admit He exists!" This was a last attempt at defiance.

"That's a decision God compels YOU to make," I replied. "He won't make it for you. He will allow you to rebel and refuse to worship Him. But He did set laws in motion, and whatever you sow, that shall you reap!"

The young lady did not laugh. It was not funny!

A few weeks later I met this man on the street

584

corner. He made one last effort at brave retaliation to salve over his wounded pride.

"I'll never bend MY knees to your Christ," he said.

"Oh, yes, you will!" I replied firmly. "There is a judgment day coming for you, and the Creator that lets you breathe says EVERY knee shall bow to Christ—even if He has to break the bones of your legs!"

I encountered this man many times on the street after that, but he never again discussed religion. He always treated me with respect.

My First Wedding

I must go back a bit now, to recount an incident that occurred in February or March of 1934. It was shortly before my wife and children had moved to Eugene from Salem.

I was asked to perform my first marriage ceremony. Ernest McGill, one of the twelve children of Mr. and Mrs. J. J. McGill, whose names have appeared before in this autobiography, asked me to perform the ceremony for him and Ora Lee Wilcox.

It caught me by surprise. It was the first time, since my ordination, I had been called on for such a ceremony. I was totally unprepared.

My first thought was to go to the pastor of some church in Eugene and ask him for his form of marriage ceremony. But on the heels of that thought flashed in the next second the thought that I had found the Bible entirely different from modern-day religious beliefs, forms and ceremonies. I realized then that instead of going to MEN to learn how to perform a marriage ceremony, I should go direct to the Bible. Instead of learning from men, I should learn of GOD.

Immediately I studied all I could find in the Bible about marriage. I did not find the words of a specific

585

ceremony written out, but I did find God's PURPOSE in marriage—that God had instituted it—and God's requirements of both husband and wife. The wording of the specific ceremony, itself, came naturally by putting together the essential scriptures concerning marriage.

When the wedding day came, the ceremony was simple, plain, taken from the Scriptures. I had seen that it is GOD and not man, who joins husband and wife as one flesh. Therefore they were married, not by me, but by GOD during a prayer. Everyone thought it was the most beautiful wedding ceremony they had ever seen. God's ways *are* beautiful! That same ceremony, with very few alterations, is still being used today, in our hundreds of churches worldwide.

But I must recount here an accompanying incident. I had, of course, written my wife that I was to marry Ernest and Ora Lee. A little later she found our elder son, "Dickie," age five, missing. When he didn't show up she became frantic. Finally she found him hiding under a bed, sobbing as if his little heart would burst.

"Why, Dickie," she called, "what's the matter?"

"I don't want Daddy to marry Ora Lee," he sobbed. "He married you, and he's my Daddy, and it's *wrong* for him to marry another woman."

Of course his mother explained. Later he, himself, performed marriage ceremonies, and I performed his wedding ceremony.

Our "New" Office

Following the evangelistic meetings in the old Masonic Temple in downtown Eugene, April and May, 1934, I had retained for some time, as mentioned above, the use of one of the smaller rooms as an office. I do not remember just when, but later—probably early autumn, 1935—Mr. Frank Chambers, owner of the building (and somewhere near half of all downtown Eugene, it was rumored), told me he had a tenant for the entire building, and I would have to move. Up to that time he had not charged any rent for this smaller office room. He said he had a vacant room in the Hampton Building, across from the Post Office (a new Post Office has been built since) on the southwest corner of Sixth and Willamette. However, he would have to charge me $5 per month office rent.

Well, we seemed to be getting up in the world. From no office rent we now advanced to paying $5 per month office rent!

However, it was an inner room, without windows for ventilation. There was a transom over the door leading into the hall. There was another transom over a locked door leading into the Labor Union Hall adjoining. But instead of fresh air, the stale tobacco smoke wafted regularly through this transom on mornings following a union meeting. There had been a skylight in the ceiling, but it was so dirty very little light filtered through.

During the years we occupied this office we were able to work only about two hours at a stretch, then having to vacate the office for an hour or so while the air changed a little. After some months we did manage to afford a small electric fan which kept the stale air circulating.

There were two or three old tables in this room. Unable to afford a desk these were used as office desk, and tables for printing, folding and mailing the mimeographed *Plain Truth*. There were also a couple of old chairs in the room.

For filing cabinets in which to keep folders of correspondence and records we went to a grocery store and asked for some cardboard cartons. The ones they

587

gave me apparently contained bottles of whiskey, since they had big whiskey labels printed on the sides. I pasted plain wrapping paper around the outside to conceal these labels.

Into this office we moved the very old second-hand neostyle—ancestor of the mimeograph—and our old second-hand ten-dollar typewriter. This constituted our entire printing equipment, on which *The Plain Truth* was printed for the first few years.

I wrote the articles, then cut the stencils. The local mimeograph representative permitted me to visit his office once a month and cut the headline on one of his "scopes." It was Mrs. Armstrong's job to grind out the sheets on the old hand-cranked neostyle. Every sheet had to be fed in by hand, then slip-sheeted by hand after each sheet was printed. She then assembled the pages, folded them, and addressed them by hand in pen and ink. She maintained the mailing list—all written in ink on sheets of paper.

What a far cry that was from the way *The Plain Truth* is printed and mailed today! But in one respect we did have an advantage in those days. Mrs. Armstrong and I were able to carry the entire mailing of the mimeographed *Plain Truth* in our arms across the street to the post office—and before we did, we always knelt and prayed over them, laying our hands on all the copies asking God to bless them and those who received them.

35

Uphill All the Way

W E HAD come, in the previous chapter, to the spring of 1935. Now I should like to backtrack briefly.

The broadcast had started the first Sunday in January, 1934. The first issue of *The Plain Truth*, mimeographed, came out February 1, 1934. The third point of the "Three-Point-Campaign" got under way the first of April, with the small-scale evangelistic campaign in downtown Eugene, Oregon.

Old Notation Discovered

In an earlier chapter I mentioned that the broadcast was started with pledges for slightly more than half of its $2.50 weekly cost. That $2.50 per half hour on radio station KORE was almost a donation from its owner, Mr. Frank Hill. He probably gave the $2.50 to the announcer as a slight bonus for opening the station 30 minutes earlier. KORE had been going on the air with its Sunday programming at 10:30 a.m. To clear time for my half hour, Mr. Hill simply moved his operating schedule up a half hour earlier.

Now $2.50 per week may seem a little ridiculous today, as the price of a half-hour broadcast. It was not a bit absurd to me, in those days! We were at the very bottom of the depression. I had, only a few months earlier, given up the $3 per week salary I had received. A single dollar was a considerable item to us then.

When I stated, earlier, that almost half of that $2.50 radio charge per week had to be undertaken on sheer faith, I was quoting from memory. The last few chapters were written in England.

Since returning to Pasadena, I have researched in the dusty old files of the years 1933 to around 1940. The papers in filing folders are still intact in the cardboard cartons I obtained without cost at a grocery store. We could not afford the luxury of steel filing cabinets in those days. In those old files, stored in a basement store-room of one of our buildings on the Pasadena campus, I have culled out a number of interesting papers, letters, bulletins, and copies of mimeographed *Plain Truths*. Among them I found an old yellowed sheet on which I had penciled notations of the pledges for the beginning of the radio program.

Under "Pledges for Radio" are the following:

J. J. McGill $.50	Ernest Fisher 1.00
Mrs. C. A. Croffoot 2.00	T. P. Madill 1.00
John Davison & family .50	Edgar W. Smith 1.00
Mrs. J. W. Snyder .25	Mrs. Gemmel .25

———

$6.50

It may seem a little strange today that some were able to pledge only 25¢ or 50¢ per month. Perhaps we have been spoiled by today's prosperity. Perhaps we have forgotten those bottom depression days. But at that time 25¢ or 50¢ per month, over and above tithes and regular offerings, as a special pledge, may have meant considerable sacrifice. Anyway, those are the names that made possible the start of the broadcasting work that now covers every inhabited continent that has, today, probably become the most powerful broadcasting work on earth, worldwide!

And today, I say, all honor to those people for that initial sacrifice! It was not so little as it might seem, at first glance, today! God has multiplied that many thousands of times over!

When Almighty God does something Himself, by His own power alone, He does it in a manner so mighty and so vast our minds cannot comprehend it. But when God does a work through human instruments, He always starts it, like the proverbial mustard seed, the *smallest*. But it *grows* to the BIGGEST!

And so I honor those eight original Co-Workers. Most, if not all, are now dead, but what they helped to start *lives on*—in *multiplying* POWER!

On this same yellowed sheet of paper is the notation of tithes and offerings received of $11.75— probably an entire month's income for my family's living! Also special offerings for the "Bulletin" I was then issuing, $4.25. But under it appear the notations: "Spent for Bulletin: stencils $1.75; 1 ream paper, $1.35; ink, $1.25; brush, $.15; postage, $1.50; miscellaneous, $1.52; total, $6.02. That was $1.77 more than offerings received for the purpose. I presume the $1.77 was paid out of the $11.75 family income, leaving less than $10 for a month's living.

I have taken this brief "flash-back" because I feel that few readers, adjusted to the prosperity and luxuries

591

of today, would otherwise realize the rough going under which this work of God was forced to start.

Actually, at $2.50 per Sunday broadcast, I did have a little over half of the amount pledged. When there were five Sundays in the month, the broadcasting cost $12.50, and when four Sundays it was $10.00. The average cost was $10.83 per month. The $6.50 pledged was actually 60%. But taking that additional $4.33 per month on sheer faith was a bigger test of faith, *in those days,* than it is easy to realize today!

I had no idea, then, where that additional $4.33 per month was to come from! But I felt positively assured that GOD had opened *this door of radio,* and expected me to walk on through it! And I relied implicitly on the PROMISE in Scripture that "my God shall supply *all your need* according to His riches in glory by Christ Jesus." And although God has allowed many severe tests of faith, *that promise has always been kept!*

Smashing Your Idol

I think it well that the reader be given some idea of the financial hardship under which God's present world-wide work got under way. Some persecutors imply that I was in it for the money! Perhaps it is well to set the record straight.

And further because an advanced student here on the Ambassador College campus expressed great surprise, the other day, to learn that I had been forced to labor along for 28 long and lean years in economic hardship. He had heard that I had been "knocked down" by God economically, somewhat as the Apostle Paul was by blindness, and plunged into God's service. But he had supposed that the financial test of faith had consisted of some three or four comparatively short periods of perhaps a few weeks or a few months.

So let me say right here something about conversion I find most people do not understand.

The REPENTANCE required as a *condition* to being truly converted by receiving God's Holy Spirit is something far different than most people suppose. It is infinitely more than merely "seeing" God's TRUTH, or some of it, and being good enough to embrace and accept it. It is something altogether different from merely *agreeing with certain doctrines.*

Whoever you are, YOU HAVE, or you *have had,* an IDOL. You have had another "god" before the true living Almighty God. It might be your hobby or your habitual pastime. It might be your husband, or wife, or child or children. It might be your job. It might be your own VANITY, or the lipstick you paint on, or your business or profession. Very often it is the *opinion of your friends,* your family, your group or social or business contacts.

But whatever it is, that idol must first be CRUSHED, SMASHED—it must be literally *torn out of your mind,* even though it hurts more than having all your teeth pulled out and perhaps a jawbone, too! I don't believe that many people experience this painlessly. I don't know of any anesthetic that will render it pleasurable. Usually it seems like something more excruciating than the agony of death by the cruelest torture.

Now I had an idol. My whole mind and heart was set on that idol. I had worked hard, night and day, for that false god. My false objective was the intense desire—the desperate, driving, overpowering ambition—to become "successful" in the eyes of important business men—to be considered by them as outstandingly "IMPORTANT" in the business world—to achieve status. I did not have a love for money *as such.*

After establishing my publishers' representative

business in Chicago, I aspired someday to own, or build, one of the finest and largest homes in the north-shore aristocratic suburb of Winnetka—with large spacious grounds constituting an important-appearing estate. I wanted to be considered important *by* the important.

Crashing Down to Reality

I was so zealously set on that accomplishment that it became the god I worshipped and served.

God could not use me as long as I had another "god" that was more important in my eyes than He. Yet tearing that ambition out of me was like yanking out, root and branch, my very life itself. It was smashing dead everything I felt I lived for, and worked for.

So God first took away my business in Chicago by bankrupting every major client. Twice, later, He again swept businesses that promised multi-million dollar rewards right out from under my feet. He brought me down to poverty and to hunger.

But the bigger they come, the saying is, the harder they fall! And all this swelled-up EGO came crashing down, *down, DOWN!* I had been so big—so important—*in my own sight,* there was no room left for GOD! But God whittled self-righteous Job down to size! God drove strutting King Nebuchadnezzar out to eat grass with the beasts! God struck down Saul with blindness, changed his direction, and then his name to Paul. And God was certainly able to knock me down off my imaginary high perch—again, and again, and again! I had to come to realize that all this self-"IMPORTANCE" was pure illusion! I was brought down to earth and reality with a THUD!

Instead of ego, vanity, and self-IMPORTANCE, God fed me, for 28 long years, on the raw and scanty diet of humiliation and poverty!

Had God merely let me suffer financial reverses, even to the point of experiencing real hunger, for short periods of a few weeks, I would have bounded back and quickly set back up my idol to serve again! Had God let me suffer that kind of humiliation and poverty even for a period of a year—or even six or seven years—I probably would have resumed the same sense of ego once back on my financial feet.

But God had in mind, as life-long events have since proved, using me as His instrument in preparing the way for the World Tomorrow—for world peace—for universal happiness, joy and prosperity, for a growing worldwide work involving tremendous expenditures in HIS SERVICE. And He knew that He could never entrust me to handle HIS money, in the administration of HIS work, as long as I set my heart on money or the things money would buy.

Please do not misunderstand. It is not wrong to have or enjoy the good material things of life. What is WRONG, and therefore harmful to our own selves, is *setting our hearts on these things*, instead of on the TRUE VALUES! The LOVE of material things—the VANITY of wanting to exalt the SELF instead of God—of wanting the worshipful praise of MEN by being considered "IMPORTANT"—these are the wrong things to set our hearts upon. When the heart is set on such false values, the soul shrinks inwardly and dries up! THANK GOD! He saved me from such a fate by that 28 years of poverty and humility!

Dying to LIVE

I was never *converted* until I was brought to the place where I realized my own nothingness, and God's all-encompassing GREATNESS—until I felt completely whipped, defeated. When I came to consider myself as a

595

worthless burned-out "hunk of human junk" not even worth throwing on the junk-pile of human derelicts, truly remorseful for having imagined I was a "somebody"—completely and totally and bitterly SORRY for the direction I had traveled and the things I had done—really and truly repentant—I told God that I was now ready to give my SELF and my LIFE over to Him. It was worthless, now, to me. If He could use it, I told Him He could have it! I didn't think, then, it was useable—even in God's hands!

But let me say to the reader, if God could take that completely defeated, worthless, self-confessed failure to which I had been reduced, and use that life to develop and build what He has done, He can take YOUR LIFE, too, and use it in a manner you simply cannot now *dream*—if *you* will turn it over to Him without reservation and leave it in His hands! What has happened since gives me no glory—but it magnifies again the POWER OF GOD to take a worthless tool and accomplish HIS WILL through it!

But don't ever suppose it came easy. If a mother suffers birthpangs that her child may be born, most of us have to suffer that WE may be born *again* of GOD—even in this first begettal stage we call conversion!

And what does all this mean? It means that *millions* of professing Christians have been deceived into believing in a FALSE CONVERSION! It means, as Jesus said, "whosoever will save his life shall lose it: and whosoever will lose his life for my sake shall find it." Or, in another place, "He *that loveth his life* shall lose it."

It means that the individual must be CHANGED! It is a change in *what you ARE!* Jesus Christ never pictured the way of salvation as the broad and easy and popular road. Rather, He said, that popular road is the way that leads to destruction—and the MANY are traveling that road. He said that *many* would desire to enter the Kingdom of God, *and should not be able!* Why? Because they are not able to *give up* this world—this world's WAYS—to give up being concerned primarily with "what will my friends—my club—my associates—my relatives say?"

Repentance means GIVING UP *your way*—the world's way—the world's opinion of you! It means turning to the WAY OF GOD—the way of His law! It means SURRENDER—unconditional surrender—to live by EVERY WORD OF GOD. Since the Bible *is* the Word of God, it means to live by the BIBLE! It means utter voluntary submission to the AUTHORITY of God, as expressed in HIS WORD!

When you come to fully realize what is the full implication of your rebellion against the AUTHORITY of God—of the Bible—it is not so easy to give up! It is much more than a change of direction. It is a change in *what you ARE!* That old SELF doesn't want to DIE! This *true repentance* is excruciatingly painful. It is agony! Jesus said FEW find that way!

It wasn't easy for me. How about you?

The only people of God, going His way, that we knew at that time were at the opposite extreme of human society from the great and the near great I had been proud to associate with. I thought immediately, of course, of what my former friends and business associates would think of me. They would regard me as a fanatic embracing superstition. It was humiliating. I knew it meant giving up all such associations. I knew it meant giving up my life's ambitions. It meant giving up everything I had driven myself so hard to attain. But now I was disillusioned. All that had been pure ego—pure inflation of VANITY. It was a blown-up balloon—and the balloon had been punctured.

When I literally *gave* my life over to God, I meant it! I did not count it mine any longer. Yet, had God brought me merely to this agonizing experience of conversion, and then restored me to economic ease and prosperity, I probably would have reverted back to the same goals and ways. The old cocky SELF-confidence probably would have returned. I probably would not have endured as a Christian.

So God not only brought me low. He *kept* me that way for 28 long years!

Yet living without this former "god" was no longer painful, once I gave it up. I had found the true GOD instead. I had found the overflowing JOY of receiving new UNDERSTANDING of God's TRUTH out of the Bible. I now plunged into the study of the Bible with an energetic zeal surpassing any efforts I had expended in the quest of material success. I found a new happiness and joy in the fellowship of those humble and lowly folk that was infinitely greater than any enjoyment experienced before. Mrs. Armstrong and I were now seeking *first* the KINGDOM OF GOD, and His righteousness. We learned that happiness does not consist of material acquisitions.

When God Opens Doors

Among old papers, letters, bulletins in those dusty old files I find a mimeographed letter addressed to co-workers. Our little family of co-workers making possible this work of God was still very small—perhaps a couple dozen or so. The letter is dated December 20th, 1934.

It started out: "I am overjoyed to be able to make a most wonderful and important announcement. The

598

Lord has very graciously blessed the work. . . . And now He has opened the way for far greater influence during 1935. . . . A wonderful opportunity has come for The RADIO CHURCH to go on the air *IN PORTLAND!* This may be done by a hook-up between our present station, KORE in Eugene, and KXL in Portland."

A few other excerpts from this letter should prove interesting.

Here is one—and how true this is, still today! "But there is one fact I want you to realize. It has been said that if a minister would DARE to stand before his congregation and preach the PLAIN TRUTH OF THE BIBLE, he would not have a dozen members left. That is about true, for God's Word is profitable for REPROOF, for CORRECTION (II Tim. 3:16), and the minister who will use it to reprove and rebuke (II Tim. 4:2) as God commands, will find the time has come when people have adopted FABLES! We have DARED to preach the TRUTH! We have not minced words, nor toned down the Word of God. And but *FEW* will *support* such preaching.

"Yet," continuing the letter, "we have found a peculiar paradox. We have learned that people WILL LISTEN, *over the radio,* to the straight truth that would cause them to get up and walk out if their own ministers preached it in their own churches! They will LISTEN, *over the radio,* but they WILL NOT SUPPORT SUCH PREACHING! We cut ourselves off totally from their financial support —yet they LISTEN! And do you know, there are MILLIONS over the United States who will never listen to the last Gospel warning in any way EXCEPT OVER THE RADIO? They can be reached BY RADIO—*and by radio ALONE!"*

How true that has been! That is one reason GOD ALMIGHTY opened the door of mass evangelism by radio and, later, by television. Today, scores of millions listen every week—yet the numbers who support this great worldwide work, even today, are only a few hundred thousand worldwide, and many of them in the lower income brackets!

Yet, even from those early days in 1934, we have made financial needs known *only* to those FEW who had voluntarily, without solicitation, become active co-workers! We have never begged for financial support over the air. We have never taken up collections in evangelistic campaigns. We have never put a price on any Gospel literature! People must send in offerings or tithes, voluntarily and without solicitation—or else tell us they wish to become co-workers—before we consider them as such, or acquaint them with the financial needs of the work!

That financing policy was in effect from the very first broadcasting year—1934! Every co-worker who helps support this work of God is individually responsible for reaching THOUSANDS with Christ's Gospel—because only one in thousands is a co-worker!

But the point I wish to make is that, by the end of our first year on the air, CHRIST opened *another door!* He opened the door for us to go on station KXL, Portland, then only 100 watts.

But at that time I was afraid to walk through that door—until *after* co-workers had PLEDGED enough money to pay for it. This very letter quoted above went on to ask co-workers for those pledges—totalling only $50 per month, for the year 1935. A coupon form of pledge was mimeographed at the bottom of the second page of the letter.

Our co-workers failed to pledge the needed $50 per month. As I remember, they pledged only about half that amount. And I failed to walk through the door Christ had opened. We had to wait almost two more years before

God gave us another opportunity for His work to expand into Portland! Later other doors were opened, when I wanted definite pledges before walking through those doors. But definite pledges was not FAITH.

We had to learn, by experience, that when God opens doors for CHRIST's GOSPEL, He expects us to start walking on through, IN FAITH, trusting HIM to supply our every NEED!

Whenever we have done this, God has always supplied the need—though He has given us severe tests of faith. Whenever we have refused to follow where Christ leads *until the money is on hand,* the money has never come!

And so the entire year 1935 went by and we were still on only the one little 100-watt station in Eugene, Oregon!

My First Car

During the year 1935, we continued grinding out a hand-made *Plain Truth* on the antiquated neostyle. The mailing list had started with 106 names. But through 1934 and 1935 it continued to grow as a result of the radio program.

Evangelistic meetings continued, Sunday nights, through most of 1935 at our "Little Church at the End of West Eighth Avenue." I had taken out time for a short six-nights-a-week campaign of perhaps two weeks at the Clear Lake schoolhouse between Eugene and Alvadore. Also I had conducted a two- or three-week campaign at a schoolhouse near Globe, Oregon, some 40 miles north of Eugene.

A Bulletin dated March, 1935, announced the addition of 200 copies to the *Plain Truth* circulation, and a radio listening audience estimated, by the mail response, at 8,000 every Sunday.

By August, 1935, the radio audience was estimated at 10,000.

I find a letter dated September 19, 1935, sent out by three members of the Eugene church, telling members and co-workers of our dire need of an automobile. I had not owned a car since leaving Salem for Astoria in December, 1931. For all these meetings I had held 8 miles, 12 miles, and 15 miles west of Eugene, I had been forced to hitch-hike a ride or be taken by someone attending who had a car.

A few excerpts from this letter may throw additional light on the circumstances of the time. Here are a few:

"Dear Friend: We want to bring to your attention a few facts that have not been known, about the work, ministry, and circumstances of your radio pastor and editor.... He started this work of Bible evangelism without any money or income of his own. He has received no salary or income from any organization, but solely on sheer faith in the Lord to supply his needs and those of his family.... To do this, Brother Armstrong and his family have sacrificed in a way you little dream of.... Most of the time Brother Armstrong has been preaching six to nine times a week. He and his wife do all the work of printing, folding, addressing, stamping and mailing out *The Plain Truth*, themselves, to save expenses.... We are three of the many who have been converted by his preaching during the past year. Now this work is expanding.... He has urgent call to open evangelistic meetings at once near Salem. The way is opening for him to go on the air in Portland.... But Brother Armstrong is severely handicapped, and may be prevented from expanding this great work, because he has no car. The time has come when he must take quick trips back and forth between Portland, Salem, and

Eugene. He must also have a way to get around to visit more of his radio audience, especially the sick and afflicted who call upon him for prayer. So we, the undersigned, have taken it upon ourselves as a committee of three, to try with the Lord's help and blessing, to provide a car for this great purpose. . . . We have in mind not even the lowest priced new car, but a used car, the lowest priced car that will serve the purpose and cover the mileage he now will have to cover. One of the undersigned is an experienced mechanic and automobile man, and will select the right car for the purpose. We three are starting this fund, at a sacrifice to ourselves."

As a result of their letter, a fund of $50 was raised. We purchased a used 1929-model Graham-Paige, in Portland. The price was $85. We signed papers for paying the additional $35, with the understanding I was to have ten days to pay it in cash and save the carrying charges of a year's payment contract. I borrowed the $35 and paid for the car. Afterward the man from whom I borrowed it—and I believe it was Ernest Fisher—figured that he owed that amount of tithe money, and cancelled the note.

Back in the proud old Chicago days, it would have been a very painful blow to pride to have accepted a car in that manner.

Along in those early years, 1934 to 1936, I sometimes laughingly boasted that "I have a suit of clothes for every day in the week—and *this* is it!" But that one suit finally became threadbare. It became a handicap to the work. Mr. Elmer Fisher decided I had to have a new one, and took me to the Montgomery-Ward store and bought me a new $19.89 suit. It may have been a year and a half or two years later when that one was looking equally unpresentable. At that time Milas

Helms, near Jefferson, formed two committees, one headed by him at Jefferson, and the other at the Eugene church, to solicit contributions from members for another new suit. They raised $35.

Through these years my wife wore used clothes her sister sent her, and how we shifted to keep our children clothed I do not remember—except that one woman at Alvadore stopped tithing by saying:

"Well, I'm not going to let any of *my* tithes go to buy silk stockings for those Armstrong girls." She said cotton stockings were good enough for them. Yet ALL other girls in high school wore silk stockings! This was before the days of nylons. Had our girls worn cotton stockings, they would have been ridiculed and laughed at by the other girls. Mrs. Armstrong did not want this to happen. She prevented it by accepting worn silk stockings from others, with runs in them, and sewing up the runs—for both her daughters, and herself.

It was incidents like this that soured and prejudiced our children against God's truth. Through those years most of the members of the church in Eugene lived better, economically, than we.

I have a letter written November 13, 1935, showing that at that time, after almost two years on the air with the radio program, the income of the work was running around $40 to $45 per month.

It was sometime during 1935 that opportunity came to purchase a small house of our own on West Sixth Avenue in Eugene. Certain of the church members raised the down payment. On this I have to trust memory. No figures are at hand, as I write. But I believe the price was $1,900, with 10%, or $190 down and 1% of the $1,710 balance, or $17.10 per month payments. The church members agreed that if I were able to keep up the payments, the property, when paid out, should be deeded to me. It was deeded to the three officers of the church and myself, as trustees for the Church, which made it church ownership.

More Persecution

There had come a request for me to hold evangelistic meetings of about three weeks in the Eldreage schoolhouse on a country road 12 miles north of Salem, Oregon.

In previous chapters I have had a great deal to say about Mr. and Mrs. O. J. Runcorn. We had come to regard them as our "spiritual" parents. They lived in Salem during these years. Their son, Fern Runcorn, and his family lived in this community close to the Eldreage school, and Mr. Fern Runcorn was a member of the school board. It was through him that permission was obtained by the board to hold the meetings. I was invited to be his guest while they were being held.

This school was one of the newer two-room schools. The rooms were divided by folding or sliding doors. These could be opened so that the two rooms became one larger auditorium room.

While it was a country community, we had an attendance running from 50 to 70 each night. Among them were some 15 teen-agers, including a few husky 16-year-old overgrown boys. They did not come because they hungered and thirsted for God's Truth. They came for mischief. They sat in the rear seats, making loud cat-calls and weird noises, trying to disrupt the preaching.

Mr. Runcorn had warned me about them in advance. He said that if I attempted to quiet them or discipline them in any way, I would find all the adults resenting it, and attendance would stop. I could not understand why, but he warned me that the people

605

there were accustomed to this noisy confusion, and would resent any effort of mine to stop it.

Consequently, when the nuisance started, I stopped my preaching long enough to say that I had been warned against trying to stop it.

"Now," I said, "if that's the way you people want it, that's the way you may have it. These boys are sitting at the rear. They are closer to you people than they are to me. If you can stand it, I can. But if and when you get tired of it, and want it stopped, I shall STOP IT!"

When these young rowdies saw they could not break up my meetings that way, after a few nights they broke into the school one night after midnight, breaking a window, and stealing a number of books.

Next evening Mr. Runcorn said the chairman of the school board had called a board meeting, and he and the third member had voted to refuse permission for the meetings to continue, on the ground that my presence there was endangering school property. But I learned also that the chairman of the school board was a member of a certain church, of which about half of all the residents of the neighborhood were members, and that he, himself, had deliberately instructed these boys to break into the school building, in order to give him the opportunity to deny the use of the building to me.

That rather aroused my indignation. I was to be allowed this one more service that same night. At this service, I announced to the congregation what had happened. I told them I did not want to be a party to a religious war in this religiously divided community, but I believed God would give me wisdom to handle the situation. I felt confident the board decision would be reversed before the following night, and advised all to come.

Next morning I drove to the Sheriff's office in

Salem. I asked him if his office was willing to uphold the Constitution of the United States which guarantees the right of peaceful assembly.

"Mr. Armstrong," he said, "if there is anything this office will stand firmly behind, it is the right of peaceful assembly. What's your trouble, and what can we do for you?"

I explained what had happened. I asked for two deputy sheriffs to be present each night, beginning at the time of the meetings, until about two hours after midnight, to prevent further breaking in or destruction of school property. He assured me his men would be glad to put down the disturbance of these young ruffians by arresting them and taking them to jail if they disturbed the meetings further, provided I would prefer charges. It was agreed. The deputy sheriffs were to remain in the school play-shed just outside the school.

Next, I went immediately, with two witnesses, to the home of the chairman of the school board.

"Now, Mr. X," I said when he came to the door, "I understand that your only objection to my meetings is your fear of destruction to the school property, and your desire to have the property protected. Is that correct?"

"Oh, yes, of course," he replied.

"And of course," I pursued, "there is no religious persecution or bigotry in your action, is there? You are not trying to start a religious war in this community where half are of your religion and half of the other kind of Christianity?"

"Oh, no, of course not," he said, his face turning red.

"Well, then, since you are not doing this as a matter of religious bigotry and intolerance, but only to protect school property, I'm sure you'll change your vote on this, for there will be no further danger to the school property. I have seen to that. The sheriff's office is sending two armed deputy-sheriffs out every night from here on. They are going to guard the school property until long after midnight—as long as there is any danger. So you have no other objection, now, have you?"

"Well," he stammered, "I - I g-guess n-not!"

"Thank you," I said. "These men are my witnesses that we now have your permission to continue the meetings."

We left, and drove to the home of the third board member. I told him what had happened.

"You might as well make it unanimous," I said, "since the other two board members have given permission, anyway."

He was glad to do so.

That night we had a good crowd.

"At the outset tonight," I said, "I want to say that I am sure, after this breaking into the school building and the robbery, that you people will be with me in demanding the constitutional right of peaceful assembly. There are two sheriff's deputies just outside this door. The first one of you young bullies that makes a single disturbing sound is going to be yanked right out of your seat, and thrown in jail for the night, and I will appear against you and demand the severest penalty of the law!"

At the end of three weeks, the interest had increased, and the meetings were continued for six weeks.

36

Broadcast Work Expands

WE COME now to the year 1936. The meetings being held 12 miles north of Salem, Oregon, had started around the 12th of December, 1935. Originally scheduled for three weeks only, they were continued an additional three weeks because of local interest— especially after the episode of bringing two sheriff's deputies from Salem to guard the school property every night.

Going to Heaven?

One night I spoke on the reward of the saved. Most people, of course, suppose it is a matter of *destination* — going to heaven. In other words, a matter of *where*, instead of *what* we are to be.

I had shown that Jesus Christ came to "confirm the PROMISES made unto the fathers." Whatever the PROMISES made to the fathers, Jesus *confirmed* them as

609

the reward of the saved. Then I showed by both Old and New Testament Scriptures that Abraham, Isaac, and Jacob were "the fathers."

Next, starting with the 12th chapter of Genesis, I showed that Abraham was not promised heaven, but rather *this earth* for an *everlasting possession.* The words "everlasting possession" simply mean ETERNAL LIFE. The same promises were re-promised to Isaac and Jacob. This was confirmed by Christ, who preached ETERNAL LIFE as the gift of God.

Of course most people have been taught, and carelessly assumed, precisely *the opposite* of the Biblical teaching on this, and many other basic truths. The BIBLE says: "The wages [reward of] sin is DEATH; but the *gift* of God is ETERNAL LIFE, through Jesus Christ our Lord" (Rom. 6:23). Yet nearly every professing Christian believes exactly the opposite. Most believe the wages of sin is ETERNAL LIFE—*in hell fire.* They do not believe eternal life is the GIFT of God — the REWARD of the saved. They believe we already possess eternal life. They believe the pagan Plato's teaching that we are "immortal souls" living in a fleshly body which is merely our temporary cloak we have put around us.

The original Hebrew word translated "soul" is *nephesh* which MEANS animal life—*mortal* existence, subject to *cessation in death.* The very word "soul" has the *opposite* meaning to eternal life. The expression "immortal soul" is as impossible and self-contradictory as that silly poem circulated some 50 years ago, about the "barefoot boy with shoes on" who "stood sitting in the grass, while the rising sun was setting in the west as it rained all day that night."

The BIBLE says positively, and TWICE: "The soul that sinneth, *it shall DIE*" (Ezek. 18:4, 20).

Teaching the Teacher

Many do not realize that the idea of going to heaven did not come from the Bible, but from pagan superstitions. Anyway, in the course of the sermon, I offered $5 to anyone who could show me any place in the Bible where it gives any plain statement or promise that the saved shall go to heaven.

After the service, one of the two teachers of that two-room country school house came to me, and with a tantalizing grin said, "Mr. Armstrong, I'm just mercenary enough to take that $5 from you. Here, read this."

She had a Bible opened to the Beatitudes in the "sermon on the mount." She pointed to verse 3 of Matthew 5: "Blessed are the poor in spirit: for theirs is the kingdom of heaven."

I smiled, too.

"Well," I exclaimed with a glint in my own eye, "now please read verse 5."

She read: "'Blessed are the meek: for *they shall inherit the earth.*'"

"Now that is a plain statement of what they shall INHERIT —the *earth.*" I said. "Doesn't that contradict your idea of going to heaven? How do you explain that?"

"Well, I don't know—unless," she said, suddenly jumping to an explanation, "unless the people who are meek have to stay on earth, but the poor in spirit get to go to heaven."

"Now, come—you know better than that," I smiled. "Are you not one of the teachers in this school?"

"Yes, I am."

"Well, now," I persisted, teasing her a little, "do you think you are qualified to be a teacher, when you

611

don't know the difference in meaning between the simple little words of 'in' and 'of'? You have heard about the famous "Bank of Morgan" in New York, haven't you?"

"Oh, yes, of course."

"Well, is that bank *inside* of Mr. Morgan?"

"I see what you mean," she smiled. "The word 'of' denotes ownership—it is not the bank *in* Mr. Morgan, but the bank he owns."

"Right! And the Kingdom of heaven is not referring to a kingdom that is *in* heaven, but one that is to be on earth and OWNED or RULED by heaven. Now turn to Luke's account of the same saying: 'Blessed be ye poor: for yours is *the kingdom of God.*' Here the expression is 'Kingdom of GOD.' It is not speaking of a kingdom inside of God's person—but the earthly kingdom GOD RULES and POSSESSES!"

Then I explained how Matthew consistently employs the phrase "Kingdom of Heaven," where Mark, Luke and John, often quoting the same words of Jesus, always use the expression "Kingdom of God." Both expressions mean the same.

"Now do you still think I should give you the $5?" I asked.

"No," she replied, "thanks for the free lesson."

As always in the evangelistic meetings I held through those years, we reaped a "harvest." There were conversions. The little group was formed into a small local church—but there was no pastor to leave there to "feed the little flock."

The details of what followed that campaign are very dim in my memory now. A general mimeographed letter to Co-Workers dated March 30, 1936, shows I had been continuing to spend some little time visiting converts and interested people in that vicinity.

But it was the same experience as other evangelistic efforts. There were results—converts baptized—but without a local minister, the "flock" was soon devoured by the world, the flesh or the devil. Few seem to be able to endure without a minister to feed them spiritually, counsel with them in their problems, and keep the "wolves" away. So far as I know, just one of that group who attended the Eldreage school meetings continues to endure at the time of this writing!

Still, this voice of experience did not sink into my consciousness sufficiently to produce the solution until ten years later. It was in 1946 that the Eternal God finally got through to me the fact that He intended to use me in founding His own college, out of which were to come forth the ministers and pastors so direly needed for the growth of God's Work!

This same general letter also records the fact that there had been no issue of *The Plain Truth* for several months—since starting these meetings. Still, I find in this mimeographed letter the statement: "As you know, I have never begged for money over the air." And, "For more than two years we have conducted this Radio Church on SHEER FAITH."

The latter part of May or early June Mrs. Armstrong and I drove our aging second-hand car to Hawthorne, California—a Los Angeles suburb—to pick up a tent which the "Sardis" people had purchased the year before. We towed it back on a trailer. I set it up in a good location on the edge of the downtown district in Springfield. Springfield adjoins Eugene to the east—a somewhat smaller city.

Of course we had a good radio following in Springfield. The tent seated around 400. We had a nightly attendance that must have averaged 150 to over 200. However, just as interest was increasing, at the end of two weeks, the "Sardis" people needed the tent. One of their men was going to hold meetings in the little town of Stayton. They had a small tent, maximum seating capacity fifty people, which they brought me to replace the bigger one.

For the remainder of the Springfield meetings we were forced to raise the side flaps straight out, with 50 people seated inside, and 100 or more having to sit outside—except the night it rained. Then only the first 50 obtained seats. The others had to return home. Meanwhile, it was privately reported to me that most nights over at Stayton there was no attendance whatever—one night two people came, and another night there were four, who had a full sermon preached to them. This was just another of the many experiences trying to co-operate with these people.

A Tough Lesson in Faith

In the preceding chapter, I quoted penciled notations from an old now-yellowed sheet showing that $6.50 per month was pledged by eight Co-Workers to start off the radio broadcasting. Actually, the original pledges were only $5.50. Three others, totalling $1 per month were added a little later.

When the first opportunity came to go on the air regularly, the owner of station KORE, Eugene, Oregon, offered me a Sunday morning half hour at the astonishing low rate of $2.50 per half hour. During a four-Sunday month that totalled $10, and in a five-Sunday month, $12.50. Actually, before starting, only $5.50 per month was guaranteed by pledges. That is, roughly, only *half* the required amount. But, *in active faith*, I did walk right on through the radio door Jesus Christ had opened.

And I have explained how, in those bottom-depression days, this took real living faith! When 25¢, 50¢, and $1 per month was all that people felt they could afford to pledge, you may realize how big the unpledged balance appeared.

At that time Jesus Christ *opened the door!* I walked through it. I *trusted Him* to keep the balance coming. HE KEPT IT COMING! Sometimes the necessary $2.50 was not on hand up to 30 minutes before broadcast time. Then one of the brethren might knock at our front door and *just happen* (?) to leave some tithe money, or an offering, at that psychological minute!

Never once did Christ fail to provide. Never did we have to miss a broadcast! Real faith requires the *courage of believing,* and *acting* on it! This, let me explain, was not like going in debt for something consumed and unpaid for. We didn't go into debt. We trusted Christ to send the money to pay *before* each program, in advance.

But I had not yet fully learned this lesson of *active faith.*

By December that first year of broadcasting— 1934—Christ OPENED A SECOND DOOR. His time had come for the broadcast to leap to Portland, with ten times the potential listeners. In fact, a hook-up was opened to us for *two* additional stations, KXL, Portland, and KSLM, Salem—both at that time only 100-watt stations. The cost was to be $50 per month.

But I had grown more cautious, apparently. I wanted *more* than Christ's assurances—I wanted tangible pledges in black and white that I could see! In the preceding chapter I quoted from the letter sent out December 20, 1934, asking for those pledges. Not enough was pledged. I let the opportunity slip. Then it was too late!

On September 3rd, 1936, after almost three years of

broadcasting, I sent out a letter to Co-Workers. One paragraph said: "Do you realize that KORE, our present radio station, is only a small local station of 100 watts? That it reaches only 50 to 75 miles from Eugene? Did you realize that people north of Salem, south of Roseburg, east of the Cascades, are never able to hear the message being broadcast? Yet, over this local station, in this small territory, we have established a regular weekly audience of around TEN THOUSAND people."

Did God reject me because I had not yet learned that lesson in faith? No, I had exercised faith in other ways many times, and answers had been miraculous. But He let me *pay* for this mistake! I had to wait *two more whole years* before Christ again opened the door to Portland! Here we were, September, 1936, and still on only that one little local station!

Yet, on the other hand, I had worked hard and remained faithful. I had held repeated evangelistic campaigns. I had kept up the publishing work, with Mrs. Armstrong's full-time help. Scores had been converted and baptized. I had preached God's TRUTH fearlessly.

From another paragraph in this general letter of September 3, 1936, I quote: "Nero fiddled while Rome burned! Many churches and religious broadcasts are today giving the people *a sleeping potion* in the form of nice, soothing, pleasing, comforting programs—lulling the people to sleep—while the JUDGMENTS OF GOD ARE FAST COMING UPON THEM! Why, in Jesus' name, do they not wake up and fearlessly SHOUT THE WARNING? This is no time for soft and smooth platitudes. It is time to AWAKEN people! It is time to WARN THEM!"

And that is precisely what this program was doing then—and is doing on many thousands of times greater power, TODAY! Even then, in that little section of one state, it was like a voice in the wilderness—the ONLY voice on the air fearlessly proclaiming CHRIST'S OWN GOSPEL MESSAGE of the Kingdom of God!

No, God did not reject us. But He did try us. He did let us suffer to learn lessons. He did let us go along on that one low-powered station, unable to leap out into greater fields, for two additional years!

At Last — Into PORTLAND!

This same letter of September 3, 1936, told Co-Workers of how I planned now to get on Portland's most powerful station. Actually, CHRIST had not opened that door. Herbert W. Armstrong *tried* to open it. Here is another excerpt from that letter:

"Consequently, the Lord willing, we plan now to extend the radio broadcasting to a powerful Portland station—if possible the most powerful station in Oregon. This station has FIFTY TIMES the power of KORE. After sundown this station reaches out all over Oregon, Washington, Idaho. After 6 p.m. the cost is just *double,* but if we are able to secure a 30-minute period between 5 and 6 p.m., Sunday evenings, which will be after sundown in the months just ahead, we can send the program out over this large territory at a cost of only $110 per month."

But *again* the pledges fell short—less than half!

Christ had not opened that door. I had to learn to wait until He did, and then to walk on through the doors HE opens!

But by November 8, another letter to our Co-Workers shows that Christ finally *had* opened the door once again in Portland. Not the door of the biggest, most powerful station in Oregon. *The same identical door* HE had opened two years before—the *smallest* power of only 100 watts, as it was then, KXL!

617

Here are portions from the letter dated November 8, 1936, which tell the story:

"I was in Portland this week, and learned that, beginning November 1st, KEX (the station I had wanted) goes off the air on a silent period at 4:45 in the afternoon, before dark. We cannot afford to pay their high rate for a day-time broadcast. We now have subscriptions for only about $40 per month, and it began to look like we would have to give up the whole program.

"And so I am sure you will rejoice with me to know that *the Lord has opened to us* a BETTER broadcast than would now be available on station KEX, and at half the cost. The owner of another smaller station, KXL, who also owns the Salem station, made me a proposition for hooking up by wire hook-up with both these stations, at our regular Sunday morning time, 10 a.m., over KORE, at Eugene, at a reduction of one-third from the regular rate. These three stations form the Oregon Network, and are connected by wire hook-up. . . . It is not as big a program as we had hoped for, but it is what the Lord has provided, and will multiply the number of listeners to between seven and ten times the number we now reach. . . . It is *a stepping stone*. Often the Lord does not let us progress as rapidly as we would like, and HE KNOWS BEST. I believe that this will soon lead to other larger stations, so that soon we shall be covering the entire Coast, and later the entire nation. . . . We can now hope to start off this extended program by next Sunday."

The next Co-Worker general mimeographed letter in my files is dated December 9, 1936. It tells its own story:

"GREETINGS in Jesus' name! I know you will rejoice with me that the extended broadcast over the Network is already bearing fruit!

618

"We are now in the second month of this broadcast, and are receiving letters from listeners every day.

"I have just returned from Portland, with good news that I know will cause you to rejoice as it did me. The way is now open, as soon as finances permit, to extend the broadcast still further, into Washington."

Once we broke out of Eugene, and learned to follow through where CHRIST leads in HIS work, we were allowed to begin expanding with increasing momentum.

37

A Costly Lesson Pays Off!

BEFORE going on to the year 1937, I'd like to backtrack again for just a moment to point out some very important lessons.

Our Sons Start School

By September, 1935, we were living in a small church-owned house on West Sixth Avenue in Eugene, Oregon, as I have recorded earlier. At this time my wife decided to start both our boys in school together.

"Dicky" (Richard David) was then six, and to reach his seventh birthday in October. "Ted" (Garner Ted) had reached five the preceding February. We might have started "Dicky," as we then called him, in school in September of 1934. He was then within about six weeks of reaching six. But Mrs. Armstrong had her mind set on starting the two boys in school together. They each had little sailor dress suits—"whites"—and of course we thought they looked very cute together. They really were pretty "sharp" in those neat and immaculate white suits.

I did not think well of putting both boys in school together. The matter had first come up in August of 1934. We discussed it a great deal. Both Mrs. Armstrong's sister and one of her brothers were school teachers—her sister of first grade. They advised strongly against putting the two boys in school together.

I am mentioning this, because the problem might confront some of our readers, and I should like to help them to profit from our experience.

My wife's brother and sister advised definitely against starting little "Teddy," as he was then called, when he was barely past 5½ years—and also against putting the two boys in the same grade when one was a year and four months older than the other. Had they been twins, it would have been different, of course.

Although I thought it unwise, it seemed to mean so much to Mrs. Armstrong to see the two boys starting off to school together that I acquiesced. So, on what probably was the morning after "Labor Day" in September, 1935, I saw my very pleased wife walk with her two smartly attired little boys on the way to school.

However, we did come to feel, later, that it had been a serious mistake to start the two boys, more than a year apart in age, in school together. Most of the reasons for this I shall relate farther on. Little "Teddy," during the growing years, was *much* shorter than his brother "Dicky." Richard David was at least of normal height for his age—but Garner Ted was short for his age— until maturity, when at last he grew up to exactly the same height as his elder brother.

Because he was so "little" during those years, his

women teachers thought "Teddy" was cute, and he was continually pushed to the front. This, naturally, resulted in giving "Dicky" an inferiority complex.

Later, during noon hour the day the boys started Junior High School, they themselves changed their names to "Dick" and "Ted." And at age 13, I took Dick in tow with me at the time we were starting on the air daily, in Hollywood, and managed to apply a treatment that snapped him completely out of his feeling of inferiority. That, however, I shall leave to be related when we come to it. It was a most interesting experiment. And it worked!

The Costly Lesson

I have already mentioned how Jesus Christ, the real HEAD of this work, had said in advance (Rev. 3:8) that, at this time, He would OPEN DOORS that His Message might go to the world IN POWER! And, further, how, after first opening the MIGHTY DOOR of radio—just the narrowest *start* of an opening first, in January, 1934, on one smallest-powered station—I had lacked the FAITH to walk on through when it opened a little wider, in November of the same year.

Instead of trusting God *fully,* I wanted the assurance of MEN. I sent out letters to our few Co-Workers, asking MONTHLY pledges. I have mentioned how that door then swung *shut,* and did not again open to us for two and a half years.

But that was not all. We were really punished much more than that. I didn't recognize it as punishment at Christ's own Hand, then. It seems plain, looking back on what happened, now.

God says, plainly, "Whatsoever is not of faith is SIN" (Rom. 14:23). And "without faith it is impossible to please Him" (Heb. 11:6). Of course this was not knowing or deliberate sin—but it certainly did not please God, and He impressed the lesson.

Not only was the expansion of the broadcasting withheld two whole years, but *The Plain Truth* was suspended from publication, also! After I failed to TRUST GOD by going on KXL when He opened its door to us, we were allowed to print and send out only *two* more issues of *The Plain Truth*—March and July issues, 1935—AND THEN *The Plain Truth* WAS ENTIRELY SUSPENDED FOR TWO AND A HALF YEARS!

After the issue of July, 1935, there was not another issue that year. There was not a single issue of *The Plain Truth* during 1936. There was not one number of *The Plain Truth* all during 1937. Not until January, 1938, did *The Plain Truth* appear again!

We were dramatically *reminded* of the lesson that GOD EXPECTS HIS PEOPLE TO TRUST HIM IN *LIVING FAITH!*

The Lesson Applied Before YOUR Eyes!

We learned our lesson! That is one reason why, today, the radio log shows many very powerful and leading radio stations broadcasting *The World Tomorrow*, worldwide.

Our living and guiding HEAD, Jesus Christ, has begun opening radio doors more rapidly than ever before. He has also been opening *other* doors for the expansion of this work in an amazing, breathtaking manner! Even in times of economic recession—WHEN OUR FAITH HAS BEEN MOST SEVERELY TRIED! Even when we have felt the imperative need of reducing expenditures in the work, not increasing them. God has provided the means.

When a radio station agrees to accept our program, and clears a definite time, that means TAKE IT—walk through that opened door NOW—or the door will be slammed SHUT—perhaps forever! Forty years of experience has taught that stern lesson. Every time I glance at the current volume number of *The Plain Truth* and see those two years missing, I have to be reminded that GOD TAUGHT ME A STERN LESSON—when He opens such doors He expects me to walk on through, TRUSTING HIM!

Would you say this takes COURAGE? Well, not exactly. Not after so many years of experience learning that GOD CAN BE TRUSTED!

It's a mighty PRACTICAL lesson!

38

Work Grows—Despite Hardships and Persecution

Now we come to the year 1937. I've explained how, in about mid-November, 1936, we started on KXL, smallest-powered 100-watt station, in Portland. With it, using Postal Telegraph wires for a hook-up, we included station KSLM, in Salem. This was our first network!

Truth About Networks

I think it will be interesting here, to give our readers a few facts they probably do not know about radio networks. The telephone companies have a very efficient system of network broadcast lines feeding the various major network stations—CBS, NBC, and ABC—coast to coast.

These are very *special* lines, specially engineered, and of far greater efficiency than ordinary telephone lines. They are specially boosted at intervals of about every fifty miles. This is necessarily a very costly service—but the quality is as near perfection as human technology can make it. Sound is carried instantaneously from originating stations in Hollywood, New York or Chicago, to all parts of the United States with no detectable loss in tonal quality. The voice is transmitted as naturally as if the speaker were in your living room or your car. Music, at both highest and lowest frequencies, is transmitted just as naturally.

The installation and maintenance of these special lines is a costly operation. In 1936 and 1937 we were not able to afford such perfection in network lines.

But at that time the Postal Telegraph company offered far less costly lines. These were just the ordinary telegraph wires—far, far from the quality of telephone special network lines. There were no boosters along the way, and even the lines themselves were inferior, for our purpose. Often they would fade down or out. Frequently they didn't work at all. The reception at the other end was far from perfect. But we were *on our first network,* nevertheless! We called it the "Oregon Network."

Everything God starts through humans must, it seems, start the very smallest—and sometimes the crudest. BUT IT WAS A START! And, once started, the WORK OF GOD *never stops!* Not only that, it never stops *growing!*

We were to use Postal wires in immediate future years to Seattle and Spokane. Later, the Postal company was absorbed by Western Union. But they helped us get a start while they lasted!

Even at that time I had my sights on extending the broadcast into Seattle and Spokane, though I was forced to learn patience, and wait until God opened those doors. I knew we could not call it the "Oregon Network" when it extended into Washington, so, in my mind, I had it named already the "Liberty Network," ready for the future!

Gospel to the Holy Land

Meanwhile, I was continuing to hold regular Sunday night evangelistic services in our little church building at the end of West Eighth Street, in Eugene. Interest and attendance gradually were increasing.

It was either the last Sunday in December, 1936, or the first Sunday night in January, 1937, that a former leader of that Church of God we find described in Revelation 3:1 as the "Sardis" church—with which I was trying, in those days, to cooperate—appeared with a professed converted Jewish evangelist.

This particular church leader, whom I will not name since I can say nothing good about him as an individual, had a scheme to get the Gospel to the Jews in the Holy Land. They had arrived a day or two before, and explained their plan to me. It sounded real good. In fact, the *idea,* itself, *was* good.

The reason evangelists generally were failing to convert the Jewish people to Christ, he explained, was their wrong approach. This may not be the whole reason—but the approach of most evangelists assuredly *had been wrong!* They customarily started by trying immediately to preach the name of Christ to the Jews. But, explained this Jewish evangelist, all Jews have been taught from babyhood to virtually hate, despise, and reject the name of Christ. To mention this name was to set up immediate prejudice. It raised an immediate impenetrable barrier.

This evangelist, being Jewish, said Jewish people would not be prejudiced against him, but would listen. Instead of preaching Christ, direct, he proposed to approach them with the Jewish Scriptures—Old Testament *only*. After arousing their interest with prophecies being actually fulfilled today, he would then turn to a few passages such as Isaiah 53, Micah 5:2, Isaiah 7:14, describing how the Messiah was to be born as a baby, of a virgin, in Bethlehem, to grow up as a child, to be despised and rejected and crucified.

He said that when he approached Christ *from* the Old Testament Scriptures—from the Jewish point of view—they would listen.

Whether or not many would listen very far, this was the *only possible approach,* I knew, that had a chance.

The plan was to raise enough money to send this man to Jerusalem, from where he would work throughout the Holy Land in getting the Message of the Saviour to the Jewish people there. I agreed to help.

The Deception

On that Sunday morning I interviewed both this church leader and the Jewish evangelist on my radio program, and announced public meetings where the converted Jew would speak at our little church on Sunday night.

That night our church building was filled. I sponsored the idea of the tour of the Holy Land, and asked for liberal donations. Never, except for something very special like this, did we take up offerings in any service. The response was liberal.

The next night we had a packed house at Harrisburg. Again, the donations were liberal, and the evangelist was on his way.

But a year later, after other unpleasant experiences with this church leader during 1937, the Jewish evangelist again visited our home in Eugene.

He had a sad report to make. His effort had not been altogether honest and sincere. It had weighed on his conscience. He knew he ought to return the money I had helped raise, but he didn't have it to repay.

He had gone to Jerusalem, all right. But he had found that the church and church members supposed to exist there were nonexistent, he said. The man whose name was used as a representative of the church also proved, he reported, to be a representative for other churches, drawing financial compensation from all of them.

The "converts" being made in the Holy Land, he reported, were not Jews at all, but Arabs—who were not really converted.

The procedure used in the Holy Land, he reported, was this: These supposed missionaries, evangelists, or "representatives" who drew money from several Protestant denominations, and reported "large harvests" of "converts," each had a small tent, in which they served tea and cookies. Like a barker at a circus sideshow, they shouted, beat tin pans, made noises to attract a crowd, announcing free cookies and tea. When the crowd gathered, the "missionary" went through a short two- or three-minute "spiel," after which he offered the free cookies and tea to all who would raise their hands and say they accepted Christ.

The natives all raised their hands, partook of the tea and cookies, and then proceeded to the next tent where they got "converted" all over again!

Well, as the saying goes, *"Live and learn!"*

I have learned many lessons, in more than half a century in Christ's ministry—and I have been completely disillusioned in regard to the sincerity of a lot of professed religion in this world!

Radio Audience Grows

In a letter to Co-Workers who were regularly supporting

God's Work with tithes and offerings, dated February 12, 1937, it was estimated that the listening audience had grown to some forty or fifty thousand, every Sunday. It was steadily growing "toward our goal of 100,000" the letter reported!

WHAT A GOAL!

That looked mighty BIG, then! Yet today our listening audience is immensely larger.

But the point is, as I mentioned once before, I did not, in those days, have any remote idea that this work ever would reach even a fraction of its power of today!

I think I have stated, before, that I did have vision. I did, at that time, look forward to going on small stations in Seattle and Spokane. My horizon had expanded to include the entire Pacific Northwest—and at times I even envisioned the entire coast. But the vision of a God-empowered work on the vast worldwide scale of today was that of our living Head and Chief Director, Jesus Christ—not mine! This is His work. I, and our Co-Workers with me, have been merely instruments in His hands! But the present size and scope and power of this great work is testimony to the POWER of GOD to build, and increase HIS WORK, and keep it growing until, like the grain of mustard seed, it FILLS THE WHOLE EARTH!

Whatever plant my heavenly Father has *not* planted shall be *rooted up!* But God says He will *never* stop the work HE has begun! Whatever is of MAN is destined to come to naught! But whatever is of God *cannot be stopped!* Through the years we have met hardship, persecution, disillusionment—every obstacle! But none could stop us, or prevent this work growing and MULTIPLYING in scope and power!

Compare the mail response of the broadcast today with 1937. A general letter sent Co-Workers on March

19, 1937, reported the following "BIG" mail response: In the past 2½ weeks, 26 letters from KXL, Portland; 20 from listeners of KSLM, Salem; and 12 from KORE, Eugene. Total 58. The letter then asked: "Brethren, is *this* worth while?" That seemed BIG then. Today, we receive tens of thousands of letters *per week*. And that is from the UNITED STATES, *only*. Besides this there is a receipt of mail at our offices, worldwide, *much larger* per day at each office than we then had in 2½ weeks back in 1937.

This letter of March 19, 1937 started out: "I am more than gratified at the evidence of rapidly increasing audience, growing power, and mounting influence." This mail count inspired us to increased activity then. And, by comparison with what God now grants us, that same report gives all of us, whose hearts are in God's Work, great inspiration to further increased activity, today!

I wonder if the reader can realize, as I read over these letters and reports from dusty files of long ago, how much deep down satisfaction and inspiring GRATITUDE to our God it gives me, today! It was a real struggle, then. It always has been! But the results with which we have been blessed—the assurance of continued MULTIPLYING growth from here on—mighty gratifying and worth all it has cost many thousands of times over!

There is a REASON for this rapid and consistent growth over the years. That reason is partly stated in a letter dated April 8, 1937: "This is *not* just another religious broadcast. It is utterly DIFFERENT! as I'm sure you realize by this time. It DARES TO PROCLAIM THE BIBLE *TRUTH* straight from the shoulder! It dares to WARN people of the fast-approaching dread DAY OF THE LORD, and to preach the only *true* Gospel—the Good News

631

of the KINGDOM OF GOD! It dares to *correct* modern fables!"

The same remains true today!

More Persecution

On Sunday, May 2, 1937, the program on the three network stations was dedicated to high school students. By arrangements with the Principal of Eugene High School, the combined boys' and girls' glee clubs of that school furnished the musical portion of the program. The Message was directed to high school students, in their own language, captioned: "Getting a Real Kick Out of Life." A special notice was sent on the Monday preceding to Principals of the High Schools of Oregon and southwestern Washington, asking them to announce the program to students in assembly.

About the first week in July, another six weeks' campaign was started in Eugene. The attendance was good—averaging 150 to 200 per night. As usual, there were a number of converts.

August 20th to 29th, inclusive, a camp meeting was held in "Cabin City," on the highway just north of Eugene.

This particular camp meeting was the last of our cooperation with the Salem, West Virginia branch of the Church. The son of one of the so-called "12 apostles" of that church informed me of a plot, hatched at a meeting he attended with his father, in which the so-called "leading ministers" of that group intended to use this camp meeting, of which we at Eugene were hosts, to attempt to discredit and ruin the radio broadcast.

I had announced the camp meeting over the air, weeks ahead, and invited all listeners to attend. Immediately, on learning of the plot, I appointed a Committee to be in charge of the camp meeting, and had

632

them go to the "leading ministers" who already were in Oregon, demanding that all antagonisms and derogatory insinuations against me personally and the radio program be withdrawn from their plans. They refused, saying other ministers from the east coast were coming, whom they could not muzzle, and they were determined to ruin the broadcast if possible.

Thereupon, I announced there would be no camp meeting. In two days the "apostle" customarily in charge of these annual camp meetings arrived in Eugene from Southern California. He came straight to our home.

What was this, he asked, about my threatening to call off the camp meeting?

"That's right," I said, explaining to him the conspiracy to defame the broadcast and ruin it.

"But you *can't* stop the meeting from being held," he exclaimed.

"But I *can,* and *will,*" I replied. "You see, I have rented this camp grounds in my own name, and I alone control it. I will not allow the grounds to be used. I have the entire member mailing list. I shall send out notices informing all of the FACTS, telling them it is cancelled, and not to come. About 85% of all expected to attend are members of the two churches at Eugene and up at Jefferson, of which I am Pastor—and they will do exactly as I say. There is no other possible place where such a meeting could be held. On next Sunday, I shall announce to the radio audience that the camp meeting, to start that night, has been cancelled. NOBODY WILL COME! Now tell me, please—how are *you* going to stop *me* from stopping the camp meeting, and saving the broadcast?"

His wife intervened, and advised him to realize that I "had him over a barrel."

He then begged me not to stop it, *promising* there would be no attacks against me or the broadcast from the pulpit or otherwise during the meetings. But I remained adamant.

"Do you question my word?" he asked, a little indignant.

"It isn't your veracity but your *ability* to stop this vicious and evil attack that I question," I replied.

He reminded me that he was a cousin of the leader in the church, who held all these ministers under his thumb. He said he would GUARANTEE that nothing hostile would occur. Finally, on this, I relented and agreed to let the meeting go on.

But there was an undercurrent of bitterness and hate. Whenever I preached, the next minister to preach devoted his sermon to an attempt to refute, disagree with, and tear down everything I had said. I tried hard to preach on subjects that could not be disputed or disagreed with—yet they found a way to twist what I had said and attempt to cast reflection against me.

Then, at a ministers' meeting, this very "apostle" who had always appeared so friendly to me, proved himself willing to give a "Judas kiss." Having the floor, he said, in pretended sympathy, that *dear* Brother Armstrong had worked *so hard,* and was *so overworked,* that they decided to "help" me by relieving me of some of my "burdens." Therefore, they had decided to appoint another of their ministers (one totally hostile to me), as pastor of the church up at Jefferson. He almost wept crocodile tears of pretended sympathy.

One elder and one deacon of the Jefferson church, shocked and thoroughly aroused at this SO EVIDENT subterfuge and bit of deceitful hypocrisy, as a plot to "take over" that church, and thus rob the broadcast of its tithes and offerings, resigned immediately.

All of us at Eugene church, and half the members at Jefferson severed all connection and effort at cooperation with those who had proved themselves willing to serve Satan and their own personal greed, and to injure the very work of GOD! I am going to END all comment about that group here, with the epitaph that—like a dead tree—they have since split and resplit into so many little tiny groups, all hating one another, that no one seems to know where all of them are.

These harrassing events were unpleasant. It really did hurt Mrs. Armstrong and me, and all loyal to God's true Work, very deeply to see some we loved very much willing to be misled by greedy and self-willed little powerless preachers. But such is life, and such is this world!

Jesus Christ said the gate is narrow, and the road hard, difficult, that leads to LIFE, and only the FEW find it. We certainly have found His words true! It has not been an easy road. I know WHY Jesus was a man of sorrows. It was not because of persecution against *Him,* or personal suffering, but the anguish of seeing those He loved reject the truth and be willing to turn the wrong way to their own perdition! It hurts, deeply, to see people drop by the wayside!

But in the Work of God, the great blessings outweigh the sorrows 100 to 1.

39

The Plain Truth
Revived!

USING Postal Telegraph wires, we continued on the local network, feeding the 10:00 a.m. Sunday morning program from KORE, Eugene, Oregon, to *two* additional stations, KXL, Portland, and KSLM, Salem.

These, like our original KORE, were the smallest-powered commercial stations in operation—a mere 100 watts.

Weekly Portland Jaunts

But we stayed, at that time, with KXL for only about ten months. On September 5, 1937, we moved up to a 500-watt station, as it then was—KWJJ. The new time on KWJJ was 4:00 p.m. Sundays. We continued on KORE and the Salem station.

This not only was another increase in power, it started weekly trips to Portland that were to continue several years. Later these trips were extended on to Seattle.

At this time I put the program on KORE, broadcast simultaneously by wire hook-up over KQLM, Salem, at 10 each Sunday morning. Then came the 123-mile drive to Portland for the 4:00 p.m. broadcast.

By this time we were using a mixed quartette on the program. As the program started out, our concept had been to condense a regular church service into a half hour, using radio techniques. The program started with a fast-moving theme hymn, then two verses (never more) of a lively hymn, followed by prayer during which the singers usually hummed—or followed it with a threefold "Amen"—then announcements about the program, *The Plain Truth* or other free literature. Then followed a sermon of about 22 minutes, then sign-off with a closing theme hymn.

In using this type of programming, in those early days, I was merely following the custom of religious programs generally. Nearly all other religious programs on radio have continued that format to this date. But later, as we branched out onto larger stations in larger areas, we began to learn that this style of program is all wrong.

It is based on the assumption that a regular Sunday church service is being brought to people in their homes. It assumes one of two fallacies: either, 1) that all radio listeners are church-going people who *want* to sit in a church service—which is true of not more than 2% of radio listeners, or, 2) that radio is the proper medium for holding a church service with our own particular church members.

We discovered later that such type of programming causes about 98% of radio listeners to tune to some other station, or tune out. The minute the average person hears a hymn, he says: "Oh-oh! There's another one of those sentimental, pestering religious broadcasts!"—and he flips the dial.

It was some years later, but eventually we learned. Then we began programming for the other 98%—the people who are not religious—the unchurched—instead of what radio men call "the religious audience." Years ago we dropped off hymns and singing altogether.

But in those days, and for some years to come, we did use singing. Our mixed quartette was hardly of Metropolitan Opera quality—yet, as religious programs went, it was very creditable. Some of the time we used eight voices in a double mixed quartette.

Customarily, however, we used the four singers, which included my wife and eldest daughter. The quartette, a pianist, and I drove directly from the studios of KORE to Portland, usually taking lunch along to eat in the car en route.

Portland Tabernacle Offer

Shortly after going over to KWJJ, opportunity came to purchase a tabernacle in Portland. This brought us to the crossroads decision for the entire future of the work.

I had to learn, here, that all that glitters is not gold. This offer glittered. It flattered. It was tempting.

A Portland radio evangelist, Willard Pope, had built this tabernacle a few years earlier. He had now built a new and slightly larger tabernacle and vacated his former one. He was conducting one of these local religious broadcasts, holding nightly evangelistic services in his tabernacle and regular Sunday service for his church members which this program brought him.

The idea of having what then appeared to me as

such a nice large auditorium of our own in Portland was enticing. This tabernacle seated 800 people.

But soon I began to realize that, although this tabernacle was offered on terms that amounted virtually to rent, with no down payment for about a year or so, it would change the entire direction and future course of our work.

It would mean tying me down to Portland—preaching in Portland six nights a week to those attracted by the radio program. It would mean trying to BUILD A LOCAL CHURCH. It would have tied me down, locally, in Portland. I had from the start realized that the first and major commission to which I had been called, was *not* to build up a church and to bring in members, but to proclaim the true and original Gospel of Christ, which the world had rejected and lost for 18½ centuries. I saw our commission, in Christ's prophecy of Matthew 24:14. The Gospel was to go out, *not* to cram it down people's throats—*not* to try to force conversion on them, *but as a witness*—perhaps even a witness *against them!*

Of course I did see that Christ had said it was to go *into all the world,* and as a witness *to all nations;* but I had no delusions of grandeur—I never thought of myself as reaching more than a segment of the whole earth. I assumed God would raise up others to reach the rest of the world. But I did realize I was called to preach that very Gospel to as many as God made possible.

This tabernacle offer, I began to realize, would mean diverting the work from that path. I began to realize that it might prevent the radio work and *The Plain Truth* from expanding into wider areas. And already I envisioned a program expanding to reach the entire west coast—and possibly even, in time, the entire United States.

For some three or four months I weighed the matter, prayed over it, sought advice and counsel from those whose judgment in such matters I respected. And finally, on the grounds it would divert us from our divinely ordained course, which I felt sure I realized at last, the tabernacle offer was turned down.

It was a wise decision. It was a test in wisdom. I think I have mentioned before that I had discovered, very early in my ministry, that I lacked natural wisdom. I had always craved UNDERSTANDING. I had absorbed a reasonable share of KNOWLEDGE. But WISDOM is ability to put both of these together and form a right DECISION. I had read God's instruction in James 1. If any man lacks wisdom, he is to ask God for it; and, believing, he shall receive it. I had asked God for wisdom. God granted it. But, even though it comes as His gift, He lets it develop gradually, and through experience. This was one more experience in WISDOM. I have always been sure the decision was God's. The work would not be where it is today, otherwise.

Atheists at a Funeral

In February, 1937, I had sent out a letter to Co-Workers saying that the mail response indicated a radio audience of between forty and fifty thousand each Sunday— growing "toward our goal of 100,000." By April the mail response indicated 60,000 listeners. By November 26th we had reached our goal—100,000 weekly listeners was announced! We set new goals—and continued to *grow!*

On November 30, 1937, the father of the former atheist Secretary of the local Communist Party, whose conversion was recorded in a preceding chapter, died. This precipitated a nerve-testing experience.

The mother of the young lady ex-Communist had also come into the Church. But it was a fairly large

640

family, and nearly all the other members of the family were professed atheists. There was some kind of a controversy within the family concerning who was to officiate at the funeral. The professed atheist members were violently opposed to me. They wanted a Mr. Herbert Higgombotham, pastor of the Unitarian Church in Eugene. However, in deference to their mother, they acquiesced.

"Oh, well," they said, "we'll sit there and endure the ignorant, superstitious, medieval mouthings of this stupid God-believing minister, and then we'll have a good laugh picking to pieces his ridiculous 'funnymentals' after it's over."

I realized what I was facing.

I spoke on the meaning of death, and the question of life after death. I mentioned that among *men* there are various IDEAS—the immortality of the soul, which is pagan; conditioned immortality and the resurrection of the dead; and the atheist idea that death ends all. Then I pointed out that the reasonings and inventions of human imagination carry no weight of authority—they are only *ideas*—and other people have *different* ideas. Nobody has ever yet come back to tell us his experience, except the resurrected Christ whom they deny. Science can contribute NOTHING. We, therefore, have one of two choices: 1) accept the revelation of the Creator God—who *knows*—in the Bible, or, 2) *admit we are absolutely IGNORANT!*

The pagan, I said, is IGNORANT—he has only his imagined and superstitious ideas. The atheist, I affirmed, is even MORE IGNORANT—he has only his *prejudiced refusal* to accept truth, without any proof or scientific knowledge whatsoever; he has no authority; he, like a fool, ignorantly believes what he *wants* to believe, because he is *unwilling* to believe the truth.

641

Then I said that I would now read to them what GOD says, and that we have the choice of accepting this AUTHORITY or confessing that we are ignorant.

En route to the cemetery from the mortuary, I rode on the driver's seat of the hearse, and with us was a cousin of the sons of the deceased.

"Mr. Armstrong," he said, "you probably didn't know it, but you had several professed atheists and scoffers before you today. They came to ridicule and scoff, but you certainly closed their mouths! They intended to go home and pick your sermon to pieces—but their home will now be as quiet as a morgue!"

Of course, I *did* know what I was up against. I had prayed to the God they denied for wisdom. I believe He granted the request. They fell into the pit they had dug for me—being labeled IGNORANT. They had no answer.

Our Car Gives Out

By December, our old second-hand several-year-old Graham-Paige car laid down on the job, like a worn-out, tired old horse ready to lie down and die.

At this time we had one secretary—Mrs. Helen Starkey. She was working without salary. Later, I think, we managed to pay her $5 per week, but even that was only a fraction of a salary.

Without my knowledge, she sent out a letter over her own signature on December 21, 1937, asking Co-Workers for a special love-offering for a new second-hand car to enable us to continue the weekly broadcast trips to Portland. It was that or go off the air.

Enough came in to purchase a 1934-model used Graham—*on monthly payments!* It lasted until 1941.

Helen Starkey died in 1959, faithful to God's work

to the end. But a year or two before she died—having moved to Pasadena—I learned that she and her husband were trying to purchase a small home, but lacked a few hundred dollars of being able. It was a very rewarding privilege for Mrs. Armstrong and me to be able now, at last, to pay her the few hundred dollars as back salary she had really earned, some twenty years before. She lived in the home they bought the short remainder of her life.

More Tests of Faith

There had been no issue of *The Plain Truth* since July, 1935. The reasons have been fully explained before. During this period, I did manage to turn out, frequently—though not monthly or with regularity— printed sermons that had been broadcast.

These had been months of trial and hardship, persecution, plots by the very ministers I was working with to wreck the broadcast, struggle to meet rising expenses and keep the work alive.

I will mention briefly one such incident. On November 22, 1937, I had managed to afford enough paper and ink to mimeograph a printed sermon. But we lacked enough to pay for postage to send it out until November 26. Here are a few brief excerpts from the letter I sent along with it. This letter was sent only to those who had become regular Co-Workers:

"Again, with the printed sermon, I send greetings in the Lord. I want to thank you from the bottom of my heart for your interest in God's truth. But this month I must take you into my confidence about some of the problems we are facing in this work. Right now Jesus Christ is opening up the most wonderful opportunities for the expansion of the work. And yet, instead of taking advantage of these opportunities, *I am faced with having to stop what we are doing, and going off the air altogether, after next Sunday's broadcast!*

"Most of you must have thought that with our vast radio audience, so many people would be sending in money that we do not need YOUR help. A HUNDRED THOUSAND *listen*, every Sunday, but only a *very FEW* of them send any money. And I have never asked for money over the air! We preach the Word of God—and the Scriptures are profitable for reproof, correction, and instruction in God's way. It is not a popular Gospel. People do not pay to be told their sins—to be reproved and corrected. They would walk out of church if their pastors hit them with the Bible TRUTH. Their pastors would lose their jobs. Yet we have found that people who would not tolerate such preaching in their churches, where their friends see them being told their sins, *will* listen privately, in the secrecy of their own homes by radio. For some reason, they cannot resist LISTENING— over the radio! But they will not support it with their money.

"The cold facts which I must face are that we have not been able to send out this printed sermon earlier because there has not been enough money to pay postage—we do not at this writing even have enough money on hand for the trip to Portland for the Sunday broadcast, and must trust God to send it before Sunday morning. I do not like to tell you these things. Brethren in Christ, this is one of the discouragements I must face—the responsibilities I must carry—in order to bring YOU the spiritual benefits and blessings so many of you have written you are receiving from this work.

"I wish you could sit at my desk a few days, and read the letters that come in. Some of them would tear at your heartstrings! You would come to really REALIZE the wonderful amount of real good this great work is doing—already on a large scale, covering most of Oregon and southwestern Washington. Thousands are hearing the true Gospel and God's warning, WHO NEVER HEARD SUCH THINGS BEFORE! Conversions are actually taking place while our program is coming in over the air!

"When I look at this world and see the people hurrying here and there, absorbed altogether in their wordly cares and pleasures—yet really miserable and unhappy and LOST—heedless, knowing NOTHING of the terrible things soon to come on those who have not put themselves under God's protection; and when I look into my Bible, and see how REAL these things are, and how SOON they are coming, I am appalled, and my heart BURNS to shout out the warning to more and more people, before it is too late!"

I felt it might be worth the space to reprint the above portions of that letter—just to show what we faced, and how we felt, at that time.

AT LAST—a Plain Truth

But, patience, faith, and struggle were rewarded—as they always are.

January 1, 1938, we finally were enabled to bring *The Plain Truth* back to life! It was the first issue in two and a half years!

But it still had to be a hand-produced mimeographed "magazine." A letter sent out with it said: "We cannot, yet, afford to have it printed. So we mimeographed it ourselves. This work has been done mostly by Sister Helen Starkey, Mrs. Armstrong, and myself, with a few of our good friends coming to the office for volunteer work the past few days, to help with the folding, addressing, stamping, etc." Mrs. Starkey was still working daily without salary.

A bulletin sent to local Oregon church members,

645

dated January, 1938, announced the *Plain Truth* mailing list was now 1050.

It had outgrown Mrs. Armstrong and me. It was becoming too large to mimeograph. In February, 1938, we were forced to reduce *The Plain Truth* down to *3 pages*—its smallest size ever. There were two sheets of paper, and the back page was devoted to a letter!

At this time I learned that we could have the March number *printed,* at a local printing plant, on cheap paper, 8 pages, for $30 more than the cost of mimeographing. *But we didn't have the $30!*

So the March and April numbers were still mimeographed.

March 18, 1938, I sent out a letter showing that the expenses of the work (including our family living) had risen to $300 per month. But we were running behind on part of the family living. Legal action was being instituted to foreclose and take from us our small home! In some manner I do not now remember, this trouble was met, and we managed to keep the home. But this only added to the harassing discouragements in the struggle to keep the work going.

First *PRINTED* Plain Truth!

Finally, after more than four years on the air, we managed to produce the *first* really printed *Plain Truth!*

This was done by combining May-June into one number! It had to be printed on inexpensive newsprint paper. The page size was larger than the present magazine, but it contained only 8 pages.

This was the first issue that carried under the masthead the slogan I had always wanted: "a magazine of understanding."

(*To be continued in Volume II.*)

646

RESEARCH CENTER